Electronic Swing Trading for Maximum Profit

Discover the Professional Trading Strategy That Combines Day Trading with Long-Term Investing Techniques

MISHA T. SARKOVICH, PH.D.

PRIMA MONEY
An Imprint of Prima Publishing
3000 Lava Ridge Court • Roseville, California 95661
(800) 632-8676 • www.primalifestyles.com

Library of Congress Cataloging-in-Publication Data on File
ISBN 0-7615-2518-1
00 01 02 03 HH 10 9 8 7 6 5 4 3 2 1
Printed in the United States of America

How to Order

Single copies may be ordered from Prima Publishing, 3000 Lava Ridge Court, Roseville, CA 95661; telephone (800) 632-8676 ext. 4444. Quantity discounts are also available. On your letterhead, include information concerning the intended use of the books and the number of books you wish to purchase.

Visit us online at www.primalifestyles.com

Acknowledgments

I dedicate this work to my family, my wife Kimberly and our sons Stefan and Marco, whose continuous love and support made this conceivable.

Sincere thanks must also go to my parents-in-law, Eleanor and Ned Keech, for their proofreading of the manuscript and their valuable comments.

The last word of acknowledgment delightfully goes to Prima Publishing editors David Richardson and Susan Silva for their professional assistance and continuous faith in this work.

Disclaimer

Because the topic of this book is securities trading, I will start with disclaimers. The swing trading business involves money (sometimes a lot of money), and we live in a litigious society:

- This book is designed as an introduction to swing trading for educational purposes. The book can never be 100 percent complete, as the stock trading business is evolving continuously. The book is intended only to give readers a general idea of how the business of trading works and how to get started.

- The information in this book represents my opinion only. I encourage all readers to complete their own research and to verify the information presented in this book for themselves.

- Trading is an inherently risky business. Because traders open and trade the margin accounts, it is possible to sustain losses that are greater than the initial trading capital. Do not trade money that you cannot afford to lose.

- Traders must be responsible for their own actions. Each trader is accountable for every completed trade, even if the trader did not intend to do it. When you begin trading, please, be careful when executing trades. Start slowly.

- I do not recommend a purchase or sale of any particular security. I do not guarantee any potential return that can be achieved through swing trading. Furthermore, I do not guarantee suitability of any particular trading transaction or trading strategy.

- Electronic stock trading is on the cutting edge of technology, and traders must accept all the associated risks of computer equipment, network, and software failures.

Introduction to Stock Trading

It may seem peculiar to commence a trading book with an ancient Chinese curse that states, eloquently, May you live in interesting times. When it comes to stock trading and investing, we certainly do. The digital information revolution, and particularly the Internet, has fundamentally changed the way Americans trade stocks. The Internet has opened the floodgates, and the balance of power in the securities industry has shifted. The stock market has undergone a metamorphosis: Hierarchical structures, such as Wall Street firms, have been torn down, empowering the networks of amateur traders and investors.

Just a few short years ago, stock trading was characterized as the domain of professional stock traders, or a "private club" with restricted access. But no longer. In the past few years, legions of small investors have become stock traders. They now do their own research, access stock exchanges directly, and execute their own trades, at a fraction of the cost of a few years ago. Just a decade ago, you could not trade stocks directly for your own account from your home. As an outsider, you were commonly told that the field was too risky, too complex, and too difficult to learn, and, most importantly, that it required specialized information and order-execution tools. It used to be that only established Wall Street firms had access to better information and trade execution, and thus had a clear trading advantage. The new trading environment has changed all that.

For the first time, amateur traders have the necessary tools, such as access to real-time stock quotes, order executions, and the Electronic Communications Networks (ECNs), to compete effectively with the professionals. Today the average American can directly trade any stocks from anywhere in the United States, which has caused substantial commotion in the securities business. It marks the democratization of stock trading. Main Street has moved closer to Wall Street.

The explosion in online investing and trading and the emergence of deep-discount brokers—as well as the huge increase in the number of mutual funds and 401(k) pension plans—have made the stock market more accessible to average Americans than ever before. At the beginning of 2000, 48 percent of U.S. households owned stocks. Just four years earlier, that number was 41 percent, and 10 years earlier, 32 percent. I believe that the high stock-ownership rate among the general populace is a positive development for American capitalism. Just as a high home-ownership rate is important for the social stability of a local community, a high stock-ownership rate promotes greater individual interest in the national economy.

It is deceptively easy today to buy and sell stocks online. Anyone with Internet access can join the trading revolution and "click" his or her way into the stock trading business. As with all revolutions, however, this one has its casualties—the small investors-turned-traders who jumped in this stock trading field too quickly, without acquiring the knowledge and skills required to survive the ubiquitous learning curve. They learned firsthand that the stock trading field is easy to enter but difficult to master. They learned that "buying low and selling high" is easier said than done.

New Trading Environment

The new trading environment owes its existence to the following:

1. *Low-cost commission structure.* This trading revolution actually began more than a quarter of century ago, in May 1975, when Wall Street firms ended the practice of charging fixed commissions. This deregulation resulted in the emergence of discount brokers. Technological advances in the 1990s resulted in the emergence of Internet brokers and electronic day-trading firms. The new competition decreased trading transaction costs even further, with the commission charges for the market order dropping to $5. This low-cost commission structure made short-term in-and-out stock trading financially feasible. Stock traders

could make many trades in a month, and commissions did not eat up their potential profits.

2. *SEC regulations that mandated direct trading access.* Further changes occurred following the stock market crash of 1987. The crash propelled the Securities and Exchange Commission (SEC) to mandate National Association of Securities Dealers Automated Quotation (NAS-DAQ) market makers to provide individual investors with better access to trade execution. In October 1987, when stock prices were free-falling, some market makers simply refused to pick up their ringing phones and execute sell orders for panicked sellers. In 1987, the SEC mandated market-maker participation in the NASDAQ Small Order Execution System (SOES) to ensure small traders access to the posted market price and to ensure public confidence in the NASDAQ market. That marked the beginning of deregulation of the stock trading industry.

In addition, in January 1997, the SEC made a ruling regarding limit-order display, which dramatically changed how execution orders were handled when buying and selling securities in U.S. equities markets. The rule has ensured that individual stock traders have the same access to the most favorable pricing available as their professional and institutional counterparts have. Thus outsiders became an integral part of the stock trading world.

3. *Technological advancements in computer hardware.* During the past decade, improvements in computer hardware have resulted in computers and servers that are affordable and extremely fast and that have large amounts of the memory required to reliably process a large flow of the stock market real-time data.

4. *Technological improvements in networking science.* Computer networking and Internet advances in the past several years, such as the availability of fast T-1, DSL, and ISDN lines, have made real-time financial data feed and trade-order execution feasible and affordable to most. This access to real-time financial information and order execution has leveled the playing field for all participants. For the first time, amateur stock traders have access to nearly the same quantity and quality of real-time financial information and the execution tools that were once used only by professional traders.

5. *Increasing price volatility.* In the past ten years, the U.S. stock market has become increasingly more volatile, a result of the current

dynamic, interdependent, and global U.S. economy. This price volatility is here to stay, which is exactly what fuels stock trading profit opportunities. The objective of an experienced stock trader is to trade volatile stocks in large-share blocks and then profit from their price movement.

Basics of Stock Trading

These days Americans can trade almost anything, from soybean contracts to crude oil contracts, from S & P 500's index futures to U.S. Treasury bonds and Eurodollars, at many different national or regional exchanges. Most likely, as a reader of this book, your intent is to trade equities. Therefore, this book focuses on the U.S. equities being traded at the NASDAQ and NYSE. However, the technical analysis principles can be applied to trading any financial instrument. I believe that anyone considering this risky business must adequately understand the following:

1. Where to trade
2. How to trade
3. When to trade
4. What to trade
5. Why the trade is or is not working

Section I of this book defines swing trading, as well as the other forms of short-term trading. The section explains the core of the swing trading business. The discussion then turns, in section II, to a brief coverage of different trading environments and trading brokers. This second section attempts to answer the first question listed above, where to trade.

The next question, how to trade, is addressed in section III, which covers the basic trading terminology and the actual mechanics of different order executions. The trader must learn to execute trades efficiently. Therefore, this section describes the different trade order executions, risk management tools, trading software tools, and margin accounts. (Trader's tax issues are covered in appendix 2.)

Timing is everything in this business. Therefore, the third question is the most important for the stock trader—when to trade. The answer to this question, which involves technical analysis and which is addressed in section IV, makes all the difference between success and failure. Section IV explains the most commonly used technical analysis indicators, which generate the trading signals to buy or sell stocks. In essence, these indicators help traders time and optimize their trade entry and exit points for higher profitability (and long-term survival).

Even if we narrow the field of trading to equities, there are many different stocks to screen, from IPOs to penny stocks, from Internet stocks to utility stocks. What stocks do you trade? How do you get alerted that a particular stock is gaining momentum? Section V of this book answers the question, what to trade.

Finally, section VI covers fundamental stock analysis. I am the first to admit that fundamental stock analysis is much more relevant to the traditional stock investor than to the stock trader. Subsequently, this topic is covered last. Nevertheless, fundamental stock analysis provides traders with the foundation to understand and appreciate the broader relationship between the stock market and the business environment. In other words, traders that understand stock market fundamentals can answer many "why" questions. In the long run, the trader will master the field of trading only when the trader knows all the facts. And those facts are stock market fundamentals.

Stock Trading Rules

It's a safe bet that you have seen the many television commercials that promote online trading and investing. The advertisements reflect, to a great extent, the general public's myths about trading and investing online. Have you seen the commercial in which a tow-truck driver, who is also an online trader, picks up a stranded car, which is owned by an elitist "old world" business executive? The executive notices a postcard on the tow-truck dashboard and asks the driver, "Vacation?" "No, that's my home," replies the driver. "Looks more like an island," continues the executive. "Technically, it's a country!" the driver modestly responds.

Obviously, there are no guarantees in this business. I do not promise readers that their stock trading will result in successful and prosperous endeavors and ultimately lead to owning a country. There is no single magical secret or stock trading Holy Grail. Trading is not an exact science. Stock trading is an art.

What I do offer in this book, however, are three simple steps—all commonsense advice—that will enhance your probability of becoming a successful stock trader:

1. Learn as much as possible about stock trading.
2. Test your trading hypotheses.
3. Trade more frequently and in larger volumes.

I do not think that anyone will dispute the first point. Knowledge is power. Anyone trading stocks should read as much as possible about stock trading in general. Reading books, such as this one, is the most economical way to learn about stock trading. A wealth of stock trading information is published, and most likely it is reasonably priced. (see appendix 1 for a list of additional information resources). As a stock trader, you are competing against the knowledgeable and experienced stock market professionals, such as the NASDAQ market makers, NYSE specialists, and other traders. Subsequently, more trading knowledge is always preferred, as it is your first line of defense.

After you acquire the required trading knowledge, you will be able to evaluate different trading styles logically and select ones that make sense to you. Although some trading styles might seem logical, they might not be appropriate for a trader given his or her risk tolerance or the skill set required for the execution of the particular strategy. Even if the particular trading style makes sense and fits your personality, skill set, and trading budget, please, do not just jump in. Test your hypothesis. See for yourself if the trading style works. Do not take someone else's word (including everything you read in this book) as absolute fact. Put a little bit of your risk money on the line and go live. Testing a different trading style live, online, with a small number of shares will generate the actual trading experience. And there is no substitute for experience.

The third point is not intuitively obvious, and yet it represents the core of stock trading. Stock trading is a business. As a participant in this business, you must be actively engaged in it. As a trader you are actively taking many stock positions. This business is not based on a few home runs, but on many incremental profits. The only way the small incremental profits can translate into large absolute-dollar gain at the end of the trading period, whether the period is one day or one week, is to trade in large-share blocks (i.e., 1,000 or more shares per trade).

Conversely, trading in large-share blocks is a double-edged sword. Because you are making many trades in increments of 1,000 or more shares per trade, you stand to quickly gain or lose large absolute-dollar amounts. Therefore, stock trading is risky. The only thing that determines whether you will gain or lose large absolute-dollar amounts is your trading knowledge and discipline—a point that is elaborated in great detail throughout the book.

Stock Market Essentials

Before we go any further, I would like to outline a few of my basic views about the stock market and trading because they underscore points that permeate this book. I believe that most stock market participants would concur with my assessments.

1. The Stock Market Is Not a Zero-Sum Game

Many have called the stock market a "zero-sum game," which means that for every winner there is a loser. I believe that the stock market is anything but a zero-sum game; however, other markets, such as futures and options and so-called derivatives, certainly are. Unlike the derivatives market, the stock market does not have contracts with an expiration date that must have an equal number of winners and losers. Options and futures trading involve executing contracts between the sellers and the buyers that have stipulated expiration dates. At the end of the contract-expiration period, either the contract buyers or the contract sellers have made the money. Options and futures trading are, thus, extremely competitive and efficient. I believe that in this particular trading environment there is a transfer of wealth from the less experienced and knowledgeable options and futures amateur traders to the more experienced and knowledgeable options and futures professional traders. I feel that trading equities is easier than trading options and futures.

In the long run, the overall stock market has a positive average rate of return. In other words, the stock market has a positive long-term bias. Since 1926, the stock market returned approximately an average annual 11 percent return, which is a higher annual rate of return than the risk-free Treasury bond market's 5.2 percent. And the past few years have been even better. Stocks in the S & P's 500 index (which represents 80 percent of the overall market capitalization) increased in value 21 percent in 1999. In addition, the average annual returns for three-year, five-year and ten-year periods were approximately 28 percent, 29 percent, and 18 percent. Where is the zero-sum game here?

The equities market has many diverse and heterogeneous market participants. Investors, traders, mutual and pension funds, institutional holders—each have diverse objectives and holding periods that range from the extreme short-term period (i.e., day traders) to the extreme long-term period (i.e., pension funds). Subsequently, different participants in the equities market will have different price targets and time frames for their decisions. It is quite feasible for a trader to sell to an investor a stock at a price that is overvalued at that time (and thus the trader would make money on the trade) and for the long-term investor to make money on that stock many years from now when the stock is sold. In other words, it is possible for short-term traders to make money in the short run and long-term investors to make money in the long run.

Finally, the total amount of funds in the stock market is not fixed. There is a continuous inflow and outflow of funds from the bond or fixed-income markets and from abroad. I perceive the stock market to be an alpine lake with an inflow and outflow. The water level of that lake is sometimes rising, and sometimes declining, but it never remains constant. For instance, if short-term interest rates drop, there will be outflow of funds from the bond market into the stock market. If the Japanese yen appreciates in value against the U.S. dollar, the U.S. stock market will become cheaper for the Japanese investors and thus there will be an inflow of funds from Japan into the U.S. stock market. There might be even changes in the U.S. tax laws, demographics, and savings patterns that will affect the flow of funds into the stock market.

2. The Stock Market Is Extremely Volatile in the Short Run

Is this news to anyone? The stock market in the short run, and particularly the NASDAQ market, is a roller coaster. On Friday, April 14, 2000, the NASDAQ plunged a record 355 points, or approximately 10 percent, which was the worst one-day drop in history. Consider also the week before—Tuesday, April 4, 2000—when the NASDAQ initially plunged 574 points, or approximately 14 percent, in an intraday decline, before rallying back to close down less than 100 points. Altogether, April 2000 brought unprecedented volatility for the technology-loaded NASDAQ market, which declined 25 percent in value during one week of trading. The surprising element is how well the investors took this volatility in stride, without any panic. Then approximately one month later, NASDAQ recorded the best week in its history. The NASDAQ composite index rose 608 points for the week beginning May 29, 2000, which was an astounding 19 percent gain in one week.

Perhaps you recall October 28, 1997, when the Dow Jones industrial average dropped 554 points, or 7.2 percent of its value, in a single day. And think back a few years to October 19, 1987, or Black Monday, when the Dow crashed 508 points in one day, which was an astonishing 22.6 percent decline in value at that time. Bond markets are much calmer in terms of the short-term price volatility because of the fixed-income component structure.

Many Wall Street analysts are concerned that stock-market price volatility has increased in the recent past, and they believe that volatility results from increased speculation. The North American Securities Administration Association (NASAA) reported that the short-term volatility has indeed been high and is rising. For the twelve-month period in 1999, more than 40 percent of the daily closing prices for the S & P's 500 index differed from the previous day's close by more than one percentage point. This level of price volatility has been surpassed only twice during the past thirty-five years.

Is this increased short-term volatility the result of stock speculation that comes with the practice of day trading or Internet stock trading? There is no clear answer to this question. However, I question the cause-and-effect relationship. The short-term traders are attracted to volatile stocks at the outset. For instance, traders trade Internet stocks because those stocks are volatile. Otherwise, how else would a stock be traded if it did not have any price movement? The fact that traders are trading Internet stocks does not make Internet stocks volatile by themselves. The real reason Internet stocks and other high-technology stocks are volatile is because the Internet and high-tech firms have the expected corporate-earnings stream, which is uncertain and volatile.

3. Risk and Returns Are Positively Correlated

This statement is intuitively clear and should be no surprise to anyone. And yet I am always amazed to hear people compare stock trading with investing. Stock trading is not investing. A stock trader's objective is to earn a high income now, whereas the investor's objective is to receive a high percentage rate of return in the future. To earn that high level of income, the short-term trader must increase his or her trading activity and thus command greater financial leverage. In other words, the trader will execute many trades with limited-risk capital during the year and, as a result, will end up purchasing a large amount of stocks during the year.

If the trader is successful, the absolute dollar amount of income, when translated into percentage terms, represents an extremely high rate of return. The only way anyone can earn that high rate of return on a limited investment is to assume higher risk and leverage. Therefore, you cannot compare returns between the stock trader and the investor, because the risk factors are dramatically different.

Likewise, you cannot compare the failure rate between stock traders and investors, because the risk-reward metrics between the two groups is dramatically different. So what if 100 percent of Treasury-bond investors made money (assuming the investor is holding the bond to maturity) if the annual rate of return is 5 or 6 percent? Short-term traders seek a 500 or 600 percent annual rate of return. Is it so surprising, given the higher assumed risk, that the majority of short-term traders will lose money?

4. Short Run Versus Long Run

In the short run, a myriad of market variables, such as investors' sentiment, weather, or interest rates, can and do influence a stock's price. However, in the long run, earnings determine whether a company is a viable business enterprise. Investors buy a piece of paper (i.e., the company stock) because that paper represents an ownership claim on the company's future earnings. If the prospects for a company's future earnings are not there, there will be little demand for that paper. Consequently, investors and traders pay close attention to corporate earnings and earnings announcements or surprises.

5. Stock Trading Is Not Gambling

Stock trading is not a game of chance. The only similarity between stock trading and gambling is the probability of loss. Unlike gamblers, stock traders have the opportunity to manage their risk. Because the online traders have a wealth of financial information at their fingertips and see on their monitors more information than the great majority of participants in the stock market, they are able to take educated and calculated risks. In addition, online traders can execute their orders relatively quickly so they can get out quickly when they need to.

It is not realistic to expect that traders will be correct 100 percent of the time. Even if they are correct 50 percent of the time, which would be equivalent to a game of chance, stock traders can still be profitable if they minimize losses when they are wrong (get out quickly at a minimal loss) and allow profits to rise when they are right. To be successful in the long run, stock traders must minimize their losses and maximize their profits. Given the quantity and sophistication of the financial information presented to online traders in real time, the probability of being right should be higher than 50 percent. With the acquired trading experience (that is, at least six months of live trading), that probability should increase.

It is true that many stock traders have a gambling mentality. They enjoy the rush of adrenaline when they make the right trade. However, good traders do not gamble. A good trader will enter a position only when he or she receives a clear trading signal, such as those we will discuss in the chapters on technical analysis. My point is that good traders follow the signals from the trading system they use, and they do not gamble. Bad traders, or soon-to-be ex-traders, do not have a trading system; they gamble.

6. Stock Trading Is Not Suitable for Everyone

Stock trading is hard work, and it is not entertainment. Stock trading requires a knowledge of trading, a time to trade, the adequate risk capital, and a great deal of self-discipline. I believe stock traders are true entrepreneurs. They risk their own capital, and they make all their own business (or trading) decisions. If the trading becomes a hobby, it is an expensive one.

To be successful in this emerging profession, stock traders must be disciplined and patient. They must have the ability to assume risk. Successful traders patiently wait for the trading signal; if they are wrong, they have the discipline to get out of the trade and minimize the loss.

Not all potential traders have the required personal characteristics to be successful traders. In addition to the key personal traits of self-discipline, patience, and the ability to assume risk, successful stock traders also tend to exhibit the following characteristics:

- *Intelligence.* Trading is an extremely competitive business. At any point in time, the trader is competing against professional market makers and other traders. To survive in this business, traders must be smart.

- *Flexibility.* Market conditions are fluid and are always in a state of motion. The trader must be able to adapt to the changing trading environment. For instance, traders should be able to trade both long and short positions with relative ease.

- *Ability to work hard.* Trading is a business. People who succeed in this business have worked hard to get there, and they have paid their dues.

- *Willingness to learn.* Successful traders strive to learn something new during each trading day, if not during each trade. They know there is always room for self-improvement.

- *Confidence.* Traders are not troubled by a series of bad trades during the week. They are confident that their trading discipline, risk management, and perseverance will ultimately translate into success.

- *Ability to react under stress.* The ability to react to trading losses or respond to information overload is important for traders to succeed. Subsequently, traders should be able to make trading decisions without freezing up or panicking.

If you believe you possess these characteristics and are willing to learn and work hard, then you can certainly benefit by what this book has to offer. The book's purpose is to provide a complete, reliable, and responsibly written guide to stock trading for both future and current stock traders. The book does not profess to abolish the risk of stock trading, because that risk is always there. It only presents the tools of risk management and demystifies, in a step-by-step manner, the complex set of knowledge that is required today to trade stocks for maximum profit. Only then, with adequate knowledge, can you get in control of your trading.

XX

Defining Swing Trading

"If you ask me a question I don't know, I'm not going to answer."

—*Yogi Berra*

No single book will create a successful trader. Reading this book is only a step in the right direction. The purpose of this introductory section is to start from square one and gradually define, explain, and illustrate the most basic swing-trading terms and concepts.

1

Swing Trading

"He who doesn't risk never gets to drink champagne."

—Russian Proverb

Swing trading, an increasingly popular trading style, has alternately been called "position trading" or "momentum trading." It is my belief that the term "swing trading" most appropriately describes the true intent of this trading style—to exploit short-term price swings. Swing trading is a compromise between the high level of trading activity that accompanies day trading and the large-volume trading that accompanies high-profile, long-term investing. In my opinion, swing trading is a form of short-term stock trading, which combines the high-income potential of day trading with the lower risk of long-term stock investing.

Unlike day traders, who typically sell their stock holdings at the end of the trading day, and unlike investors, who typically hold their stock positions for many months, swing traders hold their positions for only a few days, although this can vary anywhere from two days to two weeks. A holding period that ranges from two days to a week is too short for a typical "buy-and-hold" stock investor and too long for the typical day trader; thus many traders and authors of stock trading books have overlooked this particular style of trading.

Consequently, swing traders are few in number. Swing traders still compete against day traders and investors; however, because day traders and investors have different trading objectives, the day traders and investors do not act as a monolithic and homogeneous block of traders. Not all of them will buy a particular stock at the same point in time or sell the stock at the same time. Subsequently, the swing trading field is simply less crowded, which of course acts to the swing trader's advantage.

The best way to understand the differences among swing trading, day trading, and investing is to look at the following hypothetical example, which is a generalization of the three styles. To make any serious money through stock trading you basically have only three options:

1. Trade frequently to pick up a small gain with each trade. In other words, do many trades to earn a small incremental profit from each trade. When the small profit number from each trade is multiplied with the number of many completed trades, the net is a large cumulative gain for the year. The day trading style fits this description well.

2. Trade in large-volume increments less frequently. In other words, do a few trades each year to earn a modest profit from each trade, but trade in a very large block of shares. When the modest profit from each of the few trades is multiplied with the extremely large number of shares being traded, the net annual gain is a large cumulative sum. The typical stock investing strategy, particularly growth investing, fits this description well.

3. The third option is a hybrid of the previous two. A trader using this option will trade less frequently than the day trader under option 1, but more frequently than the growth investor under option 2. At the same time, the person subscribing to option 3 will trade stocks in larger increments than the day trader in option 1, but in much smaller trading sizes than the growth investor in option 2. This hybrid style fits the swing trader rather nicely.

Table 1.1 summarizes how an individual could potentially make $125,000 per year by investing, swing trading, or day trading. I selected a hypothetical $125,000 goal because it is a round number and is, in my opinion, a reasonable and feasible goal. Please note that I do not mean to imply that anyone who starts trading stocks will make $125,000 dollars annually. (Many terms used in table 1.1 will be explained in great detail in later chapters.)

Table 1.1 *A Hypothetical Case for Grossing $125,000 Annually in the Stock Market*

Trading Topics	Day Trader	Swing Trader	Investor
Annual goal	$125,000	$125,000	$125,000
Typical time frame	1 day	1 week	1 year
Number of trading periods in a year	Approx. 250 trading days in a year	52 weeks in a year	1 year
Goal per trading period	$500 per day	$2,500 per week	$125,000 per year
Number of round-trip trades per trading period	12 round-trip trades per day	1 per week	3 per year
Number of round-trip trades per year	3,000 per year	52 per year	3 per year
Commission per round-trip trade	$32	$32	$128
Typical trade increments	1,000 shares	2,500 shares	10,000 shares
Typical goal per trade per share	$\frac{1}{8}$ or $0.125	1.75 points or $1.75	7 points or $7.00
Net gain (assuming 60% of all trades were winning trades)	$900 per day	$2,600 per week	$126,000 per year
Gross annual profit	$225,000	$136,500	$126,000
Total commission cost	$96,000	$1,600	$385
Net annual profit	$129,000	$134,900	$125,615
Total annual value purchased (assuming $50 average stock)	$150,000,000	$6,500,000	$1,500,000
Purchasing power per trade (assuming $50 average stock)	$50,000	$125,000	$500,000
Trading capital requirement (assuming having a margin account)	$25,000	$62,500	$250,000
Return on investment	500%	200%	50%

The Day Trading Style Comparison

When creating the example in table 1.1, I made the assumption that both traders and the investor have the same annual goal—a $125,000 profit. The investor's time frame is one year, whereas the swing and day traders have a much shorter time frame—one week and one day, respectively. Let us focus for a moment on how both traders and the investor approach a $125,000 profit goal, starting with the day trader.

Assuming that there are 250 trading days in a year (in reality the number is closer to 240 days), a day trader must earn $500 per day to reach the goal of $125,000. The day trader's objective is to make many trades every day to exploit the intraday price volatility and profit from the small intraday price movement. In other words, the day trader's goal is to earn a small incremental profit, such as one-eighth or 12.5 cents on each share traded. However, the day trader is trading in increments of 1,000 shares, so 12.5 cents translates into a $125 gain.

Like his two counterparts, the day trader will make trades that lose money as well as those that result in profits. So let us assume that 60 percent of all trades were winning trades. This is a conservative estimate in my opinion, as I believe that a knowledgeable and experienced trader with the appropriate trading tools and information (i.e., professional trading software with real-time financial data feed) can reach a much higher winning percentage. After all, having a 50 percent winning-trade record would be close to flipping a coin or throwing darts at the newspaper's stock market listing.

To earn $500 per day, a typical day trader must complete 12 round-trip trades, which is one buy trade or ticket and one sell trade or ticket, at $16 per each trade or ticket. That translates into 3,000 round-trip trades per year. This number of trades results in $96,000 in commission expenses. That means that even though the day trader generated $225,000 in gross revenue, after paying commissions, his or her net profit is $129,000. If the day trader is trading in increments of 1,000 shares and the average stock price is $50, then the required purchasing power is only $50,000. That can be accomplished by opening a margin account with $25,000. A return of $129,000 with the $25,000 "investment" translates into an approximately 500 percent return.

During the market turmoil that occurred in the spring of 2000, much attention was focused on the dangers of trading on a margin.

These dangers will be discussed within the chapters on risk management and margin accounts (see chapter 9). For now we need only focus on the fact that the true day trader would close all of the positions at the end of the day, and thus the true day trader would not be subject to any margin calls.

If the average stock price were $50 during the year, then making 3,500 trades would mean that the day trader bought and sold an incredible sum of $150 million worth of stocks. The $150 million in shares that a day trader might control illustrates the enormous leverage he or she commands—even if only for a few minutes or hours at a time—with a $25,000 investment. The point here is that a high level of activity and a high amount of leverage can translate into a hypothetical high annual return of 500 percent.

The Swing Trading Style Comparison

Now let us look at how swing trading fares as an alternative to day trading. Here again, let us assume the same annual goal—a $125,000 profit. The swing trader's time frame is one week. As there are 52 weeks in a year, a swing trader must earn approximately $2,500 per week. Our hypothetical swing trader's objective is to make at least one trade every week to exploit the weekly price volatility and profit from the relatively modest weekly price movement. In other words, the swing trader's goal is to earn a modest profit, such as the 1.75 points in one week. To accomplish that, the swing trader trades in increments of 2,500 shares, which is higher than the day trader's trading size of 1,000 shares but smaller than the investor's trading size of 10,000 shares.

Let us assume again that 60 percent of all trades are winning trades. One round-trip trade per week translates into 52 trades per year and generates $1,600 in commission expenses (or 52 buy-and-sell orders at $16 per ticket). That means that after the commission expense, the profit is $135,000. If the swing trader is trading in increments of 2,500 shares and the average stock price is $50, then the required purchasing power is $125,000. That can be accomplished by opening a margin account with $62,500. A return of $135,000 with the $62,500 "investment" translates into approximately a 200 percent return.

If the average stock price were $50 during the year, then 52 trades with the average amount of 2,500 shares would mean that the swing trader bought and sold $6.5 million worth of stocks. The swing trader utilizes higher leverage than does the investor, but much smaller leverage than the day trader who controls an incredible $150 million worth of stocks cumulatively during one year.

The Investing Style Comparison

Let us compare the day trading style to the other extreme—investing. The investor's time frame in this example is one year, although many investors have much longer investment horizons, and thus he or she must earn $125,000 during that year. The investor's objective is to make a few trades in a year and profit from the price movement throughout the year. Because the investor has time to wait for price movement, it is reasonable to expect that he or she could earn an average of seven points in a year on a stock that is priced on average at $50.

We also assume that our investor will be successful on 60 percent of all trades. To earn $125,000 in a year, our hypothetical investor completes three round-trip trades with 10,000 block shares with commission at $128 per trade. Commission expenses are higher for the investor due to the large size of the trade order. This generates $385 in commission expenses, which is a minuscule expense compared with the day trader's commission expense. That means that after commission, the profit is $125,000. If the investor is trading in increments of 10,000 shares and the average stock price is $50, then the required purchasing power is $500,000. This must be accomplished by opening a margin account with $250,000, which is more money than many of us have to invest.

A return of $125,000 with the $250,000 "investment" translates into a 50 percent return. If the average stock price were $50 during the year, then three trades in blocks of 10,000 would translate into the investor having bought and sold only $1.5 million worth of stocks. This is in stark contrast to the day trader's high financial leverage of $150 million. Compared with the swing trader, the investor utilizes lower leverage throughout the trading year, because the investor controls only $1.5 million worth of stocks with a $250,000 investment. The point here is that low activity and low leverage translate into a lower annual return of 50 percent, which is much lower than the day trader's 500 percent return.

Overall Trading Style Comparison

The lower trading activity and lower leverage commanded by the swing trader translates into a lower annual return as compared with the day trader (200 vs. 500 percent). However, the swing trader trades more frequently and utilizes much higher leverage than the investor. Consequently, the swing trader has a higher annual return compared with the investor (200 vs. 50 percent).

Trading $150 million worth of stocks and completing 3,000 trades in one year creates a lot of work and stress for the day trader. In contrast, the swing trader's task is dramatically simpler. Our hypothetical swing trader makes, on average, one trade per week (or only 52 trades per year) and trades $6.5 million worth of stock. Because the swing trader makes fewer trades and completes lower dollar amounts of trading, the swing trading level of risk is smaller than the risk associated with day trading.

A typical day trader practices what I call *precision trading,* which requires a great deal of trading skill. Day traders must have sharp eyes, minds, and execution skills to pick up frequently and accurately small price movements. There is very little room for error. If the day trader is wrong and the price goes against him or her by only one-fourth of a point, which is a common and minor price gyration, a good day trader would have no choice but to exit the trade and take the small loss and move on to the next trade. There is no opportunity for second chances. Time is not on the day trader's side.

The swing trader, however, can afford to weather the small and common price gyrations—such as one-fourth or three-eighths of a point—because the holding period is much longer. Assuming that the stock analysis is correct, the swing trader can afford to wait for the price reversal. The swing trader's stop-loss limit is much higher than the day trader's loss tolerance. (The topic of stop-loss limits will be discussed in chapter 9, "Risk Management.") The stop-loss limits are not as tight and precise as the day trader's are. In other words, the swing trader could be wrong initially and lose one-fourth or three-eighths of a point when entering the trade. But in the long run, the swing trader could be right and end up with a profitable trade. Time could be on the swing trader's side.

Table 1.2 summarizes the differences among each of the three stock trading styles. The table shows that swing trading is a hybrid of the investing and day trading styles.

Full-Time vs. Part-Time Trading

One of the first trading decisions a new trader will make is whether to trade on a part-time or full-time basis. My advice to new or prospective traders is to start slowly. In other words, start trading on a part-time basis. The new trader can start out in the business gradually, which is a distinct advantage. Chances are that a new trader would not quit his or her day job, and thus there will be less pressure to make money immediately. The trader would have a continuous source of income from his or her regular job. So trading and only breaking even at the beginning would not be a financial disaster. (If the trader were trading on a full-time basis and if trading were the only source of income, then breaking even would be a failure.)

Also, starting on a part-time basis limits overall risk exposure. The trader can still keep his or her job. In the event that this "career change" does not work out, the trader still has the old job. Trading on a part-time basis will also test the trader's resolve. The trader will learn quickly whether he or she has the mental constitution for this line of work. In the event that the financial, mental, and time commitments to trading are no longer present, the trader can go back to the old job.

Table 1.2 *Stock Trading Styles*

Trading Topics	Investing	Swing Trading	Day Trading
Leverage size	Low	Medium	High
Trading activity	Low	Medium	High
Trading account size requirement	High	Medium	Low
Trading commission cost	Low	Medium	High
Trading risk level	Low	Medium	High
Trading oversight	Low	Medium	High

Furthermore, trading on a part-time basis requires less capital. There is less pressure to make money immediately. The trader does not have to trade fast, expensive stocks in increments of 1,000 or 2,000 shares to maximize trading profits. The trader can start on a part-time basis with slow stocks, which are often less expensive, trading in blocks of 500 shares or fewer, rather than 1,000. Trading the slow stocks in smaller blocks requires less initial capital, although the profit potential will be smaller as well. But the pressure to make money immediately is also less, as the part-time trader has other full-time employment.

2

Short-Term Trading

"Who bravely dares must sometimes risk a fall."

—Tobias G. Smollett

Every stock trader eventually develops his or her own trading style that reflects his or her risk tolerance and individual personality. In my opinion, the short-term trading techniques can be generalized into two broad and distinct trading styles, summarized as follows:

- swing, or so-called position or momentum, trading
- day trading

In reality, most traders use hybrids of different trading styles. During any portion of the trading day, a trader could predominantly be a swing trader, but when the opportunity arrives, the trader could quickly become a day trader. All traders are opportunists, so they would quickly take advantage of a price jump for a stock that is suddenly moving up due to some exceptional good news. Traders can begin in the trading business with one style and discover quickly, after losing some money, that the style is not working for them and try another trading style. All traders are continuously in the process of testing, modifying, and evolving their approaches.

That said, swing trading and day trading have a lot in common. Both trading styles essentially employ a price-momentum trading strategy. In other words, a stock's price is the variable to which traders pay the most attention. Compared with traditional value investing, or even growth investing, swing and day traders have a rather short attention span. Their holding period is quite short. They both emphasize technical over fundamental analysis.

Swing and day trading clearly are not passive, risk-averse investment strategies. Rather, both are highly speculative, and both require a great deal of skill, oversight, and—most importantly—a great deal of risk capital. In short, both are considered to be high-risk and potentially high-reward businesses.

Table 2.1 summarizes the differences between swing and day traders on one side of the spectrum and value and growth investors on the other side.

Day Traders

Despite the superficial similarities, there are major differences between the swing trader and the day trader, the biggest difference being the average stock-holding period. For day traders, that period is extremely short, ranging from a few minutes to a few hours. The objective of day trading

Table 2.1 *Comparison of Swing and Day Traders with Value and Growth Investors*

Value/Growth Investors	Swing/Day Traders
Proactive stand, anticipate trends	Reactive stand, observe trends
Perform fundamental analysis	Perform technical analysis
Focus on corporate earnings and assets	Focus on current stock price
Long-term holding period	Short-term holding period
Few buy-and-sell activities in a month	Many buy-and-sell orders in a week
Seek capital appreciation	Seek ordinary trading income
Delayed price quotes acceptable	Real-time price-quote system important
Real-time order execution unimportant	Real-time order execution important
Passive stock performance oversight	Active stock performance monitoring

is to exploit the intraday price volatility and profit from small intraday price movements. Subsequently, the price movement during this short period is rather small, from one-eighth to one-half of a point. To make any serious money through trading, a day trader must trade in increments of 1,000 shares per trade and make many trades in a single day. When such large blocks are traded, a move of one-eighth point translates into $125. The average day trader makes approximately forty trades each day. And then, as a general rule, most day traders close out their positions before the close of the market and go home "flat" without any overnight risk exposure, which is how day trading gets its name.

There are some compelling reasons why day traders exit their positions at the end of each day. First, "going flat" eliminates any overnight risk exposure, as markets remain active through the night. Corporations wait for the market to close to announce corporate news. Institutional investors continue to trade after the market hours through Instinet ECN, as do an increasing number of individual traders. Markets in Asia and Europe operate after the United States market hours. And finally, the federal government issues economic reports at 8 A.M. EST. All of these factors can cause a stock to gap either up or down in price when the U.S. markets open the following morning. Day traders are not prepared to deal with this uncertainty or the overnight risk exposure because they are set up to profit on fractional price movements.

If the day trader believes that a stock will continue to appreciate in value, the trader always has an option to buy the same stock when the market opens. If the stock opens with the gap up, the day trader is also forgoing the value of that upward gap. But that is a big if. Day traders believe that the potential reward of earning additional money from the gap does not justify the substantial risk that comes with holding long or short positions overnight.

Swing Traders

Swing traders have a somewhat longer stock holding period than do day traders, ranging from two days to more than a week. The objective of swing trading is to exploit the intraweek price volatility and profit from price movements over several trading days. Price movements tend to be much larger over the course of several days. Ranges of 1 to 10 points are common, especially during volatile periods. To make any serious money through swing trading, a trader must trade in much larger increments of several thousand shares per trade.

Some swing traders will trade smaller blocks but of shares with higher prices, such as those of eBay, which at this writing was trading at more than $150 per share. These higher-priced shares, which are often in technology and Internet stocks, tend to trade within a wide range during the course of a week, often offering good opportunity for profit.

Regardless of what sorts of stocks swing traders use, as a general rule, most will keep their open positions overnight and, therefore, assume overnight risk exposure. They must wait for the stock price *swing* to materialize over several days, which is how swing trading gets its name.

Swing traders are much better prepared to deal with the uncertainty of overnight risk exposure because they perform a noteworthy amount of fundamental research on the stocks they trade. They know the stock fundamentals well enough so they do not anticipate any earnings surprises during the holding period. Nevertheless, to ascertain a potential for a price swing, the swing trader's tools of analysis remain predominantly the technical-analysis indicators. Table 2.2 summarizes the differences between swing trading and day trading.

In some respects, the swing trader is a hybrid between the aggressive growth investor and the day trader. The swing trader pays close attention to the technical-analysis indicators and studies the stock closely before opening a position. Because the time frame of the analysis is several days, the swing trader most likely has on his or her computer screen several different technical-analysis charts within the different time frames. The objective is to ascertain the short-term (daily), intermediate-term (weekly), and long-term (monthly) price trends.

It is essential that the trader be able to differentiate and ascertain price trends among different time frames. One need only imagine that the trader is surrounded by trees (i.e., the short-term stock price movement) and cannot see the forest (i.e., the weekly stock price trend) to appreciate the importance of this ability. The following time frames are only my suggestions, which can easily be modified.

The intraday (one-hour), weekly (one-day), and monthly (one-day) stock-price data can be illustrated in the following manner. (Don't worry if you're not familiar with the concepts discussed here, as I'll

Table 2.2 *Swing Trading vs. Day Trading*

Trading Topics	Swing Trading	Day Trading
Trading objective	Profit from intraweek price volatility	Profit from intraday price volatility
Holding period	From 2 to 5 days	From a few minutes to a few hours—less than 1 day
Analysis tools	Technical first and then fundamental analysis	Technical analysis and Level II screen information
Target gain per trade	1 to 10 points	$\frac{1}{8}$ to 1 point
Stop loss per trade	$\frac{1}{2}$ to 2 points	$\frac{1}{4}$ to $\frac{1}{2}$ point
Trading size	More than 1,000 shares	Mostly up to 1,000 shares
Number of trades	1 to 3 trades per week	20 to 50 trades per day
Total commission cost	Relatively low	Extremely high

explain them more fully in chapter 10, "Introduction to Technical Analysis.")

The first hypothetical chart—and the one with the shortest timetable—would depict the most current or intraday price data compressed and displayed in the one-hour candlestick price format with the corresponding trading volume. (Candlestick charting and moving averages are discussed in section IV.) As a comparison, a typical day trader would most likely display one-minute price data. The swing investor would then overlay this chart with two exponential moving averages (EMA): the Fast EMA, with five periods (five hours), and the Slow EMA, with fifteen-hour periods. The Fast EMA, with five periods, represents five hours of trading data, whereas the Slow EMA, with fifteen periods, represents fifteen hours of price data. In addition, the swing trader would overlay a measure of the intraday price support and resistance levels, such as the Bollinger bands, which are based on calculations of the past 14-hour periods and with the standard deviation of plus or minus 1.85.

The second required chart with the longer timeframe would display a daily time period, such as for two months' worth of data. The second hypothetical chart would show sixty days of price data, compressed and displayed as the daily price candlestick, with the corresponding trading volume. Again, the swing trader would overlay this weekly chart with two exponential moving averages: the Fast EMA, with three periods (3 days), and the Slow EMA, with nine periods (9 days). Again, the swing trader could overlay a measure of the weekly price support and resistance levels, such as the Bollinger bands, which are based on calculations of the past 14-day periods.

Finally, the third and optional chart could show a much longer time period, such as six months' worth of data, just to keep everything in perspective and to ascertain long-term price trends. The third hypothetical chart would show 180 calendar days of price data, compressed and displayed as the daily price candlestick, with the corresponding trading volume. Again, the swing trader would overlay this chart with two exponential moving averages with much longer time frames: the Fast EMA, with ten periods (10 days) and the Slow EMA, with thirty periods (30 days). Again, the swing trader could overlay a measure of the long-term price support and resistance levels, such as the Bollinger bands.

If the trader were accurate, he or she would keep that trade position open for a longer period of time than usual, perhaps even longer than five days. Swing traders tend to have trading accounts with considerable capital. Subsequently, they can afford to purchase more than 1,000 shares at a time. They might start with 1,000 shares, and if the market moves in the right direction, they would take an additional 1,000 shares or more. In contrast, 1,000-share increments tend to be both a norm and a limit for traditional day traders.

Swing or position traders often take multiple stock positions. Given a large trading account, the position trader could purchase several stocks and monitor their performance simultaneously. Sometimes, position traders create a "basket" of stocks (for example, Internet stocks) and do a *basket trade*. Several trading software packages, such as CyberTrader® and TradeCast®, have the capability of creating a basket of stocks for quick execution. If the position trader believes that the Internet sector has the potential to go up, he or she might execute a basket order with the Internet stocks.

With the click of the mouse, the swing trader would send a simultaneous order to buy several Internet stocks in 1,000-share increments. From that point on, the swing trader would closely monitor the performance of all stocks in the basket. If any stock is not performing as expected (i.e., the price is not moving up or decreasing in value), the trader would quickly sell that stock. The trader would continue to monitor the other stocks in that basket. As long as those stocks are performing as expected (i.e., the price is increasing), the position trader would keep them. In essence, the position trader would keep the winners and shed the losers.

The Specialist Swing Trader

Still other swing traders specialize in a few NASDAQ or NYSE stocks that are actively traded and have substantial intraweek price volatility or high Beta values. Usually, these are well-known stocks such as Dell, Intel, Microsoft, Cisco, or similar high-tech stocks that generate a good deal of trading volume and price volatility. Some swing traders specialize in one or two stocks from each technology-industry sector, such as semiconductors, networks, Internet, software, hardware, and database providers. Because those high-tech stocks and industry sectors have significant price volatility, there are plenty of opportunities to trade. If momentum has stalled in one industry sector, other sectors might be active and volatile.

Swing traders that specialize in a few stocks develop a very good feel for these securities. Specialist swing traders monitor the stocks' performance continually, and thus know about the stocks' monthly, weekly, and intraday price data. For instance, the specialist swing traders develop a good feel about the stocks' intraday or intraweek price support and resistance levels. In addition, these specialist traders (not to be confused with NYSE specialists) read and monitor everything written or published in the mass media on their stocks. They'll ferret out whisper numbers and product announcements, and they'll know the names of the "ax analyst," that is, the most important analyst covering each of their stocks.

Because of their intense concentration on a few stocks, specialist swing traders are willing to take on additional risk. If the stock price momentum is there, they are willing to purchase or short-sell additional shares to pyramid or increase their position from 1,000 shares to several thousand shares. Specialists believe that the additional risk associated with the higher number of shares is a calculated risk. Due to their intense monitoring of a few stocks, specialists develop a higher tolerance for the risk. If a particular stock reversed its trend by 1 point or higher, a swing trader might still elect to hold onto his or her position, confident that the trend will reverse in due course.

Being a specialist swing trader has its advantages. Traders develop a great deal of knowledge about their stocks, so they tend to have a greater percentage of winning trades. Because they monitor only a few stocks, specialist swing traders tend to make fewer trades and thus save on commission costs. In my opinion, specialist swing traders also assume lower risks. They make fewer trades each week, and when they do trade, they take positions in the stocks that they know well. Nevertheless, specialists have lower profit potential. Because the specialists monitor only a few stocks, they miss many opportunities elsewhere in the market, where stock prices could be extremely volatile. Consequently, specialists seldom realize fantastic trading profits. They assume lower risk and thus the potential for a lower rate of return.

The Scalper Swing Trader

Scalping is the most common day trading style, and it is a very common swing trading style as well. The scalper swing traders monitor a great number of volatile stocks that have a decent daily trading volume (at least 500,000 shares per day). Their goal is to find stocks that are moving up or down. They may tune into CNBC for news of volatile stock moves or use their trading software to locate stocks approaching 52-week highs and lows.

Scalper swing traders devote a lot of time and effort to scanning or screening stock data. Stock screening is essentially a process of data mining for individual stocks that meet the specified screening parameters, such as large price momentum. You can find stock-screening tools on the Web at sites such as Microsoft Network's MoneyCentral Investor section (www.MoneyCentral.MSN.com), IQC.com (www.iqc.com), and Yahoo! Finance (finance.yahoo.com), which are the more commonly used stock Internet-based search engines.

Scalpers often spend many hours on the Internet searching and sifting through different financial information Web sites. They look for clues about any stocks that might be in play the following trading day to obtain early insights into which stocks might be volatile the next day. The Internet contains countless chat rooms designed specifically for traders, such as www.RagingBull.com or www.SiliconInvestor.com. These Internet chat rooms offer rumors, tips, and advice. Beware of the quality of information provided in chat rooms, because the rooms are often the source of "pump and dump" stock schemes. My advice is caveat emptor—buyer beware!

Trading stocks based on news can be extremely lucrative. There are numerous events, such as stock upgrades (or downgrades), mergers and acquisitions reports (or rumors), or cash-dividend increases (or decreases) that could cause an immediate public reaction (or overreaction). Most likely, the market (that is, the public) will overreact, and the stock price will move greatly. A word of caution, however—the swing trader should avoid submitting a market buy order during a time when the market is absorbing positive news, because the order could get filled near the stock's intraday price high. The ensuing profit taking (that is, selling) could quickly lower the stock's price, and you could end up selling the stock at a loss. It is always a good idea to utilize a limit buy order.

If scalper swing traders believe that particular stocks have the potential to move up or down, they would add these stocks to their watch lists. For example, they might create a watch list portfolio on one of the financial Web sites mentioned previously. Or, if they utilize advanced trading software such as that available from CyBerCorp (www.cybercorp.com) or TradeCast (www.TradeCast.com), they could use that software's market ticker window. Once a scalper swing trader has established a watch list, from that time on, he or she will monitor the stocks for any price momentum. If price movement has been detected, scalpers will monitor the stocks' progress using real-time charts or Level II quotes.

Scalpers do not closely and continuously monitor the performance of all stocks, and thus they do not form a strong opinion about the stocks' weekly price support and resistance levels. As a rule, scalpers do not have a high tolerance for loss. They tend to get in and out of trading positions relatively quickly, within a few days. If they are correct about a stock, they might stay in that trading position long enough to pick up a profit of one point or higher. If the scalpers are wrong, they will quickly leave with a minimal loss of half a point.

Scalpers are not willing to absorb higher risk. They do not want to hold and wait for a stock to reverse a losing trend, because they do not feel confident that they know the behavior of the stock they're trading well enough. Scalpers also seldom pyramid or increase their positions from 1,000 shares to several thousand shares. Because they seek narrow moves in a stock, scalper swing traders tend to make many more trades than the specialist swing trader, and consequently they pay more in commissions. For this reason, day-trading shops love to have successful scalper swing traders in their trading rooms.

Because scalpers do not acquire a great deal of knowledge about any particular stock, they tend to have a lower percentage of winning trades. They simply surf the NASDAQ and NYSE markets looking for intraweek price volatility. If a stock is moving up, a scalper would buy that stock. In my opinion, scalpers assume greater risk than specialist swing traders do. However, because scalpers monitor many stocks, they have opportunities to score more "home runs." A home run would be a winning trade that moves 10 points or more in their favor. On 1,000 shares traded, that would translate into a $10,000 profit or higher. Thus, scalpers have the potential to enjoy "fabulous" trading days.

This presentation on the two groups of swing trading styles is perhaps an oversimplification. My purpose here is only to illustrate the advantages and disadvantages of the different trading styles. Eventually, all traders develop their own trading styles and philosophies that may incorporate features of either scalping or specialist swing trading.

General Trading Principles

It is more important to do the right trades than to do the trades right. Many traders become preoccupied with trade-order execution mechanics. They become very proficient in understanding the NASDAQ and NYSE market-order execution systems. They have mastered trading-execution software and are able to enter and exit trades efficiently. But these skills alone do not make them good traders.

The most important half of the equation is the ability to pick the right trades. Trading success ultimately depends on two factors:

1. The trader must have a higher percentage of winning trades than losing trades. Let us assume that the ratio of winning to losing trades is 60 to 40 percent, which is a realistic assumption. The long-term objective is to improve that winning percentage through time and experience.

2. The trader must maximize his or her winning trades and minimize the cost of losing trades. In other words, the dollar value from the 60 percent of winning trades should be substantially higher than the dollar value derived from the 40 percent of losing trades. This is when risk management (discussed in chapter 9) becomes a crucial skill.

To improve the overall percentage of winning trades, the swing trader—or any other style of stock traders—should trade only when the odds of winning are in the trader's favor; in other words, when the probability of winning has increased. It is my opinion that the probability of winning will increase when the following events occur:

■ The trader trades on the same side of the stock trend. As traders often state, "Trend is a friend." Again, a trader does not need to anticipate or predict the future market trend. All a trader needs to do is react to existing and observable price trends. The trend can be seen on the real-time technical-analysis charts or on the Level II screen. There is no need to time the market turns perfectly and buy at the bottom and sell at the peak of the cycle. It is enough to ride the stock's momentum long enough to realize a profit.

■ The trader does not buy overbought stocks or short oversold stocks. In other words, the trader is always cognizant about a stock's daily or weekly price resistance and support levels. That information is again observable on technical-analysis charts, such as the Bollinger bands.

■ The trader trades on the same side of the market as the Wall Street professionals. The probability is greater that the NASDAQ market makers can predict future market prices more accurately than can average traders. If key market makers (see chapter 6) are accumulating a stock, the probability is that the stock will increase in value. Conversely, if key market makers or specialists are disposing of a stock from their inventory, the probability is that the stock will decrease in value.

- The trader takes a trading position only after observing a clear trading signal to buy or short sell the stock (see section IV for details). Without a clear signal, the trader is gambling.

- The trader attempts to buy the stock at the BID price and sell at the ASK price, which is the basic trading strategy of the NASDAQ market makers and NYSE specialists. By cutting or eliminating the BID and ASK spread, the trader's profitability will increase by the amount of the eliminated spread.

3

Trading and Investing Strategies

*"It seems to be a law of nature, inflexible and inexorable,
that those who will not risk cannot win."*

—*Paul Jones, Revolutionary War naval hero*

This chapter begins with two questions: (1) How do you organize all of the fundamental and technical stock market data into a meaningful action plan? and (2) How do you select the right stock at the right time? The answer to both questions is straightforward—you must have a trading or investing strategy. This chapter will help you select a trading or investment strategy that's appropriate to your objectives and level of risk tolerance. At the end of the chapter, we'll discuss stock screening, which is a tool that can be found on a variety of Internet sites. Stock screening allows you to perform a database search for stocks that fit the parameters of your trading or investment strategy.

I would like to reiterate one important point here: Stock trading is not investing. I do not advocate anywhere in this book that anyone should sell his or her entire diversified investment portfolio to raise sufficient funds to start trading stocks. On the contrary—keep your long-term investment portfolio diversified. Stock diversification is the single most important step that investors can take to improve the long-term performance of their investment portfolios. Think of your diversified investment portfolio as your retirement nest.

Neither do I advocate that anyone should borrow money from credit card cash advances or second mortgages or from friends or relatives to raise sufficient funds for stock trading. You should only use your own speculative funds that you can afford to lose. Think about your trading capital as your speculative money jar, which is there for high-risk stock trading.

Strategies

There are basically three trading and investment strategies that broadly generalize and summarize the many different methods for picking individual stocks. The list is ranked in relative importance from the viewpoint of the swing trader. The key is to select a suitable investment strategy that fits your objectives and risk tolerance and then stick to it.

1. Price momentum trading
2. Growth investing
3. Value investing

As a general rule, value investing appeals more to risk-averse and long-term investors who plan to buy and hold a stock position for many years. Growth investing appeals mostly to risk-tolerant investors who are seeking higher than the average rate of return. The stock-holding period for the growth investors can range from many months to even years. Momentum trading appeals to traders who are risk takers and who are seeking an extremely high rate of return. Subsequently, the stock-holding period for the momentum traders can range from several hours to one or two weeks.

The difference among the three types of stock market participants is dramatic and is broadly summarized and generalized in table 3.1.

Momentum Trading

Momentum trading strategy appeals to swing traders. The focus of the strategy is to identify stocks whose prices are changing at a faster rate than the industry average. In other words, the strategy means "show me a stock that is moving."

Table 3.1 *Three Types of Stock Market Participants*

	Momentum Trader	Growth Investor	Value Investor
Personal style	Risk taker	Risk-tolerant investor	Risk-averse investor
Focus of analysis	Current stock price	Corporate earnings	Corporate assets
Key guide	Current stock price	Income statement	Balance sheet
Reaction stance	Reactive stance, observe current price trend	Proactive stance, anticipate short-term price trend	Proactive stance, anticipate long-term price trend
Analysis used	Technical analysis	Fundamental and technical analysis	Fundamental analysis
Holding period	Few hours to several days	Few months to several months	Several months to many years
Trading activity	Several buy and sell orders in 1 week	Few buy and sell orders in several months	Few buy and sell orders in several years
Financial goal	Seek ordinary trading income	Seek medium-term capital appreciation	Seek long-term capital appreciation
Stock monitoring	Active stock-performance monitoring	Somewhat active stock-performance monitoring	Passive stock-performance oversight
Price-quote system	Real-time price-quote system a must	Delayed price quotes acceptable	Delayed price quotes acceptable
Order execution	Real-time order execution a must	Real-time order execution unimportant	Real-time order execution unimportant

Swing traders do not really care to learn much about the company's intrinsic value. They are shareholders of record for an extremely short period of time, such as a few days, and thus they do not want to burden themselves with "extraneous" financial information. Their objective is to profit from price volatility.

Technical analysis is the best tool to use to ascertain a stock's momentum. (This topic is addressed in detail in section IV.) Nevertheless, it is feasible to attempt to glance into the future without the benefit of technical analysis. The key is to identify stocks that are going up or down at a faster rate than the average market-price index. The basic hypothesis is that these stocks will simply continue with the exhibited price trend—that the price history will repeat itself, which is truly a heroic assumption.

The two most common price-momentum purchasing tactics employed are to search for or screen the companies that have the following characteristics:

1. **Greatest three-month price gain relative to the rest of the market.** This strategy makes sense if the market indicates continued bull market conditions, as evidenced by the rising S & P's 500 index, for example. That is, search to buy the "strong" stocks with a strong positive price momentum if the broad market (the S & P's 500 index) is also increasing in value.

In the event of a bear market, the strategy is diametrically opposite. The key is to short sell stocks that have the greatest three-month price decline relative to the rest of the market. In other words, look to short sell "weak" stocks that have a large negative price momentum if the broad market (the S & P's 500 index) is also declining in value; that is, identify the stocks that have the strongest stock performance in either price direction during one quarter, and then go with the broad market trend.

2. **The 52-week high/low.** This strategy is based on the following assumption: If the S & P's 500 index is rising, then the stocks that broke the new 52-week high price or exhibited the 52-week price resistance breakthrough will continue to increase in price. Conversely, if the S & P's 500 index is declining, then the stocks that broke the new 52-week low price or exhibited the 52-week price support breakthrough will continue to decrease in value.

The price-momentum strategy has much merit if the overall market is trending. If the overall stock market is choppy or flat, it is difficult to ascertain any price trend. In other words, this price-momentum strategy works well if there is an overall bullish or bearish market sentiment.

Growth Investing

The objective of growth investing is to identify stocks whose company earnings are growing at a faster rate than the industry standard. Unlike the value investor, the growth investor's goal is not to identify the cheap stocks. On the contrary, the growth investor will pay dearly for the growth. Growth investors often end up purchasing stocks that are commonly being traded at the 52-week high price. The objective is to identify the companies that exhibit earnings-growth momentum.

Growth investors view a stock as an ownership claim on the company's future earnings. Subsequently, the company's net earnings are the focus of the analysis, and thus growth investors pay close attention to changes in the company's financial income statement (see section IV).

The growth-investing strategy means being able to identify early on those companies that exhibit continuously higher earnings. The best measure of growth in corporate earnings is the growth in the company's earnings per share (EPS). EPS is the best measure of the company's growth because it is based on the net income figure, which takes into account both the changes in the company's revenues and expenses.

A good growth-stock buy is a stock that trades at a price level that is considered reasonable, given the company's earnings growth pattern— in other words, the strategy is "growth at reasonable price." A conventional rule of thumb is that the company's price/earnings multiple (PE) should be close to the company's earnings growth rate, which is defined as the growth rate in the company's EPS.

A financial analyst pegged the "growth at reasonable price" as the PE-growth ratio, or PEG ratio. The PEG ratio depicts the absolute number of the PE multiple divided by the EPS growth rate. For instance, the PE multiple might be 40, whereas the growth in the EPS is only 20 percent, which would make the PEG ratio 2. If the PEG ratio is substantially greater than 1, then the stock is overvalued, and thus the particular stock might be a good short-selling candidate in an overall down market. Conversely, if the PEG ratio is less than 1, then the stock is priced reasonably, given the corporate earnings growth rate.

Let us use Dell Computer Corporation stock as an example. It is not surprising that value investors find Dell stock to be overvalued or too expensive. Even growth investors would agree that Dell stock is somewhat overvalued. Growth investors would compare the absolute number of the Dell PE multiple against the absolute value of the company's growth rate in EPS. For instance, Dell's EPS in 1999 and 1998 were $0.58 and $0.36, which is a 61 percent increase in one year, and thus the trailing EPS for the last 12 months increased 61 percent. Because the absolute number of the Dell PE multiple of 70 is higher than the value of 61, the PEG ratio is 1.1; thus, one can conclude that Dell is somewhat overvalued.

Defining the "reasonable price" for growth is an increasingly controversial issue for the high-technology-sector stocks in the bull market of the 1990s. For instance, the NASDAQ composite index increased in value an astonishing 85.6 percent in 1999. An amazing 800 stocks doubled in value in one year, and 37 stocks appreciated in value by an astronomical 1,000 percent. A single company, Qualcomm, jumped in price 2,600 percent in 1999. Twenty percent of the NASDAQ stocks in 1999 had a PE multiple higher than 100. Are any of these stock price increases in 1999 reasonable for the expected growth?

Technology investors simply point to the fact that we live in the age of the information-technology revolution. Growth investors point to the current technology giants, such as Microsoft, Cisco Systems, or Dell Computer Corporation, who were small technology companies a decade ago. Growth investors claim that the high-technology highfliers are the companies that create new products and new markets that don't even exist today. How can you assign a "reasonable price" to the stocks of companies that have such tremendous future earnings potential?

Growth investors argue further that traditional stock-valuation rules do not really apply to the high-tech sector. According to growth investors, the key to the appropriate stock-valuation analysis of high-tech stocks is to assign a monetary value to the technological innovation. Even more important is the fact that these high-flying high-tech firms must exhibit a pattern of continued technological innovation. Eventually the display of continued technological innovation will result in continuous and substantial corporate earnings.

Growth investors pay close attention to company earnings. They are extremely sensitive to any announcement of earnings surprises, particularly the negative ones. Growth investors believe that because they are paying premium price for a company's track record of higher and higher expected earnings, they do not want to be surprised with bad earnings news. The slowdown in the company's earnings growth rate translates automatically into unpleasant news. The company's PE multiple will increase, whereas the EPS growth rate will decrease. This unwelcome development would clearly present the stock as grossly overvalued in the eyes of most stock market participants. It would result in an increased supply and reduced demand for the stock, which then would result in a price decline for the stock.

High-tech companies, such as Dell Computer or Microsoft, are prime examples of growth companies. However, old, established U.S. companies, such as General Electric or Pfizer, can also be classified as growth companies. These mature and established growth companies have the following common characteristics:

- Produce goods and services that are continuously in demand
- Continuously develop new products and services
- Have high-profit margins
- Have excellent marketing and sales programs
- Continuously invest in research and development, new equipment, and plants
- Have well-regarded and competent management teams

Growth investing requires a great deal of skill. The following illustrate why growth investing is difficult:

1. It is extremely difficult to identify the growth companies before they are widely discovered by the general investing public. In other words, it is extremely difficult to find growth stock before the growth stocks become too expensive and thus overvalued.

2. It is not easy to identify one or two small companies that will eventually become the future leaders in that industry, even if the industry appears to have a great deal of growth potential.

3. Most of the new companies are small and perhaps struggling. Thus it is difficult to analyze the financial statements of small companies and ascertain with any degree of certainty the expected company earnings.

4. Finally, there is always the possibility of imitators entering the market and producing the same product or service cheaper than the industry leader. That is the nature of market competition. Profits attract competitors who enter the market and drive the price down,

subsequently lowering the overall industry earnings potential. The key, then, for long-term profitability is to have the proprietary technology that would discourage future competition.

Growth investors are not market contrarians. Rather, they buy the stocks that everyone else is buying. In essence, they are always following the price trend. When following a trend for a stock, growth investors must be vigilant, because the trend can be reversed quickly. This requires continuous oversight of the growth stocks they own and the willingness to get out of a stock position quickly. Because growth stocks depend heavily on the expected corporate earnings, any negative earnings surprise can send the stock into a nosedive.

Value Investing

The objective of value investing is to identify stocks that are trading below their intrinsic net asset value; that is, to identify cheap stocks or bargain stocks relative to the company's net asset value. The value is simply defined as the net worth of the company, which means the company's assets minus the company's liabilities. Thus value investors look at the stock as a claim on the company's net assets, and so the company's assets are the focus of the analysis. Consequently, value investors pay close attention to changes in the company balance sheet (see section IV).

A good stock to a value investor is a stock that is trading at a price level below the company's net assets. There may be many reasons why the stock price is below the company's intrinsic value. The company might be out of market favor for various reasons, such as poor recent earnings reports, or a loss of appeal throughout the entire industry sector, or perhaps uncertainty about the company management. The bottom line is the stock is depressed. Nevertheless, the company continues to have a strong balance sheet, and thus strong assets.

In essence, value investors look for a bargain. Ideally they seek to buy shares of quality companies whose current stock price is below the book value per share. The book value, or the net worth, is basically the company's assets less the company's liabilities. The objective is to buy the company's net assets at a discount. Their hope is that the company will turn around. Company management, which may be new management, might improve the company's performance and thus improve the company's earnings. At that time, the company will have both a strong balance sheet and a strong income statement. Stock market participants will notice this development, and the market will bid up the stock price. Only at that time would value investors make money.

Unfortunately, it takes a good deal of time, effort, and management skill to turn around a company and regenerate any excitement for the stock on Wall Street. Thus value investors must be patient—buy and hold is their modus operandi. Time is presumably on their side. Their hope is that when they purchase the stock, it will be at the bottom of the cycle (or at least at a steep price discount). Then they'll wait for the price turnaround, which may or may not happen.

What if the company does not turn around? What if there are structural business problems in the company that cause continued financial losses? What if there are industry-wide economic reasons that pushed the company into losses? What if the company assets are grossly overvalued at the outset? Company assets are extremely difficult to value or calculate, so value investors must have a great deal of financial accounting skills to sift through a firm's financial fundamental data and answer these questions. In short, the value investor must devote a lot of time and effort to studying and researching the company's financial statement and management practices.

Finally, value investors are essentially the market contrarians. They buy stocks that are clearly out of favor. They are always going against the grain of the market. When most investors are fleeing a particular stock, value investors are accumulating it. It is rather difficult to be a market contrarian. Value investors must be able to ignore and endure all of the negative stock-analysis reports made daily by the many stock market pundits on CNBC or in print media and continue to have faith in the company management.

The most common value-investing tactic is to search for the companies that have the following:

1. **Low price-to-book ratio.** For instance, a price-to-book ratio of 0.5 means that the value investor is paying 50 cents for every dollar of the company's net worth—a bargain.

2. **High current yield.** For example, if you select a stock that provides a relatively high dividend of $1 compared with the current stock price of $10, there is a high current yield of 10 percent. It is not that

the $1 dividend is an extraordinarily large dividend. On the contrary, it is the current cheap price of $10 for the stock that makes the current yield so large. Again, the high current yield indicates a bargain.

There are several popular investment variations on the theme of selecting stocks with the high current yield. One such tactic, known as the "dogs of the Dow," has its own Internet site (www.dogsofthedow.com). The strategy involves buying the worst-performing stocks (i.e., dogs) among 30 stocks in the Dow Jones industrial average.

Implementation of the "dogs of the Dow" is also simple. Each January pick 10 or fewer stocks from a choice of 30 blue chip stocks in the Dow Jones industrial average that have the highest current yield, and keep the stocks in a portfolio for one year. Next January, do the same thing. Sell your winners, or the stocks that had increased in price during the year (which means the stock's current yield had decreased). Again, buy the "dogs," or the stocks with the highest current yield at that time. The risk is minimized because you are buying stocks in the Dow Jones industrial average, so you are buying quality stocks of the most established and mature corporations in America.

Another variation on the same theme is the "SAPI slugs" strategy, which translates into buying the slowest-performing stocks (i.e., slugs) among 500 stocks in the S & P's 500 index. Again, each January pick several stocks from a choice of the 500 largest corporations in America that have the highest current yield, and keep the stocks in a portfolio for one year. Next January, sell your winners, or the stocks that had increased in price during the year so that the stock's current yield had decreased. Again, buy the "slugs," or the stocks with the highest current yield at that time in the S & P's 500 index.

You can add another element to a value-investing strategy by analyzing a company's credit. Because value investors are looking for cheap stocks, they want to be sure that there are no underlying structural reasons, such as cash-flow problems, that would explain why a particular stock is cheap. In essence, value investors want to verify that the company is financially stable in the short term. There are several fundamental-analysis ratios available for this purpose. These ratios are designed to indicate a company's ability to meet its short-term liability. The liquidity ratios, such as cash flow, current ratio, debt-coverage ratio, and debt-to-equity ratio, will indicate whether the company has the ability to convert the company's current assets into cash quickly (see section IV).

Market Capitalization

A stock's market capitalization adds another twist to all three investing strategies. Market capitalization is defined as the total value of all outstanding shares and is computed by multiplying the number of shares by the current market price. The market capitalization, or "cap," of the stock is the technique used to segment the stock market into four distinct groups. Historically, the market capitalization has been grouped into the following categories:

1. **Large cap.** Stocks with market capitalization greater than $5 billion
2. **Mid cap.** Stocks with market capitalization from $500 million to $5 billion
3. **Small cap.** Stocks with market capitalization from $150 million to $500 million
4. **Micro cap.** Stocks with market capitalization below $150 million

Any of the three general strategies—momentum, growth, or value investing—could be applied to one or more of the specific stock market segments. As a rule, larger-market capitalization has historically represented smaller risk. The old Wall Street guidelines suggest that the risk-averse investor could reduce the risk by narrowing the investment strategy to a large-cap stock segment. Again, the hypothesis holds that smaller risk would translate into smaller returns. Similarly, traders who seek substantial trading profits would end up trading in mid- or small-cap stocks because those are hypothetically more volatile than large-cap stocks. But this is not necessarily true in the current volatile stock market environment.

Stock Screening

Now that you understand the three investment strategies—value, growth, and price-momentum investing—the next step is to select the strategy that fits the investor's objectives. In essence, the investment or trading strategy is the plan of action. Once that plan is developed, it is time to pick the stocks that will meet the plan's criteria.

This is not an easy task. There are approximately 3,000 common stocks listed on the NYSE and 4,400 stocks traded on the NASDAQ exchange. How do you select a few stocks that meet a specific investor's investment criteria at that particular point in time from the universe of 7,400 stocks? The answer is, by using stock screening, which is essentially the process of searching for stocks that meet the specified screening criteria in the universe of all stocks in the stock market database.

Only a few years ago the process of stock screening was rather complicated. The investor or trader first needed to obtain the most recent stock market data from the financial-service companies that provide data feed. As a rule, that financial data was not free and was never in real time. At best, the investor or trader would analyze historical financial-market data that was one or a few days old. Occasionally, the data provider would send the trader or investor updates or the most recent market data through regular mail on diskette or electronically via e-mail.

Investors or traders then needed a computer-software program that could process the huge amount of data. At worst, the investor or trader would write his or her own "program" using the basic spreadsheet or database software, such as Microsoft's Excel or Access application programs. Clearly this was a time-consuming and laborious process. At best, the investor would purchase an expensive software package, such as the TradeStation™, designed specifically for such daunting tasks. Thankfully, the computer-screening interface was greatly simplified and automated; the trader or investor needed only to insert the investment criteria in the predesigned window and start the stock-screening process.

Today, stock screening can be done for free on the Internet. Not only is the service free, but also the search engines use the most current data available. Because the data is always kept up-to-date, there is no need for you to update your database. Microsoft Network's Money-Central Investor section (www.MoneyCentral.MSN.com) and Yahoo! Finance (www.Quote.Yahoo.com) are the two most commonly used stock search engines. There are also other free, well-designed stock search engines on the Internet, such as Stock Valuation with Sense (www.StockSense.com), Rapid Research (www.RapidResearch.com), StockScreener (www.StockScreener.com), IQC.com (www.iqc.com), and JustQuotes (www.JustQuotes.com). In addition, TraderBot (www.TraderBot.com) offers customized stock screening and ranking, using fundamental and technical inputs in real time ($39.95 per month).

Stock-screening tools allow investors or traders to be extremely creative and precise in the way they select stocks. Most of the stock search engines have pull-down menus of different predefined and common investment-criteria choices, such as the "dogs of the Dow." In addition, stock search engines can be customized to meet individual investors' criteria. All stock-screening search engines have basically three common data-inputting components, which must be populated with the following data:

1. **Field Name.** Describes which particular financial ratio or information is being analyzed. The field names are conveniently grouped under a few subheadings to simplify the screening process. For instance, the MSN stock search engine grouped hundreds of possible financial ratios into the following subheadings:
   - Company basics, such as the industry name, market capitalization, membership in the S & P's 500 or the Dow Jones industrial average index or different stock exchanges
   - Growth rates, such as EPS growth (quarter vs. quarter, year vs. year) for the firm and the industry
   - Price history, such as the 52-week high and low and percentage price change in the past week, month, quarter, six months, and year to date
   - Return on investment, such as one-year and five-year return on equity and return on assets for the company and the industry
   - Price ratios, such as price-to-book and PE ratios for the firm and the industry for different periods, from current period to one month, to six months, to one year, and to five years
   - Management efficiency, such as the revenues or income per employee for the firm and industry
   - Profit margin, such as the net or gross profit margin for the firm and the industry for one and five years
   - Financial condition, such as the current or quick ratios, debt-coverage ratio, and debt-to-equity ratio, for the firm and industry
   - Dividends, such as current yields, payout ratios, and dividend rates for the firm and industry
   - Trading, such as beta values, short-interest shares, and average daily volume, for two weeks, one month, one quarter, and one year

2. **Operator.** Describes the logical function that needs to be performed, such as "greater than," "smaller than," "equal to," "high as possible," "low as possible," and "near"

3. **Value.** Can be the actual custom value or the value in the most recent trading day, week, month, quarter, or year

If the investor seeks the stocks of only the large and established companies in America, then he or she could simply select the following:

1. In the Field Name section, select the "market capitalization" variable.
2. In the Operator field, select "greater than."
3. In the Value field, select the custom value of "5,000,000,000," which represents $5 billion.

The search engine subsequently searches the entire stock database for all companies that match the particular criteria. The result is a list of all companies that fit this description at the present time. The investor can also select multiple criteria from the wide range of fundamental analysis choices.

The price-momentum investor or trader who seeks the short-term price-movement potential would specify the following screening criteria:

1. Market capitalization greater than 500 million
2. Average daily trading volume in the past year greater than 500,000 shares
3. Percent price change in the past week greater than 10 percent
4. Percent price change in the past month greater than 20 percent
5. Rank by highest possible percent price change in the last quarter

The result is a list of large- and mid-cap companies with plenty of trading liquidity (i.e., average trading volume greater than 500,000 shares). Most importantly, the list has stocks whose current prices are changing at a faster pace than the rest of the market. If the screening-match list is too large, the next step would be to increase the weekly and monthly percent-price-change criteria from 10 and 20 percent to 20 and 30 percent, which would subsequently narrow the list of stocks.

The growth investor who seeks continued and high-price appreciation potential would specify the following screening criteria:

1. Market capitalization greater than 1 billion
2. Average daily trading volume in the past year greater than 500,000 shares

3. EPS growth this quarter vs. last quarter greater than 30 percent

4. EPS growth this year vs. last year greater than 30 percent

5. Rank by the percent price change in the past year as high as possible

The result is a list of large- and mid-cap companies that have plenty of trading liquidity and that have the greatest growth and price increase. The list can be large, so the next step would be to increase quarterly and annually the EPS growth criteria from 30 to 40 percent, which would subsequently narrow the list of companies.

The value investor, however, seeks the bargain or distressed stocks and would specify the following screening criteria:

1. Market capitalization greater than 5 billion

2. Average daily trading volume in the past year greater than 500,000 shares

3. Beta value of less than 1.5 and greater than 0.5

4. Price-to-book value as low as possible

5. Rank by the current yield as high as possible

The result is a list of the large-cap companies that have plenty of trading liquidity and limited price volatility (beta value less than 1.5); also, the current stock prices of the companies are less than the intrinsic values.

The stock-screening engines of today also have built-in search queries that will scan stocks based on common and somewhat complex criteria, such as the price-earnings-growth (PEG) ratio.

Another screening technique is to screen stocks that have a PEG ratio below the industry PE multiple. The stocks that have a lower PE multiple than their competitors might be considered undervalued and poised for a price rebound. Yet another screening method is to compare the company's price/cash flow ratio with the industry standard. If the company's price/cash flow ratio is well below the industry standard, then the company generates a lot more cash flow than its competitors, given its stock price.

I am not advocating that traders blindly buy or short sell a stock just because the stock symbol pops up at the top of the computer screen after the search. The results of stock screening are only the first line of defense. It is up to each trader to take a closer look at a particular stock and determine whether the stock deserves further consideration. Internet stock market databases have all kinds of current financial information on any public company. For example, take a look at the Zacks Research Inc. Internet site (www.Zacks.com) and see what the consensus is among the financial analysts who are following the stock.

Back Testing

Finally, there is always the option to back test the particular screening strategy against the long-term historical market data. Several stock-research software applications, such as the TradeStation (www.OmegaResearch.com), allow investors to program and input such screening criteria as the buy-and-sell signals. For example, the screening criterion becomes the buy signal and similar screening criteria generate the sell signal. Then the computer program sifts through the historical market records, simulates buying and selling of the selected stocks, and calculates the overall return. That return is then compared with the standard industry benchmark—the S & P's 500 index.

As you can see, back testing requires a lot of computer number crunching, and, most importantly, it requires an effort to "program" the appropriate buy-and-sell signals. The objective is to determine whether a certain investment strategy would have produced profitable rates of return in the past. There is no guarantee that back testing of any screening strategy will prove that the particular investment strategy would work in the future. The overall stock market environment might change, because the investors' and traders' expectations about the future change.

The accuracy of investment simulations, or back testing, is a real issue as well. For instance, let us take a look at an investment strategy based on the quarterly EPS growth rates. The first-quarter (January, February, and March) earnings figure for a company will appear in the historical records as if they were available on April 1. Thus the April 1 stock prices would be used as the entry or exit points. The simulation exercise assumes that the prices on April 1 reflect the complete knowledge available about the corporate first-quarter earnings among Wall Street participants.

In reality, the information on corporate first-quarter earnings is published and disseminated during the next several weeks in April, because different companies issue their quarterly earnings on different days during the first few weeks of April. Using this particular investment strategy, investors or traders would end up buying and selling stocks during the first weeks in April and not necessarily on April 1. Consequently, traders might obtain dramatically different prices and thus different investment returns than what the back testing results (based on the April 1 stock purchases) would have indicated.

Where to Trade

"The future ain't what it used to be."

—*Yogi Berra*

How true. The stock trading climate today is dramatically different from the trading environment a decade ago. There is no shortage of opinions among financial economists as to what the stock trading environment might look like ten years from today. As Edgar Fiedler pointed out, "Ask five economists, and you will get five different answers. Six, if one went to Harvard."

Before the reader can progress to more advanced topics of swing trading, the basic concepts of where to trade must be addressed and understood. The objective of this section is to establish a sound foundation for understanding the differences among the NASDAQ, the NYSE, ECN trading environments and the Internet, and direct access stockbrokers.

4

Trading Environments

"The market is not an invention of capitalism. It has existed for centuries. It is an invention of civilization."

—*Mikhail Gorbachev*

When William Batten, a former chairman and CEO of the New York Stock Exchange (NYSE), was asked what stock exchanges do, he eloquently replied, "We produce the price." This is so true. In a nutshell, any stock exchange is a marketplace that determines the stock price. However, different exchanges have different ways of determining the price for a particular stock at any point in time. The NYSE is an established and centralized auction-type exchange with a string of intermediaries. The NYSE is very different from the National Association of Securities Dealers Automated Quotation (NASDAQ), which is a negotiated, decentralized electronic exchange that relies on a computerized network of several hundred stock merchants. And both the NASDAQ and NYSE are dramatically different from the privately held Electronic Communication Networks (ECNs), which are the new players on the block.

All three types of the trading environments will determine the stock price, but with different levels of efficiency, cost, and fairness. The swing traders can choose to trade on a variety of exchanges or ECNs, and therefore it's important to understand how each works. It is worth mentioning that day traders largely use the NASDAQ and ECNs because they offer detailed books on the trade order flows (see chapter 6), whereas swing traders might not need to know that level of detail on the order flows.

The NASDAQ

The NASDAQ system was created in 1971 as a true electronic securities exchange. The NASDAQ market is a negotiated and decentralized marketplace. There is no centralized meeting place or trading floor. Transactions are conducted through a computer network that connects NASD brokers/dealers, who never see each other face-to-face, as do participants on the NYSE. The National Association of Securities Dealers (NASD) regulates the NASDAQ market. In April 2000, the NASD proposed to restructure and spin off the NASDAQ as a separate, for-profit, privately held company.

The NASD membership consists of securities brokers and dealers, who are authorized by NASD to transact securities business in the United States. A NASD broker is defined as any individual, corporation, partnership, association, or other legal entity engaged in transacting securities business for the accounts of others. A NASD dealer is any individual, corporation, partnership, association, or other legal entity engaged in the business of buying and selling securities for its own account. It is noteworthy that most national and regional retail brokerages are broker dealers, which means they can trade stocks on your behalf and on their own behalf.

A trading transaction on a NASDAQ listed stock is initiated when a trader places an order with the NASD broker. The NASD broker completes an order ticket, which is then routed electronically to the NASD dealer who carries that particular security in his or her inventory. The NASD dealer is required to provide continuous bids (BID is the price at which the NASD dealer is willing to buy the security) and offers (ASK is the price at which the NASD dealer is willing to sell the security). Subsequently, the NASD dealer is said to "make a market" in that security. Thus the NASD dealer is called a "market maker."

NASDAQ market makers (and NYSE specialists) are the sanctioned securities merchants. The market maker and the specialist have two distinct roles. They are, simultaneously, the brokers who transact securities business for the account of others, and at the same time they are dealers engaged in trading securities for their own proprietary accounts. It is important that traders understand this dual nature of the "market making" business. NASDAQ Trader (www.NASDAQtrader.com) is an excellent source of NASDAQ trading information.

In essence, there are two ways that the market makers and specialists can make money. The first is to earn the spread, which is accomplished by buying the stock from the public at the lower BID price and selling it to the public at the higher ASK price. Suppose, for instance, that the best BID and ASK price for DELL is $50^1/_2$ and $50^9/_{16}$, respectively. (Because this is a NASDAQ stock, I must focus on the market makers, although the same principle applies for the NYSE listed stocks.) That means that the market makers are buying low ($50.50), selling high ($50.56), and earning the spread of $^1/_{16}$, or 6.25 cents. In this case, the market makers are acting as the agents for the public that desires to buy or sell that particular stock. Keep in mind that when market makers buy and sell stock, they are either adding shares or extracting them from their own portfolios.

If one market maker buys 1,000 shares from the public at the BID price and sells the same 1,000 shares a few seconds later at the ASK price, then a $^1/_{16}$ spread translates into a $62.50 profit. If the spread remains at the average of 6.25 cents during the day, and if Dell's average daily trading volume over 52 weeks remains at 18.5 million shares, then market makers as a collective group would earn $2.5 million on that stock alone.

A brief look at the daily trading volume at NASDAQ (and NYSE) reveals the scope of the market-making business. NASDAQ's daily average trading volume over 52 weeks is approximately 1 billion shares (ranging from 775 million to 1.2 billion shares). Collectively, market makers could earn $66 million in one day if the average spread is only $^1/_{16}$. Similarly, the NYSE's daily trading average volume during 1999 was approximately 809 million shares. Collectively, NYSE specialists could earn $50 million in one day. Apparently, the market-making business is quite lucrative.

The other way that market makers make their money is to trade stocks for their own proprietary accounts. The only way to make money by trading is to buy low and sell high. In other words, all market makers and specialists want to accumulate the shares when the price is low, and then sell the stock from inventory when the price is higher. When the market makers or the specialists anticipate that the price will go up, then they become buyers of that stock. When they anticipate that the price will decline, they become sellers of that stock. At that time, the market makers or specialists start selling the stock and depleting the inventory.

Market Makers

There are approximately 500 market-making firms providing liquidity for the more than 4,500 actively traded stocks on the NASDAQ National Market System. All market makers have a four-letter identification code that is displayed on the Level II screen (see chapter 6). Because there is competition among the market makers on the NASDAQ, it is important to know who is who among the market makers. Some market makers are large, established Wall Street institutional firms that have access to enormous capital and employ the most experienced professional traders. Those firms are 800-pound gorillas capable of stopping the price momentum at any time.

Because the large firms have a large capital base, they have a huge inventory of stocks. In addition, they can borrow a lot of stock from other Wall Street firms. Those market makers are capable of "sitting" at the top of the BID and ASK quote and continuously buying or selling that particular stock at that price level. These key market makers are often referred to in the trading industry as the "axes." It is important to know who the ax is for a particular stock. (A list of the 67 most influential market makers is included in appendix 4 of this book.) Each ax has a symbol, and traders using a Level II screen (see chapter 6) can therefore recognize when a dominant market maker places an offer to buy or sell shares.

The most important ax market makers are large investment banks with sizeable amounts of trading capital and equally large corporate cultures, such as Goldman Sachs & Co. (GSCO), Morgan Stanley (MSCO), Lehman Brothers (LEHM), and Salomon Brothers (SALB). The other important market makers are the large full-service retail brokerage firms such as Merrill Lynch & Co. (MLCO), Dean Witter Reynolds (DEAN),

Paine Webber (PAIN), Prudential (PRUD), and Smith Barney Shearson (SBSH), because they have a huge order flow from their client base. In addition, Wall Street has a few wholesalers that do not transact any retail business but represent the securities discount retailers (e.g., Charles Schwab) and Internet brokers (e.g., E*Trade). Those Wall Street firms, such as Mayer and Schweitzer (MASH), Hertzog Hein & Geduld (HRZG), Knight-Trimark (NITE), and Sherwood (SHWD), pay fees to retail brokers for "order fees."

The NYSE

The NYSE is a much different animal. A NYSE member is a firm that employs one of 1,366 individuals (usually as an officer or partner) who own a seat on the exchange. Only a member of the NYSE may transact business on the floor of the exchange. Every listed stock that trades on the NYSE floor is assigned a specialist. The role of the specialist is similar to that of a market maker—to maintain a fair and orderly market in his or her specific security. The specialist must maintain a continuous market by standing ready to buy when there are no bidders (buyers) or sell when there are no offerers (sellers) at the trading post. Unlike the NASDAQ, there is no competition among different Wall Street firms to provide the liquidity for the listed stock. A specialist has a monopoly.

Like NASDAQ market makers, the NYSE's specialists also make money by trading the stocks in their own proprietary accounts. Keep in mind that this activity is much less pronounced on the NYSE than on the NASDAQ, because the specialist is a monopolist who is regulated by the exchange. The NASDAQ market, however, is much more market oriented and competitive, and thus stock dealing is prevalent.

DOT

The NYSE uses a system called Designated Order Turnaround (DOT) to route the trade orders directly to specialists. The DOT system allows orders to be entered by traders from the day-trading firm's floor directly into the NYSE computer-execution system. The order bypasses the floor broker and goes directly to the NYSE specialist for execution.

In addition, even if other regional exchanges have better prices than do the NYSE—which is not a very likely scenario—it is impossible to route that order electronically to different exchanges.

DOT is an efficient way to execute trade orders on the NYSE. For example, if there is an exact price match between the Lucent buyers and sellers, the DOT will match those orders quickly. Both the buyers and sellers will receive the trade confirmation in a few seconds. The specialist need only approve the trade by pressing a key in the DOT system. A great majority of trades on the NYSE fit this scenario. The specialist, using DOT, will pair or match the stock buyers with the stock sellers and collect a small commission. In only about 30 percent of all executions would the specialist step in and provide the other side of the trade, thereby playing the role of the market maker and providing the liquidity for that stock.

It is my opinion that it is somewhat safer and easier to trade NYSE stocks than NASDAQ stocks. The NYSE stocks are "slow" stocks. Trading them is conservative or slow compared with the volatile NASDAQ stocks. NYSE stock prices tend to move in a somewhat smoother fashion; there are fewer sharp price turns.

There are several reasons for the relatively higher intraday price stability at the NYSE. First, the stocks listed on the NYSE tend to be large and established industrial corporations. The NASDAQ, however, is laden with technology companies pursuing long-term growth strategies. Consequently, growth stocks attract stock speculators, which tend to be short-term investors who are always chasing hot stocks and jumping in and out.

Second, the NYSE companies are simply too large and established to be very volatile. Large "blue chip" companies seldom issue news that can send stock prices skyrocketing up or down. Whereas it is a rare event for a NYSE stock to lose 50 percent of its capitalization value in a few days, that happens often on the NASDAQ. NASDAQ companies are relatively young companies; a single bad corporate announcement can send the stock price into a major descent.

Finally, the intraday price volatility is lower with the NYSE stocks because there is only one specialist who controls the price for each stock. The specialist can act to absorb and soften sharp price movements. Because the specialist controls the order flow, he or she knows the exact depth of the market (supply and demand) at any time. There is little chance that the specialist will overreact.

The NASDAQ market makers, however, compete against each other and against traders. The market makers do not know the complete order flow for a stock. They know what is in their individual order book, but they do not know the order flow of other market makers. Like any other traders, market makers can see on the Level II screen the required minimum size of the BID and ASK made by the other market makers, but not the actual orders. With such uncertainty and lack of comprehensive information, market makers might overreact and send a stock deeper in either price direction. Consequently, the average Beta value (which measures the relative price volatility compared with the industry average) is higher for NASDAQ stocks than for NYSE stocks.

Because the NYSE stocks do not move very fast in either direction, traders have time to react. They can see prices going up or down. They are not easily whipsawed by sharp and sudden price reversals. As there is no true Level II information available, the traders must devote more attention to technical stock analysis. Thus charting becomes an important component of their trading style.

In addition, the competition is much different on the NYSE, where there are fewer traders and more long-term investors. It is my opinion that one is better off trading against NYSE investors than NASDAQ market makers and other traders. However, the momentum-trading opportunities are much fewer and smaller at the NYSE. And, unfortunately, smaller risk brings smaller return. Successful and experienced traders can potentially earn seven-figure incomes trading volatile NASDAQ stocks with a relatively small trading account of $100,000. Because the NASDAQ is so volatile, there are plenty of opportunities to make money.

The AMEX

The American Stock Exchange (AMEX) is the nation's second-largest floor-based or auction-type exchange. However, the AMEX is well behind the NYSE in terms of trading volume and number of listed stocks. Nevertheless, the AMEX has a significant presence in index shares and equity-derivative securities, such as options trading. Similar to the NYSE, AMEX trading is conducted through an advanced centralized specialist system, which combines the speed of computer-routed trade orders with the liquidity of customer-driven markets. AMEX members represent a cross section of the nation's largest brokerage firms, including 661 regular members who transact business in equities and options and 203 options principal members who execute transactions in options only. An interesting development is that the NASDAQ acquired the AMEX. Some Wall Street observers anticipate that the AMEX will ultimately evolve into a derivatives exchange, whereas the AMEX common-stock listings will end up being moved to the NASDAQ.

ECNs

The SEC defines Electronic Communications Networks (ECNs) as "automated mechanisms that widely disseminate market-maker orders to third parties and permit such orders to be executed through the NAS-DAQ system." In essence, ECNs are proprietary electronic execution systems that broadcast orders entered by traders and market makers. Online brokers advertise and extol ECNs as a way to improve the price and speed of trade executions as well as a way to trade outside the regular market hours. Keep in mind that ECNs are an alternative and viable trading environment for the actively traded NASDAQ stocks only. For now, the rules of the NYSE and AMEX prevent the ECNs from gaining access to these trading environments. However, given the increasing popularity of ECNs among active traders, the NYSE and AMEX are gradually changing their rules.

ECNs came about in January 1997, as a result of new SEC order-handling rules, which required market makers to display customer limit orders that were priced at or better than the market makers' current quote. If not immediately executed, the limit orders could be routed to an eligible ECN, where they would be displayed to the market. The new SEC rules created the opportunity for ECNs to interact directly with the NASDAQ market makers and to become an integral part of the NAS-DAQ system.

Subsequently, the volume of the ECNs exploded and a new industry was born. Deregulation and competition in the securities trading industry resulted in the incredible growth of the ECNs, which remain in a constant state of motion. The two large ECNs, Island and Archipelago, have filed to become fully recognized exchanges by the SEC. The future will most likely bring consolidation or mergers among the smaller ECNs. Table 4.1 shows all ECNs and their relative market share of NASDAQ trades at the end of 1999.

Like Internet auction houses, the ECNs are the computerized "marketplaces" for stock buyers and sellers to meet. The ECNs electronically match the stock buyers with stock sellers through sophisticated computerized networks that link thousands of market participants through the hundreds of NASD brokers who subscribe to the ECN service. The ECN system allows two traders to meet and trade directly with one another without any intermediary. Because all trade executions are done electronically without a great deal of manual intervention, the ECNs are extremely fast and cost effective. The cost savings are substantial because ECNs do not need to maintain large numbers of traders, floor brokers, and other fixed costs associated with operating an exchange.

A recent SEC analysis of stock trading activities produced evidence of the existence of a two-tiered securities market. The NASDAQ market makers routinely trade stocks at one price with their retail customers and at better prices with institutional clients through the ECNs. For example, a great majority of all BID and ASK prices displayed through an ECN such as Instinet were posted at better prices than those posted publicly on the NASDAQ.

The advantages of ECNs are summarized in the following:

- **Low price.** ECNs typically charge a small fee for trade executions.
- **Speed.** Direct electronic access and avoidance of any mediators make the ECN trade-execution system extremely fast.
- **Liquidity.** Given the popularity of the few large ECNs, it is relatively easy to get trade orders filled.
- **Price transparency.** At any time, a trader can open an ECN book, such as the ISLD book, and determine the supply-and-demand flow of limit orders for any stock.
- **Order tracking.** A trader can see his or her order displayed on the Level II screen immediately.
- **Better price.** Only limit price orders are accepted and executed, and it is possible to cut the market makers' BID and ASK spread.

Table 4.1   *ECNs and NASDAQ Trades (1999)*

ECN	Owners	Location	% of NASDAQ Trades	ECN Market Share
Island (ISLD) www.isld.com	Datek Online Holding	Iselin, NJ	11.7	41.9
Instinet (INCA) www.instinet.com	Reuters Group	New York	11.0	39.4
Redibook (REDI) www.redi.com	Spear, Leeds & Kellogg	New York	1.3	4.6
Tradebook (BTRD) www.bloomberg.com	Bloomberg, Bank of New York	New York	1.2	4.3
Archipelago (ARCA) www.tradearca.com	Terra Nova Trading, E*Trade Group, Goldman Sachs	Chicago	1.0	3.6
Brass Utility (BRUT) www.sungard.com	Automated Securities Clearance (also Merrill Lynch, Morgan Stanley, Dean Witter, Knight/Trimark Group)	Weehawken, NJ	1.5	5.4
Strike (STRK) www.strk.com	Strike Technologies (Bear Stearns, DLJ, Salomon Smith Barney, Herzog Heine Geduld, PaineWebber)	New York	0.2	0.7
Attain (ATTN) www.attain.com	All-Tech Investment Group	Montvale, NJ	0.0	0.0
NexTrade (NTRD) www.nextrade1.com	PIM Global Equities/ Pro Trade	Clearwater, FL	0.0	0.0

- **No spreads.** One trader sells and the other trader buys the same stock at the same price.

- **Reliability**. The ECNs are very robust and reliable because they tend to use the latest computer-networking technology.
- **Open software architecture**. The trading platform is open and accessible, so it is relatively easy for the NASD brokers to subscribe to the ECN service.

Not surprisingly, the ECNs have certain disadvantages, too:

- Low liquidity with a few ECNs
- Partial-order fills
- Difficult fills with low-volume stocks
- No guarantee of getting the best price (unless you compare the ECN order book with a Level II screen)
- After-hours prices are not reflective of the opening and can result in high volatility and enlarged spreads

Island

Island is an ECN (ticker symbol ISLD) that was developed in 1996 and is owned by Datek Online Holding. It is the fastest growing ECN, and its sole purpose is to match bids and offers electronically. In essence, Island is an electronic central auction market that automatically matches buy and sell orders. When an order is received for a particular stock, the Island limit order book is instantaneously scanned to determine if there is a matching order. If there is a matching order, the trade order is executed immediately. However, if there is no matching order, the order is displayed on the Island limit order book until a matching order is received or until the order is canceled. In addition, the top orders are represented in the NASDAQ Level II screen display. All Island orders are anonymous and are matched based on strict price-time priority without regard to the number of shares.

Retail customers cannot send orders directly to Island. Instead, Island provides execution services to brokerage firms that, in turn, offer those services to their customers. The Internet-based brokers and day-trading firms allow their customers to send limit orders instantly into the Island system. Orders that are not matched immediately in the Island book are displayed on Level II screens if the order is over 100 shares and inside BID and ASK. Unlike SOES orders (see chapter 7),

Island orders do not have tier size limits; all orders are left as day orders. Island is open every day that the stock exchanges are open for trading. In general, Island accepts orders between 7:00 A.M. and 8:00 P.M. EST, although liquidity is dramatically lower during after-hours trading.

The Island trade-order execution system is rather simple: A trader places a limit order, either buy or sell, with the NASD broker who is subscribed to and has the Island ECN servers. The broker immediately forwards the limit order to Island for processing. Island searches its order book for that stock and looks for a match. For example, brokerage firm AAAA representing trader A places an order to "buy 500 DELL at 50." Almost at the same time, brokerage firm BBBB representing trader B places an order to "sell 1,000 DELL at 50." These two orders match electronically, and the orders are executed against each other. Trader A will end up buying 500 shares of DELL from trader B, and trader B will continue posting for sale the remaining 500 shares of DELL. If no match is found at that price, the order will be placed and displayed on the Island book.

When a trade order is entered into Island, assuming that a trader is using a high-powered trading software package, such as CyberTrader or TradeCast, the Island system directs the order first to an Island server for order matching and then to the NASDAQ SelectNet system. Traders can place trades by accessing Island directly or through the SelectNet execution system. Placing Island orders directly to Island, as opposed to accessing Island via SelectNet, is the faster of the two routes. Most day-trading firms have an Island server that routes Island orders directly to the Island system. (This should be an important consideration for the new trader who is looking to open an account with a day-trading firm.)

One of the positive aspects of Island fills is that they are quick and relatively inexpensive. Island trades usually cost $1 more than NASDAQ SOES orders. If the Island system has a better BID or ASK price available than the trader's submitted BID or ASK price, Island will fill the order at that better price. However, the trader should not use "fill or kill" orders through Island, as it is likely that the orders will not get filled. The main negative aspect of Island orders is partial fills.

The Island execution system displays the trader's Island order on the Level II screen only if the trader has entered the highest BID or the lowest ASK and only if the orders are greater than 100 shares. If several traders enter multiple Island orders at the same BID or ASK price, the Island system will simply total the share sizes to reflect all submitted orders. Using the Island execution system is crucial for a successful trading business. Island provides traders with additional liquidity and the opportunity to obtain a better price. In a later chapter I will explain how traders obtain better prices when executing trades on Island (see chapter 7).

Instinet

Instinet (ticker symbol INCA) is the largest ECN in terms of total NAS-DAQ, NYSE, and AMEX volume. It is a private corporation, head-quartered in New York City and owned by the Reuters Group PLC. Instinet Corporation is registered with the SEC as an NASD broker/dealer; it is a member of all U.S. stock exchanges and other major international stock exchanges. It was created in 1969 to furnish equity transaction services specifically to an international base of institutional investors (that is, fund managers).

Instinet does not buy or sell securities for its own account. Its only business is to provide 24-hour access to securities brokerage services for the benefit of its institutional customers. The trader can execute an Instinet order by accessing INCA through the NASDAQ SelectNet. Many day-trading brokerage firms have a stand-alone Instinet order-execution computer on the trading floor. However, Instinet is important not only as a vehicle that executes trade orders with large financial institutions. Instinet transactions also represent the activities of large financial institutions, and traders therefore pay attention to Instinet transactions, because those transactions can provide insight into the activities of the Wall Street professionals.

There are a few proprietary software packages that track or filter trading activities on Instinet. The software tracks the volume of shares being bid and offered through Instinet by financial institutions. The software also tracks prices that are bid and offered by the financial institutions. Most importantly, the software keeps a record if and when there is a price differential between the stock prices on the public exchange (that is, on the NASDAQ) and on the private exchange (that is, on Instinet). This information can provide the trader with insights about whether there is the potential for a particular stock price to go up or down.

Archipelago

Archipelago (ARCA) was approved in January 1997 by the U.S. SEC and is one of the first four ECNs. In August 1999, Archipelago filed with the SEC to become a national securities exchange that will offer an electronic trading system. To ensure its chances of SEC approval, Archipelago and the Pacific Stock Exchange (PCX) announced in March of 2000 that they are jointly creating this new electronic stock exchange. Today, as an ECN, Archipelago offers an anonymous order entry (i.e., an order will show only as ARCA) and execution capabilities that give the customers access to all other ECNs.

ARCA is a unique order-execution system with a built-in set of formulas or algorithms, which will optimally route the trade order for the best execution. In other words, ARCA provides an advanced electronic order-entry and execution system for NASDAQ and NYSE stocks. For instance, ARCA will look at stocks trading at other ECNs at that specified price to fill the order. If there is no ECN at that price and if it is a NASDAQ stock, ARCA will search for the most active market makers at the inside quote. Using the NASDAQ SelectNet system, ARCA would then access that particular market maker.

The beauty of using ARCA is that the system is doing all of the thinking and processing of the trade orders for you. Consequently, ARCA provides novice traders with automatic pilot for the optimum order execution. The only problem is that ARCA orders cannot be canceled in 30 seconds. This is because while ARCA processes the order for the optimal price, a trader must wait for the order confirmation. If a trader is trading slow-moving or less volatile stocks, then the 30-second wait is acceptable. However, in a fast-moving market, a lot happens in 30 seconds. As is the case with any other ECN, individual traders cannot send orders directly to ARCA, but rather their brokerage firms must route orders to Archipelago. Unlike ISLD, ARCA also accepts both the limit and market orders.

Future Trading Environments

I believe that ECNs have a bright future. Today, they are on the cutting edge of NASDAQ stock trading. They are the young firms in the industry that are pushing the envelope and bringing vibrancy and technological innovation into this field. For instance, Island and Archipelago ECNs have already created the extended trading-hours platform. Now traders in the United States can trade from 8:00 A.M. to 8:00 P.M. EST using the ISLD. The volume is extremely small, or thin, but that is not surprising for any pioneering process. With time, there should be greater liquidity.

NASDAQ is also going international. In Japan, the NASDAQ has partnered with Osaka Stock Exchange to bring the NASDAQ model of stock exchange to Asia. Similarly, the NASDAQ plans to open NASDAQ Europe and compete head-to-head with London and Frankfurt stock exchanges. With each building block, the NASDAQ is creating a global trading network, which might soon emerge as "Planet NASDAQ." Internationalization of the NASDAQ will bring more traders from abroad, who would gain access to the NASDAQ and thus increase the liquidity.

Finally, Internet service providers are moving to provide the necessary broadband needed to increase the speed of their service. Stock trading from your home via the Internet will be much easier and more reliable once cable modems and DSL lines become the norm. In addition, the emerging wireless trading technologies will make trading even more accessible and convenient (see chapter 5). ECNs promote more active trading and thus the standard T+3 settlement cycle, which is the trade date plus three days, will no longer be the industry norm. For instance, all traders use the specialized clearing firms that settle their trades on the very same day. Why not have the same one-day trade settlements for the rest of the general public?

5

Trading Brokers

"Nobody goes there anymore. It's too crowded."

—Yogi Berra

The first trading decision a new trader will make is deciding where to trade. More than 160 brokers offer online trading services, although only 15 companies made up 96 percent of the online brokerage market at the beginning of 2000. A new trader will determine whether to trade on-site, on the trading floor of a day-trading firm's branch office, or remotely, from home via an Internet brokerage firm. There are certain advantages to both options, which are both addressed in this chapter.

Trading with Internet Brokers

The pioneer of the online brokerage business was the discount brokerage arm of the investment banking firm Donaldson, Lufkin & Jenrette. In 1987, the Internet service provider Prodigy asked Donaldson, Lufkin & Jenrette, after being rejected by Schwab, Fidelity, and Dean Witter, to set up an online brokerage business for Prodigy. That marked the beginning of the Financial Network, which later transformed into DLJ Direct. The firm's start was very slow and modest, with the light volume of a dozen trades per day. In 1999, DLJ Direct opened 700,000 online accounts and was doing 20,000 trades per day.

Success breeds imitation, or in other words, success breeds competition. Twelve years later, DLJ Direct has lost its leadership role. In terms of volume, it ranked seventh among the online brokers in 1999. However, DLJ Direct is attempting a comeback. In May 2000, PCWorld (www.PCWorld.com) ranked DLJ Direct and Charles Schwab as the "Best Bet" for online traders and investors. Table 5.1 depicts the online trading volume leaders in 1999.

All Internet brokers are not created equally. There are some dramatic differences among the Internet brokers, because they are all trying to differentiate and tailor their services to specific market segments. A one-size-fits-all approach to online trading does not work. In addition, the field of the online brokerage firms is in a constant state of motion. Internet brokers are continuously upgrading and improving their services and lowering prices. My advice is to do your research, obtain the current information, and determine which broker meets your particular needs as a trader.

Some Internet brokers, such as Schwab (www.schwab.com), E*Trade (www.etrade.com), or DLJ Direct (www.DLJdirect.com), try to provide the one-stop-shop by offering, in one seamless trading environ-

Table 5.1   *Volume Market Share of the Top Ten Online Brokers in 1999*

Broker	Internet Address	Market Share
Charles Schwab	www.schwab.com	25
E*Trade	www.etrade.com	14
Fidelity Investments	www.fidelity.com	12
Waterhouse Securities	www.waterhouse.com	12
Datek	www.datek.com	11
Ameritrade	www.ameritrade.com	9
DLJ Direct	www.dljdirect.com	4
SureTrade	www.suretrade.com	2
Discover Brokerage	www.online.msdw.com	2
National Discount Brokers	www.ndb.com	1

ment, the full menu of securities services: stocks, options, bonds, mutual funds, IRAs, research, charting, and trade execution. Then there are the Internet brokers that compete specifically in terms of the lowest possible commissions, often at less than $10 per trade, such as FirstTrade ($6.95), SureTrade ($7.95), Wang Investments ($8.00), A. B. Watley ($9.95), Trading Direct ($9.95), and Datek ($9.99). These commissions are most likely based on the market orders. The cost of the limit orders would probably be $5.00 more.

A new twist to the Internet brokerage price competition is the emergence of commission-free trades. The biggest brokerage-name entry in this field is American Express (www.AmericanExpress.com), which offers a free limit, market, and stop-orders service to its wealthier customers with accounts of $100,000 or more. American Express clients with a minimum of $25,000 in their accounts can buy stock online free of any commissions, but the sell orders cost $14.95. Another variation on zero-commission trades is available from FreeTrade (www.FreeTrade.com), which offers online traders who have a minimum of two years online trading experience free buy and sell market orders, whereas all limit orders are $5 each. Finally, a new entry in this field is San Francisco–based The Financial Café (www.TheFinancialCafe.com), which charges no commissions on market orders, whereas all limit or stop orders are $16.95.

Then there are the Internet brokers, such as Datek, E*Trade, and Schwab, that offer after-hours trading. Datek, which owns Island ECN, provides after-hours trading from 8:00 A.M. to 8:00 P.M. EST through Island. Schwab provides after-hours trading services through REDIbook ECN, and E*Trade routes its after-hours trades through Instinet ECN. Be aware that the volume of after-hours trading is extremely thin, so trading is rather difficult. Because of the lower trading volume, the spread between the BID and ASK is somewhat larger than during the regular market hours from 9:30 A.M. to 4:00 P.M. EST. In other words, due to the larger spread, the actual cost of trading during the extra hours is higher.

Then there are the Internet brokers, such as Morgan Stanley Dean Witter Online (www.online.MSDW.com; formerly Discover), Fidelity (www.fidelity.com), Schwab, DLJ Direct, and E*Trade, which advertise the ability to acquire IPOs. These brokers can make such claims because they are owned by or affiliated with the large investment banks. For instance, the investment bank Donaldson, Lufkin & Jenrette owns DLJ Direct; Morgan Stanley owns Discover. In addition, Fidelity has partnered with the investment bank Lehman Brothers, and E*Trade has an alliance with Robertson Stephens and Goldman Sachs. Schwab has a corresponding relationship with Credit Suisse First Boston, J.P. Morgan, and Chase Manhattan Hambrecht & Quist. However, the IPO allotment given to the online brokers has been extremely small, ranging from 1 to 10 percent. I believe that online brokerage firms use and advertise this potential of purchasing IPOs as an enticement to traders to open an account with their firm. In all probability, it is extremely unlikely that investors would receive any shares of the hot IPOs from any of the Internet brokers.

Some Internet brokers provide Level II quote screen for an additional monthly fee (see chapter 6). This is a very important tool for short-term traders, such as day traders. Most Internet brokers today do not provide such information at all. Those that do provide such information free of charge are A. B. Watley (www.abwatley.com), FirsTrade (www.firstrade.com), Scottsdale Securities (www.scottrade.com), Wang Investments (www.wangvest.com), Web Street Securities (www.webstreet.com), Freeman Welwood (www.FreemanWelwood. com), and CompuTEL Securities (www.computel.com). As an absolute minimum, the trader should look for an Internet broker that provides "on-screen" trade confirmations. There is no worse feeling than sending an online buy order and then not knowing whether you have the stock or not.

Full-service Wall Street brokers are the latest entry into the increasingly crowded field of Internet brokerage business, resulting in a blurring of the lines of demarcation between full-service and discount brokers. Merrill Lynch, Morgan Stanley, Paine Webber, and Salomon Smith Barney have unveiled fee-based online brokerage services that are extremely competitive. The Wall Street firms charge a large flat annual fee, such as $1,500 for Merrill Lynch or $1,000 for Morgan Stanley, for unlimited trading and free proprietary financial research and advice. For an active swing trader who makes approximately 50 trades a year, this is comparable in terms of cost to 50 trades with Charles Schwab (at $29.95) or 100 trades with E*Trade (at $14.95), which do not offer any significant in-house research capabilities.

Internet Broker Issues

When considering Internet brokers, you should always look into the level of technical support the broker offers. Will the level of support be significant for your needs? For instance, many Internet brokerage firms are not geared toward servicing the accounts of active swing traders, who might enter several dozen orders each week. The swing trader's account is one among many thousands of accounts, most of which belong to investors who are only managing their own portfolios and perhaps submitting a few trades per month. The investors, regardless of how active they might be, are not swing traders, and thus their needs are different.

There are other issues associated with Internet brokers: How fast is the data feed? Is the data feed delayed or real-time? How fast and reliable is the trade execution? Does the Internet broker route the order to a "wholesaler" for the order-flow payment? Do you get the best price? Do you have access to ECNs? (Trading access to ECNs is important for active traders, as will be explained in chapter 7.) How quickly does the swing trader receive trade confirmation? What software does the Internet broker use for executing the trades? What other features are included in the trading software offered to the trader? What is the commission cost?

It is also extremely important that the trading firm or Internet-based broker that holds the customer's trading accounts is a member of the Securities Investor Protection Corporation (SIPC). SIPC is the product of the Securities Investor Protection Act, which was passed by Congress to safeguard customers' funds and securities in the event that the NASD broker/dealer becomes insolvent. Branch offices of trading firms make sure that the SIPC label is displayed prominently somewhere on the trading floor. The SIPC provides insurance coverage up to a maximum of $500,000, of which no more than $100,000 may be for cash losses.

There are many questions to ask when looking for an Internet broker, and each Internet broker has different answers. Because the electronic brokerage business has mushroomed in the United States during the past few years, it pays to research Internet brokers. Gomez Advisors Inc. (www.gomez.com) currently ranks 55 brokerage firms that offer online stock-trading brokerage services. Similarly, Internet Investing (www.internetinvesting.com) and Wall Street Online (www.wallstonline.com) provide reference lists of the Internet brokers.

I personally like Gomez.com's scoring methodology. The ranking assists traders who want to do business on the Internet in identifying brokers whose Internet offerings best meet their needs. Gomez.com ranks the Internet brokers by how well they serve traders in each of 100 or more objective criteria categories. Table 5.2 displays the overall scores for the top twenty Internet brokers. The highest score is 10; the lowest

Table 5.2   *Top Twenty Internet Brokers*

Rank	Internet Broker	Overall Score
1.	E*Trade	7.66
2.	Charles Schwab	7.39
3.	Fidelity Investments	7.37
4.	DLJ Direct	6.84
5.	TD Waterhouse	6.43
6.	NDB	6.32
7.	My Discount Broker	6.24
8.	A. B. Watley	6.13
9.	Morgan Stanley Dean Witter Online	6.08
10.	SureTrade	6.06
11.	Ameritrade	6.05
12.	Siebert	5.99
13.	Web Street	5.95
14.	WingspanBank.com	5.90
15.	Quick & Reilly	5.81
16.	Datek	5.77
17.	WallStreet Electronica	5.72
18.	Empire	5.72
19.	American Express Brokerage	5.71
20.	Freeman Welwood	5.64

Source: Ranked by Gomez.com

is 0. Thus if the brokerage firm earns an overall score of 10, then the firm provides the best services at the lowest cost.

Finally, Gomez.com rolls up the criteria into customer profiles. In other words, Gomez.com weights the individual criteria by customer profile according to the importance of those criteria to a particular customer profile. Table 5.3 shows the overall score for the top twenty Internet brokers for the most active traders, such as swing traders or day traders. The most important factors for swing traders are low-cost trading, a simple interface, charting, online confirmations, and fast execution.

Experts estimate that 15,000 online brokerage accounts are opened every day, which puts tremendous technological strains on Internet brokers. Due to a large amount of traffic on the Internet in general and large trading volumes by online brokers, the system performance is sometimes slow. Real-time stock quotes become delayed quotes. Order confirmations are slow, often leaving the Internet trader in the dark. The traders sometimes wonder if they actually own the stock and if they can sell it now.

Therefore, the reliability of online trading becomes an important issue. The Internet trader depends on the performance of several electronic service vendors: the Internet Service Provider (ISP), the data-feed provider, and the brokerage computer system. Most Internet brokers now offer Secure Socket Layer (SSL) Java script routing of the trade orders through the brokerage firms' host servers, and not through the slow and unprotected e-mail servers. Nevertheless, serious Internet traders will build their own system redundancy, such as maintaining two trading accounts at different brokerage firms and having two different ISPs for their Internet access.

Trading with Direct-Access Internet Brokers

There are a few Internet brokers, such as Austin-based CyBerCorp (www.cybercorp.com), Houston-based TradeCast (www.tradecast.com), and New York–based TradeScape (www.tradescape.com), that have tried to bridge the gap between the trading tools available historically to Wall Street professionals and the tools available to amateur traders via the Internet. These newcomers on the brokerage scene cater specifically to more active traders. All three companies have deep roots in the day-trading business. In the 1990s, Philip Berber (CyBerCorp), Jim Howell,

Table 5.3 *Top Twenty Internet Brokers for the Most Active Traders*

Rank	Internet Broker	Overall Score
1.	E*Trade	7.54
2.	A. B. Watley	6.86
3.	FirsTrade	6.67
4.	Web Street	6.64
5.	SureTrade	6.63
6.	Empire	6.60
7.	TD Waterhouse	6.60
8.	My Discount Broker	6.39
9.	America First Trader	6.37
10.	KeyTrade Online	6.33
11.	ScotTrade	6.31
12.	Wang Investments	6.31
13.	Fidelity Investments	6.30
14.	Ameritrade	6.30
15.	Datek	6.28
16.	Trading Direct	6.18
17.	DLJ Direct	6.12
18.	NDB	6.03
19.	Brown	5.89
20.	WallStreet Electronica	5.88

Source: Ranked by Gomez.com

and Bobby Earthman (TradeCast) started two software-development companies that produced the two software-trading platforms that are the current industry standards for day-trading shops. In 1999, CyBer-Corp and TradeCast, along with TradeScape, took a giant leap into the cyberspace brokerage business. They have modified, or stripped, their sophisticated day-trading platforms, which were sold to a few day-trading firms, and packaged them for the mass Internet market.

CyBerCorp, TradeCast, and TradeScape charge a monthly fee for real-time streaming data of Level I and II information and a commission that varies from $15 to $20 per 1,000 shares. These brokerage services are designed specifically for hyperactive traders. To the active traders trading from their homes, these companies provide direct access or routing to all of the ECNs, NASDAQ market makers, and NYSE specialists. Critics point out that these brokerage services are simply stripped-down trading machines in your home. There is very little guidance, support, or handholding. In other words, you should know a lot about trading—day trading in particular—before taking full advantage of this type of Internet brokerage service.

At home, the traders have an electronic router or modem and a dedicated and fast telephone line with a large data bandwidth (a DSL line) that transmits the data. The traders receive live price quotes from their NASD broker/dealer's quote server and send their execution orders to their NASD broker/dealer's execution server through their DSL lines. Although a DSL connection is expensive, it does provide superior speed and reliability. Several Internet sites explain DSL in detail, such as DSL Forum (www.adsl.com), DSL Reports (www.dslreports.com), and XDSL (www.xdsl.com).

Staying home to trade, whether using the services of Internet brokers or the remote trading capabilities of a local day-trading firm, has its disadvantages. The trader is alone. There is very little personal interaction between the trader and the outside world. There may be no one outside of immediate family to speak to and to share the daily trading experience with. There is no one to turn to and ask a question. Some people have a hard time dealing with that kind of professional isolation. In extreme cases, the relative isolation could take a certain mental toll.

Wireless Trading

Another new twist is the emergence of wireless trading technology. To differentiate their trading services, many brokerage firms in the United States are actively and aggressively offering wireless trading options to their wealthy or more active trading clients. The wireless trading option is attractive to many active traders whose busy lifestyles are such that they spend a great deal of time away from their desks and computers, either traveling or shuttling between meetings. Wireless trading is conducted via digital cell phones, two-way pagers, or hand-held computers. The cost of such equipment ranges from $200 for a cell phone with Internet access to $450 for a handheld computer organizer, such as the Palm Pilot. Also, brokers that provide wireless trading charge a premium (about $30 per month), although Fidelity and DLJ Direct offer the service free.

However, the level of received information is rather limited. It is impossible to compress the typical stock market data displayed on a 17- or 20-inch computer monitor onto a four-line cell phone display. Likewise, it is impossible to get real-time streaming price quotes, NASDAQ Level II information, or interactive real-time technical analysis charting. Nevertheless, a four-line display is adequate for checking account balances, getting access to market price data (Level I quotes), or receiving certain trade alerts or news, while electronically executing buy or sell orders. The trades are executed just as if the trade order was submitted electronically through a PC via the Internet. Keep in mind that wireless trading technology is still in its infancy, and the wireless network can be a rather unreliable trading medium. Losing wireless connection in the middle of trade has been known to occur. Nevertheless, the most common wireless trading technology complaints concern the tiny displays and the sluggish data transmission.

Trading with Day-Trading Firms

Another method of trading is through one of several specialized electronic day-trading firms with branch offices all over the United States. Day-trading firms cater to professional traders who demand instantaneous Level I and II quotes and fast, reliable, cheap trade executions. These day-trading firms specialize in electronic stock trading only. They tend to be new, small firms. Often the day-trading branch office is one large room (i.e., the "trading floor") packed with several computers (with large, 21-inch screen monitors) connected to the firm's servers, which are then connected to the NASDAQ and NYSE computer systems. In essence, day-trading firms provide traders with immediate and direct access to the NASDAQ market makers and NYSE specialists and allow them to execute the trades themselves without the middleman—the brokerage firm.

Staying home to trade is clearly convenient. The trader does not need to fight traffic during the commute to the day-trading office. However, going to the office to trade seems to be the more professional option. First, there are fewer distractions when traders trade together on the trading floor. There are no family members to step in with questions or requests. There is also a certain synergy among traders on the trading floor. The traders communicate among themselves throughout the day and call out the stocks that are moving at that moment. This is an enormous help. Two pairs of eyes can see more than one pair of eyes can. A single trader cannot possibly monitor the entire universe of NASDAQ and NYSE stocks. Also, it is in the traders' interests to talk out their relative trade positions. If a trade position is long, the trader has a vested interest to broadcast that trade, so that other people in the shop might join in on the same side of the trade and buy that stock (and increase demand). If it were a winning trade, then they all profit. If it were a losing trade, then they all "share" the pain.

Some professional day-trading firms have created their own proprietary "squawk boxes." These firms have hired research assistants who sit in front of computer monitors and sift through the sea of real-time financial data provided by Wall Street news-service organizations, such as Bloomberg. These research assistants continuously review and analyze all available data. Often the research assistants learn about the news before it is publicly disseminated over CNBC. When they encounter news (for example, company earnings or stock-split reports) that can move stock prices, the research assistants broadcast that news immediately to all branch offices. Every office has a speaker in the background that transmits this information. Some traders choose to ignore the squawk box. They focus and specialize on only a few stocks. But for many traders who surf the market and actively seek any stock that is moving, the squawk box is an extremely valuable tool.

One common concern is the success rate among people who trade in these day-trading shops. A study conducted by the North American Securities Administrators Association (NASAA) determined that 70 percent of day traders lose money and only 11.5 percent can make a living through day trading. Not surprisingly, the Electronic Traders Association (ETA; www.electronic-traders.com) immediately questioned the methodology and validity of the NASAA study. For instance, the ETA pointed out that only 17 day traders from a single firm were part of the NASAA study. It is difficult to take seriously results from a sample of 17 among a population of 5,000 traders. What would be the confidence interval or the error term of the NASAA conclusions based on such a minuscule sample? Anyone could easily select another sample of 17 traders and obtain completely different results. This is bad science from a government agency with an agenda. The ETA plans to commission its own study, which I hope will draw from a much bigger sample and thus have a larger confidence interval.

To stay in business and to compete against the Internet brokers, professional day-trading firms must keep investing money in the best trading technology available. Day-trading firms must maintain that competitive edge by differentiating their day-trading services from electronic trading that can be practiced at home via the Internet. In addition to providing direct access to NASDAQ and SelectNet, professional day-trading firms must at least offer direct access to the Island (ISLD) ECN. Some day-trading firms offer direct access to other ECNs in addition to ISLD, such as Instinet (INCA), Archipelago (ARCA), Terranova (TNTO), or Bloomberg Tradebook (BTRD).

The professional day-trading firms must also provide their customers with a choice of several trading platforms or trading software packages, such as CyberTrader or TradeCast. These are truly sophisticated and completely integrated stock-trading packages. A good financial software package will provide more than just Level I and Level II screen information, which is readily available elsewhere. Even the point-and-click order-execution interface is a common software feature. The following trading instruments are standard features in these sophisticated financial software packages:

- "Smart" or "hot" function keys for trade executions that quickly route trade orders in the most efficient manner for the best possible price
- Different types of market alerts, such as alerts for crossed and locked markets
- Information on market makers' movements within the inside and outside BID and ASK quotes
- The trader's "account manager," which will track, in real time, the trader's pending and open trade positions, purchasing power, and current profit and loss situations

Running a day-trading branch office requires sophisticated computer and networking technology. If the network is down, the staff must be able to reboot the servers and reestablish the trading environment quickly. If traders have questions regarding the software, the tech staff must have the answers. "Downtime," which inevitably occurs in this electronic trading environment, will thus be kept at a minimum. The expertise of the day-trader staff provides an edge over trading from home, where traders have to deal with the technology issues on their own.

Traders investigating a branch office should take a look at the branch's computer equipment. They should consider what equipment traders use at their workstations. For example, how fast are the computer processors? Each trader should have at least one 21-inch monitor, if not two linked 21-inch monitors. There is so much data in this business, the monitor screen becomes the trader's "real estate." The larger the monitor screen, the more information can be displayed.

Another important advantage to trading on-site is being part of a group of experienced and profitable traders. This is the best way to learn the business. A novice trader can learn much from a successful full-time trader. Many successful traders do not mind passing along their day-trading knowledge and experience, as long it does not interfere with their individual trading. However, successful full-time traders are a rare breed. The probability is high that there will be more part-time traders than full-time traders on the floor. At some point, however, part-time traders might "graduate" to full-time trading. My recommendation to the novice trader is to look for a firm that has successful full-time traders in place. Perhaps there will be some osmosis, and some of that trading success can rub off.

Another important advantage to trading in a branch office of a professional day-trading firm is that many firms provide a structured training program, with several levels of training. The first level might be an introduction to day trading. For newcomers, that introduction is the starting point. The second level might consist of detailed coverage of different and specific day-trading topics, such as trade execution, technical analysis, trading strategies, or psychology of trading. The third level of training might include a few weeks of simulations or paper trading. The final step might be to trade live next to an experienced and successful trader, who would act as a mentor.

Be sure to ask the branch manager about the firm's training program and the cost of that program. Day-trading firms routinely charge for training to cover expenses and also to screen potential traders. If a person is not willing to pay for the training, that person will probably not open an account and trade in that office.

Finally, go to the branch office during trading hours and test the overall atmosphere. Is it friendly? Is the office staff pleasant and helpful? What kind of support and service does the branch provide to its traders? Talk to other traders in the office and ask them if they like trading there. Is the firm competitive in terms of cost? How does it calculate its commission costs? How does it charge for split orders? How does it charge for ECNs and NYSE orders? If there is more than one day-trading firm in town, shop around.

Trading Software

Many successful traders began with one of the Internet brokers mentioned previously and then graduated to a specialized day-trading firm that provides faster execution (due to direct computer access with NASDAQ market makers and NYSE specialists) and better information (through more sophisticated trading software and access to ECNs, such as Island and Instinet). It is no secret that day-trading software packages (such as CyberTrader and TradeCast, the two mainstream trading platforms used in day-trading shops) are a world apart from any trading software packages used by online brokers. These packages are sophisticated professional trading platforms developed by young, aggressive software development firms for the aggressive day-trading environment. Thus I believe that day-trading firms have better trading tools than the mainstream Internet brokers. I would even venture to argue that the day-trading software is often better and faster than the trading systems used by some of the Wall Street brokerage firms.

It is not surprising that Charles Schwab paid an astonishing sum of $400 million to purchase CyBerCorp, the developer of CyBerTrader software. Schwab paid such a high price because Internet brokers are now targeting active traders, who are requesting the "bells and whistles" of the latest trading software. The active traders are searching for that illusive comparative advantage in this competitive business of stock trading. In recent years, Internet brokers, with their huge war chests, have tried to close the software gap. In addition to purchasing CyBerCorp, Schwab also created the higher-end trading platform called Velocity™, and E*Trade created its high-end trading system called Power E*Trade™. Internet brokers are now offering the software features that have been the norm in the day-trading business, such as the dynamic Level II screen, basket trade orders (multiple stocks simultaneous order entries), and elimination of the order preview screening process.

However, it is my opinion that there is a limit to how far Internet brokers can go to bridge the technology gap. Internet brokers must standardize their order entry window and data display screens because they are catering to thousands and thousands of customers with different investment objectives. In addition, because the trading software resides on the Internet brokers' servers, even if you have a fast DSL Internet connection plugged into your home PC, your trade still must wait in queue with all the other thousands of investors. In other words, you must wait for your Internet pages to be assembled on the server for downloading.

On the other hand, the architecture of the day-trading software is fully decentralized. The actual trading software resides on each trader's workstation. The price quotes and news stream directly in real time from the stock market through the data-feed provider in raw form via a broadband connection or satellite dish. Charts and Level I and II displays are processed quickly through the fast megahertz processors right on the trader's workstation. Thus the information comes up much faster on the computer screen than it does for those traders working at home via the Internet.

In addition, traders in the day-trading office use all that decentralized computer power to keep many windows open on their screens simultaneously. Many day-trading shops place two or more 21-inch monitors on each trader's desktop. The day-trading software packages further accommodate traders by allowing users to customize the displays—from the color of their Level I and II screens to a choice of several trading alerts, to technical-analysis charting and preprogrammed executions.

Trading depends on the speed and control of the trade-order execution. One reason successful traders prefer to trade through the branch offices of day-trading firms rather than through Internet brokers is the ability to execute trades quickly. Most day-trading firms use advanced trading software packages that create sophisticated trading environments. Some software vendors provide trading software that uses macro keys, or "smart" function keys, to automate the trade-execution orders.

This type of sophisticated trading software is usually not available for traders who use Internet brokers. Consequently, traders using the software packages at day-trading firms are one step ahead of traders using Internet brokers. Please note that these advanced features are also available in a streamlined, or downsized, version for home-based traders who trade through direct-access Internet brokers such as CyBerCorp, Trade-Cast, and TradeScape.

Clearing Trades

Most Internet-based trading brokers, and particularly day-trading firms, are not self-clearing brokerage firms. Some are relatively small brokerage firms without the necessary financial and staffing resources to process, record, and administer several thousand trades every day in hundreds, and sometimes thousands, of different customer accounts. Consequently, trading firms must use or hire some other NASD broker or dealer firm to clear or process their trades. Clearing firms are specialized Wall Street firms that have the financial resources, such as the fidelity bonding requirements, and the staffing and computer-data-management expertise to process many thousands of trades every day.

There are only a few securities clearing firms (for example, Southwest Securities and Penson Securities) that are specialized to handle the trader's trading requirements. Traditional investors are satisfied if the trade settlement date is three days after the trade date, but that time is unacceptable for the active trader. Therefore, clearing firms will settle all trades on the same day that they are placed.

All of the money goes through the clearing firm as well. When a new trader opens a trading account with a trading firm, the trader issues a check in the name of the clearing firm. The clearing firm keeps track of all trades done by all traders in that trading firm. The clearing firm then calculates the profit or loss from each trade and deducts the commission cost. When the trader closes the account, the clearing firm will cut the check or transfer the money to another account. At the end of the month, the clearing firm will send a check to the trading brokerage firm for the portion of the trader's commission, which becomes the brokerage firm's income.

Trading Suitability

From the trading firm's perspective, the first and most important issue regarding the opening of a trading account is the customer's suitability for the trading business. Trading is not for everyone. It is a risky endeavor. It is an unfortunate fact that many individuals have opened trading accounts with a day-trading firm or an Internet broker without fully understanding the skill set required in this business and the associated risks. It is important that the risks are clearly disclosed up front. The risk associated with trading is usually disclosed somewhat more adequately if the account is opened with a branch office of a day-trading firm. At least the new trader has the opportunity to talk to a live person and ask questions at a branch office. On the Internet, however, a new trader can open a trading account without ever talking to a live person.

The first question regarding an individual's suitability to be a trader involves technical competence. Many new traders were lured to this career by media coverage that glamorized and romanticized trading, and few had any experience in trading securities or commodities. At best they might have had an investment account with a discount brokerage firm.

The second issue regarding an individual's suitability involves financial competence. It is important to understand from the outset that traders place their money at substantial risk at all times. Thus new traders must understand that they will use only their "speculative" money for this endeavor. The intent is to trade money that they can afford to lose. The prospective trader's net worth and liquid net-worth status would quickly reveal whether he or she could absorb the financial losses. For instance, a liquid net worth of $100,000 would indicate that the prospective trader could afford to lose $15,000 or $20,000 before becoming a proficient trader.

There might be other considerations that would point to an individual's suitability for trading. For example, there might be questions regarding future expectations: Does the prospective trader have unrealistic views on trading? Does the new trader need to earn money trading immediately to support him- or herself? Does the prospective trader have several dependents in the family? What is the source of the start-up money?

Finally, the prospective trader must sign the required forms and risk-disclosure statements to acknowledge that all the risk always resides with the trader. The trading firm will not assume or accept any risk or liability. The trader is responsible for any action regarding the trading account. The associated market risk that comes with the buying and selling of securities is just common sense—it always goes with the trader. In addition, the trader will also always assume the accompanied technology risk (for example, computer or network breakdowns).

How to Trade

"When you come to a fork in the road, take it."

—*Yogi Berra*

EVENTUALLY YOU WILL HAVE TO TAKE A FORK IN THE ROAD AND MAKE A TRADE. The question of how to trade concerns itself with basic trading terminology and the actual mechanics of different order executions. The trader must learn to execute trades efficiently. Consequently, the NASDAQ, NYSE, and ECN order-execution platforms are described in great detail in this section. In addition to learning about different trade-order executions, this section will also present the reader with risk-management tools, different trading software tools, and an explanation of margin accounts.

CHAPTER

6

Levels I and II Screen Information

"The chief value of money lies in the fact that one lives in a world in which it is overestimated."

—*H. L. Mencken*

Chapter 4 discussed the two major and distinctly different U.S. stock exchanges or trading markets. Both NASDAQ and NYSE trading information is commonly displayed as Level I screen information, which will be explained shortly. In addition, NASDAQ trading can be viewed in much greater detail through the Level II screen. The Level II screen is the most crucial day-trading tool because it reveals and alerts day traders to upcoming and immediate price changes. Given the structure of the NYSE, there is no Level II screen for listed stocks.

Some swing traders may feel that Level II screen information doesn't offer any additional price insights and that it's not worth the cost of $100 or more per month to subscribe for the Level II data feed. Nevertheless, the Level II screen does enable traders to enter and exit positions at prices better than they'd likely receive using Level I information. Over the long term, the Level II screen can improve profitability and enable the trader to better time the markets. Also, the Level II screen has become standard terminology among traders, and financial writers commonly refer to it in the trading literature. The Level II screen can be of enormous help to both day traders and swing traders alike because, as explained below, it helps them understand how the outside-market stock prices move in the short term. Although it is possible to be an effective swing trader without a Level II screen, the power of this information can help maximize your trading effectiveness. In the end, the decision is yours. But it is always helpful to understand how Level II screens work.

The Level I Screen

All stock market participants are familiar with NASDAQ and NYSE Level I stock quotes. A Level I quote displays current inside market or the best BID and ASK prices for the stock. The Level I screen is a dynamic window, and during market hours the best BID and ASK prices are continuously updated in real time. However, if the trader is using an Internet-based broker, Level I quotes could be delayed several seconds or several minutes. In contrast, trading firms or professional traders who trade from their homes subscribe to real-time data providers that supply real-time stock quotes via satellite dish or dedicated T1 communication lines.

Many Internet-based Level I stock-quote providers use JavaScript programs to "refresh" the screen every few seconds, and thus do not display true tick-by-tick data feed, which is crucial information for the traders. This can sometimes lead to inaccurate stock quotes, especially when the stock market is moving quickly. However, swing traders are not day traders, and thus having stock quotes delayed a few seconds is not as important an issue for swing traders. Although it is difficult to ascertain a trend based on Level I information alone, much information can be ascertained from the Level I screen.

BID and ASK

The Level I quote features the stock symbol. (In figure 6.1, "DELL" is used for illustration purposes.) Although Dell is a NASDAQ stock, quotes of stocks traded on the NYSE would appear in the same manner when using Level I. A Level I quote states that at the current time, the best BID price for DELL is $50\frac{1}{2}$, or $50.50, and the best ASK price is $50\frac{9}{16}$, or $50.56. This means that the trader or investor can purchase Dell stock from the market makers at $50\frac{9}{16}$ ($50.56) and sell it to them

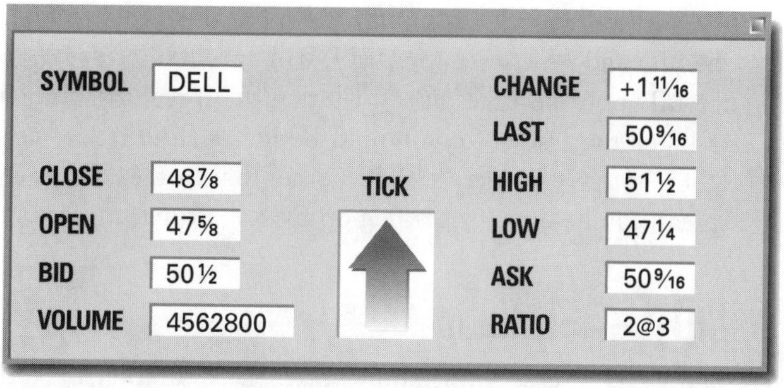

SYMBOL	DELL			**CHANGE**	+1 $^{11}/_{16}$
				LAST	50 $^9/_{16}$
CLOSE	48 $^7/_8$		**TICK**	**HIGH**	51 $^1/_2$
OPEN	47 $^5/_8$			**LOW**	47 $^1/_4$
BID	50 $^1/_2$			**ASK**	50 $^9/_{16}$
VOLUME	4562800			**RATIO**	2@3

Figure 6.1 *Level I Screen Information*

for a lower price of 50$^1/_2$ ($50.50). Therefore, traders and investors are buying stocks at the ASK price and selling them at the BID price. The best ASK price is often called the *inside offer*.

Market makers, however, are buying DELL from traders and investors at the BID price of 50$^1/_2$ ($50.50) and selling DELL to traders and investors at the ASK price of 50$^9/_{16}$ ($50.56). Anyone can see that there is a spread or difference between the BID and ASK prices. Market makers are buying low ($50.50) and selling high ($50.56) and earning the spread. In this case the spread is $^1/_{16}$, or 6.25 cents.

Spread

The spread can vary. For well-traded stocks with large daily trading volumes, such as DELL, the spread is small—$^1/_{16}$ (6.25 cents), or even smaller at $^1/_{32}$ (3.12 cents). Sometimes during trading, the spread can widen to $^1/_8$ (12.5 cents) or even more. Market forces (that is, supply and demand for DELL) will determine the size of the spread. For thinly (or infrequently) traded stocks, the spread is larger. The lower liquidity creates additional risk, and thus NASDAQ market makers and NYSE specialists are justified for maintaining a larger spread for thinly traded stocks.

When the trader purchases stock at the ASK price, he or she is already in the hole (out of money) by $^1/_{16}$. The trader could immediately turn around and sell the stock at the inside BID price, thus losing the spread. If the trader trades in increments of 1,000 shares, he or she enters the position with $62.50 in the hole. For the trader to break even, both the BID and ASK price for DELL will have to increase $1/_{16}$ of a point, so the BID price becomes $50^9/_{16}$. Cutting the spread becomes an important task for the trader, as it would be ideal if the trader could purchase DELL at the BID price ($50.50) rather than at the ASK price. Cutting the spread can be done by trading on ECNs (a topic covered in chapter 7).

BID-to-ASK Ratio

The Level I screen also shows how many market makers are buying DELL and how many market makers are selling DELL at any given time. In other words, the Level I screen states how many market makers are on both the BID and the ASK side. In figure 6.1, the ratio of BID to ASK is 2 @ 3, or 2 to 3 (see the lower right corner of the Level I screen). It means that there are two buyers and three sellers. This ratio can be expressed in terms of BID and ASK volume as well. The bullish sign would be a BID-to-ASK ratio of 5 @ 1, which means that five market makers are buying and only one market maker is selling.

The ratio does not really show the depth of the market because it does not show how many shares each market maker is selling or buying. The ratio is simply stating that there are more buyers than there are sellers. If the single selling market maker is a large established Wall Street firm selling a large block of shares for an institutional investor, then a 5 @ 1 ratio may lead a new trader to think that the market is moving up, when this is actually not the case.

Volume

In figure 6.1, the trading volume at that time for DELL is more than 4.5 million shares. This snapshot is most likely "taken" early in the morning of the trading day because DELL is a well-traded stock—it trades, on average, ten times that volume every day. The trader must trade liquid stocks, and the daily trading volume must be at least 500,000 shares. Liquidity is crucial to assure that there will be a seller to close the long position at the end of trading. It is very risky to accumulate a large share block of thinly traded stocks. Imagine holding 10,000 shares of a stock trading in the $10 range with a daily volume of 100,000 shares. If the price starts to decline, it would be difficult to unload (sell) 10 percent of the daily volume quickly without driving the price down further.

High and Low

The Level I screen also displays the day's high and low prices. In this example, the high ASK price for the day was $51\frac{1}{2}$, and the low ASK price was $47\frac{1}{4}$. That means that DELL had substantial intraday price volatility—$4\frac{1}{4}$ points for this example. This range is a good change in absolute price level. In relative terms, a $4\frac{1}{4}$ absolute change in price represents approximately a 9 percent increase from the daily low price. This level of intraday price volatility provides ample opportunity to day trade this stock. Therefore, traders should focus on and trade stocks that have at least a 2-point intraday price movement.

On the other hand, a swing trader might be better off looking at the 52-week high and low price range, which is not commonly displayed on the Level II screen. A quick way to ascertain intrayear price volatility is to look for the difference between the high and low prices for the 52-week period. If that price differential is small, then the stock is not moving much in either direction. The differential between the 52-week high and low prices is the proxy measure for the intrayear price swings. The 52-week high and low prices are standard fundamental stock market information that is commonly provided on any stock market quote system.

If the high ASK price for the past 52 weeks were $53\frac{1}{2}$, and the low ASK price for the past year were $31\frac{1}{4}$, then DELL had substantial price volatility in that year ($22\frac{1}{4}$ points). This 52-week range has substantial absolute dollar change in price and provides ample opportunity for the swing trader to trade the stock. In relative terms, a $22\frac{1}{4}$-point absolute change in price represents an approximate 71 percent increase from the 52-week low price. This level of price volatility provides ample opportunity for swing trading. Charting Dell stock using the daily closing price for the past year reveals more than a dozen substantial 10-point price swings. Swing traders should focus on and trade stocks that have many substantial (at least 5 points) intrayear price swings.

To be successful, a swing trader must trade stocks that are more volatile relative to the overall S & P's 500 price-index average. In short, the swing trader should search for the stocks that have a high daily trading volume and a relatively high Beta value. A particular stock's Beta coefficient, a common component of fundamental analysis that can be found in many financial search engines on the Internet, will provide a measure of the market volatility associated with that security.

If the stock has a Beta value greater than 1, then that stock is more volatile relative to the entire stock market. A Beta of 2 would mean that the stock went up (or down) an average of 10 percent, whereas the overall market went up (or down) 5 percent during a certain period of time (for example, 52 weeks). Appendix 3 of this book contains a list of the 100 NASDAQ and NYSE stocks with the highest Beta values (Beta greater than 1.5) and an average daily trading volume greater than 500,000 shares. My recommendation to swing traders is to trade stocks that are volatile and liquid.

Close and Open

Another piece of information that is provided on the Level I screen is the close price from yesterday and the open price for today. In figure 6.1, DELL closed yesterday on $48^7/_8$ and opened today at $47^5/_8$, or with the gap down by $1^1/_4$ points. There are many reasons why stocks open with a gap up or down (mostly down). For example, companies will wait for the market to close before announcing any news (for example, earnings or dividends). Institutional investors continue to trade after the market hours through Instinet; therefore, market forces (and thus prices) do not stop at the close of the market.

In the example shown in figure 6.1, DELL opened with a large gap down. If the trader had 1,000 shares of DELL in the overnight long position, then the trader would start that day with a $1,250 loss. This $1^1/_4$ gap down is seemingly a large gap for a $50 stock. But the gap could be a lot worse. Something could happen overnight in Asia (or anywhere else in the world) seemingly unrelated to DELL that could cause DELL to open several points lower. Then the loss would be several thousand dollars.

The experienced day trader will seldom if ever carry an overnight position. In contrast, the holding period for swing traders varies from two days to two weeks. Therefore, the swing-trading holding period would depend on many factors, such as the condition of the overall market or the particular swing trader's style and risk tolerance. If Swing traders engage in some form of fundamental stock analysis of the companies whose stocks they trade, they can usually estimate this risk.

Change

Change during the day is the last piece of information that is available on a Level I screen. In the example in figure 6.1, DELL went up $1^{11}/_{16}$ from yesterday's closing price. Most trading software packages also have a symbol for the last price tick. In this case, the symbol for the last price change is the arrow, and it is an uptick. Other software packages have "+" or "−" symbols. Some software packages use green or red color-coded BID and ASK prices. A red BID would mean that the last BID was a downtick. The last tick symbol is a very useful visual tool.

Traders should pay close attention to the current stock price in relation to the stock's daily high or low prices. The relationship between the current price and the daily high or low prices would be one proxy measure of the intraday price support and resistance levels for the stock. Therefore, day traders should avoid taking a long position if the current price is approaching the daily high price level. Conversely, they should avoid taking a short position if the current price is approaching the daily low price level.

On the other hand, swing traders pay much closer attention to the current stock price in relation to the stock's 52-week high or low prices. The relationship between the current price and the 52-week high or low prices would be one proxy measure of the stock's long-term price support and resistance levels. Therefore, swing traders should avoid taking a long position if the current price is approaching the 52-week high price level. Conversely, they should avoid taking a short position if the current price is approaching the 52-week low price level.

NASDAQ Level II Information

The Level II screen is one of the most effective day trading tools available. Figure 6.2 displays the Level I and Level II screens together.

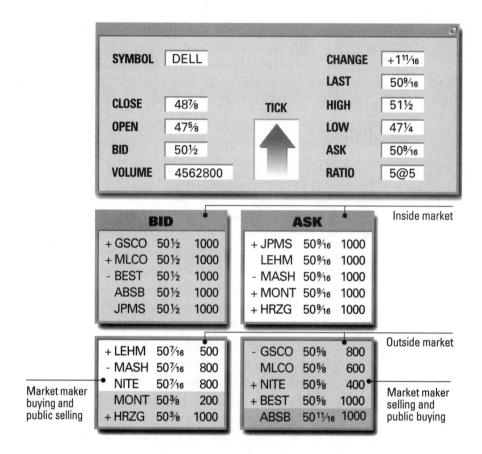

Figure 6.2   *NASDAQ Levels I and II Screen Information*

In addition to posting the inside market's BID and ASK price quotations for all market makers (which is available on the Level I screen), the Level II screen posts real-time BID and ASK prices that are outside the market. "Inside market" is the best (i.e., the highest) BID price at which the stock can be sold in the market, or the best (i.e., the lowest) ASK price at which the stock can be bought in the market at a given time. In the hypothetical example in figure 6.2, DELL has five market makers on the inside BID and ASK prices; thus the current ratio of BID to ASK is 5 @ 5, as displayed by the Level I screen. But this time we also see which market makers are buying and selling, as well as the share size that market makers are advertising for sale or purchase.

In this example, J. P. Morgan Securities (JPMS), Lehman Brothers (LEHM), Mayer & Schweitzer (MASH), Montgomery Securities (MONT), and Herzog Heine Geduld (HRZG) are selling 1,000 shares of DELL, each at $50^{9}/_{16}$. In other words, the public (traders and investors) are buying DELL at the quoted ASK price of $50^{9}/_{16}$ (or $50.56 per share) from the five market makers. The price of $50^{9}/_{16}$ is clearly the lowest buying price. A trader could buy 1,000 shares of DELL from Merrill Lynch & Co. (MLCO) at $50^{5}/_{8}$ (or $50.62 per share), but that clearly is more expensive than the best ASK price of $50^{9}/_{16}$. Subsequently, MLCO is away from the market, or in the outside market, which means, for the moment at least, that MLCO is not a seller of that stock.

Conversely, Goldman Sachs & Co. (GSCO), Merrill Lynch & Co. (MLCO), Bear Stearns & Co. (BEST), Alex Brown & Sons (ABSB), and J. P. Morgan Securities (JPMS) are buying 1,000 shares of DELL, each at $50^{1}/_{2}$. Traders and investors are selling DELL at the quoted BID price of $50^{1}/_{2}$ (or $50.50 per share) from the five market makers. The BID of $50^{1}/_{2}$ is clearly the highest selling price. The trader could sell 1,000 shares of DELL to Montgomery Securities (MONT) at $50^{3}/_{8}$ (or $50.37 per share), but that is clearly less than the best BID price of $50^{1}/_{2}$ ($50.50). MONT is away from the market, or in the outside market. In essence, MONT is not a buyer of the stock.

Each price level on the Level II screen receives a different color for easy reference, whereas in this book, which has only two colors (black and white), the difference is shown by different levels of shading. In figure 6.2, on the BID side, there are five market makers that are posting the best selling price, and they are all the same color. Note also that on the ASK side there are five market makers that are posting the best buying price; they are also the same color. Both the BID and the ASK side have four distinct columns. The first column has "+" and "−" signs, indicating whether the market maker has increased or decreased the BID or ASK price. If there are no "+" or "−" signs, then the market maker has refreshed the same BID or ASK price. The second column shows the market maker's four-letter identification code. The third column shows the market maker's BID and ASK prices. And the last column shows the number (size) of shares offered by the market makers at that BID or ASK price.

Figure 6.2 shows only ten market makers represented on the Level II screen. In reality, DELL has many more market makers on both the BID and the ASK side. For a variety of reasons, some market makers may not be active in market-making activities, but they are required to post both BID and ASK prices. These market makers would deliberately back away from the best BID and ASK prices. Their BID and ASK prices would be posted at the bottom of the Level II screen.

The Level II screen has two distinct BID and ASK sides. Market makers are required to post simultaneously on both sides. The position of the market maker on both the BID and the ASK sides reveals whether that market maker is a buyer or seller. The market maker's relative position would reveal whether he or she is bullish or bearish on that stock. Figure 6.3 illustrates this point.

Figure 6.3 reveals that MLCO and GSCO are buyers. They are at the top of the BID side, buying the stock at $50\frac{1}{2}$. MLCO and GSCO have joined the BID, and they are in the inside market. Because both MLCO and GSCO are required to be on both sides of the market, GSCO and MLCO have posted a relatively high ASK price of $50\frac{7}{8}$, which is not a competitive price. These two market makers are buyers and not sellers. One could argue that GSCO and MLCO are bullish on that particular stock. GSCO and MLCO are buying stock at the low

Figure 6.3 *MLCO and GSCO Are Buyers*

price ($50^1/_2$) and anticipating that stock will go up in value so they could sell it at the higher price ($50^7/_8$).

Why would a rational investor buy the stock from GSCO and MLCO at $50^7/_8$ when the lowest posted ASK price is $50^9/_{16}$ from JPMS and LEHM? If the investor does not have access to real-time data feed and Level II screen information, the investor would not know the best ASK price (i.e., the lowest buying price). For example, an investor who has an account with Merrill Lynch & Co. (MLCO) and who is buying that stock through Merrill Lynch might pay $50^7/_8$ (or $50.87 per share). However, traders monitoring the stock would know the difference. One of the advantages of trading one's own account is the ability to view live Level II screen information. Someone who does this knows that he or she is getting the best price.

Conversely, figure 6.4 reveals that MLCO and GSCO are sellers. They are at the top of the ASK side, selling the stock at $50^9/_{16}$. They have joined the ASK, and they are in the inside market. Because MLCO and GSCO are required to be on both sides of the market simultaneously, they have both posted a relatively low BID price of $50^1/_4$, which is not competitive. This is because GSCO and MLCO are sellers and not buyers. Figure 6.4 reveals that GSCO and MLCO are bearish on that particular stock. They are trying to sell that stock and deplete the inventory, anticipating that the stock will go down in value in the future. In other words, GSCO and MLCO are selling stock at the best ASK price ($50^9/_{16}$) and anticipating that the stock will drop in value so they can buy it at the lower price ($50^1/_4$).

Again, why would a rational investor sell the stock to GSCO and MLCO at $50^1/_4$ when the highest posted BID price is $50^1/_2$ from WEAT and COWN? The investor who has an account with Merrill Lynch & Co. and who is selling that stock would most likely receive $50^1/_4$ (or $50.25 per share), which is MLCO's buying price. How would the investor know the best BID price (i.e., the highest selling price) if he or she does not have access to real-time data feed and Level II screen information? A trader, because of his or her access to live Level II screen information, would know that he or she is getting the best price.

Thinly traded NASDAQ stocks have only a few market makers that provide liquidity. Most likely, if a stock were thinly traded, there would be only a few or one market maker at any price level. Figure 6.5 depicts a stock with no price depth. This would be a stock to avoid trading.

Figure 6.4   *MLCO and GSCO Are Sellers*

Figure 6.5   *Stock with No Price Depth*

In figure 6.5, there are only five market makers providing liquidity for the stock. The trader has an opportunity to buy the stock at $50^9/_{16}$ from JPMS and BEST. The spread between BID and ASK is $^1/_{16}$, which would mean that price would have to go up $^1/_{16}$ to break even. However, there is only one market maker that is selling the stock at $50^1/_2$. If GLCO leaves the inside BID, the price would drop to $50^3/_8$. The spread between BID and ASK would be $^3/_{16}$, which would mean that the price would have to go up $^3/_{16}$ just to break even. If the market turns quickly in the opposite (lower) direction, MLCO could leave the BID of $50^3/_8$, and the selling price would become $50^5/_{16}$.

It is very risky to trade thinly traded stocks that have little depth. A stock should have several market makers on both sides of BID and ASK at one price level. Even actively traded stocks with many market makers could, during the trading day, end up in the situation depicted in figure 6.5, which basically shows the trader that there is very little room for mistakes. The trader may not be able to liquidate a position at the desired price level when there is very little liquidity. If only one market maker leaves the inside market, the price of the stock will change.

Dynamics of the Level II Screen

The next step is to link the supply-and-demand market forces to the NASDAQ Level II screen information (see figure 6.6). There are five market makers on the BID side and on the ASK side (i.e., there are five buyers and five sellers for that stock). The equilibrium price at this time is $50^1/_2$ and $50^9/_{16}$, given that everything remains constant.

"Everything else being equal" is the crucial assumption here, because nothing in the stock market remains constant. Thus supply-and-demand lines are always shifting or moving. Whenever something happens in the market (whether it's good news or bad news), it will change

Figure 6.6 *Level II and Supply-and-Demand Forces*

the participants' perceptions about a stock. If the news is good, more buyers will enter the market and the demand will increase. Similarly, more stock sellers will exit the market, and the stock supply will decrease. The demand schedule will shift to the right, whereas the supply schedule will shift to the left. If the news is bad, buyers will exit the market, and demand for the stock will decrease. Likewise, stock sellers will enter the market, and the supply will increase. In this situation, the demand schedule will shift to the left, and the supply schedule will shift to the right. Because the world of the stock market is dynamic, supply and demand are always moving; there is always an increase or a decrease in demand or supply.

This basic economics concept of reduced supply and increased demand for a stock can be illustrated on the Level II screen as well. The Level II screen is updated dynamically (that is, continuously). Market makers continuously enter different BID and ASK prices, or join or leave the inside BID and ASK prices. Consequently, Level II screen information is always changing. This is particularly true for fast-trading technology stocks.

Figure 6.7 attempts to provide the link between the supply-and-demand market forces and the fast-moving Level II screen. The starting point is figure 6.6, where there are five buyers and five sellers who are bidding and offering the same amount of shares of the stock on each side. The equilibrium prices at that point in time were $50\frac{1}{2}$ and $50\frac{9}{16}$. Again, suppose that the stock had been accompanied by good news, and there had been a reduction in supply and an increase in demand for that stock. Imagine that we have frozen the Level II screen at that moment. Figure 6.7 will depict that change resulting from the good news.

This time there are only two market makers selling the stock on the ASK side, which translates into a reduction in the supply of that stock. The color-coded inside ASK side has shrunk from five to two market makers (represented in figure 6.7 by the up arrow on the ASK side, which shows that the color of the inside ASK is "shrinking" and "moving up"). On the other hand, there are eight market makers buying the stock on the BID side. The color-coded inside BID side has been enlarged from five to eight market makers (represented in figure 6.7 by the down arrow on the BID side, which shows that the color of the inside BID is "increasing" and "moving down").

Figure 6.7 *Level II Screen Information with Increased Demand and Reduced Supply*

The best BID and ASK prices are still $50^1/_2$ and $50^9/_{16}$. But this price will not last very long. There is a distinct possibility that the two remaining market makers (JPMS and LEHM) will eventually leave the ASK side. At that time the ASK price will increase to $50^5/_8$. Nonetheless, there are eight market makers competing to buy that stock. There is a distinct possibility that one of the eight market makers will eventually increase the BID price. At that time, the BID price will increase to $50^9/_{16}$, a development that is depicted in figure 6.8 by the "freeze-frame" picture of the Level II screen.

The two market makers (JPMS and LEHM) increased their ASK price from $50^9/_{16}$ to $50^5/_8$, and the color representing $50^9/_{16}$ "moved up" and disappeared from the ASK side. However, two market makers (MLCO and GSCO) increased their BID price from $50^1/_2$ to $50^9/_{16}$. The color-coded price of $50^9/_{16}$ moved in counterclockwise motion from the ASK side to the BID side. The dynamic Level II screen will show this counterclockwise motion whenever there is a price increase.

If the price-increase momentum continued, there would be more market makers entering the BID side (that is, buying the stock). At the same time, there would be more market makers leaving the ASK side. Figure

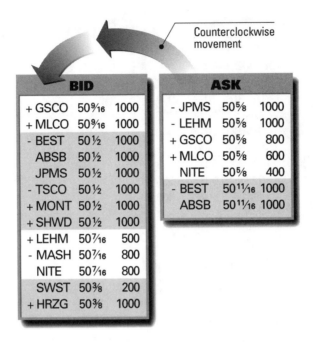

Figure 6.8   *Level II and Price Increase*

6.8 depicts that continued price-increase movement. The number of market makers on the inside ASK price has been reduced from five to two. The color-coded price block of $50^5/_8$ on the inside ASK price has shrunk and "moved up." On the other side, the number of market makers on the inside BID price has increased from two to five, and there are now more market makers on the inside BID price. The color-coded price block of $50^9/_{16}$ on the inside BID has been enlarged and "moved down." The counterclockwise motion on the Level II screen would thus continue. In short, the color-coded block of the inside BID would increase in size and, conversely, the color-coded block of the inside ASK would decrease.

For the time being, the best BID and ASK sides have remained unchanged, at $50^9/_{16}$ and $50^5/_8$. The trader who has access to a live Level II screen would receive a visual confirmation that a price-increase momentum is there, thus providing the trader with a preview of the future. If the price momentum continues in this counterclockwise motion on the Level II screen, the trader could expect new and higher BID and ASK prices of $50^5/_8$ and $50^{11}/_{16}$. The counterclockwise motion on the Level II screen would then constitute a BUY signal for the trader whose focus is on the small short-term price momentum.

Traders can observe when the counterclockwise motion on the Level II screen slows down and stops. This action means that the price-increase momentum is losing its steam. (Other investors and traders who do not have the Level II screen could not preview this slowdown in the price-increase momentum.) The inflow of money is slowing down; the demand for the stock has ceased to increase. There are no new market makers entering the inside BID, the stock supply has stabilized and ceased to decrease, and the market makers are not leaving the inside ASK price. All of this would tell traders that the momentum is shifting. Now would be a good time to exit the long position, or sell the stock—the slowdown in the momentum is a signal to SELL the stock.

Conversely, his basic economic concept of reduced demand and increased supply for the stock can be illustrated on the Level II screen as well. The starting point is again figure 6.6. In that example, there were five market makers on the BID side and on the ASK side; that is, there were five buyers and five sellers for that stock. The equilibrium prices at this point of time were $50\frac{1}{2}$ and $50\frac{9}{16}$.

Suppose that stock was accompanied by bad news, and there was a reduction in demand and an increase in supply for that stock. If you imagine a frozen image of the Level II screen for that moment, you would see what is depicted in figure 6.9. Now there are only two market makers buying the stock on the BID side, which translates into a reduction in demand for that stock. The color-coded inside BID side has shrunk from five to two market makers (represented in figure 6.9 by the up arrow on the BID side, which shows that the color-coded inside BID is shrinking and moving up). But, there are eight market makers selling the stock on the ASK side. The color-coded inside ASK side has been enlarged from five to eight market makers (represented in figure 6.9 by the down arrow on the ASK side, which indicates that the color-coded inside ASK is increasing and moving down).

The best BID and ASK prices are still $50\frac{1}{2}$ and $50\frac{9}{16}$. But this price will not last very long. There is a distinct possibility that the two remaining market makers (ABSB and JPMS) will eventually leave the inside BID side. At that time, the BID price would decrease to $50\frac{7}{16}$.

On the other hand, there are eight market makers competing to sell that stock. There is a distinct possibility that one or more of the eight

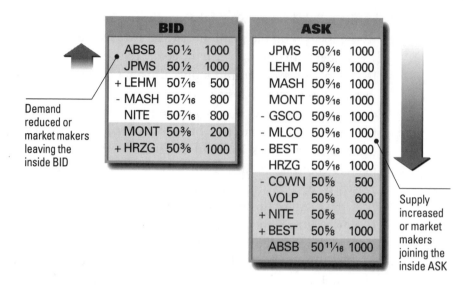

BID		
ABSB	50½	1000
JPMS	50½	1000
+ LEHM	50⁷⁄₁₆	500
- MASH	50⁷⁄₁₆	800
NITE	50⁷⁄₁₆	800
MONT	50⅜	200
+ HRZG	50⅜	1000

Demand reduced or market makers leaving the inside BID

ASK		
JPMS	50⁹⁄₁₆	1000
LEHM	50⁹⁄₁₆	1000
MASH	50⁹⁄₁₆	1000
MONT	50⁹⁄₁₆	1000
- GSCO	50⁹⁄₁₆	1000
- MLCO	50⁹⁄₁₆	1000
- BEST	50⁹⁄₁₆	1000
HRZG	50⁹⁄₁₆	1000
- COWN	50⅝	500
VOLP	50⅝	600
+ NITE	50⅝	400
+ BEST	50⅝	1000
ABSB	50¹¹⁄₁₆	1000

Supply increased or market makers joining the inside ASK

Figure 6.9 *Level II Screen Information with Increased Supply and Reduced Demand*

market makers (or new market makers who are not currently on the inside ASK) will eventually decrease the ASK price. At that time, the ASK price will decrease to $50^1/_2$. This development is depicted in figure 6.10 in the "freeze-frame" picture of the Level II screen.

The two market makers (JPMS and LEHM) decreased their BID price from $50^1/_2$ to $50^7/_{16}$. One market maker (LEHM) refreshed the same price of $50^7/_{16}$, and thus LEHM joined the inside BID. The color representing $50^1/_2$ "moved up" and disappeared from the BID side. But, four market makers (JPMS, LEHM, MASH, and MONT) lowered their ASK price from $50^9/_{16}$ to $50^1/_2$. This is shown as a new color-coded price and will show up on the ASK side. In essence, the color-coded price of $50^1/_2$ would move in clockwise motion from the BID side to the ASK side. Whenever there is a price decrease, the dynamic Level II screen will show this clockwise motion.

In addition, traders can observe when the clockwise motion on the Level II screen slows down and stops, which would indicate that the price-decrease momentum was losing its steam. (Other investors and traders who do not have access to the Level II screen would not be able to preview this slowdown in momentum.) The outflow of money is

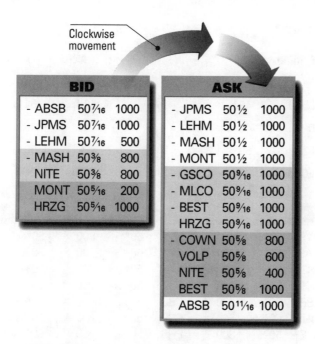

Figure 6.10 *Level II and Price Decrease*

slowing down, and the stock supply has ceased to increase. There are no new market makers entering the inside ASK, and some market makers may be refreshing at a higher ASK. The demand for the stock has stabilized, and it is no longer decreasing. Market makers are not leaving the inside BID price. All of this tells the trader that the momentum is shifting. Now would probably be a good time to exit the short position. In other words, buy the stock and close the short position.

NYSE Trading Information Screen

Because there is only one "market maker" for the listed securities, there is no Level II screen information available for NYSE securities. Traders who do not have a seat on the exchange would not know the depth of the market at any point in time, as this information is available only to the specialist on the exchange floor. Thus traders on the NYSE deal with a very limited set of stock information. Figure 6.11 displays what NYSE traders can observe on their computer screens.

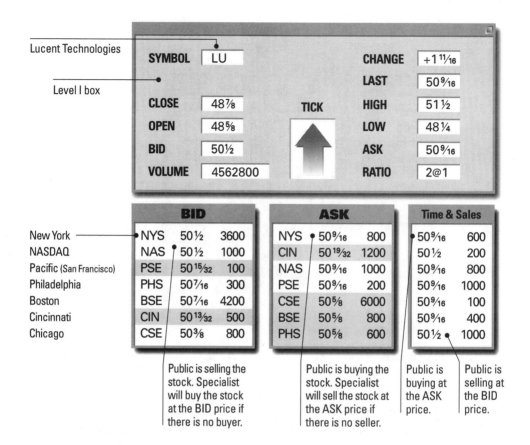

Figure 6.11 *NYSE Trading Information*

The first box in figure 6.11 is essentially the familiar Level I screen information. The only difference in the Level I information between the NYSE-listed securities and the NASDAQ-traded stocks is the "ratio" field. The ratio field for NASDAQ stocks displays the number of market makers on the inside BID and ASK side. In this example, with Lucent Technologies (LU), there is always only one specialist. However, there are several regional exchanges, in addition to the NYSE, that trade listed securities. In figure 6.11, there are two exchanges that furnish the highest BID, or the best selling price, for Lucent Technologies. On the other side, only the NYSE has the lowest ASK, or the best buying price. Thus the ratio field states that there are two exchanges with the best selling price and only one exchange with the best buying price. Because the NYSE has the trading volume advantage, the probability is great that it will provide the best prices for the listed stocks among different regional exchanges.

Another important distinction between the NASDAQ Level II screen and the NYSE screen is the NYSE screen's ability to view the size of the inside market. In this example, the NYSE specialist has sell orders for 3,600 shares of Lucent Technologies, but has buy orders for only 800 shares of Lucent. These shares are the actual size of the inside market. The trader can deduce that there are more sellers than buyers for the stock at that price level. This information could indicate a potential for the price to decrease. In this case, the ratio of selling to buying is relatively small (3,600:800), so the downward pressure is relatively small. But imagine an order to sell 36,000 shares rather than 3,600 shares. That ratio alone would indicate a large potential for the price to decline in the near future. Many traders state that this is why they decided to trade mostly NYSE stocks—there is less information to view, and they have the ability to see the true BID and ASK size.

Finally, the NASDAQ Level II screen does not show actual shares. Market makers are required to post only the absolute minimum of shares that they are willing to buy or sell. Consequently, the bid for 1,000 shares by the market maker (on the inside BID) is misleading. The same market maker could be "sitting" on the inside BID, refreshing the inside BID price, and buying, for example, 100,000 shares. However, the NASDAQ Level II screen does show the depth of the market. It displays how many other market makers are willing to pay for the stock at different price ranges. The NYSE screen does not show any of that information. Traders on the NYSE do not have access to "market depth" information.

The other useful information provided in figure 6.11 is the actual buy and sell orders that are being filled. That information is available in the "time and sales" window, which is also displayed in figure 6.11. The trader can see in real time whether the sales are being executed at the BID or the ASK price. The large number and size of executed sales on the ASK side would indicate a buying pattern, which would constitute a bullish sign. The large number and size of executed sales on the BID side would indicate a selling pattern, which would constitute a bearish sign. Occasionally, the time and sales window will display prices that are not the inside BID and ASK prices. The different prices might be old prices that are being reported with delay or the preferenced trade orders.

Therefore, there is no real Level II screen information for the listed stocks of the NYSE screen. The different exchanges are color-coded at the same price level, similar to the NASDAQ Level II screen. However, the fact remains that traders can only directly access the NYSE specialists by routing the order through the NYSE DOT system. The NYSE uses the DOT system (see chapter 4), which allows traders to enter orders from the trading firm's trading floor directly into the NYSE computer-execution system. The order bypasses the floor broker and goes directly to the NYSE specialist for execution. Therefore, even if the other exchanges listed in figure 6.11 have better prices than the NYSE, it is impossible to route that order electronically to different exchanges because the regional exchanges do not offer direct routing, such as DOT.

Level I Information and Poor Trading Stocks

A quick glance at the Level I screen at market close would reveal whether that stock is a good trading stock. Figure 6.12 depicts a recent snapshot of Ashworth Inc. (ASHW), a California-based manufacturer of golfing apparel.

ASHW is not a good swing-trading stock. The BID and ASK prices are $4^1/_2$ and $4^{19}/_{32}$. The spread is small, which is good. However, the trading volume for that particular day was only 36,900 shares, which is not enough liquidity. In fact, the average daily trading volume for ASHW's for the past 52 weeks was approximately 100,000 shares. Swing traders should trade stocks that have at least a 500,000-share daily trading volume. Thus ASHW does not have the liquidity to be suitable for trading.

Also, ASHW does not have daily price volatility. The daily price range for that day was $4^7/_{16}$ and $4^5/_8$, which translates to a price change of approximately 19 cents. That means that the maximum profit the trader could earn in one day on ASHW, if the entry and exit points are perfectly executed, is 19 cents per share. This 19 cents might be a high relative price change (4 percent) in one day for an inexpensive stock such as ASHW, but 19 cents is a small absolute change. It would be difficult to make money swing trading ASHW stock if the maximum daily-profit potential is only 19 cents per share.

SYMBOL	ASHW		CHANGE	-⁵⁄₁₆
			LAST TRADE	4 ¹⁹⁄₃₂
CLOSE	4⅞	TICK	HIGH for day	4⅝
OPEN	4 ¹³⁄₁₆		LOW for day	4⁷⁄₁₆
BID	4½		ASK	4 ¹⁹⁄₃₂
VOLUME	36900		RATIO Bid/Ask	1@2

Figure 6.12 *Example of a Poor Trading Stock*

Even the examination of the 52-week high and low prices for ASHW reveals a limited trading range in absolute-dollar terms. For instance, the 52-week high price for ASHW was 6, whereas the lowest price in the past year was $3\frac{1}{8}$. In this example, it is a $2\frac{7}{8}$-point trading range for the year, which is a small absolute-dollar change in price. In short, it does not provide many opportunities for the swing trader to trade the stock. Charting ASHW using the daily closing price for the past year reveals that the trading range was mostly between $4 and $5 during most of the year.

Swing traders should emphasize and trade stocks that have a high absolute-price change and many substantial (at least 5 points) intrayear price swings. In relative terms, a $2\frac{7}{8}$-absolute-point change in price represents a high relative-price change. For instance, a $2\frac{7}{8}$-point change in price represents an approximate 78 percent increase from the 52-week low price. The objective of swing trading is to make high absolute-dollar profits and not high relative returns. If the absolute-dollar price increase is small ($2\frac{7}{8}$), then the only way to obtain high trading profits is to increase the number of shares traded. But that can be a dangerous trading practice if the stock does not have substantial liquidity or if the daily trading volume is small. For instance, how do you get out of a stock position quickly in the event of a sharp price downturn if the swing trader is holding a huge amount of a thinly traded stock? The answer is that you cannot.

7

Trade Orders and Execution

"It's better to be boldly decisive and risk being wrong than to agonize at length and be right too late."

—*Marilyn Moats Kennedy*

Because most of this chapter discusses day trading order-execution tactics, I need to explain up front what swing traders can learn by reading it. Previously I stated that swing traders need not concern themselves with minute intraday moves in price because their time frame is much longer. If that is the case, does it mean swing traders need to learn about fast executions as well? Should swing traders worry about which ECNs they use? Do they need to know what a heavy-duty trading-execution program, such as CyberTrader or TradeCast, can do?

My opinion is yes. The fact is that day traders use the fastest execution tools available to the general public, and thus they obtain better prices and greater liquidity. Although it is possible to be an effective swing trader without using the limit orders or cutting the spread, the power of this information can help you maximize your trading profits. It is always helpful to understand how professional traders execute their trades. In other words, you can learn to drive a fast sports car but elect to drive it slowly. In the end, the decision is yours.

Trading Terminology

The following four trading terms need defining (see also figure 7.1):

1. **Bidding.** Bidding is passive buying. The trader is a price maker: He or she is trying to purchase securities at a better or lower price than the inside ASK price. Usually, the trader will bid to purchase the security at the inside BID price, or the lowest possible price at which the trader can buy the stock. If the trader is less aggressive, the trader could bid the high BID, which is the price higher than the inside BID and lower than the inside ASK. It's probable that the trader will use one of the ECNs, such as Island, to execute those trades, because he or she would more likely be dealing with other individuals instead of market makers, who are less likely to budge on price.

In either case (bidding the BID or high BID via Island or SelectNet), the trader needs a seller. There is no guarantee that the trader will find that seller or that the trade will be executed at that price level. The trader's objective is to cut the spread between the BID and ASK prices and buy the stock at the lower price. This is a difficult task if the market is moving up. If the price of the stock has a clear upside momentum, why would anyone sell the stock at the lower price?

2. **Buying.** Buying is aggressive purchasing. The trader is a price taker: He or she is sending an order to purchase a stock at the posted inside ASK price. The trader is aggressive; he or she wants this stock badly and quickly because of the upside price momentum. The trader is willing to sacrifice the spread and is taking the stock from someone who is offering it for sale at the inside ASK price through the SOES or ECNs—either a market maker posting the best inside ASK price within the SOES, or another trader offering to sell the shares at the best inside ASK price through Island. Because the purchasing price is the inside ASK price, there is a very good probability that the order will get filled.

3. **Offering.** Offering is passive selling. The trader is a price maker: He or she is trying to sell securities at a better or higher price than the inside BID price. Most commonly, the trader will offer to sell the security at the inside ASK price, or the highest possible price at which the trader can sell that stock. If the trader is less aggressive, he or she could offer the low ASK, which is the price higher than the inside BID and lower than the inside ASK. Again, the trader would use one of the ECNs or Select-Net to execute those trades.

In either case (offering the ASK or low ASK on Island or SelectNet), the trader needs to find a buyer. There is no guarantee that the trader will find that buyer, and no guarantee that the trade will be executed at that price level. The trader's objective is to cut the spread between the BID and ASK prices and sell the stock at the higher price. This is a difficult task if the market is moving down. If the price of the stock has a clear downside momentum, the buyer has an incentive to wait for the price to move further down before buying the stock.

4. **Selling.** Selling is aggressive trading. The trader is a price taker in that he or she is sending an order to sell a stock at the posted inside BID price. He or she badly wants to dump the stock quickly because of a downside price momentum. The trader is willing to sacrifice the spread between the inside BID and ASK prices. The trader is giving that stock to someone who is bidding the stock for purchase at the inside BID price through the SOES or ECNs—either a market maker posting the best inside BID price within the SOES, or another trader bidding to buy the

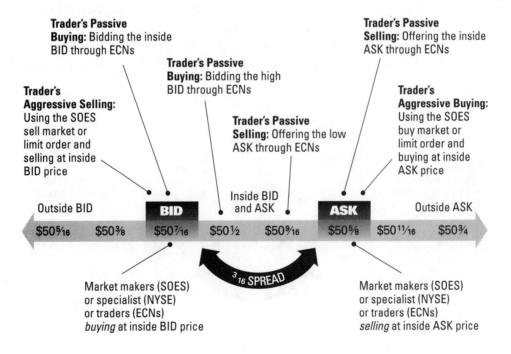

Figure 7.1 *Types of Execution Orders*

shares at the inside BID price through Island. Because the selling price is the inside BID price, there is a very good probability that the order will get filled. Figure 7.1 helps to illustrate this point.

Types of Orders

Traders can enter a number of different types of orders on the NASDAQ and NYSE. The type of order used is determined mostly by the trader's objectives. Following is a list of trade-execution orders. Figure 7.2 provides additional illustration.

1. **Market order.** The most common type of trade order is the market order. Although it does not specify a price, it is executed at whatever price is available when the order reaches the exchange floor. A market order will always be executed, but traders or investors cannot be sure of the execution price.

2. **Limit order.** When customers wish to buy or sell a security at a specific price, they enter a limit order—an order that can only be executed at the specified price or better. A buy limit can be executed at the limit price or lower; a sell limit can be executed at the limit price or higher. A buy-limit order is placed below the current market price of the security, whereas a sell-limit order is placed above the current market price. Because a limit order is entered at a price that differs from the current

Figure 7.2   *Bidding, Buying, Offering, and Selling*

best price, it is unlikely that the order would be executed immediately. Therefore, a limit order is usually given to a NYSE specialist to hold until it can be executed. It is possible that the order may never be executed, because the limit price is not reached or there are other orders at the same price with higher priority.

3. **Stop order.** A stop order becomes a market order to buy or sell securities once a specified price is attained or penetrated. The specific price indicated by the investor is called the *stop price*. Once the order is activated, the investor is guaranteed execution, but there is no guarantee of the execution price. A sell stop order is always placed below the current market price of the security and is typically used to limit a loss or protect a profit on a long stock position. A buy stop order is always placed above the current market price and is used to limit a loss or protect a profit on a short sale.

4. **Stop-limit order.** A stop-limit order is similar to a stop order in that a stop price will activate the order. However, once activated, the stop-limit order becomes a buy-limit or sell-limit order, and it can only be executed at a specified price or better. Thus, as its name implies, a stop-limit order is a combination of a stop order and a limit order. A stop-limit order eliminates the risk of a stop order when the investor is not guaranteed an execution price, but exposes the investor to the risk that the order may never be filled. A sell stop-limit order is always placed below the current market price of the security; it is used to limit the loss (or protect a profit) on a long position. Once activated, it becomes a sell-limit order. A buy stop-limit order is always placed above the current market price of the security; it is used to limit the loss (or protect a profit) on a short position. Again, once activated, it becomes a buy-limit order.

Order Qualifiers

In addition to the types of orders that an investor may enter, there are various qualifications that may be used to fill an order. The following is a list of the order qualifiers:

1. **Day order.** Every order is a day order unless otherwise specified. If not executed, it is automatically canceled at the end of the day.

2. **Good 'til canceled (GTC), or open, order.** This is an order that remains in effect until executed or canceled. The floor broker should periodically update GTC orders.

3. **At the opening.** This is an order to buy or sell at the opening price. If not executed at the opening, it will be canceled.

4. **At the close.** This order is to be executed as close to the closing price as possible. There is no guarantee that the price will be the closing price.

5. **Not held (NH).** This qualification gives the floor broker discretion as to the time and price of an order. If the floor broker does not execute or does not obtain the best price, the broker will not be held responsible. A NYSE specialist cannot accept a not-held order.

6. **All or none (AON).** According to this qualification, the entire order must be filled on the same transaction. The order does not have to be filled immediately; it can be executed during the course of the trading day.

7. **Immediate or cancel (IOC).** This qualifier dictates that as much of the order as possible must be executed immediately. The portion that is not immediately executed is canceled.

8. **Fill or kill (FOK).** This qualification combines the AON and IOC orders. The entire order must be executed immediately or the entire order is canceled.

Limit vs. Market Orders

As a general rule, the trader should use the buy-limit order rather than the buy-market order, since specifying the buying price is always a good risk-management practice. The trader needs to be in control and buy the stock at the "right" price. If the market is moving very fast and the trader is using market orders, he or she might overpay for a security. If the trader uses the buy-market order, he or she is abdicating somewhat the ability to control the price. In other words, the trader is "chasing" the stock.

If the trader has a long stock position and the price is dropping quickly, the trader could use the sell-market order rather than the sell-limit order. If the trader uses the sell-limit order, the order might not get filled, and the trader would miss the market altogether. Because the objective is to minimize the risk and get out of the stock quickly, the trader could use the sell-market order. Unfortunately, using the sell-market order is an invitation to get a fill at the bottom. A better strategy yet is to try to go out of market. In other words, the trader should try to sell the stock at the outside market (outside BID price) and not use the current inside BID price.

For example, if the stock tanks, your best bet is to take out the best Island ECN BID, even if that BID price is outside the market, because the order will be matched directly. Another option is to use NASDAQ SelectNet and preference a market maker who might be a few price notches (or color levels on the Level II screen) below the inside BID price. However, this would not ensure a fill to the same degree that routing an order through an ECN would.

Conversely, if the stock is taking off fast and you desperately want to get in (or get out of the short position), then your best bet is to take out the best available Island ASK price, even if that ASK price is higher than inside ASK and outside the market. With the NASDAQ stocks, use NASDAQ SelectNet and preference a market maker who might be a few price notches (or color levels on the Level II screen) above the inside ASK price.

The bottom line is that traders should use market orders sparingly. If a stock is appreciating in value and the trader wants to close a profitable long position, the trader should use the market order. In other words, if the trader is selling with the up-tick price, or the green BID bar on the trading screen, then a market order is the appropriate choice.

Limit Orders on the NYSE

One important distinction between the NYSE and the NASDAQ is the treatment of limit orders. To protect individual traders and investors, the NYSE enacted rules that assign priority to customers' orders over those of NYSE specialists. In other words, a customer's limit orders, up to 2,100 shares, will be placed in front of a specialist's orders, even if the specialist had been first in line. Traders trading on the NASDAQ market do not have that protection.

This is a tremendous advantage for NYSE traders. For the limit order to be executed, someone has to be on the other side of the trade to buy or sell the stock at the market BID and ASK price through the market orders. Specialists will seldom fill these orders. It is the investors on the NYSE who send the market orders that close the trade. In other words, when the trader submits a limit order to buy the stock at the BID price, the investor sells that stock at the BID price through the market order. Conversely, when the trader submits a limit order to sell the stock at the ASK price, the investor buys that stock at the ASK price via the market order. That means that traders on the NYSE can trade without paying the BID and ASK spread. The traders, therefore, are making the spread, which is a typical day-trading strategy.

Priority of Orders

Because a number of orders can arrive at the exchange floor at approximately the same time, a priority of orders has been established to determine which order will be executed first. The priority of trade orders is as follows:

1. Price
2. Time
3. Size

The first priority is always price. The highest BID and lowest ASK will always come first. After price, time is the determining factor. If all bidders or offerers are equal in price, then whoever came into the trading crowd first will take preference over later bidders or offerers. If the orders are equal in price and time, then the size of the order is the determining factor. Normally, the larger order will receive priority.

What this all means is that market orders do not have any priority over limit orders. Suppose, for example, that the best BID and ASK prices are 50 and $50\frac{1}{8}$, and the following is the order sequence received at the trading post:

1. LMT Buy $50\frac{1}{8}$ 300
2. MKT Buy $50\frac{1}{8}$ 1,000
3. MKT Buy $50\frac{1}{8}$ 2,000

If this is the order time sequence, the limit buy order for 300 shares will be executed before the two market orders. The point of this exercise is to show that limit orders do not have any inherent disadvantages over market orders if they are submitted first. Hence, it is better for a trader to be in control of his or her trading and submit a limit order rather than a market order.

NASDAQ SOES Orders

The NASD's Small Order Execution System (SOES) was designed specifically for the benefit of small investors or traders who are trading on the NASDAQ. Traders or investors always buy the stock at the posted low ASK price or sell the stock at the posted high BID price from the market makers through the SOES. The execution order is routed directly to the NASDAQ market makers. SOES orders at the same price are executed on a first-come, first-served basis. This assures that the traders or investors receive the best posted price.

The second key feature of the SOES is its mandatory nature. The NASD currently requires that all market makers post the firm BID and ASK prices and subsequently honor those trades. Because SOES orders are mandatory for the market makers and are executed automatically, the SOES is a very powerful trading-execution tool. When stock prices are moving up, the SOES buy order is a good tool for getting into the market quickly at a posted ASK price.

On January 14, 2000, the SEC approved the NASD rule-change proposal to convert and expand the SOES into NASDAQ's primary trading platform, called the NASDAQ National Market System (NNMS), which is sometimes referred to as the SuperSOES. The new SOES, or the NNMS, will be enhanced by an increase in the maximum order size for NASDAQ national market securities (from 1,000 to 9,900 shares), a reduction in the order-execution delay (from 17 to 5 seconds), and an allowance for market makers to execute their proprietary orders, thus eliminating market makers' exposure to dual liability. Dual liability results if a market maker receives and executes an order through Select-Net and immediately thereafter receives an execution against its quote through SOES.

Market makers are required to post their best BID and ASK price as well as their share size, such as 1,000 shares. This information is displayed to the entire world on the Level II screen. Under the new Super-SOES proposal, market makers would also have an option to indicate a reserve-size share amount at that BID and ASK price, which unfortunately will not be displayed on the Level II screen. However, having the reserve size indicated in the system will improve the efficiency and speed of the automatic electronic execution.

Consider the following scenario: Two market makers, A and B, are ranked in time priority. Both market makers publicly post an inside BID at $20, with a minimum of 1,000 shares and a reserve of 2,000 shares. A limit sell order is entered into the NASDAQ system at $20 for 5,000 shares. Obviously, the NNMS will first take out the displayed minimum 1,000 shares each from both market makers. Then, the NNMS will take out 2,000 shares from market maker A, followed by 1,000 shares from market maker B, for a total of 5,000 shares. Under the current system, the order would most likely get partially filled for the posted minimum 1,000 shares from each market maker (A and B).

The speed of the SOES order execution depends on how many market makers are at the inside BID and ASK market and how many other day-trading SOES orders are in the computerized queue. The unanswerable question is: How quickly are they refreshing the inside BID and ASK quotes? For instance, the market makers are only required to post 1,000 shares on the Level II screen, and that is exactly what they do. Thus the posted 1,000 shares on the Level II screen may not be the actual trading size. The market makers do not like to disclose to the public the true size or interest of their buying or selling intentions. The "ax" market maker can continue to refresh 1,000 after 1,000 shares of any particular stock at the lowest ASK price (that is, he or she can continue to sell), and thus effectively stop any price momentum.

Getting in the market with the SOES used to be the most common execution method of day traders. Once traders ascertained an upward price movement, they quickly jumped into the market using an SOES limit order. They bought the stock at the posted inside ASK price rather than bidding into the stock at the inside BID price or higher BID price. The SOES granted them quick execution at the guaranteed best ASK price at that time. The key was to get into the market quickly to pick up that price momentum.

SOES Mechanics   All NASDAQ stocks have an SOES limit. Most trading stocks currently have a 1,000-share limit, although the limits are proposed to go up to 9,900. Most trading software automatically displays the tier limit under the share amount allowed under the SOES. The trader cannot send out through the SOES an execution order for more than the tier limit. If the market makers are not available at the inside BID or ASK market, then the SOES order will be canceled automatically. If the only party available at the inside BID or ASK market is an ECN, such as Island, the SOES order will be rejected. Certain small capitalization stocks may display a few market makers on the Level II screen, but the stock may not be traded through the SOES. In that case, the trading software would generate this message: "No SOES market maker available."

From the trader's perspective, the maximum SOES order size for a security is either the proposed 9,900, or the current limit of 1,000, 500, or 200 shares, depending on the price and trading volume of that security. Only public customers' orders that are not larger than the maximum order size may be entered by the SOES order-entry firm (the day-trading firm or NASD broker or dealer) into the SOES for execution against the SOES market maker. Orders in excess of the maximum order size may not be divided into smaller parts for purposes of meeting the size requirements for orders entered into SOES.

The SOES treats limit orders priced at the current inside BID and ASK market as market orders that are immediately executed. The SOES orders are unpreferenced orders, which are executed against the market makers in rotation. Currently, the SOES does not execute an unpreferenced order against a single market maker more than once every 17 seconds, although NASDAQ has proposed a change to 5 seconds. That means the market makers can be "SOESed" by the trader, and the market makers have the option to refresh the same price or back away to the outside BID and ASK market (after the proposed 5-second delay).

The SOES previously had a 5-minute rule, which was modified in the summer of 1998. The old rule stated that if an order was filled through the SOES, the trader could not trade that same stock in the same direction within 5 minutes. In other words, the trader could not buy 1,000 shares of Microsoft and then buy another 1,000 or any other amount of Microsoft within 5 minutes of buying the original 1,000 shares. Again, that rule has been modified. Now, if the trader can show that each Microsoft order was a separate and individual trading decision, then it is OK to trade the same Microsoft stock in the same direction within 5 minutes. For instance, a trader could buy Microsoft, then buy Yahoo!, and then buy Microsoft again, which would all constitute separate investment decisions. If the price of Microsoft is different for the first and second Microsoft trade, then each order is a separate investment decision.

When using trading software, such as CyberTrader or TradeCast, placing an SOES order is a simple task. The trader simply selects the stock by typing in the stock symbol. Then he or she presses the default function key for the action to enter the SOES order. Users can choose between limit and market SOES orders by pressing different function keys.

SOES Future   SOES orders used to be the bread and butter of the day-trading business. Unfortunately, NASDAQ market makers and the NASD have instituted myriad small and seemingly innocuous rules that have transformed the SOES into a negligible percentage of the NASDAQ's trading volume today. In other words, the NASDAQ market makers pushed for—and NASD passed—several SOES rules that benefit the market makers, such as SOES limit size and the revised 5-minute rule, which have made trading with the SOES very difficult. In response to these changes, the traders simply turned their backs on the SOES and opened their arms to ECNs. In other words, ECNs ultimately provide a faster, cheaper, and friendlier trading environment than do the NASDAQ's SOES or SelectNet. Time will tell whether the proposed changes will make the SuperSOES (or NNMS) and SelectNet the trader's primary trading medium once again.

NASDAQ SelectNet Orders   SelectNet is an execution-order service owned and operated by NASDAQ. Whereas the SOES execution service is mandatory for market makers, use of SelectNet is completely voluntary. As the name implies, the trader would "select" and offer to the market makers a bid to buy or an offer to sell shares of a stock. However, the submitted order does not have to be filled by the market makers.

All orders with traditional brokers are currently routed through SelectNet. With the proposed SOES changes, all orders will be routed through the new SuperSOES. Therefore SelectNet will only be used for large orders (larger than the posted NNMS-sized orders), to hit ECNs, or to go out of market (outside market). In essence, SelectNet will become a completely voluntary and interactive marketplace for over-sized orders between the traders on one side and the market makers and

ECN market participants on the other. A SelectNet order will get filled only if the market makers perceive that the trader's bid or offer is a good deal. Traders who use trading-execution software that has the SelectNet feature can either broadcast their bids or offers to all market makers, or preference a single market maker or ECN market participant.

SelectNet Broadcast Orders   The first option is to broadcast the bid and offer. Traders can broadcast to all market makers their bid to buy a stock at the current inside BID price. They can also broadcast to all market makers their bid to buy a stock at the higher BID price. The trader's bid would be posted throughout the NASDAQ network to all market makers, but it would not show up on Level II screens. In other words, the offer to buy the stock at the inside BID price or higher BID price will be visible only to market makers.

Why would a trader want to use the SelectNet broadcast as an execution vehicle? If the buy order gets filled, the trader would buy the stock at the inside BID price. At worst, the trader would buy the stock at the higher BID price. Either way, the trader will be better off using the SelectNet broadcast than buying the stock through the SOES at the best ASK price. But isn't it always better to buy at the lower price than the higher price? Well, the trader will be better off buying the stock at the inside BID or higher BID price than at the lowest ASK price. However, the key phrase is "if the bid offer gets filled." There is no guarantee that the market makers will fill the order. The trader only hopes that the order will get filled.

SelectNet Preference Orders   The second option is to preference a single market maker through SelectNet. When the SelectNet preference order is submitted to the market maker, that order will show up on the market maker's computer screen. The market maker would then have 15 seconds either to fill the order or to move off the posted price. In essence, the trader is reminding the market maker that the posted price needs to be honored. The SelectNet preference bid forces the selected market maker to act.

If the order is not executed by the market maker and if it is not during a high-volume period, it is a good practice to refresh SelectNet orders after 15 seconds. At high-volume periods, however, SelectNet is extremely slow, and orders can stay open for minutes without the trader being able to cancel or get a fill confirmation, no matter what trading system is used. At this time the trader also cannot cancel the SelectNet order for 10 seconds. So if the market starts to move in the opposite direction, the trader does not have the option to cancel the order. In all probability, the market maker will fill the order during that time. After 10 seconds, the trader can manually send a cancel order, or the order will be canceled automatically by the software after a user-defined preset time (15 seconds). The trader will then receive a confirmation message on the computer screen that the SelectNet order has been canceled.

SelectNet Order-Execution Mechanics   When using trading software, such as CyberTrader of TradeCast, placing a SelectNet order is a relatively simple task. The trader simply types the stock symbol in the appropriate window and presses Enter. Next, the trader holds down the Shift key while pressing the default function key for the SelectNet order-routing action. Figure 7.3 displays an example of the SelectNet window that would open, along with Level II screen information.

If the asterisk (*) shown in figure 7.3 is selected, the software will send a SelectNet broadcast order to all market makers. The trader could send out a SelectNet preference order to a particular market maker with a click of the mouse button. In this example, the trader can select one market maker who is advertising to buy Dell (DELL) at $64^3/_8$: The trader could send his bid to sell Dell at $64^3/_8$ to Goldman, Sachs & Co. (GSCO), to Bear Sterns & Co. (BEST), to Smith Barney Inc. (SBSH), to J.P. Morgan Securities Inc. (JPMS), or to Herzog, Heine, Geduld Inc. (HRZG).

The trader can access any market maker through SelectNet preferencing. He or she simply selects a price, and the software will match that price with all the available market makers at the price shown on the Level II screen. In figure 7.3, clicking the price arrow in the price box changes the market-maker window, displaying the market makers and ECNs available at that price.

The trader can use the up and down arrows to the right of the price box to adjust the price. Clicking on these arrow keys will increase or decrease the price by $^1/_{16}$. When the trader clicks OK, the order is sent through the NASDAQ SelectNet network. If the trader increases the inside BID price by $^1/_{16}$, he or she is broadcasting to all market makers

Figure 7.3 *SelectNet Order Execution and Level II Screen*

in the universe that he or she is bidding to buy the stock at the high BID price, which is higher than the current inside BID price.

In essence, traders who want to buy a stock through SelectNet have two alternatives. They can bid to buy the stock at the inside BID price, or as the traders would say, "Bid the BID." Or they can bid to buy the stock at the price higher than the current inside BID ("Bid the high BID").

Conversely, traders who want to sell a stock through SelectNet would also have two options. They could offer to sell the stock at the inside ASK price, or "Offer the ASK." Or the traders could offer to sell the stock at a price lower than the current inside ASK, or "Offer the low ASK."

Unlike with the SOES, there is no tier-size limit on a SelectNet order. The trader can bid to buy or offer to sell in increments of 2,000 or more shares. Because SelectNet is a voluntary order-execution system, no one is forced to honor any trade. The market makers even have the option to execute partial orders through SelectNet at their discretion. In addition to the posted market makers, the trader can also access Instinet (INCA) and other ECNs through the SelectNet order-execution system.

SelectNet Preference Buy-Order Trading Strategy   One common day-trading strategy that swing traders can learn from is using the SelectNet preference order to get in or out of a stock when the market is moving quickly. The trader can bid or offer on SelectNet as a way to take advantage of market momentum. Figure 7.4 helps to illustrate this point.

Imagine that the inside market is $50\frac{1}{2}$ to $50\frac{9}{16}$ for this stock. Let's assume that the stock has strong upside momentum. The trader eagerly wants to buy 1,000 shares of this stock. There is only one market maker on the Level II screen who is posting the lowest ASK price of $50\frac{9}{16}$. If the trader decides to utilize the SOES buy-limit order at $50\frac{9}{16}$, he or she will probably not be the first trader in the computerized queue, and the SOES buy-limit order would probably not get filled.

If B. T. Alex Brown Inc. (BTAB) leaves the inside ASK price, the new lowest ASK will become $50\frac{5}{8}$. At that time, the trader can submit an SOES buy-limit order at $50\frac{5}{8}$. Again, he or she will be competing with many other traders who are attempting to execute the same SOES buy market or limit orders at that price. If the upside price momentum is strong, the trader might miss the market. There are only three market makers posting 1,000 shares for sale. Those market makers could refresh the price and sell more than the posted 3,000 shares. If the market is moving, it is likely that the best ASK price will go up quickly from $50\frac{5}{8}$ to $50\frac{11}{16}$.

Rather than risking the opportunity altogether to buy a stock that is moving up fast, traders can elect from the beginning to preference the

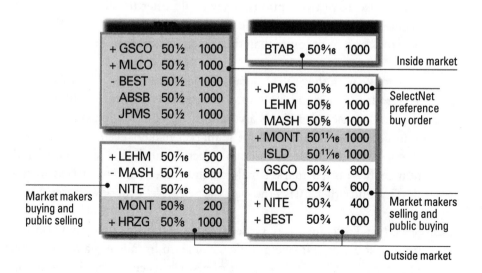

Figure 7.4 *SelectNet Preference Buy-Order Routing*

market makers who are on the outside market at that time. Using our example in figure 7.4, the astute trader could immediately submit the SelectNet preference buy order for 1,000 shares to J.P. Morgan Securities Inc. (JPMS) or Lehman Brothers Inc. (LEHM) for $50^5/_8$, although the lowest ASK price at that time is $50^9/_{16}$ (BTAB). In essence, the trader would forgo the best ASK price and pay $^1/_{16}$ more. But that would enhance the probability that the trader would end up owning the stock that is currently moving up in value.

SelectNet Preference Sell-Order Trading Strategy Conversely, let's assume that the stock has strong downside momentum (see figure 7.5). The inside market is $50^9/_{16}$ to $50^5/_8$ for this stock. The trader eagerly wants to get out of the long position and sell 1,000 shares. There is only one market maker on the Level II screen who is posting the highest BID price of $50^9/_{16}$. If the trader decides to utilize the SOES sell-limit order at $50^9/_{16}$, he or she will probably not be the first in line in the nation. The probability is that the SOES sell-limit order would not get filled.

If Mayer & Schweitzer Inc. (MASH) leaves the inside BID price, the new highest BID would become $50^1/_2$. At that time, the trader can submit an SOES sell-limit order at $50^1/_2$. The trader would compete with many other traders who would attempt to execute the same SOES sell market or limit orders at that price. If the downside price momentum is

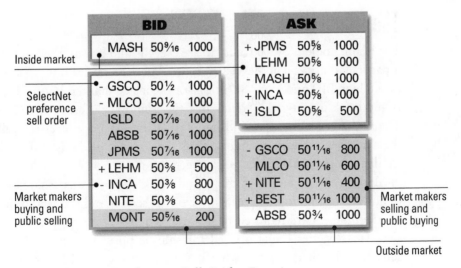

Figure 7.5 *SelectNet Preference Sell-Order Routing*

strong, the trader might miss that price as well. There are only two market makers who are each posting 1,000 shares for purchase. Although those market makers could refresh the price and buy more than the posted 2,000 shares, if the market is moving downward, it's probable that the best BID price will further decrease quickly.

Rather than risking the opportunity to dump a stock that is moving down fast, traders can elect from the beginning to preference the market makers who are on the outside market at that time. Figure 7.5 illustrates this point. The astute trader could immediately submit the SelectNet preference sell order for 1,000 shares to Goldman, Sachs & Co. (GSCO) or Merrill Lynch (MLCO) for $50\frac{1}{2}$. The trader would forgo the best BID price and sell for $\frac{1}{16}$ less. But that would enhance the probability that the trader would end up dumping a stock that is declining in value.

Island Trade Orders

When a trade order is entered into Island, the Island system directs the order first to an Island server for order matching and then, if it is not immediately filled, to the NASDAQ SelectNet system. Traders can access Island directly or through the SelectNet execution system. Placing Island orders directly to Island, as opposed to preferencing Island via SelectNet, is the faster of the two routes.

The Island Book

The Island book allows a trader to see every Island buy and sell order for a particular stock. The Level II screen allows the trader only to see the Island high BID and low ASK prices, or the inside market. In essence, the Island book displays the "depth" of the Island at different price levels. The Island book shows all bids and offers at every price level, as well as the available quantity of shares. Thus the concept of the Island book is similar to the NASDAQ Level II screen.

However, the fact that the Island book shows actual shares is an important distinction between the Level II screen and the Island book. Market makers are required to post the required minimum stock-share sizes (that is, tier limit) offered for sale or purchase on the Level II screen, and that is exactly what is shown on the Level II screen. The market makers do not wish to show their full hands. For instance, a market maker broadcasts that 1,000 shares of Yahoo! are offered for sale. In reality, the same market maker might be selling 100,000 shares of Yahoo! From the Level II screen, the traders cannot tell the actual size of the Yahoo! inside or outside market.

The Island book, however, displays the actual size of the inside or outside market for any stock. This is very useful information. Imagine that the trader can see 100,000 shares of Yahoo! being offered for sale at one price level higher than the inside ASK price. That would indicate that the supply of Yahoo! is increasing dramatically. There is a distinct possibility that the price of Yahoo! will decline in the near future. Figure 7.6 demonstrates this situation.

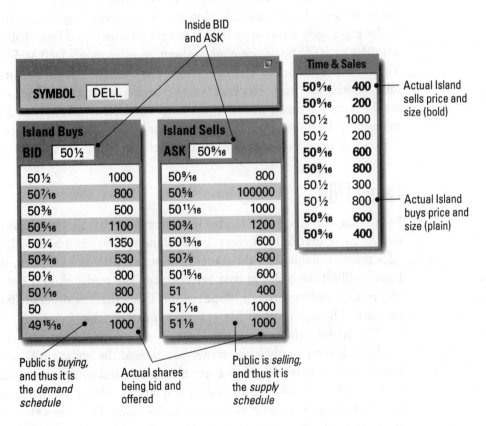

Figure 7.6 *The Island Book*

The trader can simply type in a stock symbol (for example, DELL), and the Island book will display the inside BID and ASK prices and the total number of shares available at that level. In this example, there are 1,000 shares at $50\frac{1}{2}$ at the Island buys and 800 shares at $50\frac{9}{16}$ at the Island sells. In addition, the Island book displays all available price levels and share sizes. All actual bids and offers at the same price level are lumped together. For instance, the large 100,000 offer for sale at $50\frac{5}{8}$ could be possible, as it may include many smaller orders. The "time and sales" Island window displays the price and share amount of all "prints," or actual individual buys and sells. These are commonly color-coded on the computer screen (green for buys and red for sells). In the black and white figure 7.6, bold lettering represents the red Island sells.

All Island orders are based on the FIFO system: first in, first out. It is important to know what is being traded on Island. The trader who has access to the Island book can plan an exit strategy. Suppose that the trader has a long position in Dell. If the trader observes a large 100,000 sell offer at $50\frac{5}{8}$, he or she might submit an offer to sell Dell at $50\frac{19}{32}$. This would ensure that the offer is first in line for Island execution, unless someone offers stock at a lower price. In addition, that offer would place the trader ahead of the large sell offer of 100,000 at $50\frac{5}{8}$. In essence, the trader would make sure that he or she gets out before the anticipated price decline that comes with the large sell offer.

Island Fills

Island fills are quick and relatively inexpensive. Island trades usually cost $1 more than SOES orders. If the Island system has a better BID or ASK price available than the trader's submitted BID or ASK price, then Island will fill the order at that better price. The trader should not use "fill or kill" orders through Island, as it is likely that the orders will not get filled. The downside of Island orders is partial fills.

The Island execution system displays the trader's Island order on the Level II screen only if the trader has entered the highest BID or the lowest ASK. If several traders enter multiple Island orders at the same BID or ASK price, the Island system will simply add up the share sizes to reflect all submitted orders. Island orders must be greater than 100 shares to be displayed on the Level II screen.

Using the Island execution system is crucial for a successful day-trading business. However, it is also important to swing traders because Island provides traders with additional liquidity and the opportunity to obtain a better price.

Island Order Mechanics

When using trading software, such as CyberTrader or TradeCast, placing or entering an Island order is a relatively simple task. The trader simply types the stock symbol in the appropriate window and presses Enter. Then he or she presses the Island function keys for the buy-and-sell orders. When the Island order box appears on the screen, the trader can adjust the price with the arrow keys next to the price box or use the keyboard arrow keys. The trader can adjust the price up to bid the high BID or down to offer the low ASK. When the trade order is ready, the trader sends the order by clicking OK or by pressing Enter to send the order.

Summary

Today, the ECNs have assumed the role of preferred order-execution vehicle.

Today, after a trader takes a long position in a stock, and after the stock appreciates in value, the trader commonly tries to get out of that position through an ECN, such as Island. For instance, if the BID and ASK prices are 50 and $50^1/_8$, the trader has four options for selling the stock:

1. An SOES, ARCA, or SelectNet sell-limit order at the inside BID price of 50

2. An offer to sell the stock at the current inside ASK price through the ECN at $50^1/_8$

3. An offer to sell the stock at a lower price than the current inside ASK price through the ECN at $50^1/_{16}$

4. Take out the best Island BID, even if the price is lower than the inside BID, such as $49^{15}/_{16}$

The probability is high that the trader might use either the second or third option to get a better selling price for the stock. Most likely, the trader would try to cut the spread, sell the stock at $50\frac{1}{16}$, and earn an additional $\frac{1}{16}$. The additional $\frac{1}{16}$ on a 1,000-share increment block translates into a $62.50 gain.

8

Trading Capital and Trading Account

"The easiest way for your children to learn about money is for you not to have any."

—Katherine Whitehorn

Most day-trading firms generally require a minimum capital amount of $20,000, although several established day-trading firms require at least $50,000 to open an account. Swing traders or position traders require even more capital. All of these accounts are margin accounts. A *margin account* signifies that the broker is extending credit to customers, who are purchasing stocks on "margin"—in essence, it's a credit issued to finance securities transactions.

Under the Federal Reserve Board regulation (Regulation T, or Reg. T), which governs the amount of credit that can be extended, the maximum amount that brokers can advance is 50 percent. That means that a trader's deposit of $20,000 will result in an additional $20,000 credit (advance or loan) from the broker, and the trader will thus have $40,000 worth of purchasing power. Every brokerage firm has a margin department that provides oversight and supervision of the extension of credit. Internet brokers cater to investors who might purchase stocks in increments of 100 shares, and so their minimum account is dramatically less than the minimum of $20,000 needed to open a trading account and to trade stocks in increments of 1,000 shares.

With a minimum margin account of $20,000, purchasing power is restricted to $40,000. With $40,000 purchasing power, traders have two options: (1) Trade stocks listed for $40 or less in increments of 1,000 shares, or (2) trade the expensive stocks for $80 or more in increments substantially fewer than 500 shares. Both strategies have drawbacks.

Consider the first option. If the trader were trading a less expensive stock (that is, $40 or less per share) in increments of 1,000 shares (with $40,000 purchasing power), then the stock would need to increase in value by $2.50 for the trader to earn $2,500 in one week and thus earn $125,000 annually, which was the example used of the hypothetical swing trader in table 1.1. But stocks do not usually go up $2.50 (or 6.25 percent) that easily, especially within a single week. Something must drive that stock up 6.25 percent, such as positive news (for example, higher than estimated earnings or a merger), and that does not happen very often. Traders need to be patient and spend time monitoring the inexpensive stocks for a 6.25 percent price movement that earns $2,500 per week.

Now consider the second option. If a trader with $40,000 purchasing power were trading expensive stock (e.g., $80) in increments of 500 shares, then the stock would need to increase in value by $5.00 (or 6.25 percent) for the trader to earn $2,500. Again, this does not happen very often. Either way, the trader is handicapped.

The best long-term scenario is to be well capitalized (third option), such as, for example, having a trading account with $80,000 in equity (or $160,000 in purchasing power) to trade expensive and volatile stocks in increments of 2,000 shares and profit from the small ($1.25 or higher) price movement. In other words, a swing trader could earn $2,500 in one week with the small absolute and relative price change of $1.25 (or 1.5 percent) if the trader has a large trading account. This small absolute and relative stock-price change happens frequently within one week. But in order for that to occur, one needs an adequate amount of trading capital. Table 8.1 illustrates this point well.

Please do not misunderstand this point. New traders should not begin by trading expensive, volatile stocks in increments of 2,000 shares. That is the domain of an experienced trader. Even if adequate trading capital is available, the novice trader should start slowly by

Table 8.1 *Capitalization Levels and Swing Trading*

	Capitali- zation	Trading Equity	Purchasing Power	Price	Shares	Profit Goal per Week	Absolute Change	Relative Change
Option 1	Under-capitalized	$20,000	$40,000	$40	1,000	$2,500	$2.50	6.25%
Option 2	Under-capitalized	$20,000	$40,000	$80	500	$2,500	$5.00	6.25%
Option 3	Well capitalized	$80,000	$160,000	$80	2,000	$2,500	$1.25	1.56%

trading inexpensive stocks that do not move very fast. As a rule of thumb, traders should start trading with 100 or 200 shares and increase the size of the shares traded as they gain experience, increasing the trading block by 100 or 200 shares every week until they reach the block of 2,000 shares. It is unrealistic to expect that new traders will start making money immediately. Trading is a skill that takes time to develop.

Trading Account

The issue of margin accounts, discussed at the start of this chapter, needs to be further addressed. Most traders open margin accounts for their transactions in order to secure two-to-one leverage and purchase more stocks. Traders are using the margin accounts in order to obtain a higher rate of return on their initial investment. Since the late 1990s, the total margin debt has been increasing steadily—on average, 22 percent since 1992. In 1999, on the NYSE alone, the margin debt increased to $228 billion, which is a 62 percent jump from $140 billion at the end of 1998. Most analysts attribute this increase to the recent influx of Internet traders and day traders.

Critics of Internet trading and day trading have argued that many traders are not knowledgeable enough about the inner workings of the margin-account system or that high leverage also works as a liability.

This chapter is designed to address this concern, as well as providing a brief explanation of margin-account terminology. It is important that traders be able to read and understand the margin-account statements that they will receive from the clearing firms.

The Federal Reserve Board, under Regulation T of the SEC Act of 1934, regulates the extension of credit by NASD broker/dealers to traders and investors. Regulation T is expressed as a percentage of the total purchase price. The current Reg. T margin requirement is 50 percent for long and short securities transactions. Only "marginable" securities, which include all stocks on the NYSE and NASDAQ national market system, may be purchased on margin.

When the NASD broker or dealer extends a credit to a trader who wants to trade securities, the trading transactions must be executed in a margin account. Opening a margin account requires that the trader sign a margin agreement, which specifies the following:

- The trader agrees to pledge the securities in the margin account to the NASD broker/dealer as collateral for the loan.

- The trader grants permission to the NASD broker/dealer to repledge (that is, "rehypothecate") the same securities at the bank as collateral for the loan. The bank will issue a loan to the NASD broker/dealer at a specific interest rate, which in the industry is called the "brokers' call rate."

- The trader also grants permission to the NASD broker/dealer to lend the same security to other brokers' customers who sold short that particular security.

In essence, the entire hypothecation process has four distinct steps:

1. The trader pledges (or hypothecates) securities to the NASD broker/dealer.

2. The NASD broker/dealer rehypothecates the same securities that were used as collateral for the loan to the bank.

3. The bank lends to the NASD broker/dealer money at the broker's call rate.

4. The NASD broker/dealer lends to the trader at the margin interest rate, which is a bit higher than the broker's call rate.

The Long Margin Account

Figure 8.1 shows what happens when a trader purchases a security on margin. The long market value will fluctuate with the price of the security throughout the day. Suppose the trader has purchased 1,000 shares of a stock that is priced at that time at $40. The long market value is $40,000. The debit balance represents the amount that was borrowed by the trader and is owed to the NASD broker/dealer firm. In this example, given the 50 percent Reg. T requirement, the maximum amount that the trader can borrow is $20,000. That is the base amount that will be used to calculate the interest charges paid by the customer. The annual interest rate charged is usually in the range of 8 to 9 percent. The equity is the customer's deposited money. The customer will deposit $20,000 in the margin account. That initially is the customer's equity. The equity can also be calculated by subtracting the amount owed from the current market value of the stock position. Figure 8.1 illustrates this point.

If the security appreciates in value, the long market value will increase. Because the borrowed amount remains the same (the debit balance remains at $20,000), the trader's equity increases as well. When the equity in the account exceeds the Reg. T requirement of 50 percent, the trader has excess equity in the account. Figure 8.2 elaborates further on this point.

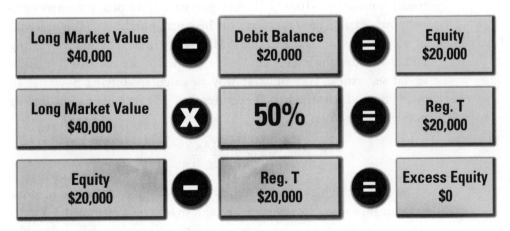

Figure 8.1 *Long Margin Account*

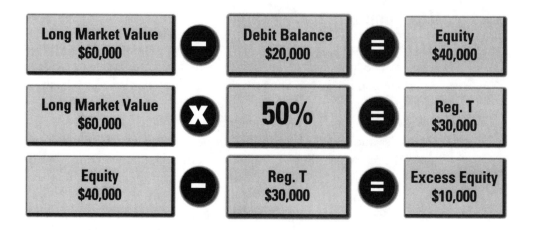

Long Market Value $60,000	−	Debit Balance $20,000	=	Equity $40,000
Long Market Value $60,000	×	50%	=	Reg. T $30,000
Equity $40,000	−	Reg. T $30,000	=	Excess Equity $10,000

Figure 8.2   *Long Margin Account with Stock Price Appreciation*

Suppose that the stock price increases from $40 to $60. The long market value is now $60,000. Because the borrowed amount (or the debit balance) remains the same (at $20,000), the trader's equity increases to $40,000. The Reg. T 50 percent requirement on the $60,000 current market value is $30,000. That means that the trader has excess equity of $10,000 in the account.

The excess equity in a margin account is referred to in the industry as the "special memorandum account" (SMA). In this example, the trader can use the $10,000 SMA to purchase additional securities or to withdraw cash. The trader can, for instance, purchase $20,000 worth of securities with the $10,000 SMA—the trader has higher buying power because the excess equity (or SMA) can be used to buy additional securities. The quickest way to calculate buying power is to divide the SMA by the Reg. T requirement. The formula for the buying power is as follows:

$$\text{Buying Power} = \frac{\text{SMA}}{\text{Reg. T}}$$

Whereas the higher price results in excess equity, a decline in stock value might cause a long margin account to become "restricted." A margin account becomes a restricted account if the equity falls below the Reg. T 50 percent requirement. Figure 8.3 illustrates this point.

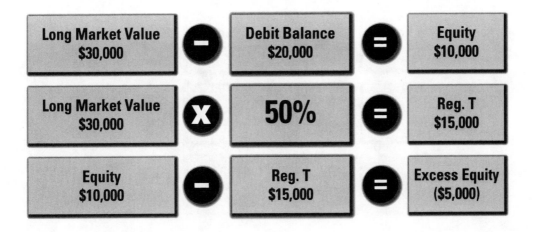

Figure 8.3   *Restricted Margin Account*

Now let us suppose that the stock price has decreased from the initial price of $40 to $30. The long market value is now $30,000. Because the initial borrowed amount (or the debit balance) remained the same (at $20,000), the trader's equity decreased to $10,000. The Reg. T 50 percent requirement on the $30,000 current market value is $15,000. That means that the trader now has negative excess equity in the account of negative $5,000. The account is now restricted.

If a margin account is restricted, the trader can continue making additional purchases by meeting the Reg. T requirement on a particular additional purchase. It is not mandatory to deposit additional money to bring the entire account up to the Reg. T requirement. With a restricted margin account, 100 percent of any sale proceeds will be used to reduce the debit balance in the margin account. If the price drops dramatically, the trader will receive a margin maintenance call from the broker. The NASD requires that all customers maintain at least 25 percent equity of the current market value in their accounts. Figure 8.4 illustrates this point.

Now let us suppose that the stock price decreased dramatically from the initial price of $40 to $25. The long market value is now $25,000. Because the initial borrowed amount (or the debit balance) remains the same (at $20,000), the trader's equity has decreased to $5,000. The minimum maintenance requirement for NASDAQ and

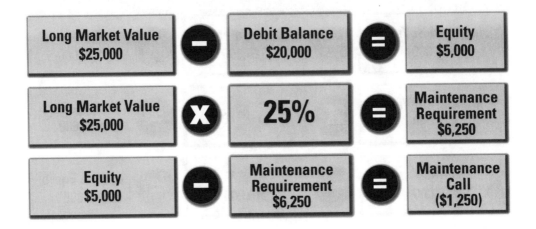

Figure 8.4 *Margin Maintenance Requirement*

NYSE stocks is 25 percent; that 25 percent requirement on a $25,000 current market value is $6,250. That means that the trader's equity in the account is below the minimum maintenance requirement. The trader will receive a maintenance call from the broker, and the broker will require that the trader deposit $1,250 into the account.

The Short Margin Account

When a trader sells short a security in his or her margin account, the trader has established a "credit balance" in the margin account. Figure 8.5 shows what happens when the trader sells short a security on margin. First, the short-sale value will fluctuate with the price of the security. Suppose that the trader has sold short 1,000 shares of a stock that is priced at $40. The short-sale value is $40,000.

The credit balance represents the total short-sale proceeds and the Reg. T margin requirement on the short-sale value. In this example, given the 50 percent Reg. T requirement, the maximum amount that the trader can borrow for the short sale is $20,000. That is also the base amount that will be used to calculate the interest charges paid by the customer. The equity is the customer's deposited money—the customer had to deposit $20,000 in the short margin account. Equity can be calculated by subtracting the credit balance from the current short market value of the security that was initially sold.

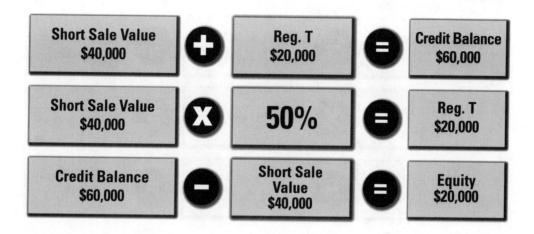

Figure 8.5   *Short Margin Account*

The trader anticipates that the security will decrease in value, so the trader has opened a short position. If the price were to decrease, the short market value would decrease. Because the borrowed amount remains the same (i.e., the credit balance remained the same at $60,000), the trader's equity has increased. When the equity in the account exceeds the Reg. T requirement of 50 percent, the trader has excess equity in the short margin account. Figure 8.6 elaborates on this point.

For example, suppose that the stock price decreased from $40 to $30. The short market value is now $30,000. Because the borrowed amount (or the credit balance) remained the same at $60,000, the trader's equity increased from $20,000 to $30,000. The Reg. T 50 percent requirement on the $30,000 current short market value is $15,000. That means that the trader has excess equity of $15,000 in the account. In this example, the trader can use the $15,000 excess equity to purchase or short sell additional securities or to withdraw cash. The trader can purchase $30,000 worth of securities with the $15,000 excess equity.

The minimum maintenance requirement for NASDAQ and NYSE stocks in a short margin account and selling for more than $5 per share is 30 percent. The brokerage firm will regard the long and short margin accounts as one margin account. The combined equity for the long and short margin accounts is displayed in figure 8.7.

It is important that traders can read and interpret their daily margin activity statements. If a trader has an overnight position, he or she must

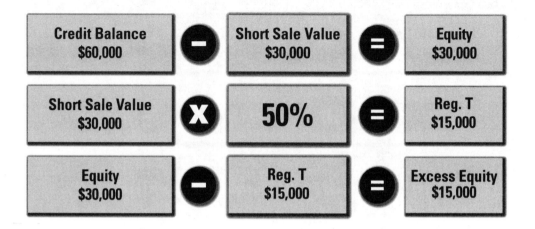

Figure 8.6 *Short Margin Account with Stock Price Depreciation*

be able to understand how the total equity and interest charges are being calculated. After all, the total equity, buying power, and margin interest charged to the trader is the trader's money.

Intraday Margin Call

If traders always close their open positions before the close of the market, they do not need to worry about the margin interest charges or maintenance calls. (Some clearing firms, however, do charge margin interest for intraday trading, even if all positions are closed at the market close. The trader should definitely inquire about margin interest charges when opening an account.)

However, many traders should worry about intraday *margin calls*. It is very common for a trader to exceed his or her buying power some

Figure 8.7 *Combined Equity for Long and Short Margin Accounts*

time during the trading day. Traders transact so many trades during the day that it is quite possible to lose track of one's daily purchasing power. Even if the trading software has an "account manager" feature, which dynamically updates the trader's buying power, it is still easy to exceed one's buying power. Also, it must be acknowledged that traders commonly try to maximize their leverage. In doing so, they sometimes "push the envelope" too far and exceed their purchasing power.

For example, if the trader deposited $20,000 into his or her account, then, given the Reg. T requirement, the trader's buying power is $40,000. Suppose that the trader makes only one trade that day. The trader purchased and sold 1,000 shares of a stock that was priced at the point of purchase and sale at $44. After the closing sale, the trader's position is "flat"—he did not make any money on this trade. Nevertheless, the trader purchased $44,000 worth of the stock, even though he or she had only $40,000 in buying power.

The trader will then receive an intraday margin call for $2,000 from the clearing firm. The clearing firm will ask that the day trader deposit into the account an additional $2,000 within the next five trading days. This is because the trader purchased stocks with credit the trader did not have. The trader needs to bring the account purchasing power to $44,000. Even though the trader is "flat" (i.e., with no long positions) in the stock, the trader would still need to come up with the extra cash. Given the 50 percent Reg. T credit requirement, a $2,000 deposit would increase the purchasing power by $4,000, and the total purchasing power would thus be $44,000.

A $2,000 intraday margin call should not be difficult to meet. But suppose that the intraday margin call is for $20,000 rather than $2,000. If the trader has net-worth liquidity, then the $20,000 intraday margin call would not be an issue. However, if the trader does not have $20,000—and the intraday margin call is not met in the next five trading days—the clearing firm will most likely close that account. If the trader wishes to continue trading with the same broker, he or she would have to open another account under a different tax-identification number. This is not an easy matter. The trader would need to establish a legal entity (that is, a general partnership or limited liability company) and ask the IRS for a new tax-identification number. This takes time and effort.

9

Risk Management

"The safest way to double your money is to fold it over once and put it in your pocket."

—*Kin Hubbard*

Stock trading is not simply a "get rich click" scheme. Many have tried it, and quite a few have failed. But for those who have succeeded, trading is a financially and intellectually rewarding way to make an independent living. In the financial world, there is a long-held axiom that there is a positive correlation between risk and reward: the higher the risk, the higher the return. This is clearly true for the business of electronic stock trading.

There is only anecdotal evidence (mostly media reports) about the profitability of stock trading, and no formal study has been completed that authoritatively documents traders' income. I suspect that the variance of income distribution among traders is huge. Several magazine and newspaper articles have mentioned or named traders who are making six- or seven-figure incomes. And it's true that a few experienced traders who have access to large amounts of trading capital can earn high levels of income. Most traders will not reach these levels. However, if properly trained, with enough experience and enough trading risk capital, a trader can earn sufficient income to take this from a part-time endeavor to a full-time profession.

Most importantly, the general public needs to understand that stock trading, such as day trading or swing trading, is trading and not investing. Although trading can be a very successful long-term business, it is a very difficult business to get started. For instance, James Lee, president of the Electronic Traders Association (www.electronic-traders.com), claims that after a six-month learning curve, a third of the traders lose money, another third tread water, and the rest do well. The following are some caveats from the Electronic Traders Association regarding the risks of day trading. I believe that these concepts apply to swing trading as well:

- Trading requires skill, discipline, and hard work.
- Successful traders regard trading as a career and not a hobby.
- Securities markets are extremely efficient and competitive. New traders will compete against professional traders who have been trading for many years.
- Financial markets are very dynamic, and competitive conditions change. What may have been a successful trading strategy in the past might not work in the future.
- Only risk capital should be used for trading. Do not trade money that you cannot afford to lose.
- Most people who begin trading sustain losses or produce only marginal profits during the first three to six months of trading. Do not trade unless you are willing to sustain losses while gaining trading experience.
- Individuals who are not highly disciplined should avoid trading.
- The new trader should limit both the numbers of trades he or she makes as well as the size of the trades to limit losses during the learning process.

In addition to the normal *market risk* (that is, price volatility), the trader is exposed to occasional trading-execution risks. The entire electronic trading platform (the computer network) could fail due to factors beyond anyone's control.

New traders should be prepared to lose money in the first few months. The amount of the initial loss will vary, depending on the trader's risk-management skills. It is possible to lose $15,000 or more before becoming a proficient trader. A new trader needs to learn quickly the tools of the profession and manage the risk, or the trader will fail. Beginning traders should be prepared to sustain a loss, and they should not trade money they cannot afford to lose. They should not mortgage their homes to obtain trading capital or obtain credit card cash advances, nor should they trade their retirement funds.

The new trader should also have realistic expectations. To expect to become a proficient trader overnight and to start making money immediately is simply unreasonable. Even if one reads all of the books written on this topic and practices paper trading (using a simulation or demonstration trading software) before going live, there are no guarantees that a trader will succeed. Most successful traders have learned this profession the hard way: making mistakes and learning from them.

In my opinion, the mission for new traders is not to make money initially. In fact, the novice trader should expect to lose money at the beginning. The learning curve for the trading profession is steep and expensive. The trader's objective should be long-term survival. If a novice trader stays in the business six months, there is a distinct probability that the trader is making a profit. If the novice trader stays in this business after one year from the opening of the trading account, then there is a strong probability that the trader is making a six-figure annual income.

Risk-Management Tools

The following are some of the risk-management tools that traders use. All traders can easily apply them. These measures are my suggestions and will only limit risk exposure, not eliminate all trading risk. Furthermore, the measures will not guarantee that a trader will be successful.

The first crucial risk-management technique is to get out of losing trades quickly. The trader must react to the market activity. If the price is going up, the trader should go with the trend and open a long position. Suppose that the trader made a wrong trade and the long position is losing money. The price of the stock has reversed its trend, and now it is going down. The trader has received a clear signal to get out. Every downtick is a signal to the trader to get out. The trader then has two distinct choices: (1) Get out of the stock immediately and minimize the loss, or (2) hold on to the long position and hope for a price reversal.

Hope is a four-letter word. It is not good to hope when trading stocks. A trader who hopes that the open stock position will turn around has abdicated control over his or her trading money. Yes, it is possible that the position could reverse and the stock price might bounce back. Yes, it is even possible that the losing position could turn into a profitable trade. Yes, everything is possible. But how likely is that to occur? What is the probability that the stock will bounce back? If a trader cannot logically ascertain the probability of a price reversal occurring, the trader should close that position immediately. It is the only prudent thing to do.

The trader should not wait for a small loss to turn into a bigger loss. The trader needs to get out of that losing long position as quickly as possible. How many price signals (price downticks) does it take to convince that trader that he or she was wrong on that trade? Is it $1/4$ or $3/8$ or $1/2$? If he or she is trading in 1,000-share blocks, does the trader need to lose $250 or $375 or $500 before admitting that he or she was wrong?

The trader must set loss limits. The level of loss limits will vary among traders. The loss limit depends on the trader's trading style, the amount of trading capital available, the level of trading experience, and individual willingness to assume risk. Nevertheless, the traders must retain those self-imposed loss limits throughout the trading. The loss limit could be as tight as $3/8$ or $1/2$ a point, or even higher, such as 1 point. However, 1 point should be the maximum loss that a trader would lose on a single trade. The only exception should be the very expensive and volatile stocks, such as CMGI and other similar Internet stocks, which routinely fluctuate by several dollars per day.

One circumstance that traders can control in their trading endeavors is the amount of their losses. They can decide whether to enter a stock position or not. But once they take a position, traders cannot influence the profits or the upside aspects of the trading business. If prices are going up, the trader will continue holding that position. And the amount of profit will depend on the strength of that price-increase momentum. However, traders can always decide when to close an open position, and thus they have control over the exit strategy. Traders must continuously manage their losses. That is the key to trading success: On one side have the control to minimize the downside, and on the other side try to maximize the upside.

If you are a trader who is taking multiple stock positions, another loss-limit device is to set an absolute-dollar amount that you're willing to lose for one day of trading. The absolute-dollar loss amount incurred in a single day will vary among traders; it will depend on the trader's available trading capital and individual willingness to assume risk. The amount could be $800 or $1,000 or higher. Everyone will have bad trading days. The key is to contain how expensive the bad trading days are. They do not have to be expensive. If your trading is not going in the right direction, close your open positions and go outside to re-energize. The next day might be different. There is always the next day.

Traders should also set an absolute-dollar amount that they are willing to lose for one week of trading. That amount should be higher than the loss limit imposed for a day's losses. However, it should not be proportionately higher (for example, five times higher). It would be unrealistic to expect that a trader will lose the maximum amount allowable every single day. If that is the case, the trader does not know what he or she is doing. Go back to the drawing board; reassess your entire trading strategy. Ultimately, appraise whether trading is a suitable business for you.

My advice is not to "marry" the losers (which also applies to other aspects of anyone's life). In other words, do not get attached to losing stock trades. Listen to the market. See the obvious. Do not fight the ticker tape. Get out of that position! New traders must learn to admit they were wrong—and that is the key: admitting that your trade was wrong and moving on to the next trade.

The second risk-management technique is to get out of a position if the stock price is moving quickly against the trader's position. The trader should use the ECN's outside market prices or a market order. Too often, the trader admits that a trade was bad and decides to get out, but instead of getting out in the fastest possible way, the trader tries to extract a better price. Instead of selling the stock at the best BID price available, the trader attempts to submit an offer to sell at inside the BID and ASK spread through an ECN such as Island.

Because the stock price is dropping fast, the probability is low that the offer to sell at the ASK will get filled. If that is the case, the trader will attempt to submit a new offer to sell at the new ASK, which is lower than the previous ASK price. Again, the probability is low that the offer to sell will get filled, because the stock price is falling quickly. By the time the trader drops the idea of offering the stock for sale through the ECNs and executes the SOES market order at the inside BID price, the BID price is already down. The trader has lost money trying to pick up a $1/16$ higher selling price. The inside BID price is now lower than it was a few moments ago.

If the stock is tanking and the trader has direct access to the ECNs, then his or her best bet is to take out the best ECN BID, even if that BID price is outside the market. In other words, suppose Cisco Systems' stock is tanking fast, and instead of hoping to sell the shares at the inside BID at 65, the trader picks up the best Island BID, which might be $64^7/_8$. At least the trader will get out. If a fast market exists, the trader's sell order probably will not get filled at 65. If the trader is trading NAS-DAQ stocks, another option is to use NASDAQ SelectNet and preference a market maker who might be a few price notches (or color levels on the Level II screen) below the inside BID price. In other words, instead of hoping to sell at the inside BID at 65, the trader quickly preferences a specific market maker who might be buying at that time at $64^7/_8$.

Conversely, if the stock is taking off fast and the trader desperately wants to get in (or get out of the short position), then the best bet is to "take out" the best available ECN ASK price, even if that ASK price is higher (higher than the inside ASK) and thus outside the market. In other words, Dell stock is moving up fast, and instead of hoping to buy the shares at the inside ASK at 50, the trader picks up the best Island ASK, which might be $50^1/_8$ or $50^1/_4$. At least the trader will get in. Again, the probability is such that in the fast upward-moving market the trader's buy order will not get filled at 50, because the trader will be one of many trying to get in. With the OTC stocks, another option is to use NASDAQ SelectNet and preference a market maker who might be a few price notches (or color levels on the Level II screen) above the inside ASK price. In other words, instead of hoping to buy the shares at the inside ASK at 50, the trader quickly preferences a specific market maker who might be selling at that time at $50^1/_8$ or $50^1/_4$.

Another way traders take on undue amounts of risk is by *pyramiding* a stock position. The trader would start with a 1,000- or 2,000-share long or short position. Then the trader would quickly add a few thousand more shares to the existing open position. (Obviously, this is subject to availability of trading funds.) If the stock price quickly reverses its course, the trader would have trouble selling several thousand shares quickly (such as 5,000 shares). The trader would eventually sell all the shares, and it is likely that the obtained average selling price for 5,000 shares would be lower than the price obtained if the trader had only a block of 1,000 or 2,000 shares.

Good traders have a motto: Do not fight the tape. The stock market is always right. If the trader has a long position and the price of the stock is declining with each tick, then the market is giving the trader a clear signal: Get out of that trade. Disciplined traders will get that message quickly and will get out.

Furthermore, the disciplined trader waits patiently for a clear trading signal to buy or sell a stock. Without that signal, the trader will not enter the trade (otherwise, trading becomes gambling). A good trader will enter a position only when he or she receives a trading signal to buy or sell short. Finally, a good trader would not let a winning trade turn into a losing trade. A trader would take the profits, regardless of how small they might be. Traders do not go broke taking profits.

Losing Money

Why is it that so many people have lost money while trading stocks when, on the surface, trading is deceptively simple? The core of trading is to exploit the *small* price swings (or the short-term price volatility) and earn incremental profits by trading in *large* increments of 1,000 or 2,000 shares. However, trading in large increments, such as the 1,000- or 2,000-share blocks, is a double-edged sword. On the upside, if the trader is trading in large increments, such as the 1,000-share blocks, a trader can quickly earn a $250 profit if the price goes in the favorable direction by a single $1/4$ of a point. Conversely, the trader can quickly lose $250 if the price goes in the opposite direction by $1/4$ of a point.

In addition, all accounts are margin accounts. So there is an issue of 2-to-1 financial *leverage*. That means a $20,000 initial deposit creates $40,000 in buying power. However, leverage works in both directions. Positive leverage happens when a trader quickly picks up $1/4$ point (or a $250 gain) on a relatively small initial investment (the initial account deposit). Conversely, negative leverage occurs when a trader quickly loses $1/4$ point and incurs a $250 loss. Because of the 2-to-1 leverage, it is possible to lose more money than one's initial account deposit.

The Losing Streak

Every trader will sooner or later face a losing streak. Sometimes that losing streak can be so pronounced and severe that it challenges the trader's confidence. The question is not whether the losing streak will happen, but what to do when it does happen. So what can be done? The following is my advice:

1. *Stop losing money.* (At first read, this advice seems comical, I realize.) If the losing streak is pronounced, stop trading for a few days. Take a break. Take time off to recharge your batteries. The market will be here when you come back. With a fresh re-energized mind, you might find the trading outcome to be different. The point is that you have stopped losing money. During the time off from trading, take a look at your losing trades. Print a price chart of the stock(s) that is/are responsible for the losing streak that day or week, and mark all of the buy-and-sell points. Examine the buying and selling decisions. Try to understand why those trades were bad. Learn from your mistakes.

2. *Go back to the basics.* Re-examine and re-evaluate your trading style. Keep a trading diary. Write down the reasons for entering trades. See whether those reasons passed the reality test. Write down the reasons for exiting trades. See whether the exit strategies are efficient. Look for your individual trading patterns. The worst thing to do is to blame something or someone else for the losses. Do not blame the losses on bad luck. Luck has nothing to do with recurring losses. Traders are responsible for their own losses.

3. *Reverse the losing streak once you come back, re-energized, to trade.* The objective is to score profitable trades, regardless of how small the profit is. In other words, place something on anything green on the board. If it is a $1/4$ gain, take it. Sell it for the small gain. The point is to rebuild confidence. Again, the objective is to stop bleeding, or stop losing, money. Any trading gain is a step in the right direction.

4. *Reduce the trading share size.* If you are commonly trading in increments of 1,000 shares, then drop the size to 500 shares. This would alleviate some of the pressure of losing a lot of money. If there is a loss, it will not be as dramatic. Again, the focus here is to stop losing money. With a few profitable days, your confidence will be regained. At that

time you can resume trading the normal lot size of 1,000 or 2,000 shares.

The Trading Plan

No traders plan to fail. They simply fail to plan. The novice trader should have a trading plan that clearly spells out what he or she will do under different trading circumstances. It is easier to visualize trading activities with a defined trading plan (or "trading map") in place. The trading plan should be very specific and state, for instance:

The following are my buy or sell signals: _____.

The following are my risk-management tools: _____.

And, I the trader, will follow my own trading rules.

To write an effective trading plan, you must be able to visualize the trading process. To visualize the trading process, you must know the trading business. And thus, the foremost requirements are trading knowledge and skill. Knowledge is power!

Anyone trading stocks should read as much as possible about stock trading in general. This book lists many stock-trading references. As a new trader, you will compete against experienced professionals, such as the NASDAQ market makers, NYSE specialists, and other traders. You must have knowledge of the NASDAQ and NYSE securities markets and their trading rules in order to survive. Acquiring those skills is time-consuming and often expensive. But it is necessary.

If your town has a day-trading firm, visit the office to see what educational programs it offers. Day-trading firms often have free seminars and classes. Sometimes firms charge a training fee. Ask if you can talk with others who have taken the training class. Find out who is presenting the course and if the training is well organized. Talk to the other traders. Ask them how they trade. Ask them if they are profitable. Pay close attention to the actions (executions) of the profitable traders. Please do not misconstrue this paragraph as an invitation to become a day trader. I am only saying that one can learn a lot about trading in the day-trading environment.

Trading-Plan Questions

Your trading plan should address the following questions:

1. *Why do I want to trade?* This is an important question. The new trader should understand his or her underlying motivation for trading. What is the attraction? Is it the lure of "quick and easy money" or the potential to make a lot of money? Is it the ability to be self-employed, or is there a passion and sincere interest in the stock market? Understanding one's own motivation is an important ingredient to success.

2. *What is my time frame for reaching profitability? In other words, when do I become profitable?* The trading plan should state that the novice trader should expect to lose up to a specific amount at the beginning, and that it may take six months to become profitable. When such losses come at the beginning, and they will, the novice trader will not panic. The losses are part of the plan. The novice trader can continue with the plan and move up the learning curve.

3. *What do I trade (i.e., what types of stocks and how many shares) in the first month, the second month, and so on?* The trading plan should call for the novice trader to trade "slow" stocks (i.e., the relatively inexpensive NASDAQ or NYSE stocks that do not move rapidly) in the beginning. If the trading plan requires the novice trader to trade slow stocks in increments of 200 shares for the first week (and then increase the trading amount each week by an additional 200 shares), the novice trader should follow that plan.

4. *What should my trading style and philosophy be at the beginning?* Do I start as a specialist trader (specializing in a few NASDAQ or NYSE stocks, for instance), or do I adopt a scalper's method (seeking price momentum anywhere on the NASDAQ or NYSE)? What style better suits my personality? How much risk am I willing to tolerate?

5. *How do I prepare for the next trading day?* The trading plan should state how you would prepare for each trading day. Will you start off by reading *Investor's Business Daily* before the markets open? Will you watch CNBC early every morning to ascertain the public's market sentiment?

6. *What do I do when a trade goes against me?* This answer should be the most prominent part of the trading plan. In other words, what is my

loss limit for one trade? Do I lose $^3/_8$ or $^1/_2$ or higher before getting out of the trade?

7. *What are my stock buying and selling signals?* This is the trading plan's most important question. The plan must be very specific about trading signals. The new trader must know exactly what signs or signals he or she is waiting to receive from the stock market. For example, is it:

- The crossover between the fast and slow exponential moving averages?

- The price approaching the support or resistance levels (upper or lower Bollinger bands)?

8. *What are my exit points or exit signals?* In addition to being specific and stating when the trader will enter the market (that is, take a long or short position), the plan should also state when to exit the position. In other words, what is the trading signal to close a profitable position? Is it:

- The crossover between the fast and slow exponential moving averages?

- The price approaching the intraday support or resistance levels (upper or lower Bollinger bands)?

- A specific price increase (for example, 2 points)?

Paper Trading

All active trading brokerages use sophisticated financial software packages that have a training module (demo or simulation mode) that will provide real-time data flow and somewhat realistic simulated trade executions. New traders can sit in front of the computer monitor during market hours, view real-time quotes and charts, and "paper trade." Paper trading means that buy-and-sell orders are not actually executed, but only processed and confirmed by the traders' computers. The computer will keep track of trading activities and update trading statistics. Any losses are only paper losses. Paper trading is an easy and comfortable way to become familiar with trading software and the NASDAQ and NYSE markets. New traders should practice paper trading for several weeks before beginning to trade live.

Before a new trader graduates from paper trading to live trading, he or she should consistently make a thousand dollars in paper-trading profits every day for several weeks. Consistency is crucial. The new trader should then discount the paper-trading profit by at least one-half. I suggest this because live trading is dramatically different from paper trading. All paper-trading market or *limit orders* (orders to buy or sell at a specified price or at a better price) are filled automatically at the requested limit price or posted market price. In reality, that does not happen very often. Traders will learn quickly that live market orders are not filled at the expected price, and often limit orders are not filled at all.

For example, if a trader is watching real-time quotes on the screen, and there is one market maker with the best posted selling price (ASK), and the trader submits a buy market order for a NASDAQ stock, that order goes into a computerized queue. If the trader is first in line, the order will be executed; however, it is rare that a trader is first in line. One of two things could then happen. The trader's order could be executed at the same price if the market maker elects at his or her discretion to refresh the same selling ASK price. However, if the price is moving up fast, then the market maker will not refresh the same ASK price but will instead back away and post a higher ASK price. The trader's market order would then get executed at a price higher than expected. If the market is moving up very fast, the trader might end up with a substantially higher price than anticipated.

Similarly, when a trader electronically submits a buy limit order for a NASDAQ stock, this order might never get executed at the specified price. If the price trend is up, the market maker will increase the ASK price. That would mean the limit order would never get executed at the lower price. In other words, the stock price may be moving too quickly and could simply pass over the limit order before it is executed.

Finally, paper trading does not involve real money, and thus there is no real risk. Without the genuine risk of losing money, the trader's emotions are not involved. Fear, greed, panic, and hope do not interfere with trading judgments, so it is easier to be a disciplined trader. However, there is no substitute for real-life experience. Paper trading is at best only a predictor of future trading results.

The most expensive and reckless trading education is to start live trading without undertaking an adequate and sufficiently long training program. New traders will make mistakes. Some mistakes will simply be the wrong trades (for example, buying a stock when the market is going down). Some of those mistakes will be execution errors (pressing the wrong key, for instance). If you are in a day-trading shop, the trading software used by day-trading firms is sophisticated and complex, and it takes time to master it. The same would be true if you traded online using an active trading brokerage. However, new traders are better off making mistakes in a demo mode than in a live mode. Mistakes committed in a demo mode are much cheaper!

Starting to Trade

It is easy to lose money trading. Experienced traders commonly trade the most volatile and expensive high-tech NASDAQ stocks in increments of 1,000 or 2,000 shares. A 1-point loss trading 1,000 shares of a volatile Internet stock translates into a $1,000 loss. Before one is ready to trade the expensive and volatile Internet stocks in large increments, one has to go up the learning curve, and that learning curve is steep. However, the learning curve does not have to be expensive. It is my opinion that most people lose money trading because they start live trading before they are ready. Furthermore, when they do start trading, they immediately start trading volatile and expensive stocks in large increments. This is a recipe for losing a lot of money quickly.

The key to survival is to start slow, and gradually move up. A child has to learn to crawl before that child can walk. Only after the child has mastered walking can that child attempt to run. I remember how long it took my son to learn to hold a pencil properly. For years, he would hold a pencil as a stick. It took three years or so for my son to master a skill that seems by adult standards to be notably elementary. The same analogy can be applied to trading. What seems simple and obvious for experienced traders is obscure and complex for the novice trader. It takes time to pick up those trading skills.

Starting slowly is the paramount consideration. It is the best way to ensure that the novice trader does not "blow up" in the first few months of trading. It is very easy to blow up at the beginning. The novice trader will make many errors and mistakes. Those mistakes could be inputting order errors (pressing the wrong key) or misreading the market direction (making the wrong trade). The novice trader could not possibly eliminate all the errors and mistakes; mistakes are part of the learning process. Thus, the first objective is to minimize the number of mistakes. The second objective is to minimize the cost of those mistakes and to learn from them. Those mistakes do not need to be expensive.

The Slow Trading Approach

The "slow" trading approach is the conservative approach. This slow approach provides an opportunity to learn the business gradually without losing a lot of money. The first step is to select "slow" stocks. These are stocks that do not move very fast. They tend to be relatively stable and do not move very much or very fast in either price direction, so the reaction time is much longer. Thus the novice trader has plenty of time to react to the price movement and to get the order executed.

Slow stocks tend to be inexpensive stocks with a price less than $20 and more than $5 per share (there is no point in trading "penny stocks"). Because they are relatively inexpensive, the stocks do not move a lot in absolute-dollar terms. The slow stocks might be as volatile as the fast stocks in relative (that is, percentage change) terms. The 5 percent price change for the $20 stock is only 1 point. However, a 5 percent price change for a $100 stock is 5 points. For the novice trader, it is easier to follow stocks that move 1 point in a day than those that move 5 points in a day.

A price movement of $3/_8$ is a real price trend for the slow stocks because it represents a relatively high percentage change in price. That is a real price movement, so it is possible to observe the market forces of supply and demand that generated the price movement. For example, one could observe a buildup of market makers on the inside BID side and a reduction in the number of market makers on the inside ASK.

The $3/_8$ price movement is, however, a relatively small percentage change in price for fast, expensive stocks, such as Internet stocks. It is a simple noise in the market and is thus not real price movement. It is more difficult to detect the market forces of supply and demand that generated the price movement for fast stocks. The fast stocks could continuously gyrate up and down without any discernible price pattern. And thus it is easy to get "jiggled out" when trading the fast stocks.

The slow approach, which consists of trading the slow-moving and inexpensive stocks, would assure that market gyrations would not easily jiggle the novice trader out. The novice trader would be able to ascertain or visualize real price movement. At that time, the novice trader would go with the trend.

In addition, trading the slow stocks would also limit the initial number of trading transactions. Fewer transactions would limit the number of possible mistakes, which would further enhance the trader's probability of long-term survival. Fewer transactions, of course, would also limit the potential to make money. However, the objective of the novice trader is not to make money initially, but to learn to trade. Again, the focus is on long-term trading. In order to make money trading in the long run, the novice trader must survive in the short run.

The most important step that the novice trader can undertake initially is to start trading in increments of 200 shares. Trading the slow stocks will minimize the total number of losing trades. Trading in increments of 200 shares will minimize the cost of those mistakes. For instance, the novice trader cannot avoid making losing trades. It is realistic to expect that a novice trader will have winning trades two-thirds of the time and losing trades one-third of the time. With time and experience, the percentage of winning trades should increase. The objective is to minimize the cost of the losing trades. If the novice trader starts trading in increments of 1,000 shares, then one small trading mistake with a price change of $3/_8$ would translate into a $375 loss. It is easy to make a $3/_8$ mistake, and $375 mistakes can quickly add up.

It is preferable to start trading in increments of 200 shares. Then one small trading mistake with a price change of $3/_8$ would translate into only a $75 loss (and not a $375 loss), which the novice trader can afford to absorb. In other words, the novice swing trader can afford to make many $75 mistakes (that is, $3/_8$ price-change mistakes), learn something from each mistake, and almost still be as well off as with a single $1/_{16}$ small mistake when trading in 1,000-share blocks. It is my firm advice to all new traders to start trading in increments of 200 shares.

It is also true that it is very difficult to make money trading if one trades in increments of 200 shares. It is my recommendation that a novice trader start with 200 shares and increase the trading allotment by

200 shares each week. With each passing day, the novice trader should learn something from past mistakes. Trading in allotments of 200 shares would ensure that mistakes are not expensive, and the trading capital would be preserved. In the second week, the novice trader could increase the allotment from 200 shares to 400 shares. That would be my recipe for minimizing the overall cost of learning the trading business.

The Fast Trading Approach

The "fast" trading approach should be the domain of experienced traders. The fast trading approach results in aggressive trading. The focus of attention is on "fast" stocks: those stocks whose prices move extremely fast. These stocks tend to be the expensive (greater than $50 per share) Internet and high-technology stocks. These stocks move notably fast in either price direction.

Most importantly, fast stocks have a great deal of absolute-price volatility, and it is the absolute-dollar price change that counts. A 5 percent price change for a $150 stock is 7.5 points. The fast trader must be attentive throughout the day in order to follow a stock that moves 7.5 points in a day. A $1/2$ point or even 1 point is a relatively small percentage change in price for stocks priced at $150. It is a noise in the market and not a real price trend. The $150 stock would constantly gyrate up and down by $1/2$ or 1 point without any discernible price pattern. It is very easy to get jiggled out when placing a stop order for these fast stocks.

The fast stock trader usually trades in increments of 1,000 or 2,000 shares. Trading in increments of 1,000 shares exposes the trader to substantial loss due to bad trades. But high risk is associated with high returns. Trading in increments of 1,000 or 2,000 shares is the best way to make a lot of money. If the round-trip trading-transaction cost is approximately $32, and if the trader is trading in increments of 1,000 shares, then the stock price needs to go up or down only $1/32$ per 1,000 shares to break even on that trade. Again, a price movement of approximately $1/32$ is immaterial and common. It happens all the time. However, a $1/32$ price movement can go in the wrong direction as well. Trading in an allotment of 1,000 shares would guarantee that trading mistakes would be expensive.

Summary

The risk of loss in trading is substantial; at best the trader can only manage or control the risk. It can never be eliminated completely. Anyone considering stock trading should evaluate his or her suitability in light of his or her financial resources and individual circumstances. Many individuals have opened trading accounts with electronic day-trading firms or through Internet brokers without fully understanding the skills needed or the risks involved. The learning curve is steep, but it does not need to be expensive. It takes time to acquire trading skills, so start slowly. Start trading slow stocks in relatively small increments and then, with time and experience, gradually move up.

When to Trade

"You can observe a lot by watching."

—*Yogi Berra*

ONE CHART IS WORTH A THOUSAND WORDS. WE CAN GAIN A GOOD DEAL OF insight about the stock market by watching a price chart. In addition, the technical-analysis tools clarify and present a wealth of financial data in a format that can be easily reviewed and interpreted by swing traders. Thus the technical-analysis tools are important in reducing a great deal of the market "noise" that is always present in the dynamic financial markets. The purpose of this section is to focus on the basic technical-analysis tools and concepts that are often used by professional traders to determine when to enter or exit a position. Timing is everything in this business.

10

Introduction to Technical Analysis

*"Not everything that counts can be counted,
and not everything that can be counted counts."*

—*Albert Einstein*

Technical stock analysis sounds a lot more intimidating than it really is. It began in the 1900s, when Charles Dow, of DowJones publishing fame, became the first "technician" to plot and publish stock price trends in a consistent format. Today, *technical analysis* means different things to different people. On one end of the technical-analysis spectrum, there are chartists who continuously search for an emerging visual pattern of price fluctuations. At the other extreme are computerized stock market technicians who continuously crunch huge volumes of price and trading data to produce mathematical technical-analysis indicators. We'll discuss both schools of thought in a moment. But first, let's explore the reasoning behind some of the harshest criticism of technical analysis.

Perhaps the strongest criticisms are voiced by the man known as the "father" of the fundamental stock analysis, Benjamin Graham, who wrote the following in his 1949 book *The Intelligent Investor*: "In our own stock-market experience and observation, extending over 50 years, we have not known a single person who has consistently or lastingly made money by thus 'following the market' (i.e., technical analysis). We do not hesitate to declare that this approach is as fallacious as it is popular."

Another and more balanced criticism of technical analysis was delivered by author Burton Malkiel, who questioned in his 1973 book *A Random Walk Down Wall Street* whether technicians can predict price momentum over several time periods, such as minutes, days, or weeks. "Stocks are likened to fullbacks who, once having gained some momentum, can be expected to carry on for a long gain. It turns out that this is simply not the case." Malkiel noted that sometimes one gets positive rising prices for several days in a row, but that sometimes when you flip a coin you also get a long string of "heads" in a row. This is what economists mean when they say that stock prices behave much like a random walk.

In addition, Malkiel argued that technical analysis does not automatically translate into better or superior results. According to Malkiel, when the buy-and-hold strategy is compared with the technical strategies, the technical schemes often do make profits for their users, but so does a buy-and-hold strategy. Only if technical schemes or systems produce better returns than the average market returns can the technical analysis be judged effective. Malkiel said that, to date, none has consistently passed the test.

It is my belief that technical stock analysis, in and of itself, is not the Holy Grail of stock trading. A technical stock analyst cannot forecast with certainty what a stock price will be in the future. Nobody can do that. Even if the recognized price pattern has any foundation in historical price data, there is no guarantee that history will repeat itself. However, although I believe that technical analysis does not guarantee success in stock trading, it can improve the probability of making more profitable trades. In other words, technical analysis helps traders time the entry and exit points better and thus minimize the risk and maximize the return of stock trading.

Charting vs. Mathematical Technical Analysis

The first broad area of technical analysis we'll discuss is charting. There is an old saying that holds "There are no rich chartists on Wall Street." There is a good amount of truth to this old adage. I personally do not believe that there is an exact science behind any of these descriptive charting patterns. Interpretation of the charting pattern is always subjective. Nevertheless, I can see some benefit in attempting to visualize the price support and resistance levels by plotting and superimposing charting patterns over the price data. Plotting of price patterns is essentially a harmless activity, and it can only help to visualize the pattern.

In essence, charting is an art. Before computers and the Internet provided traders with real-time charts, adherents armed themselves with pencils, paper, and price data. A chartist might superimpose a pattern on the given paper price chart and visualize a pattern on the graph that would become a trading signal. Most often the chartist would draw a linear pattern on a given price chart and assign it a technical-sounding name. Charting patterns have an impressive array of esoteric names: triangles, head and shoulders, double bottoms or tops, saucers, flags, and other patterns. This book covers only the most basic and common chartist price patterns.

Mathematical Approach

The advent of computerized technical-analysis tools has provided more valuable insights about stock prices than charting patterns could provide. Computers can crunch huge volumes of price data quickly and efficiently and display instantaneously the price patterns that are not immediately self-evident. In other words, the computer can help probe the price data much deeper and much more precisely than the human eye can. In addition, technical-analysis software programs are increasingly the standard fare of any trading software package.

Using the computer to process huge volumes of price data mathematically is only half of the equation; understanding the output is the other half. Understanding and correctly interpreting the results of the mathematical technical analysis is much more critical than being able to use technical-analysis software packages.

Using the computer as a trading tool does not inherently give you a trading advantage. Author John Murphy eloquently wrote the following in his 1986 book *Technical Analysis of the Financial Markets:* "The amount of impressive technical data at one's fingertips sometimes fosters a false sense of security and competence. Traders mistakenly assume that they are automatically better simply because they have access to so much computer power."

All software stock-trading packages contain a library of technical-analysis indicators. This book focuses on the technical-analysis indicators that use the current closing price as the basic unit of analysis. The current price and the last closing price are the most important stock market variable because they depict the balance of power between the buyers and sellers at that point in time and at the end of the game. In addition, there are other technical-analysis indicators that utilize information on the stock's opening prices, the highest or lowest stock price in the selected time period, and trading volume.

Because the objective of the swing trader is to exploit the present short-term price volatility, it is irrelevant to chart and analyze the longer term historical prices. Do you really need to know such historical prices as the 60-day moving average for this time last year? This might be an issue only if you believe that the particular stock might have a strong seasonal trading pattern.

Instead, a day trader, for instance, would wish to chart and analyze intraday prices based on one-minute intervals. For their part, swing traders plan to hold stock positions for several days (or in some cases, a few weeks), and thus would chart and analyze the stock prices on a daily or one-hour interval basis. In either case, the objective of the swing trader and the day trader is to exploit the short-term price volatility. Nevertheless, it is always useful to look at the long-term price trend, as it provides information on the long-term historical price support and resistance, such as the 52-week price support and resistance levels.

As a rule, I believe in keeping things as simple as possible, especially when it comes to technical analysis. There is so much financial data coming across the computer screen that it is easy to get bogged down in sophisticated and esoteric technical information. And thus I have narrowed the technical-analysis discussion to the basic price-trend indicators and oscillators. For additional information, I recommend Steven Achelis' book *Technical Analysis from A to Z*, which is the most complete reference guide on technical analysis.

Technical Analysis Formats

A picture is worth a thousand words. And a quick look at a price chart loaded with technical-analysis data would immediately reveal the current status of the stock. Constructing technical-analysis charts is not a difficult endeavor. Technical-analysis software packages are relatively user friendly. Most of them are Microsoft Windows–based products with pull-down options menus. All you have to do is click with your mouse on the technical-analysis indicator option and the computer program will do all of the number crunching. Interpreting the results of the technical-analysis study is entirely a different matter. It is much more difficult to understand the meaning of all these lines, bars, or histograms on the price chart. It takes time to become proficient in reading, interpreting, and understanding technical analysis tools.

A short-term trader can pack many technical-analysis tools into a single price chart. A trader can decide to overlay simultaneously the stock-price information on the chart with several technical-analysis indicators. And each technical-analysis indicator can be subsequently marked and color-coded for easy viewing and reference. Finally, the selected format determines only how the price data is displayed on the screen. The data format is not in itself the technical stock analysis.

Time Frame

All stock-trading software packages contain a technical-analysis library, which includes many of the most commonly used technical indicators. These technical-analysis indicators can be modified to suit any trading preferences by changing the format of the input values. For instance, a trader with an extremely short time frame would most likely elect to use the option of analyzing one-minute-interval price data. A swing investor, however, with a longer time frame would likely use the hourly price data.

As a trader, selecting the time frame you use to view price data is an important decision. A graph of a stock at the same point in time can look dramatically different between the short- and long-term frames. Figures 10.1 and 10.2 illustrate this point for 3Com Corp. stock. Both figures also demonstrate tremendous price volatility at both the short- and long-term levels.

A day trader who has selected the one-minute price data could observe on the screen a short-term trend that indicates that the stock is increasing in value in the last few minutes. In the meantime, a swing

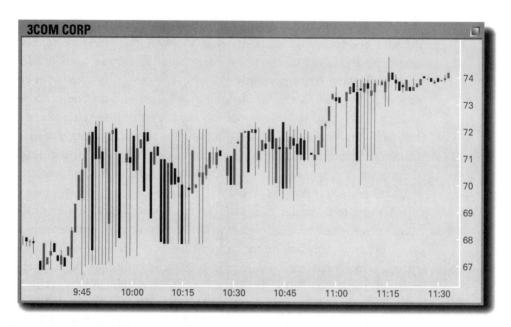

Figure 10.1   *Different Time Frames for the Same Stock at the Point in Time: One-Minute Data Compression for 3Com Corp.*

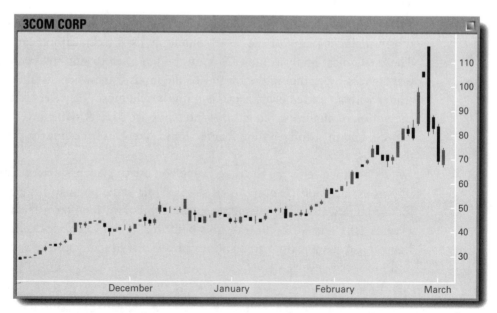

Figure 10.2   *Different Time Frames for the Same Stock at the Point in Time: Daily Data Compression for 3Com Corp.*

investor who has selected the daily price data could observe on the screen a decrease in the last few days.

Given different time frames and trading objectives, it is possible that both the day trader and the swing investor are correct. A day trader could decide to open a long position on that stock for a few minutes or hours and have a profitable short-term trade. Meanwhile, a swing investor could decide to open a short position on that stock for a few days or a week and have a profitable longer-term trade as well. It is always a good idea to look at the same stock in different time frames. Sometimes, day traders are too close to the "trees" to see the "forest." It is always a good idea to pull back, open another chart on the same stock but with a longer time frame, and see the "forest."

Tick-by-Tick Price

Many popular charting programs allow you to plot stock prices in real time, as each trade takes place. This is called tick-by-tick data. It is awfully difficult to perform any kind of formal technical analysis based on the tick-by-tick prices. My advice is to use tick-by-tick charts only to visually follow the stock executions after the trade position has been taken. The graphical presentation of the tick-by-tick price chart is shown in figure 10.3.

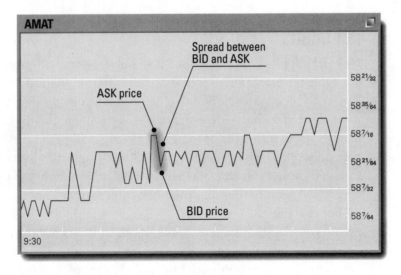

Figure 10.3 *Tick-by-Tick Price Chart*

The tick-by-tick price chart displays a zigzag-pattern line chart. The current ASK price, which represents the market buying price, is at the top of the zigzag pattern. The current BID price, which represents the market selling price at that point in time, is at the bottom of the zigzag pattern. In other words, the buying price is always higher than the selling price at any point in time. The spread is the difference or distance between the top and bottom. Usually the spread is relatively constant (i.e., $\frac{1}{16}$ or $\frac{1}{8}$, depending on the trading volume), so the distance is almost always the same. Sometimes, the spread narrows, and the gap between the top and bottom becomes smaller. Sometimes, the spread expands, and the gap between the top and bottom becomes larger.

As previously mentioned, a trader must decide what interval he or she will use to monitor price data: one-minute intervals or one-hour price intervals. Following that, you have to decide on what component of price data you'll use within that time frame: the open BID, close BID, open ASK, close ASK, high BID, low BID, high ASK, or low ASK. My strong preference is to select the close ASK price for the input-format price. The close ASK price represents the last market buying price in that particular time interval. In other words, if you are entering a long stock position for the first time, then the close ASK price is the most important price.

Bar Charts

Now let's look at another—perhaps simpler—way to represent price data: the bar chart. The tick-by-tick price chart in figure 10.3 contains a large amount of information that can be conveniently summarized into a bar chart. Bar charts are expressed as vertical lines, with left and right handles representing the opening and closing ASK prices for the selected period. Suppose that the entire figure 10.3 graph represents price data collected during just one minute of trading. Note how the next figure, figure 10.4, summarizes all of the tick-by-tick price data into one vertical bar-chart line.

As you can see, that one simple bar-chart line is packed with a lot of data. In our example, one minute of trading is summarized in a single bar chart. The same approach can easily be extended to one day's worth of price data. In other words, a daily bar chart would summarize data

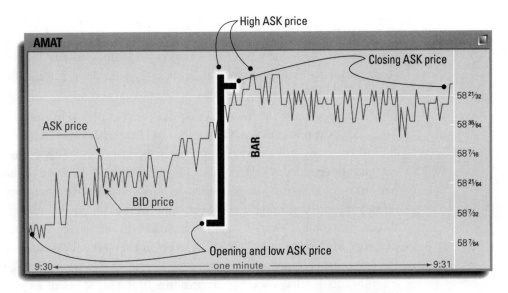

Figure 10.4 *Summarizing Tick-by-Tick Data into a One-Minute Bar Chart*

for the entire day of trading. For instance, a bar chart would show the following:

1. Opening ASK, which is represented by the left handle on the bar, is the buying price of the first trade in this time period. The opening ASK price at the start of the day's trading is especially important because it reveals the opening market sentiment. Looking again at the chart, note that the left handle represents the opening consensus price after all stock buyers had the opportunity to digest the market information overnight.

2. Closing ASK, which is represented by the right handle on the bar, is the buying price of the last trade in that time period. Again, the closing ASK has a great deal of importance when the bar chart represents the daily price data. In other words, the right handle represents the closing consensus price after all stock buyers and sellers had an opportunity to digest all of the market information during the entire trading day. The technical analysts pay close attention to the relationship between the daily open and close ASK prices. For instance, bullish traders would like to observe the closing ASK exceed the opening ASK.

3. High ASK represents the highest ASK price for that period of trading. High ASK is represented at the top of the vertical bar chart, and it represents the highest price that buyers are willing to pay for the security during this time interval. If we are using daily price data, then high ASK represents the peak price for that day.

4. Low ASK represents the lowest ASK price for that period of trading. Low ASK is represented at the bottom of the vertical bar chart. In case of the daily price data, it represents the lowest price that buyers paid for the security during this day-long interval. The size of the bar chart, or distance between the top and bottom of the bar, represents the trading range during this time frame. Often the vertical distance of the bar chart is small, which indicates a narrow trading range or little price volatility. Conversely, if the vertical distance of the bar chart is large, then this would indicate a wide trading range or substantial price volatility during this time period, such as one day.

Line Charts

The stock-price data can also be expressed visually as a line chart. However, the line charts are not used frequently. Line charts basically connect the same type of price information over time. For example, the trader can select to plot as a line chart format all the close ASK prices on a one-minute interval basis. In essence, opening BID, closing BID, open ASK, and high and low BID and ASK data would be ignored. This would provide one clean and continuous price line.

The advantage of this format is its simplicity. It is easy to ascertain a price trend by monitoring the slope of the line chart. The disadvantage of this format is that other price data, such as the opening BID, closing BID, open ASK, and high and low BID and ASK data, are simply disregarded. The trader may elect to track different price-data points, such as the close BID price. My strong preference is to select the close ASK as the preferred input price for a line chart.

Bar and line charts are the two most common formats of technical analysis. The only technical-analysis format that is missing in this chapter is the candlestick chart. Candlestick charting is an increasingly popular method of displaying price data, and thus chapter 11 is devoted exclusively to this particular charting format.

11

Candlestick Charting Format

"A man with a watch knows what time it is.
A man with two watches is never sure."

—*Segal's Law*

Candlestick charting originated in Japan in the 1600s as a method of analyzing the price movement of rice contracts, and thus it has certain mystical Oriental qualities. Some pattern names still have Japanese names, such as *doji* or *harami*, whereas other patterns have exotic, mystical-sounding translated names, such as *dark clouds, morning star,* or *evening star.* Many technical analysts like to use candlesticks because of that mystique.

I personally like to use candlesticks because they are very descriptive and easy on the eye. Candlestick charting displays the same information as a bar chart, but it brings an additional visual dimension. For instance, the colors of the several candlestick bodies illustrate bullish or bearish activity that is easy to visualize. Most importantly, candlesticks pack a lot of information about the relationship among the closing, opening, high, and low prices in the current and previous periods. For additional information on candlestick charting, I strongly recommend the 1991 Steve Nison book *Japanese Candlestick Charting Techniques.*

All popular charting software packages let you create candlestick charts by simply selecting the candlestick charting option. Instead of receiving price data displayed in the default format of bar charts, a trader can elect to modify the software chart-formatting options and choose the candlestick charts.

Similar to bar charts, candlestick charts also display the following price information:

1. Opening ASK
2. Closing ASK
3. High ASK
4. Low ASK

A single candlestick goes a step further than bar charts by revealing which market side prevailed during the time period. If the market bulls beat the market bears in that period of time and the closing price is higher than the opening price, the candlestick body takes on a green shade. The green candlestick body is much easier to view than the position of small left and right "handles" that represent the opening and closing prices on the bar chart. Conversely, if the bears beat the bulls within the time period, and the closing price is lower than the opening price, the candlestick body becomes red.

Candlestick charts are plotted as vertical rectangular boxes that connect opening and closing prices for a defined time period. Vertical lines called "wicks" extend from the rectangles to denote extreme high and low prices for the period.

In this chapter, for easier visual identification and because we have only two colors, the color black identifies when the closing price ends above the opening price (bullish candlestick). When the closing price for a time period finishes below the opening price, then the rectangular box is colored gray (bearish candlestick). When the opening and closing price remain the same, no rectangular boxes representing the candle body are depicted (see figure 11.1).

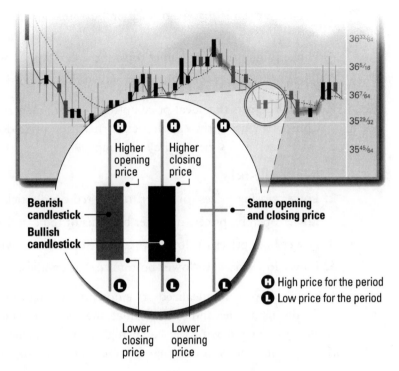

Figure 11.1 *Candlestick Chart*

Candlestick Patterns

Candlestick charts make it easier to view a price trend, whether the stock makes an uptrend, downtrend, or lateral movement in the time period.

Using the candlestick format, the price uptrend can be generalized and defined as a series of the following:

1. Green candlesticks

2. Higher closing prices (or higher tops of green candlestick bodies)

3. Higher opening prices (or higher bottoms of green candlestick bodies)

4. Higher high prices (or higher tops of the candlestick wicks)

5. Higher low prices (or higher bottoms of the candlestick wicks)

Figure 11.2 depicts this ideal price uptrend environment.

Conversely, using the candlestick format, the price downtrend can be summarized as a series of the following:

1. Red candlesticks

2. Lower closing prices (or lower tops of red candlestick bodies)

3. Lower opening prices (or lower bottoms of red candlestick bodies)

4. Lower high prices (or lower tops of the candlestick wicks)

5. Lower low prices (or lower bottoms of the candlestick wicks)

Figure 11.3 depicts an idealized price downtrend environment.

Finally, using the candlestick format, the neutral or sideways market can be summarized with the equal highs, lows, opening and closing prices, or continuous interchange between the same-size green and red

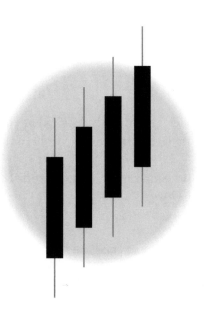

Figure 11.2 *Price Uptrend*

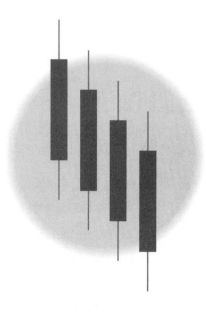

Figure 11.3 *Price Downtrend*

candlesticks (i.e., one green candlestick followed immediately in the next period by a red candlestick of the same size). Figure 11.4 depicts this ideal sideways market environment.

Obviously, the three trend patterns illustrated previously are over-simplifications of the real price trend. I wish that all trends would be that clear and obvious. The following illustrations present more realistic up, down, and neutral price trends as expressed in the candlestick format. Figure 11.5 depicts four more realistic bullish candlestick patterns. These patterns occur commonly enough to have names.

- *Hammer.* This pattern displays a significantly low price for the time interval (long lower shadow), which is substantially lower than the opening and closing price.

- *Piercing line.* This displays two candlestick lines. The first line is a bearish candlestick where the first interval closing price is lower than the opening price. The second line is a bullish candlestick where the second interval opening price is lower than the previous period closing price. However, the second interval closing price ended at a higher level than the second period opening price and the previous period closing price.

- *Bullish engulfing lines.* The first line is the small bearish candlestick. The second line is the strong bullish candlestick where the second interval opening price is lower than the previous period

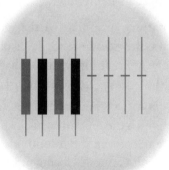

Figure 11.4 *Neutral Market*

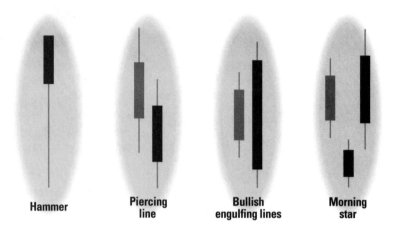

Figure 11.5 *Bullish Candlestick Patterns*

closing price, and the closing price is higher than the previous period opening price.

- *Morning star.* The first line is the bearish candlestick. The second line is the small bullish candlestick where the second interval opening and closing prices are lower than the previous period closing price. The third line is a large bullish candlestick where the third interval opening and closing prices are both higher than the second period closing price.

Figure 11.6 illustrates the four most common bearish candlestick patterns, which are summarized as the following:

- *Hanging man.* The pattern is similar to the hammer, except it occurs after a substantial price uptrend. It displays significantly low prices for both time intervals (long lower shadows) and a very small range between the opening and closing prices.

- *Dark cloud.* This displays two candlestick lines. The first line is a bullish candlestick in which the first interval closing price is higher than the opening price. However, the second line is a bearish candlestick in which the second interval closing price is lower than the previous period closing price and lower than half of the first candlestick body.

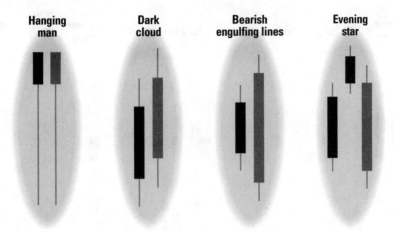

Figure 11.6 *Bearish Candlestick Patterns*

- *Bearish engulfing lines.* The first line is the small bullish candlestick. The second line is the strong bearish candlestick because the second interval opening price is higher than the previous period closing price, but the closing price is much lower than the previous period opening price. In essence the bearish candlestick engulfs the small bullish candlestick.

- *Evening star.* The first line is the bullish candlestick; the second line is a smaller bullish candlestick. The second interval opening and closing prices are higher than the previous period closing price. However, the third line is a large bearish candlestick where the third interval opening and closing prices are both lower than the second period closing price.

Figure 11.7 shows the five most common neutral candlestick patterns, which are summarized as the following:

- *Spinning tops.* The pattern displays a relatively small range between the opening and closing prices and high and low prices for both time intervals.

- *Doji.* This pattern displays a line where the interval closing price is the same as the opening price.

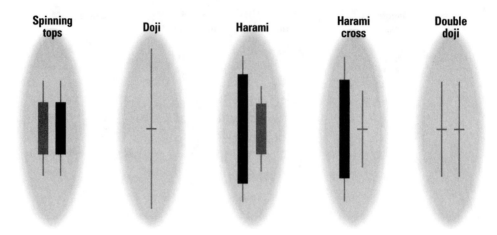

Figure 11.7 *Neutral Candlestick Patterns*

- *Harami.* The first line is the large bullish candlestick. However, the second line is the small bearish candlestick because the second interval opening price is lower than the previous period closing price. The closing price is higher than the previous period opening price. In essence, the bullish candlestick engulfs the small bearish candlestick, which indicates a decrease in the positive price momentum.

- *Harami cross.* The first line is the bullish candlestick. However, the second line is the doji candlestick. In other words, the second interval opening and closing prices are the same, which depicts a decrease in the momentum.

- *Double doji.* The last candlestick pattern consists of two doji lines, which implies continuous indecision. That stock price will eventually break out in either direction.

Now that we have the three possible price trends presented in the most common candlestick patterns, I present for illustration purposes a simplified buy signal using the hypothetical candlestick patterns. Swing or day traders can also use this simplified candlestick buy signal. The swing trader would examine the daily or hourly candlestick price chart, whereas the day trader would focus on 1-minute or 5-minute compressed price data in the candlestick format. The buy signal pattern consists of three distinct stages:

1. *An established downtrend pattern, which is depicted by a series of "red" candlesticks.* In other words, the candlesticks display lower closing prices, lower opening prices, lower high prices, and lower low prices for three to five periods.

2. *An established neutral trend, when prices are basically going sideways.* This neutral position is depicted by the continuous interchange between the same-size green and red candlesticks. This would also symbolize the end of the price downtrend. It would also indicate that the trader is buying at the price-support level.

3. *After observing the two established downtrend and neutral-trend candlestick patterns, the swing trader would patiently wait for the beginning of the price uptrend.* In other words, the emergence of the uptrend would constitute the buy signal. The first sign of the uptrend pattern can be any of the previously mentioned bullish candlestick patterns, such as the hammer, piercing line, bullish engulfing lines, or morning star. Figure 11.8 illustrates the hypothetical buy signal using the bullish engulfing line as the sign of the uptrend.

Conversely, the following list presents a simplified short-sell signal using the candlestick patterns. This simplified candlestick buy signal can be used both by swing or day traders. Again, the sell signal pattern consists of three distinct stages:

1. *An established uptrend pattern, which is depicted by a series of "green" or up-tick candlesticks.* In other words, the candlesticks display higher closing prices, higher opening prices, higher high prices, and higher low prices for three to five periods.

2. *An established neutral trend, when prices are basically going sideways.* This neutral position is depicted by the continuous interchange between the same-size green and red candlesticks. This

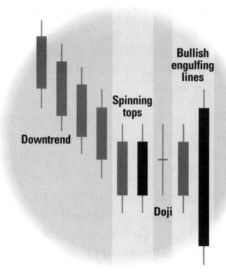

Figure 11.8   *Hypothetical Buy Signal*

would also symbolize the end of the price uptrend. It would also indicate that the trader is short selling at the price-resistance level.

3. *After observing the two established uptrend and neutral-trend candlestick patterns, the swing trader would patiently wait for the beginning of a price downtrend.* The emergence of the downtrend would constitute the short-sell signal. The first sign of the downtrend pattern can be any of the previously mentioned bearish candlestick patterns, such as the hanging man, dark cloud, bearish engulfing lines, or evening star. Figure 11.9 illustrates the hypothetical short-sell signal using the bearish engulfing line as the sign of the price downtrend.

Because candlestick charts are a very visual tool, I use them as the standard charting format throughout this book. Chapter 12 depicts the most basic and common charting patterns, again using the standard candlestick format.

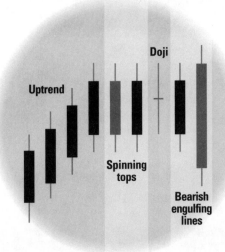

Figure 11.9 *Hypothetical Short-Sell Signal*

CHAPTER

12

Charting Patterns

"Things should be made as simple as possible, but not any simpler."

—Albert Einstein

There is an old Wall Street adage that holds that "Price charts do not lie." This is very true. The charts display historical prices, and thus there's no disagreement about past prices. Numbers do not lie. Chief executive officers (CEOs) or chief financial officers (CFOs), however, often do. A company's financial accountants, however, are capable of displaying financial data in a much more favorable light. In addition, CEOs and CFOs commonly put a favorable spin on company financial documents. For instance, declining company revenues are presented as the "new challenge," and mismanagement is labeled as the "strategic paradigm shift." All of this suggests that fundamental analysis does not provide an exact or precise representation of a company's financial position, because the data are not perfect and company management often obfuscates the true financial information.

However, there is another important Wall Street adage worth bearing in mind: "Price charts have no memory." This is an important qualifier to the maxim that price charts do not lie. And the reasoning here is simple: Just because prices exhibit the beginning of a certain visual pattern, there is no guarantee that the price will continue that pattern or that the pattern will automatically result in the desired price movement. In other words, there is no scientific law dictating why a stock price should go in a particular direction.

Rather, charting is a subjective art. There is no one best method for visually identifying the short-term trading range between price support and resistance levels or for establishing an emerging price trend. Different traders could look at the same price chart and identify different charting patterns and reach different conclusions about future prices. My objective in this chapter is only to present the charting patterns most frequently used by traders.

Horizontal Lines of Price Support and Resistance

Trader and psychiatrist Alexander Elder, who wrote the classic trading book *Trading for a Living*, stated that the support and resistance price patterns exist because people have memories. Traders and investors simply get used to buying and selling stocks within a certain price range. When a stock price drops to the lower edge of a trading range, it attracts buyers who perceive that the stock is undervalued. The lower price range becomes the price support. Conversely, when a stock jumps to the upper edge of a price-trading range, it attracts sellers who perceive this to be an opportunity to take some profits. Subsequently, the stock selling at the upper price range creates the price resistance.

One easy, quick, and subjective method of identifying support and resistance levels within a trading range is to draw two horizontal price lines around the price-congestion area. The price-congestion area defines the trading range for that period of time. The top horizontal line connecting the top edges of the price-congestion area is the price-resistance level. Conversely, the bottom horizontal line, which connects the bottom edges of the price-congestion area, becomes the price-support level.

The longer the price stays in the established trading range or the congestion area, the stronger are the price support and resistance levels. In addition, when the price range of the congestion area is relatively wide, then the support and resistance levels are much stronger. Furthermore, traders pay attention to the level of the trading volume in the price-congestion area. If the trading volume is substantial, then the price support and resistance levels are considered to be strong. Finally, the horizontal price support and resistance lines tend to have more meaning for the longer term than over the short run. For example, the horizontal price support and resistance lines based on the daily or hourly price data have a lot more relevance than the lines based on the 1-minute price data.

The chartist's objective is to look for the stock to break out of its congestion area. Sooner or later the stock price will penetrate the established horizontal lines of support and resistance. However, that alone does not mean the emergence of a new price trend. Experienced traders will argue that stocks spend more time in the trading range than in the newly established trend. In other words, most breakouts are false breakouts. The price quickly reverts to its common price-trading range. The experienced traders perceive this as an opportunity to take the opposite position.

For instance, if the price climbs above its resistance level, experienced traders will look for a slowdown in the momentum in order to short sell the stock. Conversely, if the price drops below the stock's support level, experienced traders will look for signs of increasing buying activity in order to take the long position. Professional traders use the term "fading the breakout" to describe such a trading strategy. Fading the breakout trading strategy means that swing traders should observe the breakout, wait for the slowdown in the price momentum, and then take the opposite position. When a breakout does turn out to be real, the price-support line often becomes the new resistance line in the case of a downward move. Conversely, when a stock breaks out from its resistance level, the resistance line becomes the support line.

Figure 12.1 depicts the support and resistance levels for CMGI, using daily price data. Again, the key is to draw horizontal lines through the upper and lower edges of the "congestion" price areas. The bottom horizontal line represents price support, and the top horizontal line represents price resistance. This type of stock chart is useful for short-term swing investors who might use the hourly price-data points.

Trend Lines

The trend line will point the direction of the trend. However, the key feature of a trend line is not the direction of the line, which is obvious, but the slope or the angle of the trend lines. The slope of the trend line reveals the relative market strength of the established price trend. The predominant bullish market sentiment at any point in time is displayed through the steeper positive slopes of the emerging trend line. If the

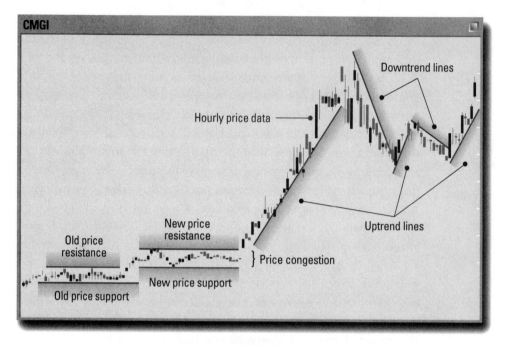

Figure 12.1   *Horizontal Price Support, Resistance, and Trend Lines*

trend-line slope is positive but the angle of the slope is relatively small, then the bullish market sentiment is rather weak. Conversely, the predominant bearish market sentiment is displayed by the steep negative trend-line slope.

As a general rule, the longer the trend line, the stronger the trend. A long trend line basically means that there are more price-point observations to support the trend. Another factor that indicates support of the emerging trend is the trading volume. A relatively high trading volume confirms and supports the uptrend. Conversely, a declining trading volume confirms the down price trend. Often the trend line breaks, which indicates that there is a change in the level of the market sentiment. For instance, the trend line could still be positive, but the slope of the emerging trend line has diminished. This would indicate that the bullish market sentiment for this particular stock is losing its momentum. It might even indicate the potential for price reversal.

As was the case with support and resistance lines, there is a quick and easy way to identify the general trend lines of an existing price trend. Simply draw the positively or negatively sloped price line around the price area at the bottom and the top. It's all right to leave out the extreme price fluctuations and focus instead on the area of price trend. It is important to emphasize here that stock prices remain within a trading range between their support and resistance levels more often than they exhibit a trending pattern. Several continuous upticks do not constitute a price uptrend. Similarly, a few continuous downticks do not constitute a downtrend either. The price could fluctuate between the established support and resistance levels for a prolonged period of time.

Gaps

Gap ups and downs are a common feature of today's stock market. The dictionary defines *gap* as an "unfilled space or a wide separation or break." For traders, a gap means an interruption in price continuity during a certain time interval. The reason we observe price gaps so frequently is because the stock market is highly dynamic. There will be periods of market disequilibrium when either the demand or supply shifts suddenly and dramatically, leaving a temporary imbalance between the number of available stock buyers and sellers.

When monitoring daily opening price data, a gap up indicates that no trades transpired within the certain price range between the highest price in the previous day and the lowest price in the next day. Likewise, a gap down indicates that no trades have occurred within the range between the lowest price in the previous day and the highest price in the next day. Figure 12.2 illustrates this point.

Gaps occurring at the market open have greater importance to short-term investors and traders than gaps that occur in the intraday (if using hourly or minute price data), simply because they are more frequent and more pronounced. Gaps at the opening indicate the overnight Wall Street reaction to news announced most likely after the market has closed. If the news is positive and significant, the gap up in price can be substantial when the market opens the following day. Such gaps indicate that buy orders have accumulated before the market opening. Market makers react to this increase in the stock's demand by adjusting the opening price above the closing price from the previous day.

If the positive news is announced during the market hours and if the traders are using the short-term interval, such as the 1-minute price data, then the price-gap up might be rather small. The continuous stock

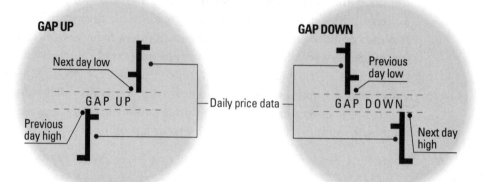

Figure 12.2   *Price Gaps*

trading will display a gradual price increase. In other words, it is unrealistic to expect that a preponderance of buy orders will reach the market makers in the same minute.

Conversely, if the news is negative and significant, the gap down in the daily price chart is even more pronounced than the gap up. Fear and panic selling generate a large preponderance of sell orders that reach the brokers before the market opening. Subsequently, the NASDAQ market makers and the NYSE specialists react to this increase in the stock's supply by adjusting the opening price much below the closing price from the previous day. If the negative news is announced during market hours, the news will show only as a large trading range for that day if you happen to be viewing it using daily charts.

In addition to price-gap ups and price-gap downs, there are differentiations between the two basic types of price gaps.

1. *Common gaps.* Common gaps are simply too common and they seldom translate into a continued trend. Here's an example: Suppose positive news brings disproportionately more buyers than sellers into the market in a short period of time. The result is an opening price gap. After the opening, the stock price can continue to go up quickly, but the momentum is short-lived. The trading volume is initially high but quickly returns to normal levels. Profit taking by short-term traders will reverse the price trend and the price will drop. The prices revert back to the old trading range, and there are no new higher closing prices in the vicinity.

2. *Breakout gaps.* Breakout gaps are an infrequent occurrence, as they result in a new and higher price trend. A continued high trading volume characterizes the breakout gaps. The positive price trend is confirmed by the sustained increase in the trading volume. Any technical-analysis trending indicator, such as the moving average, should likewise point to a new and higher price-momentum trend.

It's difficult to trade simply using daily price charts and price-gap information. How do you know whether a price gap is a breakout or a common gap? It is my opinion that most price gaps are common gaps, and subsequently the price reversal occurs quickly. Most traders will look for short-selling trading opportunities after first observing the price-gap up, followed by the slowdown in the price increase. In trading technical jargon, the traders would "fade" the common price gaps. In other words, the traders would go against the gap after observing the price slowdown. The lesson for swing traders is that a "fading the gaps" trading strategy means that swing traders should observe the gap up or gap down, wait for the slowdown in the price momentum, and then take the opposite position.

Head and Shoulders

The most common and most recognizable charting pattern is the "head and shoulders" pattern. The pattern will typically play itself out over a period of days or even weeks, and for that reason it is especially relevant to swing traders. The name comes from the pattern's slight resemblance to a human head and shoulders, and it represents a bearish signal. By contrast, an inverse head and shoulders pattern is a bullish sign. Both patterns indicate price reversal.

The head and shoulders pattern indicates that the market bulls are running out of steam, and thus the peak of the second shoulder is lower than the peak of the head, pointing to a bearish price reversal. Chartists will pay close attention to the trading-volume level that corresponds with the head and shoulders. The declining trading volume associated with the second shoulder is confirmation of future declining prices. The head and shoulders pattern also indicates the potential for a price breakdown or penetration of the established price-support line. Figure 12.3 depicts the pattern using daily price data on Amazon.com stock. Note

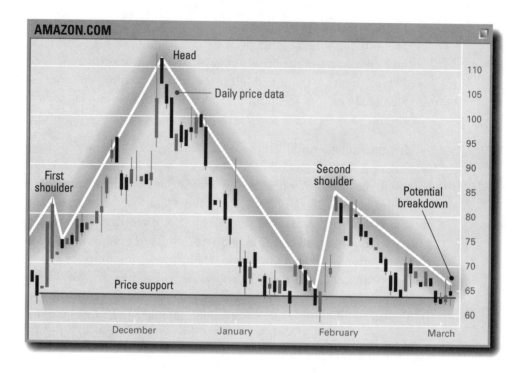

Figure 12.3 *Hypothetical Head and Shoulders Pattern*

that this pattern is usually more clearly indicated using a simple line chart, rather than the candlestick chart format.

Conversely, the inverse head and shoulders pattern points to the fact that market bears are running out of steam, and thus the bottom of the second shoulder has a higher price than the bottom of the head, pointing to a bullish price reversal. The increasing trading volume associated with the second shoulder of the inverse head and shoulders pattern provides confirmation of an expected future price increase. The inverse head and shoulders pattern also indicates the potential for a price breakout or penetration of the established price-resistance line. Figure 12.4 illustrates the inverse head and shoulders pattern using the daily Intel stock price data.

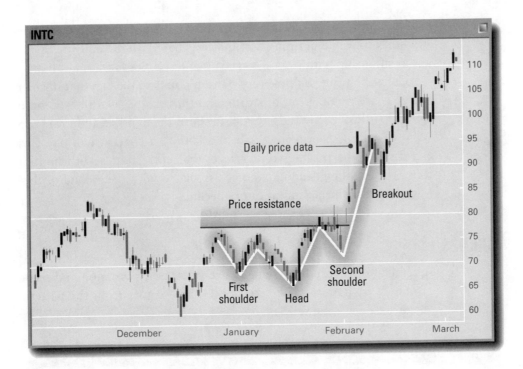

INTC

Daily price data

Price resistance

Breakout

First shoulder

Head

Second shoulder

December   January   February   March

Figure 12.4 *Inverse Head and Shoulders Pattern for INTC*

Multiple Tops and Bottoms

Another common and recognizable charting pattern is the "multiple tops and bottoms" pattern. In this case, the name comes from the pattern's resemblance to multiple tops and bottoms, such as the double or triple tops and bottoms. In other words, this pattern derives its name from its appearance—several higher and higher bottoms or lower and lower tops. The multiple tops represent a bearish signal, whereas the multiple bottom pattern is bullish. Again, both patterns indicate a price reversal. You will see that the multiple tops and bottoms pattern is a variation on the head and shoulders pattern.

Multiple bottoms indicate that the market bears are running out of steam, and thus the floor price of the second or third bottom will be higher than the first bottom price—a bullish sign. Increasing trading volume associated with the higher second or third top is confirmation of the expected future price increase. Figure 12.5 illustrates the I2 Technologies Inc. stock multiple bottom chart that was based on the daily price data and relationship with respect to the price-resistance level.

Conversely, the multiple tops pattern points to the fact that the market bulls are running out of steam, and thus the peak of the second or third top is lower than the first top. In short, the multiple and lower tops point to a bearish price reversal. In addition, a chartist will pay close attention to the trading-volume level that corresponds with multiple tops. The declining trading volume associated with the second or third lower top is confirmation of future declining prices.

Triangles

Ascending or descending triangles are yet another common and recognizable chart pattern. The "triangles" name comes from the pattern's

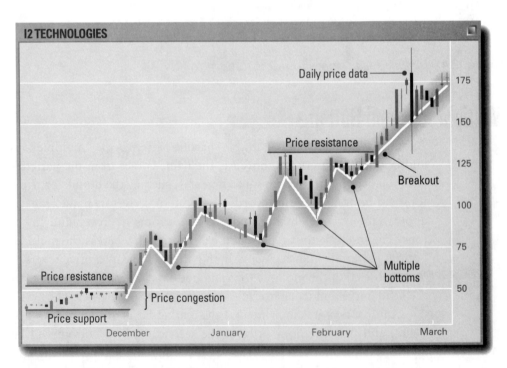

Figure 12.5 *Multiple Bottoms Pattern*

resemblance to ascending or descending triangles. Each triangle is defined by two converging lines. The upper line connects two or more period tops, whereas the lower line connects two or more bottoms. The descending triangle represents a bearish signal, whereas the ascending triangle is bullish. Both patterns indicate price congestion that might result in a price breakout or breakdown. The ascending or descending triangles are similar to the horizontal lines of support and resistance.

The descending triangle pattern occurs when the upper boundary of the triangle is declining. The descending triangle points out that the market bulls are running out of steam, and thus the next period's high price is continuously lower than the previous period's high price. In short, the continuously lower high prices point to a bearish price reversal.

Here again, chartists pay close attention to the trading-volume level that corresponds to a descending triangle. The declining trading volume associated with the continuously lower high prices is confirmation of possible future declining prices. Finally, the descending triangle pattern indicates the possibility of the price breakdown or penetration of the established price-support line. Figure 12.6 illustrates the hypothetical descending triangles pattern and relationship with respect to the price-support level for Lucent Technologies.

Conversely, the ascending triangle pattern occurs when the lower boundary of the triangle is rising. The ascending triangle pattern points out that the market bears are running out of steam and thus the next period's low price is continuously higher than the previous period's low price. In short, the continuously higher low prices in the period point to a bullish price reversal.

Increasing trading volume associated with continuously higher low prices is confirmation of possible higher prices. The ascending triangle pattern indicates the possibility of price breakouts or penetration of the established price-resistance line. Figure 12.7 illustrates the hypothetical ascending triangle pattern and relationship with respect to the price-resistance level for CMGI stock.

A symmetrical triangle is defined when both the upper (price resistance) boundary and the lower (price support) boundary are converging. In other words, prices are continuously making lower highs and higher lows, and thus the congestion area is being narrowed. Imagine adding a descending triangle on top of an ascending triangle and thus creating one

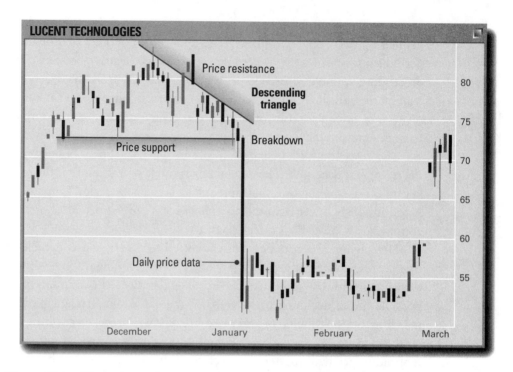

Figure 12.6   *Hypothetical Descending Triangles Pattern*

symmetrical triangle. Because the triangle is symmetrical, it is impossible to predict which market force (bulls or bears) will prevail out of the price congestion. That is, the symmetrical triangle can result in either a price breakout or a price breakdown. Figure 12.8 illustrates the hypothetical symmetrical triangle pattern and relationship with respect to the price-resistance level for LCOS stock.

Flags

The "flag" pattern is another consolidation or congestion pattern. The flag pattern name comes from the pattern's resemblance to an ascending or descending flag. Each flag is defined by two narrow parallel lines with an up or down slant. The upper flag line connects two or more period tops, whereas the lower flag line connects two or more bottoms. The

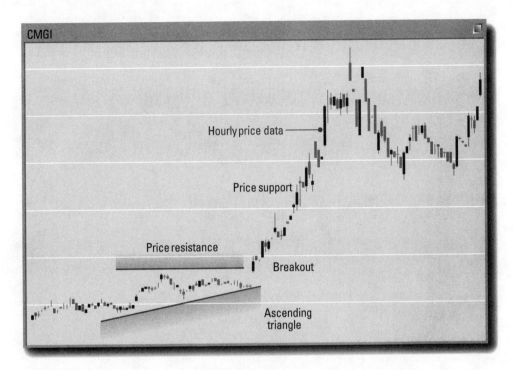

Figure 12.7 *Hypothetical Ascending Triangles Pattern for CMGI*

ascending flag represents a bearish signal, whereas the descending flag pattern is bullish. Both the upside and downside flag patterns indicate price congestion that might result in price breakdowns or breakouts. Subsequently, the ascending or descending flags are similar to the trend lines that also represent price support and resistance levels.

The downside flag pattern is defined when the upper and lower boundaries of the flag are declining. The downside flag pattern represents a period of price congestion, which is supposedly followed by the breakout (or price increase). In other words, the appearance of the downside flag pattern is a bullish charting indicator. Figure 12.9 illustrates the downside flag pattern using Microsoft daily price data and its relationship to price-support and price-resistance levels.

Conversely, the upside flag pattern is defined when the upper and lower boundaries of the flag are increasing. The upside flag pattern

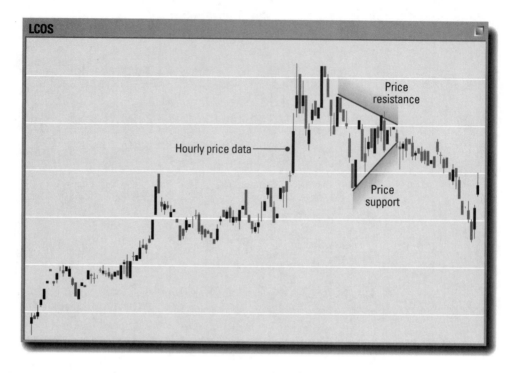

Figure 12.8 *Hypothetical Symmetrical Triangles Pattern for LCOS*

represents a period of price congestion, which is supposedly followed by the breakdown (or the price decrease). In other words, the appearance of the upside flag pattern is a bearish charting indicator.

In summary, I am not a big fan of charting price patterns because, in my opinion, charting price patterns are rather too subjective. Nevertheless, charted price patterns are always the starting point for anyone using technical analysis. There is, however, a better and more exact approach to technical analysis—the mathematical approach, which is presented next in the following three chapters.

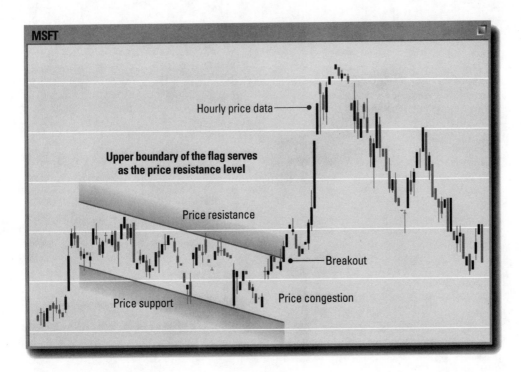

Figure 12.9 *Downside Flag Pattern for MSFT*

13

Moving Averages and MACD

"There are three kinds of lies:
lies, damned lies, and statistics."

—Benjamin Disraeli

For traders who use computerized technical analysis, the most common indicator—and often the starting point—is the moving average (MA) indicator. MA is the average price of a stock at a given point in time for a given number of periods. The technical analyst arbitrarily determines the number of periods when calculating an MA. As you'll see shortly, it can range from 3 to 120 periods. In addition, the MA periods can be defined to be any time interval, such as 1-minute, 15-minute, hourly, or daily data. If you are a day trader, then 1-minute price data is the most appropriate time interval. If you are a swing trader with a longer time horizon for analysis, then hourly price data is the most appropriate time interval. If you are an investor, then daily price data is the most appropriate time interval.

There are many reasons that make MA analysis the most frequently used technical-analysis tool. MA is a simple mathematical concept, so most people find it easy to understand. A primary benefit of MA is the fact that it eliminates some of the market noise. Traders use MA indicators to filter out tick-by-tick price gyrations and to provide a view of a price trend. In other words, the MA line will smooth out the sometimes-confusing actual price fluctuations. For that reason, it is a good tool to use to confirm a price trend. The MA line would emphasize the direction of a trend and confirm a trend reversal. However, the MA system does not work very well in a "choppy" market where there's no clear short-term trend. It does work well in a trending market where prices are clearly going up or down.

The MA's most notable drawback is the fact that it's a lagging indicator. There is a time lag between the actual price line and the MA line because the MA line is the average of the last several data observations, and thus it always trails behind the actual most current price input. This lag limitation will be explained in detail shortly.

Simple, Weighted, and Exponential Moving Averages

A moving average is the sum of a selected number of previous price values divided by the total number of those values. In other words, a 3-hour MA would be the sum of the prices of the previous 3 hours divided by 3. However, all 3-hour segments are not created equally. The last or the most recent hour is more important than the previous hour or the first hour. Thus the technical analysis differentiates between the simple moving average (SMA), the weighted moving average (WMA), and the exponential moving average (EMA).

The simple moving average is the most basic. With it, every hour has equal weight. Thus the last or the most recent hour has $1/3$ weight, the previous hour also has $1/3$ weight, and the first hour has $1/3$ weight. But this is too simplistic. Let us instead assign a weight to each hour interval, as all three hours do not have equal importance. Because the last or the most recent hour is the most important observation, let us assign 50 percent weight to that price value. The previous hour would have 30 percent weight, and the first hour would have 20 percent weight. All together, the three hours of price values would account for 100 percent of the SMA value. These assigned weights are purely arbitrary. Most technical analysts strictly use the exponential moving average. EMA uses a mathematical method that automatically provides the greater weight to most recent price actions.

Figure 13.1 is a graphical presentation of a hypothetical exponential function that is used to assign a relative weight to each time period used to calculate an EMA. If there are only three periods in the MA analysis, the relative weights are allocated by the exponential function as illustrated in figure 13.1. If there were nine periods in the MA analysis, the relative weights would be assigned automatically by the same exponential function. I plan to use EMA exclusively in this book.

Fast and Slow Exponential Moving Averages

Figure 13.2 presents two EMA lines. The first line is the fast EMA of three observations of the 1-hour intervals. This EMA is called the "fast EMA" because it will follow or "hug" the actual price movement very closely. There will be very little time lag between the 3-hour fast EMA and the actual price change. The fast EMA will smooth out to some degree the actual price fluctuations, so it would be easy to spot a trend in almost real-time terms. In essence, the fast EMA will eliminate some of the market "noise" or brief gyrations.

The second line in figure 13.2 is the slow EMA of nine observations of 1-hour intervals. A rule of thumb is that the period of the slow EMA should be three times greater than the period for the fast EMA. The trader could select any two periods of 1-hour data intervals that have the 3-to-1 ratio—3-hour and 9-hour or 5-hour and 15-hour observations. If the trader wants to reduce more of the market "noise" and obtain fewer trading signals, then the trader would select longer time periods for the fast and slow EMA—9-hour and 27-hour observations.

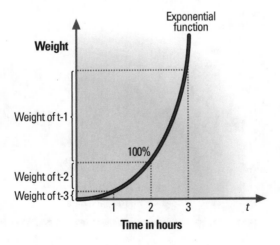

Figure 13.1 *Exponential Moving Averages*

This EMA is called the "slow EMA" because it does not follow the actual price movement very closely. There will be a substantial time lag between the 9-hour slow EMA and the actual price change. The reason for that is simple. The 9-hour slow EMA incorporates the stock price of 9 hours ago and thus has to lag the current price. That lag can be very visible when there is a sharp change or movement in prices. Figure 13.2 graphically points out the slow EMA lag. The slow EMA will greatly smooth out the actual price fluctuations. It would be easy to spot the longer price trend. In essence, the slow EMA will eliminate to a greater extent the market "noise" or price gyrations.

When fast and slow EMA lines are plotted together we get what's known as a crossover or trading signal. When the fast EMA (3-hr.) line is greater than or above the slow EMA (9-hr.) line, then stock prices are going up. This is a mathematical truism. The fast EMA (3-hr.) line must be greater than the slow EMA (9-hr.) line in order to pull the slower EMA line to a higher price value.

Conversely, when the fast EMA (3-hr.) line is smaller than or below the slow EMA (9-hr.) line, then stock prices are going down. Again, this is a mathematical truism. The fast EMA (3-hr.) line must be smaller than the slow EMA (9-hr.) line in order to pull the slower EMA line to a lower price value. Figure 13.2 illustrates this point.

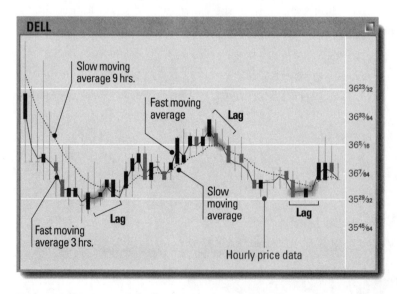

Figure 13.2 *Fast and Slow Exponential Moving Average Lines*

There are two trading signals or crossovers in figure 13.3. The first signal occurs when the fast EMA (3-hr.) line crosses over and goes above the slow EMA (9-hr.) line. It is a signal that stock prices are going up and thus a signal to open a long position on that stock. Note that prices were already moving up when the crossover occurred. Again, that illustrates the time lag. Subsequently, a trader following the EMA crossover signals will never pick the stock price at the bottom and at the peak. However, as the swing trader is plotting the EMA of the three periods of 1-hour-interval price observations in real time, that time lag is minor.

The second signal occurs when the fast EMA (3-hr.) line crosses and goes below the slow EMA (9-hr.) line. It is a signal that stock prices are already going down and thus a signal to sell. Note again that prices were already moving down when the crossover occurred, a consequence of the time lag.

After closing the long position, a trader would immediately enter into a second trade. He or she would sell the stock short. The short position would be closed when the fast EMA crosses over and above the slow EMA. That would constitute a signal to buy the stock and cover the short sale. At the same time, it would be a trading signal to open the long position as well.

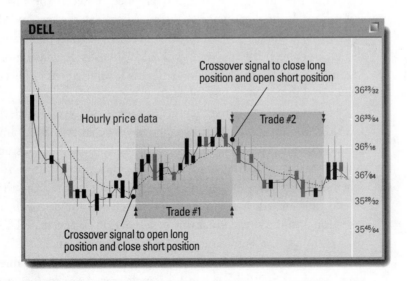

Figure 13.3 *Fast and Slow Exponential Moving Average Lines Crossover*

Note that the trader is always in the market. There is always a signal to open a long or short position. The danger here is that there is a clear and distinct possibility that the trader will overplay the market. For example, if the market is not trending—that is, if only small, random price gyrations are taking place—then the trader might enter the long position and quickly discover that prices had reverted back. He or she would end up being whipsawed by the market price gyrations. In other words, the stock prices might go up only $1/_4$ of a point and then decline, forcing the trader to quickly sell.

To avoid being whipsawed, the trader could increase the number of time intervals in the slow EMA line from 9 to 12. That would make the slow EMA slower, and thus it would avoid many crossover buy or sell trading signals. However, the slower EMA line would result in increased lag time.

Moving Average Convergence/Divergence

You can use another technical-analysis tool called the "moving average convergence/divergence" (MACD) to gauge the strength of the upward or downward price movement. Basically, MACD lets you measure the extent of the divergence and convergence between the fast and slow EMA lines. If the divergence or distance between the fast and slow EMA lines is increasing, then the price movement is gaining strength. If the distance between the fast and slow EMA lines is decreasing or converging, however, then the price movement is losing strength. This concept is elaborated in the MACD analysis.

Moving average convergence/divergence analysis was developed by Gerald Appel in 1985. MACD is a derivative of two EMA lines, and it is an excellent price-trending indicator. MACD is also considered to be somewhat of an oscillator tool. An oscillator is a line that indicates whether a stock is overbought or oversold. In other words, an oscillator would indicate whether prices have moved too far or too fast in either direction and thus are vulnerable to a reaction or reversal. The best way to explain MACD is to construct MACD from scratch.

To do so, we begin by subtracting the fast EMA (3-hr.) line from the slow EMA (9-hr.) line. When the stock prices are increasing, the fast EMA (3-hr.) line is greater than the slow EMA (9-hr.), and thus the MACD line is positive. If stock prices continue to increase at a rapid rate, then the gap between the fast EMA (3-hr.) line and the slow EMA (9-hr.) line will also continue to increase, and thus the MACD line will be positive and continue to grow as well. Figure 13.4 illustrates this point.

Conversely, when a stock's price decreases, the fast EMA (3-hr.) line is below the slow EMA (9-hr.) line, and thus the MACD line is negative. If the stock's price continues to decline, then the gap between the fast EMA (3-hr.) line and the slow EMA (9-hr.) line will continue to increase also, and thus the MACD line will continue to be negative. In essence, the MACD line will quickly tell the trader if the price trend is up or down and whether that positive or negative price trend is increasing or decreasing.

If the MACD is positive or above the zero line and if there is a divergence (i.e., an increase in the spread) between the MACD and zero line, then the trader would interpret that as a bullish sign. If MACD is still positive and there is a convergence (i.e., a decrease in the spread) between the MACD and the zero line, then the trader would interpret that as a sign that the bulls in the market are losing steam. The trader would then expect a price reversal. In essence, the trader would receive

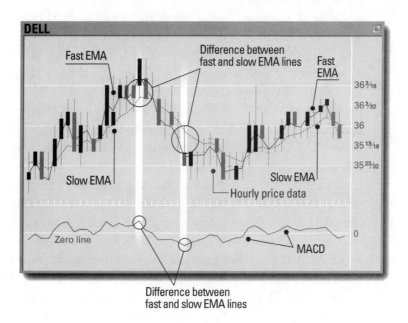

Figure 13.4 *Moving Average Convergence/Divergence (MACD)*

a warning sign that stock prices would probably stop increasing and would begin to decline.

By the same token, if the MACD is negative and below the zero line, and if there is a divergence (i.e., an increase in the spread) between the MACD and the zero line, then the trader would interpret that as a bearish sign. If MACD is still negative and there is a convergence (i.e., a decrease in the spread) between the MACD and the zero line, then the trader would interpret that as a sign that the bears in the market are losing steam. The trader would then expect a price reversal. In other words, a trader would receive a warning sign that stock prices would most likely stop decreasing and would begin to increase.

The crossover between the fast and slow EMA lines corresponds to the crossover between the MACD and zero line. In essence, the MACD line is a derivative of the two EMA lines. The MACD conveys the same information as the fast and slow EMA lines. However, information on the direction and strength of the price movement is easily visualized with the MACD line.

The next step is to create a MACD signal line. The MACD signal line is the exponential moving average of the calculated MACD. For example, the MACD signal line is the EMA of the 9-period MACD values. The signal MACD line will smooth out the actual MACD fluctuations. The signal MACD line is needed in order to get the clear buy-or-sell signals, which are the crossovers between the MACD and signal MACD lines. These crossovers between the MACD and signal MACD lines are often used as the buy-or-sell signals. In essence, the MACD is the fast line and the signal MACD is the slow line. When the MACD crosses over and above the signal MACD line, that would indicate a bullish signal to buy. When MACD crosses below the signal MACD line, that would constitute a bearish signal to sell the stock.

The final step is to plot the MACD histogram. The size and the pattern of the MACD histogram bars would act as an oscillator indicator. The MACD histogram is displayed as the difference between the MACD and signal MACD lines. When the MACD crosses over and above the signal MACD line, then the MACD histogram would have positive values. A positive MACD histogram would indicate a bullish signal to buy.

The MACD histogram also helps the trader to visualize the level of price divergence or convergence between the MACD and MACD signal lines. The actual absolute-price differential between the MACD and signal MACD values is rather small, but the computer program will automatically resize that small value. The key is to visualize whether there is convergence or divergence between the MACD and signal MACD lines. If the MACD histogram is increasing in value, then the bullish sign has intensified. If the MACD histogram is decreasing in value, however, then the bulls are running out of steam.

When the MACD crosses below the signal MACD line, then the MACD histogram would have negative values. A negative MACD histogram would constitute a sell signal. The key is to focus and visualize whether there is convergence or divergence between the MACD and signal MACD lines. If the MACD histogram is negative and decreasing in value, then the bearish signal has intensified. If, however, the MACD histogram is negative and decreasing at a diminishing rate, then the bears are running out of steam.

The MA and MACD are the starting points (or entry level) of computerized technical analysis. I'm not saying that MA and MACD indicators are the *best* computerized technical-analysis tools, because there is no single best technical-analysis indicator. But despite MA and MACD limitations, they remain the most popular and commonly used computerized technical-analysis tools because their underlying foundations are scientifically sound.

14

Price Volatility and Oscillator Indicators

"Oil prices have fallen lately. We include this news for the benefit of gas companies, which otherwise wouldn't learn of it for six months."

—*Bill Tammeus, in Toronto's* National Newspaper, *1991*

Imagine having a technical tool that tells you where the current stock price is relative to the most recent high and low price range. There are technical-analysis tools called *oscillator indicators* that were specifically designed to accomplish this objective. As there are several oscillator indicators available, I will focus on the most relevant and popular ocillators used for short-term stock trading.

An oscillator is defined as a line that indicates whether a stock is overbought or oversold. In other words, an oscillator would indicate whether prices moved too far or too fast in either direction from the average price and thus are vulnerable to a reaction or reversal. In essence, an oscillator indicator is a tool that monitors the risk of price volatility. It is important that we differentiate between the two different risk measurements of price volatility:

- Absolute price volatility, which is measured by a standard deviation
- Relative price volatility, which is measured by a Beta coefficient

Absolute Price Volatility

The most basic method of ascertaining the risk is to look at the high and low stock prices during a certain period of time, such as 52 weeks. The range between the high and low tells us only the difference between the two extremes. If the range between the high and low is substantial, then the security carries substantial risk. As a general rule, a small price range between the high and low prices would constitute a lower risk.

A more useful approach is to plot the distribution of all daily stock prices, from the low to high price extremes, during the 52-week period. Figure 14.1 depicts that hypothetical price-distribution pattern between the high and low prices of 250 daily closing price observations. Assuming normal distribution, which is the most common assumption in statistics, we can observe that prices would cluster around the mean value, with an equal number of price observations being higher and lower than the average price.

It is possible to have two stocks with the identical average price for the 52-week period but having a different degree of risk. For instance, one stock (A) might have more of the extreme high and low price values, and thus the distribution tails would spread farther from the mean. Another stock (B) might have prices that gathered closely around the

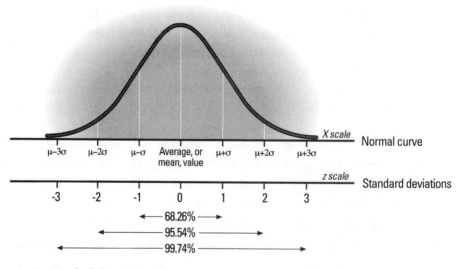

Figure 14.1 *Probability Distribution*

mean, and thus the tails are closer to the average value. Which of these two stocks would have the lower absolute price-volatility risk?

Stock B has a lower price variance from the average price, and thus stock B has a lower standard deviation. Stock A, however, has a greater variance from the average price, and consequently stock A has a higher standard deviation and thus greater absolute price risk. Conversely, the lower standard deviation means smaller variance from the mean value and thus smaller risk. Hence, the standard deviation is a measure of absolute risk.

Relative Price Volatility

Suppose that we have collected daily stock price data for a particular stock for a year, and thus we have 250 data observations (given approximately 250 trading days in a year). Compare that information to the S & P's 500 index prices for the same period of time. In other words, on a horizontal axis we measure the daily S & P's 500 index return, and a vertical axis measures the daily stock prices for this particular stock. Using a basic econometric regression analysis, we develop a linear line of the best data fit, which has an intercept value (Alpha) and a slope (Beta). The Beta coefficient (or the slope coefficient) is a statistical measure of the price volatility of a particular stock in relation to the entire stock market's volatility (i.e., the S & P's 500 index). In other words, the Beta coefficient for a stock will provide a measure of the relative market volatility associated with that security.

The Beta coefficient is a common part of any fundamental analysis and can be found on many financial search engines on the Internet, such as on Yahoo.com or MSN.com. Figure 14.2 illustrates three hypothetical Beta values with distinctly different relative price-volatility measures. If the returns of the S & P's 500 index increase by 10 percent, then the stock with the Beta value of 0.5 would increase in value only by 5 percent. If the Beta is 1, then stock return will increase proportionately by 10 percent as well. Similarly, if the returns of the S & P's 500 index increase by 10 percent, then the stock with the Beta value of 2 would increase in value by 20 percent.

The Beta value can range from 0 to a positive number, such as 3. Some financial analysts argue that gold-mining stock, for instance, could have a negative Beta value, but there is no empirical evidence to support

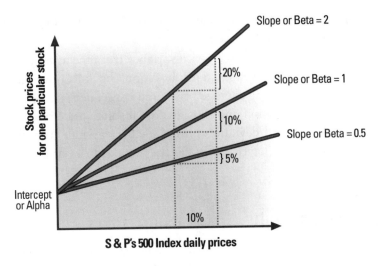

Figure 14.2 *Calculating Beta*

this claim. Stocks that have a Beta value less than 1 are considered to be stable stocks, as these are less price volatile than the overall S & P's 500 index. If the Beta value is equal to 1, then the stock price volatility is identical to the overall average market volatility. If the stock has a Beta value greater than 1, then that stock is more volatile relative to the entire stock market's volatility. Table 14.1 summarizes all possible Beta values.

My recommendation to swing traders is to trade stocks that are volatile and liquid. In other words, look for stocks that have a Beta value greater than 1.5 and have substantial average daily trading volumes

Table 14.1 *Relative Price Volatility: Beta Values*

Beta Value	Explanation	Example
Negative beta	S & P's 500 index goes down and the stock price goes up	Gold-mining stocks
Beta less than 1	Stable and less price-volatile stocks	Utility stocks
Beta equal to 1	Overall market and the stock have the identical price volatility	S & P's 500 index fund
Beta greater than 1	More volatile stocks	Internet stocks

(greater than 500,000 shares). (See appendix 3 for a list of such stocks.) Another investment strategy for the investor is to buy stocks with a high Beta value (large price volatility) in the bull market and then move to stocks with a low Beta value (low price volatility) in the bear market.

Bollinger Bands

A few years ago I encountered in a book on stock trading an analogy about oscillators that was very instructive. Imagine walking a large dog on a long leash in fresh snow. The dog is pulling you and refuses to walk in a straight line. Instead, it continually bounces from side to side. If the dog scrambles too far to one side, he would feel the resistance from the leash and would turn in the opposite direction, or the direction that has the least resistance. Furthermore, every now and then the dog would be so enticed by something (i.e., a cat) on the left or right side that he would exert enough force to pull him in that direction.

Imagine drawing an analogy between the dog's footprints in the snow and stock prices. Most of the time, the dog's prints (or the stock prices) stayed within the left and right boundaries of the long leash. Imagine that the left- and right-side boundaries of your dog leash are your price support and resistance boundaries. Well, the Bollinger bands indicator is essentially your stock price "leash." Among the several oscillators, the Bollinger bands oscillator is my favorite. It is commonly used by traders and is available in today's trading-software packages.

The Bollinger bands indicator was developed by John Bollinger. This technical tool is an excellent way to determine the price support and resistance levels. Price resistance is a price level at which prices have stopped rising and have either moved sideways or reversed direction. In other words, the price-resistance level indicates an overbought market. Price support, however, is a price level at which prices have stopped falling and either moved sideways or reversed direction. In other words, the price-support level indicates an oversold market. The Bollinger bands oscillator is an indicator that monitors the risk of price fluctuations within price support and resistance levels.

The Bollinger bands indicator is an improvement from the standard fixed-percentage bands, which were commonly used by professional traders. For instance, traders commonly used two bands around the current price as the support and resistance levels. A plus 10 percent from the current price would become a price-resistance band. A minus 10 percent from the current price would become a price-support band. As is apparent, fixed-percentage bands were not very flexible. The fixed-percentage bands created two parallel lines that did not change with the increased or decreased price volatility.

The Bollinger bands indicator uses standard deviations for the two bands instead of the fixed-percentage lines. The standard deviation of the stock price is the measure of the absolute risk arising from the stock's price volatility. The starting assumption is that the stock prices during a certain time interval have a normal distribution around the average. For short-term stock trading, let us use, as an example, 14 price observations of 1-hour interval data. You can vary the number of observations in the Bollinger bands calculations. However, I chose to keep the trading-software default at 14 periods for calculating the Bollinger bands. That would mean that swing traders should also use 14 hourly periods if they are using hourly data. In essence, I am analyzing the absolute price volatility for the stock in the last 14 hours of trading. Figure 14.1 illustrates the normal price distribution (or bell-shaped distribution) that results if the stock prices are normally distributed around the mean price and if the prices are deviated equally on the plus and minus side from the existing moving average price. The average stock price is in the middle, and high and low prices are on the ends.

Statistical theory tells us that 68 percent of all price observations would reside on a +1 standard deviation (+1 St.D.) and a –1 standard deviation (–1 St.D.) from the mean. Furthermore, 95 percent of all price observations would reside on a +2 standard deviation (+2 St.D.) and a –2 standard deviation (–2 St.D.) from the mean. If we select +1.85 St.D. and –1.85 St.D. for the upper and lower Bollinger bands lines, then we could assume that there is an approximate 80 percent probability that all prices will fall within the upper and lower bands.

As the price volatility increases for a particular stock, then the price variance would increase as well. A higher price variance from the average price would automatically increase the standard deviation. In times of decreased price volatility, the high and low prices will be relatively close to the average (or mean) price, and thus the standard deviation would be rather small. Conversely, in times of increased price volatility, the high and low prices will be relatively far apart from the mean price, and thus the standard deviation would be large.

In essence, the standard deviations automatically adjust for the increased or decreased intraday or intraweek stock price volatility. If the Bollinger bands increase (i.e., widen), then that would automatically indicate a higher price volatility, or higher standard deviations. If, however, the Bollinger bands decrease (i.e., become narrower), then that would automatically indicate a lower price volatility, or more stable prices.

The upper band of +1.85 St.D. above the moving average point constitutes the price-resistance level at that point of time. The lower band of −1.85 St.D. below the moving average point constitutes the price-support level at that point of time. The statistical theory dictates that there is an approximate 80 percent probability that all prices would fall within the upper and lower Bollinger bands. In other words, there is only a 20 percent probability that actual prices would go above or below the two Bollinger bands lines.

A trader should always try to stay within the Bollinger bands trading range (see figure 14.2). After all, there is an approximate 80 percent probability that the price will remain in this range. Would you bet your money on a 20 percent probability? It is not a good idea to open a long position (i.e., buy the stock) when the price has reached the price-resistance level

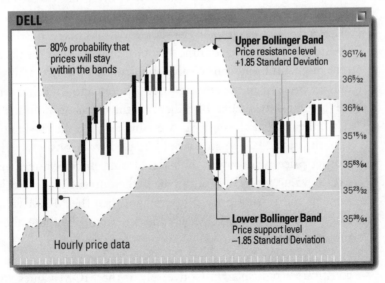

Figure 14.2 *Bollinger Bands*

(i.e., the upper Bollinger band). When the stock prices approach the upper Bollinger band, then the stock is overbought.

Conversely, it is not a good idea to open a short position (i.e., sell short the stock) when the price has reached the price-support level (i.e., the lower Bollinger band). When the stock prices approach the lower Bollinger band, many traders are convinced that the stock is oversold.

Momentum Indicator

The momentum indicator (MOM) is another technical-analysis tool that can be useful to swing traders. The MOM is an oscillator-type indicator used to ascertain whether there is an upward or downward price momentum and to determine overbought or oversold markets. In this chapter, the momentum indicator is plotted as a line attached to the main diagram. With some software packages, the MOM is plotted as a histogram (i.e., as bars). The momentum indicator helps to visually determine the pace or strength at which stock prices are going up or down. In essence, this indicator will ascertain whether the price momentum, be it positive or negative, is gaining or losing its steam or strength.

The MOM is calculated simply by subtracting the current closing price from the closing price several periods ago. The past period can be any period selected by the trader. It is my preference to use the same period that is being used for the slow EMA, which was discussed in chapter 13. In this chapter, the slow EMA has been constructed by using the stock closing price of nine 1-hour intervals. That means that the current momentum-indicator value is calculated by subtracting the current closing price from the closing price 9 hours ago. In other words, MOM $= P(t) - P(t - 9)$. Figure 14.3 displays the momentum indicator.

If the current closing price were higher than the closing price 9 hours ago, then the MOM value would be positive. Conversely, if the current closing price were lower than the closing price 9 hours ago, then the MOM value would be negative. If the current closing price were the same as the closing price 9 hours ago, then the MOM value would be zero. Therefore, the MOM would oscillate or fluctuate above or below the zero line.

If the MOM values were positive and increasing, then that would constitute a bullish sign. Conversely, if the MOM values were negative and decreasing, then that would be a bearish sign. If the MOM were to

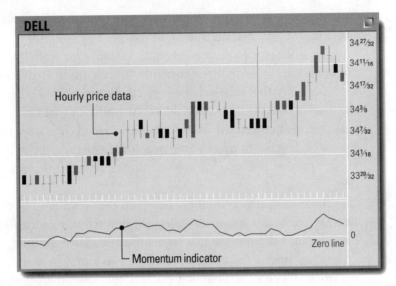

Figure 14.3 *Momentum Indicator*

systematically fluctuate around the zero line between the positive and negative values, that would point to a choppy market. It is difficult to trade stocks that have extremely choppy MOMs.

If the MOM values were to rise too far above the zero line, that could indicate an overbought market. If the MOM values were positive but the MOM were to reverse its direction and start to move down toward the zero line, then that would indicate an early sign that the positive (i.e., upward) price momentum was losing its steam. Conversely, if the MOM values were to fall too far from the zero line, that could indicate an oversold market. Also, if the MOM value were negative but the MOM were to reverse its direction and start to move up toward the zero line, then that would indicate an early sign that the downward price momentum was losing its steam.

Stochastic Oscillator

George Lane developed the stochastic oscillator indicator in the 1970s. It is one of the most popular overbought/oversold indicators available. Most of today's trading software products incorporate stochastic analysis. The indicator was designed to show when the stock becomes overbought or oversold within a certain trading range.

The stochastic indicator generates readings between 0 and 100. It is commonly accepted that readings over 75 constitute an overbought market. It is likely that relatively high prices have attracted sellers who enter the market, sell the stock, and make the profit. In that case, it is possible that the price movement would reverse its trend. It is a signal (or warning) to traders not to open a long position. In essence, the overbought stochastic market line at 75 would constitute an arbitrary price-resistance line.

Conversely, it is commonly accepted that readings under 25 constitute an oversold market. An oversold market exists when stock prices have declined rapidly due to a large influx of sellers. At that time, the relatively low prices would attract buyers who enter the market to pick up the stock at a perceived bargain price. In that case, there is a distinct possibility that the price movement would reverse its trend. It is a warning not to sell short the stock. Instead, it signals to traders to look for the possibility of opening a long position if an uptrend emerges. In other words, the oversold stochastic market line at 25 would constitute an arbitrary price-support line. Figure 14.4 depicts the stochastic oscillator.

As you can see from the chart, the stochastic oscillator fluctuates between the two market extremes. When plotted on the chart, the stochastic indicator appears with very jagged peaks and troughs. Anything in between 25 and 75 on the oscillator readings would indicate the normal trading range. Again, the indicator refers to the location of the current price in relation to its price range over the specified period of time. As I have been using nine 1-hour intervals throughout most of the technical-analysis material (except when we used 14 hours with Bollinger bands), then the chart in figure 14.2 will use the stochastic oscillator that is based on the nine 1-hour intervals. As a default, the time period most commonly used by trading software products is 14 bars, or 14 hourly intervals.

Fast and Slow Stochastic

The stochastic oscillator, or the "fast stochastic," is often labeled in the technical-analysis literature as the %K. The fast stochastic is defined as the difference between the current stock price and the lowest stock price

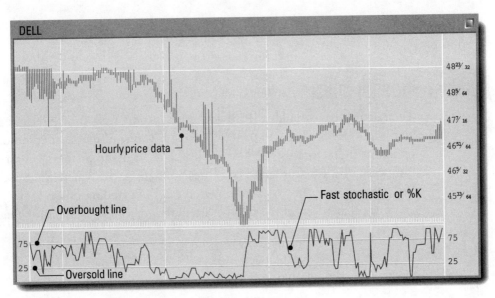

Figure 14.4 *Stochastic Oscillator Indicator*

in the last 9 hours, which is then divided by the difference between the highest and lowest prices in the last 9 periods. In other words, %K is defined as [P(t) – Lowest P(t – 9)] divided by [Highest P(t – 9) – Lowest P(t – 9)], where the [Highest P(t – 9) – Lowest P(t – 9)] represents the price-trading range in the last 9 hours, and the [P(t) – Lowest P(t – 9)] represents the location of a current price in relation to the lowest price in the last 9 hours.

The stochastic indicator chart appears to have very jagged peaks and troughs. Many traders prefer to use "slow stochastic" (or %D), which is the slower or smoothed-out stochastic oscillator. The %D is basically a moving average (MA) of the %K. Therefore, the moving average stochastic line (%D) will smooth out some of the jagged peaks and troughs of the fast stochastic line.

Some technical analysts plot the %K line next to the %D line. The two lines would generate many crossovers. The crossovers can be interpreted as the buy-and-sell signals. For example, if the %K crosses over and goes above the %D, that would constitute a buy signal. If the %K crosses and goes under the %D, that would constitute a sell signal. My personal preference is to treat and use the stochastic oscillator indicators strictly as overbought and oversold indicators and not as the trading buy-and-sell signals.

Relative Strength Index

The relative strength index (RSI) was developed by well-known technical analyst J. Welles Wilder in the late 1970s. It is one of the most common oscillator indicators used by swing investors. Similar to the stochastic indicator, the RSI indicator was designed to show when the stock becomes overbought or oversold within a certain trading range.

The calculation for the relative strength index (RSI) is the following:

$$RSI = 100 - \frac{100}{(1 + RS)}$$

where RS is the relative strength, or:

$$RS = \frac{\text{(Average net positive closing price changes for selected time)}}{\text{(Average net negative closing price changes for selected time)}}$$

Suppose we are dealing with daily price data and our selected time period is 14 days, which is commonly the default period for most RSI oscillator software applications. If fewer days, such as a 9-day period, are used to calculate the RSI, then the RSI indicator will be more volatile or choppy. If the closing price in one period, such as one day, is higher than the previous day's closing price, then that day will have a positive net-price change. However, the closing price in one period could be lower than the previous day's closing price, and thus that day will have a negative net-price change.

If positive net-price changes are greater on average than negative net-price changes average (indicating a bullish market condition), then the numerator will be larger than the denominator and the RSI index will increase in value. For instance, imagine that the average of net positive closing-price changes for the selected 14-day period is 80, and suppose that the average of the net negative closing-price changes for the selected 14-day time period is 40. Then, the RS is $^{80}/_{40}$ (or 2), which would result in the following:

$$RS = 2$$
$$RSI = 100 - \frac{100}{(1 + 2)}$$

$$RSI = 100 - 33.3$$
$$RSI = 66.7$$

In this hypothetical example, the RSI is relatively high at 66.7, which indicates that prices are approaching an overbought market level, such as the RSI overbought benchmark of 70. At that overbought price level, there is a distinct possibility for price reversal or price decline. In other words, stock prices have reached such a high level as to attract profit taking or selling.

If negative net-price changes are greater than positive net-price changes (indicating a bearish signal), then the numerator will be smaller than the denominator and the RSI index will decrease in value. Conversely, imagine that the average of the net positive closing-price changes for the selected 14-day time period is only 40, and suppose that the average of the net negative closing-price changes for the selected 14-day time period is substantially higher at 80. Then, the RS is $^{40}/_{80}$ (or $^1/_2$), which would result in the following:

$$RS = 0.5$$
$$RSI = 100 - \frac{100}{(1 + 0.5)}$$
$$RSI = 100 - \frac{100}{1.5}$$
$$RSI = 100 - 66.6$$
$$RSI = 33.4$$

Conversely, a relatively low RSI (33.4) indicates that prices are approaching an oversold market level, such as the RSI oversold benchmark of 30. At that oversold price level, there is a distinct possibility for price reversal or price increase. In short, stock prices have reached such a low level as to attract new investors or greater buying.

Similar to the stochastic indicator, the RSI generates readings between 0 and 100. It is commonly accepted that readings over 70 constitute an overbought market. Again, the term *overbought* implies that the stock prices went up too fast and too far with the high influx of buyers and that there is a distinct probability that the high prices will attract sellers who would sell the stock to make a profit. The RSI reading at 70 is a signal to traders not to open a long position because the RSI has approached an arbitrary price-resistance line. Traders should, then, consider looking for the short-selling opportunities.

Conversely, it is commonly accepted that RSI readings under 30 constitute an oversold market. An *oversold* market is a situation where stock prices have declined rapidly due to a large influx of sellers, which would then attract buyers who would buy the stock at the perceived bargain price. Subsequently, it is a signal not to short sell the stock. The low RSI reading is not in itself the buy signal. Rather, it is a signal to look for the possibility of opening a long position if the positive trend is ascertained. Finally, for all technical purposes, the RSI value of 50 can serve as the zero line used by other oscillators. Figure 14.5 depicts the RSI oscillator for Dell Computer Corporation.

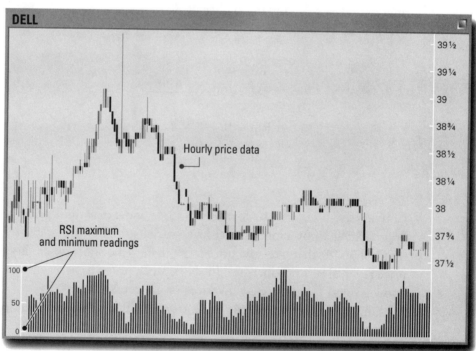

Figure 14.5 *Relative Strength Index*

The key to reading the RSI oscillator is to look at these two RSI characteristics:

1. Level of the RSI reading, whether the RSI reading is high or low
2. Direction of the RSI oscillator, whether the RSI reading is going up or down

The bullish trading signal is to see the RSI readings at the low level, such as at around 30, along with an increase in each RSI reading. In other words, the RSI reading must be higher than the previous RSI bar reading, or the RSI is going up. Conversely, the bearish RSI signal is to see the RSI readings at the high level, such as the 70 reading, and that there is a continuous decrease in each RSI reading. In other words, you start with the high RSI, and each additional RSI reading must be lower than the previous RSI bar reading.

In summary, the oscillator indicators are popular technical-analysis tools that tell you where the current stock price is relative to the most recent high and low price range. Oscillators help traders avoid buying a stock at the relative high price or short selling a stock when the price is at the relatively low level. Consequently, they are crucial tools for monitoring the trading risks associated with price volatility.

CHAPTER
15

Broad Market Measures and Trading Volume

"There was a time when a fool and his money were soon parted, but now it happens to everybody."

—*Adlai Stevenson*

An old stock market adage states that "a rising tide lifts all boats." And though this is certainly true of boats, it is not always true for the stock market. The rising stock market "tide" will lift the price for most of the "boats," but not for all of them. Some "boats" are beyond hope. Even with the strong rising market "tide," there will always be laggards.

Nevertheless, it is important to always monitor the broad stock market. The trader must be aware at all times of the direction and intensity of overall market sentiment. Monitoring the movement of a broad market index will, in essence, show one the current overall price momentum. It is my opinion that it is a good idea to go along with the overall market direction. The late Mao Tse-tung once advised that one should not "piss against the wind." If a trader were going against the overall market, there is a distinct possibility that he or she would end up getting "wet."

If the overall stock market prices decline, then it would not be a good idea to open a long position. It's possible you're right in thinking that the particular stock will appreciate in value, but the odds are against it. If the trader is opening a long position and the overall advance-to-decline value is negative for that day, then the probability of having a winning trade is diminished. The advance-decline value is negative if the number of declining issues is greater than the number of advancing issues.

Market Indices

The most frequently asked question in the stock market is, "How is the market doing today?" The correct way to answer this question is to quote the price change in a market index. A market index is an important stock trading tool. It reveals the overall market price performance at any point in time. It also provides the benchmark used to compare individual stock returns to the overall market at any point in time. The most common market indices are the S & P's 500 (INX), the Dow Jones industrial average (INDU), the NASDAQ Composite (COMPX), the NASDAQ 100 (IQX), the NYSE Composite (NYA.X), the Russell 2,000 (IUX), and the Wilshire Small Cap.

Several studies have indicated that there is relatively high correlation between the major stock indices—most of the time the market indices move in tandem. When the S & P's 500 index increases in value, then most likely the Dow Jones industrial average index also goes up in value. For instance, the coefficient of correlation between the S & P's 500 and the Dow Jones industrial average is approximately 0.96. The coefficient of correlation of 1 indicates perfect correlation, whereas the coefficient of correlation of 0 indicates no correlation. The high correlation is not surprising. The companies that are part of the two indices are both operating at the same time in the same economic environment. Secondly, there is an overlap—30 companies in the Dow Jones industrial average index are also part of the broader S & P's 500 index.

Although market indices tend to move in the same market direction at a different pace, occasionally the two market indices might diverge. A recent example of this is the market performance divergence between the NASDAQ Composite index and the Dow Jones industrial average in the first months of 2000, when the NASDAQ Composite index increased approximately 13 percent and the Dow Jones industrial average declined 14 percent in the same time period. Subsequently, financial commentators began speculating about a dual stock market. In other words, the technology-driven—and, particularly, the Internet-growth-driven—NASDAQ stock market is appreciating in value, whereas the stock prices of the old industrial companies are declining due to the impact of higher interest rates on future corporate earnings. Then, in April 2000, a major price correction in the technology sector occurred. For instance, on Friday, April 14, 2000, the NASDAQ plunged a record 355 points, or approximately 10 percent, which was the worst one-day drop in history. All told, April 2000 saw an unprecedented decline in the technology-loaded NASDAQ market, which declined 25 percent in value during one week of trading. The prices of the NASDAQ Composite index and the Dow Jones industrial average are thus now a good deal more balanced.

Index Construction

The important difference among different indices is the method of index construction. There are basically two issues regarding the development of a market index:

- Sample size
- Weighting scheme

The sample size discloses the number of stocks in the index. A large sample size means that the index is designed to monitor a broader stock market. It is a statistical truism that the larger the sample, the more accurately the sample measures the broad market performance. For instance, Standard and Poor's 500 index, with its sample size of 500 stocks, is a much better indicator of the overall market performance than the Dow Jones industrial average, which has a sample of 30 stocks.

There are a number of specialized indices that have, by design, a small sample. The specialized indices are designed specifically to monitor a single industry sector that might have a limited number of firms. For example, the Semiconductor index (or SOX) monitors only a small number of stocks in this particular industry. In essence, the sample is by necessity small, because the population of the entire industry sector is small.

The second issue is the index-weighting scheme, which reveals how much importance is assigned to each stock. There are basically two main stock-weighting approaches:

- Market-capitalization weighting
- Price weighting

Market-capitalization weighting means that each stock is assigned a weight based on the firm's relative market value or size in the stock market. Large firms, such as Microsoft, Intel, or Dell, would carry more relative weight in the index than the firms that have smaller market capitalization. The S & P's 500 index is an example of the market-capitalization-weighted market index. Most market indices are market-capitalization-weighted indices.

Price weighting, however, means that each stock is assigned a weight based on the firm's relative stock price in the market at that point in time. Companies that exhibit high prices carry more relative weight in the index than the firms that have low prices. The Dow Jones industrial average is an example of a price-weighted market index. Table 15.1 illustrates the difference between the two weighting schemes for five hypothetical stocks.

The calculation of the returns for two market indices reveals the dramatic difference in the outcome. The same five stocks display different returns under the two different market-indices construction approaches. For example:

$$\text{Return based on the price-weighted market index} = \frac{(162 - 149)}{149} = 8.72\%$$

Table 15.1 *Market Index Construction*

Stock	Price at the Beginning Period	Market Capitalization Number of Shares	Price at the Beginning Period	End Period	Market Capitalization at the End Period
AAAA	20	1,000,000	20,000,000	22	22,000,000
BBBB	24	1,800,000	43,200,000	29	52,200,000
CCCC	30	1,500,000	45,000,000	32	48,000,000
DDDD	35	800,000	28,000,000	36	28,800,000
EEEE	40	1,200,000	48,000,000	43	51,600,000
Total	149	6,300,000	184,200,000	162	202,600,000

$$\text{Return based on the market-capitalization-weighted market index} = \frac{(202,600,000 - 184,200,000)}{18,400,000} = 9.99\%$$

Finally, the computational procedure adds another twist in the market index construction. Some indices use a simple arithmetic average in the index calculations, whereas other indices use a geometric mean. Different indices also use different methods for adjusting for the stock splits, stock dividends, and changes in the number of outstanding shares.

The S & P's 500 Index

One way to monitor the broad market is to monitor Standard and Poor's 500 index (the S & P's 500), which is an indicator of the general stock price movement for the 500 largest companies in the United States. Many trading software packages allow the trader to overlay a stock index such as the S & P's 500 index next to any stock prices being monitored. The S & P's 500 index values are commonly quoted by the stock data-feed providers. The software automatically resizes the index next to the prices of a particular stock. It is an easy way to ascertain if prices of a particular stock are moving in the same direction with the broad market.

Figure 15.1 provides an example of a technical-analysis chart that has a broad market overlay. If the trading software does not have the overlay feature, my recommendation is to open a separate window and monitor at least one broad market index. In this particular example, the stock price of Dell (DELL) was highly correlated at that moment of analysis with the broad stock market as measured by the S & P's 500 futures.

A good way to understand the S & P's 500 index is to visualize it as a lake filled with 500 stocks. Just like any other lake, this lake has its water inflow and outflow. Membership in the S & P's 500 index is based on a company's current market capitalization, which continuously changes with stock prices. There are always companies that are appreciating in value at a much faster pace than the rest of the market, and consequently these stocks will reach the benchmark and qualify to be added to the index. Inclusion into the index generates an immediate boost in demand for these stocks. Many investors invest in the S & P's 500 index fund on a regular monthly or biweekly basis through investment plans, such as 401(k) plans. Thus stocks that are added to that purchase mix will have a continuous built-in demand. Conversely, the stocks that are

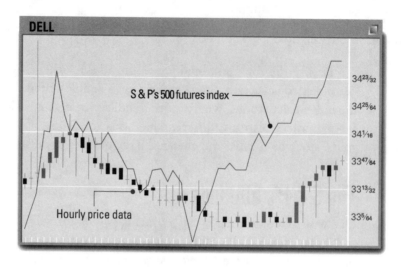

Figure 15.1 *Broad Market Index Overlay*

dropped from the index are subsequently dropped from that purchase mix, so the stock will suffer a decrease in demand.

There are approximately 35 NASDAQ-listed companies that are in the S & P's 500 stock index. Perhaps the S & P's 500 index is too broad a measure of the overall market. Some traders who trade mostly NAS-DAQ stocks pay much closer attention to the narrower market indices, such as the NASDAQ 100. Some traders who specialize in a few technology stocks closely monitor certain sector indices, such as the Internet index (INX), the Technology index (TXX), the Software index (CWX) on the Chicago Board Options Exchange (CBOE), or the Semiconductor index (SOX) on the Philadelphia Exchange.

Many traders pay very close attention to the S & P's 500 futures trend line. The S & P's 500 futures are standardized futures contracts with an expiration date, and the contracts are being actively traded on the Chicago Mercantile Exchange. In essence, the S & P's 500 futures contract is a financial derivative. The value of the S & P's 500 futures contract is tied directly to the underlying cash value of the S & P's 500 index. In fact, the delivery of the contract is the cash settlement of the difference between the original transaction price and the final price of the index at the termination of the contract. The price of the index futures will be highly correlated with the value of the corresponding index. The activity of the index arbitrageurs ensures that the deviations between the price of the index futures and value of the underlying cash index are relatively minor.

Many traders believe that the S & P's 500 futures is a leading market indicator. By contrast, a cash index, such as the S & P's 500 index or the Dow Jones industrial average index, is a lagging indicator. It reflects the actual or historical price changes of the underlying stocks that comprise that particular cash index. The futures index, however, reflects to great extent anticipation about the future of the broad market by the market professionals and speculators. In essence, the broad market sentiment is quickly and efficiently reflected in the price of the S & P's 500 futures contract. Because the S & P's 500 futures contract is actively traded, the trader can plot and overlay the price value of the futures contract against the stock price. Instead of plotting the value of the S & P's 500 index (i.e., the lagging indicator), the trader can plot the price of the S & P's 500 futures index (i.e., the leading indicator).

The Dow Jones Industrial Average Index

The Dow Jones industrial average index (INDU) is one of the first published stock market indices. Charles Dow, founder and editor of the *Wall Street Journal,* published the index in the journal on July 3, 1884. At that time, the index consisted of only nine stocks, and most of them were railroad companies. Today, the index consists of 30 large and established U.S. industrial companies. In addition, today we have the Dow Jones Transportation index (TRAN), consisting of 20 large transportation companies, and the Dow Jones Utilities index (UTIL), consisting of 15 large utility companies. Finally, the Dow Jones Composite index (COMP) combines the three Dow Jones indices into one merged price index consisting of 65 stocks.

Market Breadth Indicators

"Advance decline issues," "advance decline ratio," "advance decline line," and TRIN are some of the several indicators measuring broad market breadth that are available on most sophisticated trading software platforms. They all have the same foundation and objective:

- They are designed to measure the broad market price momentum.
- They are based on the difference in the number of advancing and declining issues.

The difference between the advancing and declining stock issues is the starting point of the analysis. There are approximately 3,000 common stocks listed on the NYSE. If the overall market is flat, and one ignores those stocks that are unchanged in price, one can expect that 1,500 stocks would advance and 1,500 stocks would decline in value. That would mean that advance decline issues would be set at zero.

Suppose that 2,000 stocks advance and 1,000 stocks decline in value, which would cause the advance decline issues to be +1,000. Any advance decline issues reading over 1,000 indicates a strong bullish market sentiment. Conversely, imagine that only 1,000 stocks advance, whereas 2,000 stocks decline in value, which would cause the advance decline issues to be –1,000. Any negative advance decline issues reading at –1,000 indicates a strong bearish market sentiment.

Instead of subtracting the number of declining issues from the number of advancing issues, imagine that we simply divide the number of advancing issues by the number of declining issues. From our earlier example, where 2,000 stocks advance and 1,000 stocks decline in value, the advance decline ratio is 2, which would indicate a strong bullish market sentiment. Conversely, when only 1,000 stocks advance, whereas 2,000 stocks decline in value, the advance decline ratio becomes 0.5, which represents a bearish sign. Therefore, when the advance decline ratio is greater than 1, then the overall stock market is increasing in value. When the advance decline ratio is less than 1, then the stock market is decreasing in value.

The next step is to run a cumulative total of all advance decline issues on the NYSE. If we plot that cumulative total of all advance decline issues over time in a line format, the result is the advance decline line, which is one of the most popular market breath indicators. The actual figure of the cumulative advance decline line has no practical meaning. The important thing is the direction and slope of the advance decline line. The slope and direction reveal the overall trend and the strength of the broad market. For instance, a positive and steep line would indicate strong bullish market conditions, whereas the positive and relatively small slope would indicate a weak bullish market sentiment. Conversely, a negative and steep line would indicate strong bearish market conditions, whereas the negative and relatively small slope would indicate a weak bearish market sentiment.

Table 15.2 depicts calculations for different market breadth indicators, using hypothetical daily data for two weeks of trading on the NYSE. The time interval could be adjusted to any particular time frame to reflect the focus of the analysis, such as hourly or daily data.

Finally, TRIN is a market breadth indicator that expands on the previously mentioned advance decline issues, advance decline ratio, and advance decline line indicators. In addition to monitoring the number of advancing and declining issues, TRIN also adds the measure of trading volume associated with the advancing and declining issues. TRIN is the ratio derived from two independent ratios—advancing/declining issues ratio and advancing/declining volume ratio. In other words:

Table 15.2 *Hypothetical Advance Decline Issues, Advance Decline Ratio, and Advance Decline Line*

Time Interval	Advance Issues	Decline Issues	Advance Decline Issues	Advance Decline Ratio	Advance Decline Line
1	2,000.00	1,000.00	1,000.00	2.00	1,000.00
2	1,600.00	1,400.00	200.00	1.14	1,200.00
3	800.00	2,200.00	−1,400.00	0.36	−200.00
4	1,200.00	1,800.00	−600.00	0.67	−800.00
5	1,100.00	1,900.00	−800.00	0.58	−1,600.00
6	1,000.00	2,000.00	−1,000.00	0.50	−2,600.00
7	1,200.00	1,800.00	−600.00	0.67	−3,200.00
8	1,700.00	1,300.00	400.00	1.31	−2,800.00
9	1,900.00	1,100.00	800.00	1.73	−2,000.00
10	2,000.00	1,000.00	1,000.00	2.00	−1,000.00

$$TRIN = \frac{\text{Advancing issues/declining issues}}{\text{Advancing issues volume/declining issues volume}}$$

This ratio was developed by Richard Arms in the late 1960s. *Barron's* weekly business newspaper, which reported it first, called the ratio the "short-term trading index." Today, it is simply referred to as the trading index, or TRIN. Most traders use TRIN as an overbought and oversold indicator rather than as a broad market price-momentum indicator. As a general rule, an overbought market must have a TRIN ratio less than 1, and a TRIN ratio reading below 0.8 would constitute a warning to traders that the NYSE is overheating.

The following is an example of hypothetical NYSE trading data:

If advancing issues = 2,000
Declining issues = 1,000
Advancing issues volume = 750,000,000 shares
Declining issues volume = 250,000,000 shares
$$\text{Then TRIN} = \frac{(2,000/1,000)}{(750,000,000/250,000,000)} = \frac{2}{3} = 0.66$$

Conversely, an oversold market must have a TRIN ratio greater than 1, and a TRIN ratio reading above 1.1 would constitute a warning to traders that the NYSE prices are declining too far too quickly and that a price reversal is a strong possibility.

For instance, suppose the opposite is true:

If advancing issues = 1,000
Declining issues = 2,000
Advancing issues volume = 250,000,000 shares
Declining issues volume = 750,000,000 shares
$$\text{Then TRIN} = \frac{(1,000/2,000)}{(250,000,000/750,000,000)} = \frac{0.5}{0.33} = 1.5$$

Trading Volume

Stock price movement is the most important dimension of technical analysis. However, trading volume is the fuel that generates that price change. For many technical analysts, the volume is a proxy variable (i.e., a substitute variable) of the money flow. The "time and sales" window clearly provides the actual and exact size and direction of the money flow. A trader can quickly ascertain in real terms whether the public is buying or selling. For instance, the "time and sales" window prints the actual share size associated with the BID and ASK prices. If 10,000 shares were traded at the ASK price and only 1,000 shares were cleared at the BID price, then the public bought 10,000 and sold only 1,000 shares at that point in time. This information alone indicates the potential for a price increase—quantity demanded exceeds the quantity supplied.

Plotting the raw trading volume in real terms on the chart, however, would reveal only the combined buying and selling size of the trading, not its direction (whether it is buying or selling). In other words, the entire public buying and selling volume is presented as a single volume statistic.

Finally, most stocks that are commonly traded by traders always have substantial daily trading volume. Thus the technical analysis focuses on the deviation from the normal trading activities. Increasing volume often accompanies higher prices. Conversely, declining volume is an advance warning of a possible price correction. Most traders use the trading volume statistics to confirm the existing price movement. However, the volume statistics are always subject to brief distortions. For instance, option expirations and program trading can clearly affect the intraday volume without providing any underlying cause for price increase or decrease. In addition, spikes in the trading volume without any gradual increase over several hours may be the result of news leaks, or certain stock-analyst comments.

On-Balance Volume Indicator

One of the simplest volume indicators is the "on-balance volume" (OBV) indicator. Joseph Granville developed the OBV indicator in the 1960s. On-balance volume is plotted as a line representing the cumulative total of the trading volume. When the closing price for the 1-hour trading interval is higher than the closing price for the previous 1-hour trading interval, then that trading volume is assigned a plus (+) sign. If the closing price ends up on the uptick, then the OBV indicator assumes that the stock is under accumulation. If the closing price for the 1-hour trading interval is lower than the closing price for the previous 1-hour trading interval, then that trading volume is assigned a negative (−) sign.

In other words, if the closing price ends up on the downtick, then the OBV indicator assumes that the stock is under distribution. The OBV is a simple running cumulative total of the plus and minus (i.e., upside and downside) trading volume.

The OBV indicator can be overlaid on the price data or plotted in a separate subgraph. The OBV illustrates the trading volume flow in order to determine whether there is buying or selling pressure. Figure 15.2 illustrates the on-balance volume (OBV) indicator for the intraday 1-hour interval prices and volume of Dell (DELL).

A trader would like to see the price and the OBV indicator moving in the same direction. If both the price and OBV are moving up, then the trend is considered strong. If the price is going up but the running cumulative OBV line is declining, then divergence exists and there is a distinct possibility of a price reversal. Conversely, if both the stock price and the OBV indicator are moving down, then the downward trend is considered strong. However, if the stock price is going down but the running cumulative OBV line is increasing, or if the stock price is going up while

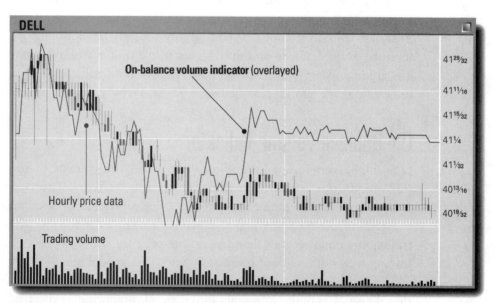

Figure 15.2　*On-Balance Volume Indicator and Trading Volume*

the running cumulative OBV line is decreasing, then there is a distinct possibility of a price reversal.

Technical Analysis Chart with Combined Indicators

Finally, traders can combine several technical-analysis indicators into a single chart. Figure 15.3 is an example of such a combined effort. The graph is crowded with several technical-analysis indicators, such as the fast and slow EMA lines, Bollinger bands, and the momentum indicator. Sometimes it is difficult to differentiate among different lines on a small chart, although the lines could be color-coded for easier reference. The trader can, however, pack a lot of analysis in a small chart. It is my opinion that more is preferable to less information. However, novice traders usually start with a few basic technical-analysis indicators and then add additional indicators as they gain experience. Too much analysis can, at times, cause confusion or can even lead to trading paralysis.

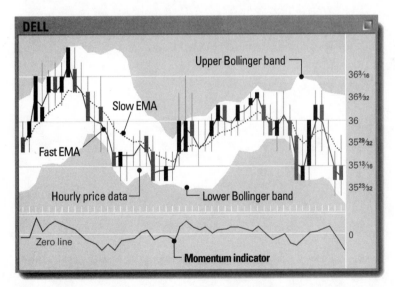

Figure 15.3 *Combined Technical-Analysis Indicators: Fast and Slow EMA Lines, Bollinger Bands, and the Momentum Indicator*

V

What to Trade

"We're lost, but we're making good time."

—*Yogi Berra*

THERE ARE SO MANY DIFFERENT STOCKS TO WATCH, FROM THE IPOs TO PENNY stocks, from Internet stocks to the utility stocks. How do you select a stock to trade out of the universe of approximately 8,000 NASDAQ and NYSE stocks at any point in time? What stocks do you trade? How are you alerted when a particular stock is gaining momentum? Section V of this book will attempt to answer the question of what to trade.

16

Trading Alerts

*"In the long run, we get no more than we have been
willing to risk giving."*

—*Sheldon Kopp*

The dictionary defines the noun "alert" as "an alarm of danger." In the stock market, an alert is an alarm of opportunity. Being an alert stock trader or investor basically means being continuously watchful and prompt in greeting the opportunity in an increasingly more volatile stock market. Swing traders use basic trading alerts to be prompted to take a closer view at a particular stock where the price momentum is changing. That alone can make the difference in being successful or unsuccessful in the market.

That said, in my opinion, an alert is not a signal to buy or sell stocks. An alert only prompts you to take a closer look. No one should jump in and buy or short sell a stock just because the stock symbol popped up in one of the computer alert windows. After being alerted that the stock has the potential to move up or down in price in the near future, the trader should conduct some form of technical analysis. The trading signals would confirm or reject the trader's hypothesis that the particular stock has the probability to move in the desired price direction.

It is naive to expect that all alerts will occur simultaneously in order to give a clear indication. The universe does not have to be lined up perfectly in order for a swing trader to obtain a clear signal that there is a price-momentum shift. It is only important that he or she recognize the great majority of the listed alerts in order to examine and analyze closely one particular stock, rather than another stock. In addition, the listed alerts are presented in a particular order. Shorter-term alerts that have an immediate price impact and are used most commonly by day traders are presented first. Longer-term alerts that have lasting or prolonged price impacts and are used commonly by swing traders and investors are presented last.

The NASDAQ Level II Screen

The shortest-term alert and the most important day trading alert tool is the NASDAQ Level II screen. As we learned in chapter 6, the NASDAQ Level II screen provides insight into the activities of many competing market makers who are dealing in the same stock. The NYSE stocks do not have the Level II information because there is only one assigned specialist that makes the market for a particular stock. There are several trading software products that package Level II screen information in formats that are relatively easy to track. It takes time for a new trader to become familiar with the Level II format and to interpret such information as the trading alerts. As the Level II information is crucial for the short-term traders, such as day traders, the presentation on the Level II screen is covered in a separate chapter.

Time and Sales Window

Not all trading software depicts the time and sales information in a separate window. The time and sales window is another short-term alert tool that is frequently used by day traders, as its focus is on minute intraday price swings. I must tell readers that the discussion to follow assumes you are using one of the more sophisticated trading software platforms, developed by CyBerCorp or TradeCast or similar software developers. Most significantly, the time and sales data is relevant to swing traders, in addition to day traders, because it will confirm the short-term price movement and whether the swing traders are getting in and out of positions at the very best price. This tool is important because it prints tick-by-tick what is actually being traded. In essence, time and sales reveal whether the public is buying or selling the stock. In addition, it reveals the actual size (i.e., number of shares) and the respective price of all buying and selling transactions.

You cannot see that information on the NASDAQ Level II screen. The time and sales window complements the Level II information. It informs traders not only what the market makers are willing to do, but also what is actually being executed right now in terms of price and size. There are traders that need only the Level II screen with the time and sales window in order to trade proficiently.

Figure 16.1 represents the time and sales window. In this particular example, the inside ASK price is $50^9/_{16}$, which represents the price at which the public is buying that particular stock. So all trades that were executed at the ASK price of $50^9/_{16}$ represent stock purchases. If the trader is considering taking a long position, then it would be reassuring to see the public buying that stock as well. A preponderance of buying transactions in the time and sales window can be translated as a bullish signal.

One way that the stock would go up in value is for the public to continue to buy it. The trader would like to see in the time and sales window that trades are being executed at the ASK price ($50^9/_{16}$). In addition, the trader needs to pay close attention to the size of the purchase. It would be reassuring to see the public buying that particular stock in

Figure 16.1 *Time and Sales Window with Purchasing Trades*

increments of 500 or 1,000 shares. Small lots of 100 or 200 shares do not really move the market.

Figure 16.2 represents the time and sales window with the preponderance of sales. A preponderance of selling transactions in the time and sales window can be interpreted as a bearish signal. In this particular example, the inside BID price is $50^{1}/_{2}$, which represents the price at which the public is selling that particular stock. All trades that were executed at $50^{1}/_{2}$ represent stock sales. If the trader is considering taking a short position (i.e., selling the stock first in anticipation of the price decline), then it would be a positive sign to see the public selling that stock.

Continuous stock selling is one way that the stock would decline in value. An indication of this is that the sales are being executed at the BID price. Again, the trader needs to pay close attention to the size of the sales. It would be reassuring to see the public selling that particular stock in increments of 500 or 1,000 shares, as small lots of 100 shares do not push the price down.

For liquid or actively traded stocks such as DELL, INTC, or MSFT, buy and sell trades are continuously being executed. Subsequently, the executed trades are continuously running in the time and sales window. For instance, all trades displayed in the time and sales window in figures 16.1 and 16.2 occurred that moment. However, the less liquid stocks need to have a stamped time next to each trade, so that the trader can

Figure 16.2 *Time and Sales Window with Selling Trades*

ascertain a momentum. The trader should be extremely cautious about trading stocks with little activity in the time and sales window. If the time and sales window does not show any activity, then there is no point in trading that stock.

In addition, the time and sales window might display prints of the trading activities where the executed price was in between the BID and ASK prices. That indicates that market makers either purchased the stock from the public for a price that is higher than the posted BID price, or sold the stock to the public for a price that is lower than the posted ASK price. Most likely, these trading transactions were completed through one of the ECNs, such as SelectNet. Finally, some displayed prices in the time and sales window are simply not accurate at that point in time. They might be old prices that are being submitted late.

The following is a summary of observable events displayed in the time and sales window that characterize a price increase or the potential for price momentum for a particular stock:

1. Buying trades executed at the ASK price in the time and sales window (indicating that the public is buying) represents the basic price-increase alert.

2. Buying trades at the ASK price executed in 500- or 1,000-share lots (indicating that the public is buying a substantial quantity of shares) also represents the price-increase alert.

3. Selling trades going off at BID price in the time and sales window (indicating that the public is selling) represents the basic price-decrease alert.

4. Selling trades executed at the BID price in lots of 500 or 1,000 shares (indicating that the public is selling a substantial quantity of shares) also represents a price-decrease alert.

Market Ticker

The market ticker is an alert tool often used by day traders that is commonly available in sophisticated trading software packages, such as CyberTrader and TradeCast. It reports on any inside BID and ASK quote changes for any stock. It can be set up to track price changes for the entire universe of NASDAQ or NYSE stocks, or it can be customized to follow only a select group of stocks. Market tickers are often used to track a group of commonly traded large-volume volatile stocks and to spot their price momentum. The trader can individually select particular stocks to be tracked.

For example, the trader might have a list of 10 or 20 stocks that meet his or her trading criteria. The trader would enter stock symbols of that list into his or her personal ticker. From that point on, the ticker would basically highlight all changes in the inside BID and ASK prices. In the event that the trader does not have such a personalized list of stocks, then the ticker can be programmed to track a universe of all NASDAQ or NYSE stocks that meet certain trading criteria. For example, a trading criterion could be: "stocks greater than $20 per share, with the spread less than $1/4$ and daily trading volume over 500,000 shares."

Ticker reports can have two distinctly different formats. The first option is to customize the ticker to report only the actual changes in the inside BID and ASK prices. This type of ticker format basically reports on change in the Level I price information. If the trader monitors only twenty stocks, this type of ticker would not move very fast. The ticker would report only when the actual price has changed. Therefore it is easy to follow. The other, less popular option is to customize the ticker to report all the changes within the inside BID and ASK side made by all market makers or ECNs. This is basically the Level II information limited to inside BID and ASK quotes.

Figure 16.3 represents the Level I and II ticker. The ticker report is also color-coded for easy reference. All stocks with the last uptick (or price increase) are reported in green. Stocks with the last downtick (or price decrease) are reported in red. Because figure 16.3 is not colored, all "green" upticks are displayed in bold, and all "red" downticks are displayed in shaded color. The most recent inside BID and ASK price change is reported on the top of the ticker page.

Usually, the trader would position the ticker window so it is prominently visible on the monitoring screen. For instance, the trader would notice that the Level I market ticker reported DELL twice, as illustrated in figure 16.3. Initially, the best BID and ASK price for DELL was $50^{1}/_{2}$ and $50^{9}/_{16}$. The ASK price for DELL was increased to $50^{9}/_{16}$, as indicated by the "green" (i.e., bold) ASK color. The next DELL showing was also "green." On this occasion, both the BID and ASK prices for DELL were increased.

MARKET TICKER (Level II)				
DELL	[MONT]	50½	50 ⅝	+ 1⅛
CIEN	[MLCO]	27¼	27 ⁵⁄₁₆	+ 1¼
DELL	[TUCK]	50½	50 ⅝	+ 1⅛
AMZN	[GSCO]	110⅞	110 ¹⁵⁄₁₆	+1¹⁄₁₆
DELL	[NEED]	50½	50 ⅝	+ 1⅛
DELL	[HRZG]	50½	50 ⅝	+ 1⅛
DELL	[PRUD]	50½	50 ⁹⁄₁₆	+1¹⁄₁₆
CSCO	[NAWE]	99⅞	99 ¹⁵⁄₁₆	+ ⅞
DELL	[RAGN]	50½	50 ⁹⁄₁₆	+1¹⁄₁₆
YHOO	[ABSA]	150	150 ⅛	+ 2¼

MARKET TICKER (Level I)			
DELL	50⁹⁄₁₆	50⅝	+ 1⅛
CIEN	27¼	27⁵⁄₁₆	+ 1¼
SUNW	101¹⁄₁₆	101 ⅛	- ⁵⁄₁₆
AMZN	110⅞	110 ¹⁵⁄₁₆	+1¹⁄₁₆
INTC	130⅜	110⁷⁄₁₆	+ ⁷⁄₁₆
INWO	26¹⁵⁄₁₆	27	- ⅝
DELL	50½	50⁹⁄₁₆	+1¹⁄₁₆
CSCO	99⅞	99 ¹⁵⁄₁₆	+ ⅞
WCOM	83¹⁵⁄₁₆	83⅞	+1⁵⁄₁₆
YHOO	150	150⅛	2¼

Figure 16.3 *Market Tickers (Level I and II Information)*

This display of a series of "green" DELL on the market ticker would alert the trader that DELL is moving up. In essence, the ticker report would be used as a stock-alert tool. At that time the trader would open the Level I and II screens for DELL, along with the time and sales window. Then the trader would open a chart of DELL with some technical charting analysis. The technical charting analysis window is already on the monitoring screen and loaded with a certain type of technical analysis (i.e., two exponential moving averages).

The following is a summary of observable events on the market ticker that characterize the potential for price momentum for a particular stock:

1. "Green" (or uptick) BID and ASK price on the Level I market ticker window represents the potential for a positive price momentum.

2. "Red" (or downtick) BID and ASK price on the Level I market ticker window represents the potential for a negative price momentum.

Top Advances and Declines

The "top advances and declines" report is an alert tool commonly used by swing traders. It shows the top ten stocks in terms of volume and largest dollar advance and decline for that particular point in time that day. Figure 16.4 displays such a report. The report is updated dynamically in real time, and thus it is always current. Most trading software packages provide this alert feature for the NASDAQ and NYSE stocks.

A trader would most likely focus on the top ten advances and declines. The volume indicator does not really change much. For the NASDAQ stocks, as illustrated in figure 16.4, it is always the same large-capitalization technology companies, such as Microsoft, Dell, Intel, and Cisco, that are being actively traded and thus displayed in the top volume window. However, the top ten advances and declines window is a different story. Different stocks each day will populate this window. The top advances and declines report is also biased toward the expensive and volatile technology stocks. Some screens let you select for dollar or percentage price changes. It would be more useful for swing traders to select absolute-dollar rather than the percentage changes, because the goal of swing trading is to exploit high absolute price change.

Because the report is ranked in absolute-dollar terms, expensive stocks are usually listed first. Some expensive Internet stocks with high intraday volatility are commonly on the top advances and declines list. For those expensive and volatile stocks, a $10 absolute price change is still a small relative percentage change. At one point in time, Amazon.com (AMZN) and Yahoo! (YHOO) were trading at the range of $200 plus per share. A $10 price change would constitute a 5 percent relative price change, which was quite a common occurrence at that time.

Some NASDAQ stocks that show up in the top advances and declines window are not really good stocks to trade. They tend to be small companies that have a low daily trading volume. It is difficult to get the buy-and-sell orders filled at the price the trader wants. Also, they

NASDAQ VOLUME		NASDAQ TOP ADVANCES		NASDAQ TOP DECLINES	
MSFT	9,852,700	ASDV	$+4\frac{5}{16}$	CPWR	$-2\frac{7}{8}$
DELL	8,752,300	NETA	$+4\frac{1}{4}$	PSQL	$-2\frac{5}{8}$
INTC	5,653,000	SDTI	$+3\frac{7}{8}$	MICA	$-2\frac{1}{4}$
WCOM	4,823,500	AMZN	$+3\frac{3}{8}$	DCTM	-2
CSCO	4,230,200	CIEN	$+2\frac{1}{4}$	PLAT	$-1\frac{15}{16}$
COMS	3,860,400	SEBL	$+2\frac{3}{16}$	AMAT	$-1\frac{7}{8}$
ORCL	3,243,100	HYSL	$+2\frac{1}{8}$	SYBS	$-1\frac{5}{8}$
AMZN	3,105,500	LGTO	$+2\frac{1}{16}$	JDEC	$-1\frac{7}{16}$
YHOO	3,025,820	CTXS	$+2$	BMCS	$-1\frac{5}{16}$

Figure 16.4 *Top Advances and Declines Alert*

show up all of a sudden after some particular bad (or good) news. The volatility is then short-lived. The stock price would then tend to stay at such levels. Subsequently, the traders cannot really trade these stocks.

52-Week and Daily High and Low

The "52-week" and "daily high and low" are two additional alert tools available to swing traders. The 52-week high-and-low alert is particularly important to swing traders, because it might indicate a price breakout above the long-term price-resistance level or below the long-term price-support level. This alert window is available in most trading software packages for the NASDAQ and NYSE stocks. It shows the top ten stocks that hit the new intraday or 52-week high and low prices. Some software packages have a price filter so the trader can exclude inexpensive stocks. The report is updated dynamically in real time. It is always current for that particular point in time. Figure 16.5 displays the 52-week highs-and-lows report for NASDAQ stocks. A similar report can be displayed for NYSE stocks.

The objective of this 52-week high is to focus on price breakouts. A breakout is a movement of a stock price out of an established trading range. The new 52-week high price would be interpreted as a stock-price breakout above its long-term price-resistance level. Resistance is the upper boundary of the trading range, where selling pressure tends to keep the price below the established range. When the new stock

NASDAQ 52 WEEK HIGH		NASDAQ 52 WEEK LOW	
AMGEN	78	JDEC	13 $15/16$
BMET	44½	BPAO	7 ¾
CHANF	10	ADSC	4
CPWM	28⅞	CDEN	6 $1/32$
CPTL	16½	CMDL	6 ¼
CSTR	17 $11/16$	DTLN	18 ⅜
KIDE	38⅞	DYMX	2 ¼
JAKK	18⅞	INPR	3 ¾
WCOM	93¾	LKFNP	10 $1/16$

Figure 16.5   *52-Week Highs and Lows*

symbol is being displayed on the day highs report, the trader could interpret this event as a stock-price breakout above the intraday price-resistance level.

If the price breaks out of the 52-week high price, the trader would expect the stock's momentum to continue. At that time, the trader would start to monitor that particular stock in anticipation of continued momentum. In other words, the trader would add that stock to those tracked by the market ticker. If the stock keeps showing up on the market ticker as a green uptick, then the trader might open Level I and II screens and technical-analysis charts for that stock.

The new 52-week low price would be translated as a stock-price breakout below the long-term support level. Support is the lower boundary of the trading range, where buying pressure tends to keep the price from decreasing below that established range. If the price breaks below the 52-week low price, the trader would expect that the stock price would continue to decline. Again, it's key here that the trader was alerted to the possibility to short sell that stock. Just as some traders mainly utilize the Level II screen and time and sales window, others trade profitably day in and day out by simply buying the 52-week high stocks and short selling the 52-week low stocks. This could be a risky strategy for swing traders, because—as I mentioned in chapter 10 on technical analysis—most price breakouts are false breakouts and will not sustain themselves over a period of days or weeks.

Earnings Reports

The quarterly earnings reports are by far the most important fundamental-analysis alert. There have been several academic studies designed to measure the impact and price reaction of the corporate quarterly earnings reports. The most often quoted study is the work by Rendleman, Jones, and Latane, which was published in November 1982 in the *Journal of Financial Economics*. In that study the authors compared the firm's actual quarterly earnings numbers to the financial analysts' estimates of the corporate earnings. The authors ranked all of the firm's positive and negative earnings surprises into 10 possible categories.

The extremely high positive earnings surprises were grouped into the top categories. For instance, category 10 represents the great earnings surprises of the firms whose actual quarterly earnings were greater than

2 standard deviations from the analysts' consensus earnings estimates. Category 9 represents the firms whose actual quarterly earnings were higher than expected but by a smaller margin than in category 10.

Category 5, in the middle, represents the firms that reported the same earnings as estimated by the financial analysts. The standard deviation between the actual and estimated earnings was close to 0. This group can be labeled as the "no earnings surprises" group.

The extremely negative earnings surprises were grouped into the bottom category 1, which is labeled "negative earning surprises." This category represents the firms whose actual quarterly earnings were less than the 2 standard deviations from the analysts' consensus earnings estimates. The higher category 2 represents the firms whose actual quarterly earnings were lower than expected but by a smaller margin than in category 1.

Figure 16.6 depicts this relationship between the price reaction and quarterly earnings reports. The authors measured on a horizontal axis the time in terms of days before and after the quarterly earnings reports were issued. On the vertical axis, the authors measured the cumulative average excess return above or below the average stock market return.

Please note that stock prices began to react several days before the actual date of the announcement. The stock prices of the companies that would have positive earnings surprises were going up dramatically in value two to three days before the actual earnings reports were issued. Conversely, the stock prices of the companies that would have an announcement of negative earnings surprises were going down in value continuously and substantially twenty days before the actual earnings reports were issued. This is most likely the result of information leakage by the company insiders.

After the issuance of the earnings report, the stocks that could be labeled as the positive earnings surprises continued to increase in price. The pace of the price increase is dramatically smaller, but nevertheless there is a positive price momentum. Conversely, the stocks that could be labeled as the negative earning surprises continued to decrease in price after the earnings report's issuance. The rate of the price decline is dramatically smaller than what was experienced before the earnings report, but nevertheless the negative price momentum exists. Companies who did not have any positive or negative earnings surprises continued to perform comparable to the stock market average.

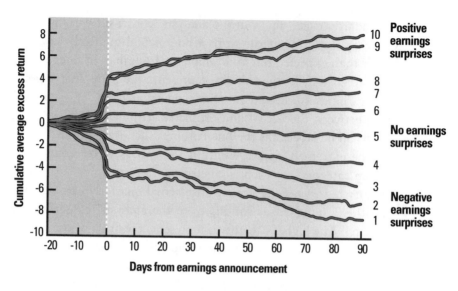

Figure 16.6 *Price Reaction and Quarterly Earnings Reports*

The point of the study is that public information, such as corporate quarterly earnings reports, continue to have an impact on prices long after the announcement. Most of the price change is incorporated before the actual quarterly earnings reports were made public. This study would support the claim that the stock market is less than efficient when it comes to the announcement of the quarterly earnings reports. My recommendation to swing investors and traders would be to closely monitor the quarterly earnings reports.

The advent of eavesdropping on earnings conference calls through the Internet and the deliberate practice by companies of understating earnings estimates prior to announcement in order to achieve a positive surprise have greatly complicated the use of earnings announcements as a viable tool. There are several Internet sites, such as www.vcall.com, www.bestcalls.com, www.streetevents.com, and www.streetfusion.com, that provide live audio public access to earnings conference calls between the corporate executives and Wall Street professionals. Keep in mind that these conference calls tend to be rather long and provide a mountain of financial fundamental-analysis data that is rather difficult to interpret.

Earnings surprises, either positive or negative, are clearly a major development. This is particularly true for the growth stocks in the high-technology sectors, which have the exceptionally high price earnings (PE) multiple. The only reason that the market is paying a premium price for these stocks is because of the anticipation of a proportionately high earnings growth. When earnings do not materialize, many growth investors feel cheated, and thus there is a mass exodus. Analysts' stock recommendation upgrades and particularly downgrades are relevant because a few analysts that are employed by large retail brokerage firms are influential and have substantial followings.

Cash Dividends

Although dividend-paying stocks tend to be less price volatile and more established "old economy" companies, these stocks are nevertheless still viable swing-trading stocks. Declaration of higher cash dividends serves as a bullish trading alert because it is interpreted as a sign of the management's confidence in continued prospects of higher future earnings.

The board of directors commonly declares cash dividends on a quarterly basis on a date that is commonly known as the "dividend declaration date." The declared dividends are paid out of corporate net earnings and are most likely in the same magnitude as the last declared quarterly dividends. The board is authorized to announce dividends of any size, even larger than the current corporate earnings. The board will also establish the "date of record" for the cash dividend, which means that the cash dividend is paid only to current shareholders of record at this specified date.

To "simplify" the process and answer the commonly asked question of who is entitled to the declared cash dividends, the brokers have created the ex-dividend date. The ex-dividend date basically takes into account the time required to clear the trading transaction between the stock buyer and seller. The settlement date is the date when a buyer pays for the security and a seller delivers the security and receives the proceeds of the sale. The standard settlement date is three business days after the trade day, or as the brokers call it, T + 3. The transactions carried out on a cash basis settle on the same day as the trade.

June 15 →	July 12 →	July 13 →	July 15 →	Aug 20
Declaration date	Trade date	Ex-dividend date	Date of record	Payment date

Figure 16.7 *Settlement Dates*

Therefore, in order to receive the cash dividend, the investor must be identified as the shareholder of record at the date specified by the board to be the date of record. Because the standard settlement takes three business days, the investor needs to purchase the stock before the ex-dividend day, which is two days prior to the date of record. In addition, the board will also pick an arbitrary date when the dividend checks are physically mailed or electronically deposited to the investors' brokerage accounts. This "simplified" process is summarized and explained in figure 16.7.

Declaration of increased cash dividends has a tangible economic meaning. The higher cash dividend goes directly into the shareholders' pockets. It boosts the future stream of income to the shareholders, which will automatically increase the net present value of that investment. In other words, higher declared dividends add additional value to the shareholders.

In addition, the higher declared dividends translate into a clear market signal that the company management is confident about the continued prospects of higher future corporate earnings. The corporate management is reluctant to cut the existing dividends because it will translate into the public acknowledgement that the company has declining future earnings. Subsequently, management will cut the cash dividends only as the absolute last resort. Conversely, management will increase cash dividends only if it is absolutely convinced that there has been a permanent increase in corporate profitability and thus the prospect of higher future earnings. Consequently, the increased cash dividends serve as a clear signal from the corporate insiders that the corporate-earnings capabilities are lastingly enhanced.

The February 1969 paper by Fama, Fisher, Jensen, and Roll, published in the *International Economic Review*, attempted to examine the nature of the stock market reaction to the announcements of higher cash dividends. The authors looked at the stocks' excess investment return as compared to the average S & P's 500 index return in the vicinity of the declaration event. They concluded that the price behavior of common stocks following the declaration of a cash-dividend increase deviates significantly from the average returns of all other stocks.

The results of the study are depicted in figure 16.8, which shows the price reaction for all stocks that had declared higher cash dividends. The study revealed that the stocks had begun to increase in price prior to the higher-cash-dividend announcement. Again, that makes sense. The corporate earnings went up, so the stock prices went up, and thus the stocks' return exceeded the market average. The increase in price is substantial. It occurred many days or weeks prior to the declaration of the higher cash dividend. The relatively high corporate earnings are the leading force or cause that directed the company's management to declare the higher cash dividend.

After the higher-cash-dividend announcement date, the stocks' prices, and thus the stock returns, continued to increase somewhat compared to the overall stock market return. The stock market has received a clear confirmation that corporate earnings were permanently enhanced. In other words, the higher cash dividend resulted in continued higher prices or higher returns after the announcement date. Figure 16.8 demonstrates this point clearly.

Stock Splits and Stock Dividends

A stock split does not impact any corporate revenues or expenses, and it does not change the firm's total market capitalization. The stock split only changes proportionately the size of the stock units in which the ownership is bought and sold. For instance, when the corporation announces a stock split of two for one, the corporate pie is still the same, except there are now two smaller pieces instead of one large piece. Instead of having one ownership share bought or sold at $100, we now have two shares being traded at $50 a piece.

It is often argued that all stock market participants respond favorably to stock splits because the split brings the stock price into a more affordable trading range. After the stock split, the lower stock price might have stronger appeal to investors and thus increased demand for the stock.

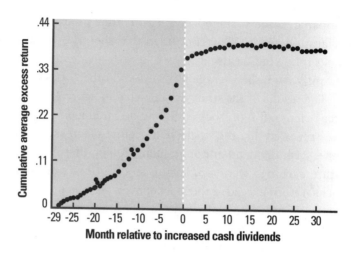

Figure 16.8 *Stock Price Reaction to Increased Cash Dividends*

Some market participants believe that stock splits act as leading indicators for a future increase in dividends. They claim that a stock split is often followed by the corporate announcement of increased dividends. However, other market analysts believe that a preponderance of many stock-split announcements in the stock market is an early indication of an overvalued stock market. When the corporate stocks are expensive, the board of directors might announce the stock split just to keep the stock prices in a reasonable trading range. Subsequently, some analysts believe that too many stock splits in the market are the early signs of an overpriced stock market, and thus a general price correction might be forthcoming.

Several academic studies were undertaken to examine the nature of the stock market reaction to the announcements of stock splits. The most often quoted result is the February 1969 research paper by Fama, Fisher, Jensen, and Roll that was published in the *International Economic Review*. The authors looked at the stocks' excess return as compared to the average S & P's 500 index return in the vicinity of the event. They concluded that the price behavior of common stocks following the declaration of stock splits does not deviate significantly from the average returns of all other stocks.

The results of the study are depicted in figure 16.9, which shows the price reaction for all stocks that had declared stock splits. The study revealed that the stocks had begun to increase in price prior to the stock-split announcement. This makes sense. Most likely, the corporate earnings are increased, stock prices are going up, and thus the stocks' return exceeds the market average. The increase in price is substantial and it occurred during many days or weeks prior to the declaration of the stock splits, so it cannot be attributed to insider trading. In fact, the relatively high stock price is the leading force or cause that directed the company to declare a stock split.

However, after the stock-split announcement date, the stocks' prices and return remained flat and steady compared to the overall stock market return. In other words, the stock split did not result in continued higher prices or higher returns after the stock-split announcement date. Figure 16.9 illustrates this point clearly.

In contrast, reverse stock splits create a smaller number of outstanding shares. The reverse split results in an upward stock-price adjustment. For instance, a 1-to-4 stock split would increase the stock price by 4 times and decrease the number of outstanding shares by 4 times as well. The corporate management will authorize the reverse split in order to raise the price of the stock. The exchanges usually require

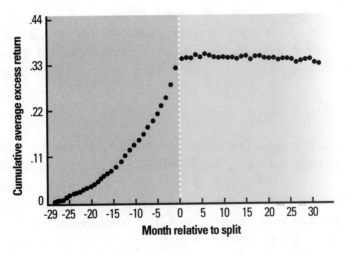

Figure 16.9 *Stock Price Reaction to Stock Splits*

that the stock prices remain over a certain threshold in order for the firm to remain listed on the exchange. (The minimum stock price is only one of several exchange listing requirements.) The reverse stock split is the easiest way to keep the price over that level.

The relationship between the stock price reaction to reverse stock splits is diametrically opposite from the previous figure 16.9. Most likely, corporate earnings were already declining and stock prices were therefore going down. Thus the stocks' return was already below the market average. The price decrease most likely occurred during many days or weeks prior to the declaration of the reverse stock split. Indeed, the relatively low stock price is the cause that directed the company to declare the reverse stock split. After the reverse-stock-split announcement date, the stock returns remained low and steady compared to the overall stock market return. In other words, the reverse stock split alone does not result in continued lower prices or lower returns after the reverse-stock-split announcement. The company's stock prices are declining due to the company's adverse economics and are not the result of a reverse-stock-split announcement.

Stock dividends are very similar to stock splits and are fairly rare, especially among the technology stocks preferred by swing traders. Nothing of substance happens. The firm's board of directors has the discretion to declare or "pay" stock dividends to the company's shareholders. For instance, a 10 percent stock dividend means that a shareholder of record who owns 100 shares will receive 10 additional shares of the stock. It must be noted that the price of the stock will also be adjusted accordingly downward by 10 percent. The stock dividend only changes proportionately the size of the stock units in which the ownership is bought and sold.

News

News is an important factor that will drive the stock price in the short run. Under the "news" heading I do not include any news about corporate earnings, declaration of cash dividends, or stock splits because this crucial financial information deserves (and has received) separate headings. *News* is narrowly defined here as the reports of recent business events, such as mergers, acquisitions, changes in management, new products, and new accounts, which all have the potential to impact a stock's price.

The news of corporate mergers, acquisitions, changes in management, new products, and new accounts has the potential to quickly influence the opinion of many stock buyers and sellers, and thus it can dramatically shift the demand for the stock. In the short run, the stock price can jolt out of the equilibrium and quickly go up or down.

Mergers and Acquisitions

News about mergers and acquisitions has a lasting impact on stock prices. As a general rule, when a publicly held firm is acquired, then that firm's stock price will inevitably go up. The reasoning is straightforward. In order to agree to be acquired, the company demands and receives a stock price that is a premium over its current price. Why would the company's board of directors agree for the firm to be acquired if the price is not right?

The opposite is true for the acquirer, or the new parent firm. The acquirer firm will most likely end up paying for the acquisition with its own stock. That simply means stock-ownership dilution. After the merger or acquisition, there will be proportionately more shareholders having an ownership claim on the corporate earnings. Most likely, the corporate parent earnings would not increase proportionately after the merger or acquisition. The merger or acquisition is also a costly endeavor that will reflect on the company's bottom line. The merger or acquisition will also disrupt business operations for both firms. It will take some time for the new management to complete the merger or acquisition. Subsequently, it is anticipated that the acquirer firm (the new parent firm) will experience a stock price decline in the short run.

The monster merger between the Internet pioneer America Online (AOL) and media and entertainment giant Time Warner is a good example of the merger-and-acquisition effect on stock prices. After the merger announcement, the stocks of the firm to be acquired, Time Warner, skyrocketed 39 percent in one day, whereas the shares of the acquirer (the new parent firm), AOL, declined approximately 2 percent.

In addition, the AOL shares kept declining in the following days of trading. As the AOL shares kept declining in value, the merger deal became less and less attractive for the Time Warner shareholders who were paid with AOL shares. As the AOL shares started declining in value in the following trading days, so did the shares of Time Warner.

Trading on News

For the long-term investor, the good and bad news and its impact are only blips on the price chart or in the regular short-term price fluctuations. All companies, including the strong blue chip companies (which are the established and mature companies in their industries), have occasional bad news. The strong companies eventually overcome their short-term business difficulties, and the stock will rebound. Time is on the side of the long-term investors. However, swing traders do not have the benefit of time to weather the storm and wait for the stock to rebound. If their capital is tied up in that stock, they are out of business. Thus the short-term traders cannot afford to ignore the news about the company.

Then, all news is not created equal. The media has a vested interest in hyping up the story and making a lot of noise. "Noisy" investment headlines sell the papers and grab our attention. Investment noise is always a part of stock market news. It is up to the individual trader or investor to filter out the noise and concentrate only on important news about the company.

The important news is quickly disseminated throughout the stock market. The individual traders or short-term investors are not the first recipients of such news. It's likely that any important news was already leaked to the large shareholders and the press before it was publicly announced. The stock market has, in all probability, already reacted to such news before the public announcement. With the shift in the stock's supply-and-demand schedule, the stock price would change. If the news is perceived by a majority of the market participants to be favorable news, then the stock price would increase. That increase in price would already be displayed in one of the earlier price alerts, such as the real-time Level II screen, the time and sales window, the market ticker, and the daily high and low.

For instance, the traders or short-term investors who are monitoring Cisco stock, as an example, would already notice and observe the positive price momentum on the Level II screen, in the time and sales window, on the market ticker, or in the daily high and low window. They would have already seen Cisco's green symbol on the market ticker, its counterclockwise movement on the Level II screen, and large buy orders going off at the ASK price in the time and sales window. Depending on the relative importance of the news, the traders and short-term investors would see the Cisco symbol (CSCO) popping up in the daily high or even the 52-week high window. They would see the positive price movement, although they would not know why the stock is moving up. The public announcement of the news would only provide the confirmation and explanation of the underlying reasons for such a price increase.

The traders or investors who are not monitoring Cisco stock at that time will most likely receive the alert about Cisco's good fortunes from the electronic news reports, such as CNBC or Bloomberg. At that point in time, the astute traders or investors must assimilate and quickly interpret the news about Cisco and quickly decide whether such news will have a lasting impact on Cisco stock. Although they are not the first individuals in the stock market to receive such news, they are not the last investors or traders to receive it either.

It takes time for news to reach most market participants. There are many investors, particularly the long-term investors, who will read about such news in the newspaper on the next business day. Again, the key to trading on news is to assimilate the news quickly and interpret the relative importance of the news on Cisco's future-earnings potential. If your analysis concludes that Cisco's corporate earnings will improve in the future, then higher earnings will attract more buyers and fewer sellers of Cisco stock. At that time, the demand schedule for Cisco stock would continue to increase, and the supply schedule would continue to decline. The ultimate result is the stock-price increase.

The trader then needs to act quickly, before the new information is fully appreciated by most of the market participants and thus fully reflected in the new equilibrium price. Act quickly, because the probability is high that he or she is not the only one who interpreted such news as being important and having a lasting positive impact on the corporate earnings. Other investors and traders are already buying the stock and driving the price up.

Swing traders can afford to pay less attention to such macroeconomic news as the performance of the general economic indicators. This is true because there is a buffer between the individual stock impact and general economic developments. It will take time for the general macroeconomic news to alter demand for the stock; it will take time for such news to trickle down through the market and impact the individual stock, because the news is not directly related to the individual company.

Unfortunately, that time frame can be rather short. For example, changes in the Fed's monetary policy will have a quick impact on the interest-rate-sensitive stocks, such as the bank stocks. Likewise, the Federal Reserve chairman's comments before a congressional committee can result in a substantial and general sell-off or acquisition and thus affect the swing trader's stock positions.

Direct company news, however, such as mergers, acquisitions, changes in management, new products, and new accounts, have a direct impact on the company's stock price. It is not a question of whether the direct company news affects the stock price through a shift in the company's supply and demand of the stock, but rather what the magnitude of the supply-and-demand shift is. In other words, how many new stock buyers and sellers will enter or exit the market for this stock based on the new information?

In my opinion, swing traders should pose two basic questions regarding the announcement of direct company news:

1. What is the direction of the stock's supply-and-demand shift? Will the news bring more or fewer buyers and sellers for that stock? In other words, will this news indicate an increase or decrease in future corporate earnings?

2. What is the magnitude of the shift in the stock's supply-and-demand schedule? If the news is important, or perceived to be important by many stock market participants, then many stock buyers and sellers will simultaneously enter or exit the market for that stock and the stock will quickly and dramatically adjust to a new equilibrium. With that in mind, ask yourself, what is the magnitude of the news impact on future corporate earnings?

Any news that deals with the firm's core business is important. If the firm is in the high-technology sector, then anything that impacts the firm's proprietary technology is important. Does the news mean that the firm is losing its technological advantage? Is there a new firm with a "killer application" software product that will make the firm's product technologically obsolete?

Finally, trading on news does not mean blindly buying or selling stocks just because the stocks were mentioned favorably on CNBC or through another media outlet. Favorable or unfavorable company news only serves as an alert to take a closer look at one particular stock. There is no substitute for more thorough analysis. Examine one or two technical-analysis charts, such as the moving averages crossover for asserting the price trend and the Bollinger bands for determining the price supports and resistance. If you are a trader, look on the Level II screen for market makers' movement. Research a few fundamental-analysis ratios. But do not blindly chase the media's hot stocks of the day or the week, because such a strategy is costly. You might simply end up buying the stock at the top.

Seasonal Events

The writer Mark Twain once observed a simple and universal stock market seasonal rule that was true a century ago and is still true today. He wrote, "October is one of the dangerous months to speculate in stocks. The other months are July, January, April, September, November, May, March, June, December, August, and February."

All truisms aside, seasonal indicators are difficult to defend. If the seasonal rules are true and effective, then all market participants would eventually use the rules, and thus all of us would be on the same side of the market exchange during that part of the year. And, it must also be noted that the seasonal effects do not appear to be substantially large. In other words, the magnitude of these events is relatively small, and thus no one will become rich by simply implementing the seasonal trading "rules."

If you're a buyer and adhering to the conventions of the seasonality effects, you should buy before the seasonality effects kick in to capture the effect and to buy the stocks at the lower price. If you're a seller, you should sell after the seasonality effects kick in to capture the effect and to sell the stocks at the higher price. It must be noted that the seasonal stock market effects have a larger price impact on smaller-capitalization firms than they do on the large-cap stocks.

The most common stock market seasonal rules are summarized as follows:

1. The summer doldrums effect
2. The January effect

3. The pre-holiday effect

4. The month-end effect

5. The day of the week effect

An old Wall Street adage is "Sell in May, then go away." There is a great deal of truth to this adage. Simply stated, investors and traders are less active in summer months because they go away on vacation. Trading volume drops dramatically in summer months. For instance, the monthly change in the NYSE trading volume from the previous month average drops significantly in the summer months of June, July, August, and September. On the other hand, the beginning months in a year (January, February, March) exhibit substantially larger average trading volumes. With the trading volume down in summer months, the price volatility is up.

Also, it is not surprising that both the S & P's 500 and the NASDAQ Composite indices have underperformed in the summer months as compared with the rest of the year. With a lower trading volume in the summer months, stock prices tend to decline as well. Since 1982, the S & P's 500 index monthly percentage gain for the months of August, September, and October was less than 0.5 percent. On the other hand, months at the beginning and end of the year seem to generate the largest monthly gains for the S & P's 500 index. For instance, since 1982, February produced on average a more than 2 percent monthly gain, followed closely by January, March, November, and December, which recorded on average more than 1.5 percent monthly gains.

The January effect exists because investors tend to oversell stocks in the previous December for tax purposes. In other words, investors shed (sell) their "dogs" from their investment portfolio in order to minimize their tax liability for that year, and the subsequent selling surge results in lower stock prices for the month of December. Professional fund managers also sometimes tend to sell the underperforming stocks in December in order to avoid having these stocks appear on year-end reports.

In the next year there is a resurgence of buying interest. Investors and mutual funds have cash to invest, and some stocks look like bargains now. Subsequently the market tends to rebound in the first several trading days of the following month, and thus we see the January effect. Indeed, the average return in January tends to be approximately

3 percent higher than the average return for the other months in the year.

The 1988 "Incredible January Effect" study by Haugen and Lakonishok estimates that a large percentage of all average differences between the rates of return for small and large capitalization firms comes in the first 5 trading days in January. The first 5 trading days in January account for approximately 27 percent of the annual differences between the returns of small and large firms during the period between 1963 and 1979. Table 16.1 depicts this January impact.

The pre-holiday effect means that stock prices tend to go up each trading day before the holiday market close. There are 10 holidays for which the major stock exchanges close: Martin Luther King Day, Presidents Day, Good Friday, Memorial Day, Independence Day, Labor Day, Election Day, Thanksgiving, Christmas, and New Year's Day. The only logical explanation for this effect is that short sellers tend to close their short positions before the holidays because they may fear that the companies might announce some good news while the market is closed.

The month-end effect basically derives from the propensity for stock prices to increase during the last day of every month and the first four days at the beginning of the month. In essence, the five continuous trading days tend to be good for investors with long positions. The following are the reasons for this:

- Mutual funds investment of monthly proceeds from the monthly stock purchase plans

Table 16.1 *Annual Extra Difference by Trading Day*

Trading Day	Percentage Difference
First trading day in January	10
Second trading day in January	6
Third trading day in January	4
Fourth trading day in January	4
Fifth trading day in January	3
All other trading days in the year	73

- Mutual funds investment of monthly proceeds from the monthly 401(k) deferred-compensation plans
- Month-end portfolio adjustments by financial institutions

The day of the week effect states that there are some differences in the expected percentage changes in stock prices depending on which day of the week trading is conducted. Review of the historical records between 1962 and 1978 revealed that the S & P's 500 index had a propensity to decline in value on Monday, whereas Wednesday, Thursday, and Friday tended to exhibit higher prices. The financial analysts refer to the observation that Mondays exhibit negative returns as the "weekend effect." Most of the price decline on Monday occurs within the first hour of opening. Finally, Tuesday tended to have positive returns, but with a much lower price increase than Wednesday, Thursday, and Friday. Figure 16.10 depicts this effect. Please keep in mind that the results reflect the stock market data from the 1960s and 1970s, and that a study of the present stock market environment might generate a different outcome.

In addition, there is one more general and commonly accepted effect—the presidential election effect. The presidential election effect is not really a seasonal effect because, thankfully, we do not have annual presidential elections. Nevertheless, the presidential elections have a pervasive impact on the overall U.S. economy and thus subsequently on the U.S. stock market.

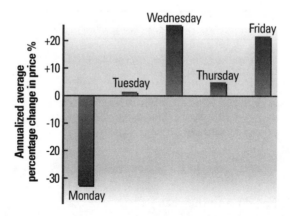

Figure 16.10 *Days of the Week Effect*

The logic behind the presidential election effect is straightforward. White House incumbents tend to sponsor expansionary fiscal and monetary policies in order to ensure a booming economy during the election year to assure the president's reelection or to help his or her party win the election. The market data supports this hypothesis. There is a strong positive correlation between the presidential election and the S & P's 500 index performance. The S & P's 500 index increased in 11 out of 12 presidential elections since 1952, with the exception of the 1960 election. The average annual increase in the S & P's 500 index during the 12 elections was approximately 11 percent.

Stock Screening

Stock screening is essentially the process of data mining for stocks that meet the specified screening criteria in the universe of all stocks in the database. Microsoft Network's MoneyCentral Investor (www.Money Cen tral.MSN.com) and Yahoo! Finance (Finance.Yahoo.com) are the two most commonly used Internet-based stock search engines.

These two stock search engines have a pull-down menu of different predefined and common investment criteria. The price-momentum trader could specify the following stock screening criteria:

1. Market capitalization greater than 500 million
2. Average daily trading volume in the last year greater than 500,000 shares
3. Percent price change in the last week greater than 10 percent
4. Percent price change in the last month greater than 20 percent
5. Percent price change, by rank, in the last quarter

The result is a list of the large- and mid-cap companies with plenty of trading liquidity (i.e., the average trading volume is greater than 500,000 shares). Most importantly, the current stock prices of the companies on the list are changing at a faster pace than the rest of the market. If the screening-match list is too large, the next step would be to increase the weekly and monthly percentage price change criteria from 10 and 20 percent to 20 and 30 percent, which would subsequently narrow the list to fewer stocks. The result of the stock screening is only the first alert. It is up to the investor or trader to take a closer look at the stock to determine whether the stock deserves additional consideration.

Insider Trading

Insiders are any officers or directors of the company, or any person that owns 10 percent of the company stock, or anyone with nonpublic information about the company. The SEC stipulates that it is illegal for anyone to trade a security on an organized exchange if the person has taken advantage of material inside information that is not disclosed to the general public. This statement begs the question, What constitutes material inside information? The answer is rather vague. Material inside information can be any information of which public dissemination can affect the market price of that security.

The SEC requires that all insiders report to the SEC within 10 days of the following month any trading transactions they have made in the company's shares. The SEC will summarize and publish this information monthly in the "Official Summary of Insider Transactions." The SEC information is then analyzed, repackaged, and published by several financial information services companies. One such service is the Vickers Stock Research Corporation of New Jersey, which publishes the "Weekly Insider Report." In addition, Value Line Inc. (www.value line.com) issues an index of the insiders' decisions. Another source is the Insider Trader (www.insidertrader.com), which publishes weekly a free listing of the select companies that filed the SEC insider activity reports. Another online insider trading resource is Thomson Financial (www.thomsoninvest.com), which also chronicles insider activities.

It seems intuitively clear that a large selling volume by the company insiders would indicate a bearish sign, whereas a large buying volume would constitute a bullish signal. However, interpretation of the limited insider trading data that is available is not that simple. First of all, the data on insider trading is published rather late. By the time the SEC receives the insider trading form (within 10 days of the following month) and issues the report ("Official Summary of Insider Transactions"), the market has most likely already reacted to the company news that prompted the initial insider trading in the first place. My point here is that it is probably too late for the general public to take advantage of this information about the insider trading, because the market already made the price correction on that stock.

In addition, the SEC prohibits corporate insiders from short selling their stock. That means that there is no clear bearish signal derived from the insiders' actions. Also, insiders do not have any incentive to engage in short-term trading in the company stock. The SEC rule stipulates that any short-term trading profit made by the company insiders (where the short term is anything less than six months) must be returned to the company treasury. Consequently, insiders may only take long-term stock positions. Because the company insiders are not active traders, there are only a few trading signals at hand.

Most importantly, insiders buy and sell the company's shares for many different and personal reasons, which have little to do with the company's business performance. Sometimes the senior executive managers are buying the company's shares in order to exercise a stock option, which was most likely granted by the board of directors several years ago. Often, the insiders are selling the company's shares in order to raise money to buy or build new homes (or for any other large purchases). Frequently, the insiders are selling their shares simply to diversify their investment portfolio. Some are simply cashing out in order to retire. All of these sell orders do not indicate any potential for an adverse price trend. Indeed, there are plenty of circumstances where a few insiders sell the company shares, whereas the other insiders are buying the shares.

Some insiders, such as the company founders, are prohibited from selling the company's shares for several years after the initial public offering (IPO). Some insiders, such as the executive managers, are fully vested with the stock only after waiting a few years following the IPO. These conditions were inserted in the IPO documentation to promote the long-term tenure of the initial ownership and management structure. In other words, the company founders and senior executives have a vested financial interest to remain in the company for at least a few years following the IPO. After a few years, these insiders are free to sell their shares, which they generally do. And thus the consequent selling activities do not disclose any additional insight about the future of the company.

Some insiders sell some company shares every year for tax purposes. Tax accountants call this selling activity "tax planning," and the objective is to minimize the long-term tax liability. In addition, SEC rule No. 144 provides restrictions on the sale of the so-called "control stocks," which are the stocks owned by the company insiders. The SEC restrictions stipulate how many and how often the insiders can sell the company's shares on the open exchange. For listed stocks, the company insider cannot sell more than 1 percent of the total shares outstanding, or the average weekly volume within one quarter. Subsequently, the insiders tend to sell some shares every year when they are allowed to sell, and thus this does not represent a selling signal.

Finally, insiders are afraid of the potential liability if they trade the company stock. They do not want to be caught up in a legal quagmire and be charged by the federal government with insider trading. The insiders cannot trade during any of the four months in a year when the company's quarterly earnings are announced. If they do, then they are trading based on inside information, which has not yet been disclosed publicly. During other times of the year, insiders may know information about some new material developments—such as the potential for a merger, acquisition, or new account—or anything that can be construed or misconstrued by our litigious society as "material insider information." Consequently, insiders are often advised by their legal counsel to simply avoid trading the company's share.

I believe that tracking insider trading activities is a time-consuming endeavor that seldomly provides any meaningful information. The information that the general public receives about insider trading is always late (i.e., several days after the insiders already bought or sold the stock). Most importantly, it is extremely difficult to interpret such information precisely and accurately. In short, company insiders buy or sell the company shares for many different and personal reasons. If you do not know the reasons behind the insider trading, then do not trade on such information.

CHAPTER
17
Trading Initial Public Offerings

"Save a little money each month, and at the end of the year you'll be surprised at how little you have."

—*Ernest Haskins*

Initial public offerings (IPOs) are not for everyone. IPOs are inherently volatile, explosive, extremely difficult to acquire, and, most significantly, different than seasoned stocks. Because the rules for trading IPOs are different than those you'd apply to seasoned stocks, I have decided they warrant a separate chapter.

From the perspective of the more mundane world of stock trading and investing, IPOs are shrouded in mystique, which is due to the fact that they remain off limits to most traders. Yet IPOs seem to have a great deal of popular appeal. This is not surprising. Some of the fastest and most spectacular gains made in the equity markets in 1998 and 1999 came from IPOs. Conversely, the stock market's brutal sell-off of technology stocks in April and May 2000 battered the high-flying dot-com IPOs. Some of these high-flying IPOs, such as TheGlobe.com and DrKoop.com, which made spectacular first-day trading gains, are now trading for $5 or less, and thus have been reduced to the status of "penny stocks."

One explanation for the IPO popularity can be found with the popular press, which publishes story after story about huge IPO successes.

For instance, Microsoft was trading close to $120 at the end of 1999, which was a record level since its November 1986 IPO. When the price adjustments for eight stock splits since 1986 are made, the Microsoft IPO price would have been approximately 12.5 cents. A $1,000 investment in Microsoft in November of 1986 would have been worth approximately $958,000 thirteen years later at the end of 1999.

The more recent IPO history is just as impressive. By all accounts, the IPO market was extremely hot in 1999. Unprecedented economic prosperity, a strong bull market, and a revolution in information technology fueled IPOs in 1999. The amount of equity capital raised in 1999 IPOs reached an unprecedented level of $69 billion. A total of 546 IPOs debuted in 1999, which was less than the record 872 IPOs in 1996, which raised $50 billion. The average IPO in 1999 raised $126 million in equity capital. The largest IPOs came from United Parcel Service Inc. ($5.4 billion) and Goldman Sachs Group ($3.6 billion).

1999 Hot and Not-So-Hot IPOs

Many Wall Street players allege that IPO stands for "immediate profit opportunities." It is clearly an opportunity for profit if you were one of the privileged few able to obtain shares of the new hot issues. The hot IPO market in 1999 was driven mostly by the huge retail demand for the new issues of start-up Internet companies. It seems that small investors wanted to get in on the ground floor of the potential high-tech stars.

Hot IPOs are often oversubscribed to by a huge factor. If there are only 2 million IPO shares available and there is demand for 10 million shares at the given public offering price, then it is not surprising that the new issue will open up in the aftermarket with a huge gap up. Underwriters also indirectly benefit from the big jump upward in the first day of trading because such news will create additional excitement for the stock and for the underwriting business as well. As the stock price continues to go up, the underwriter will have an easier time selling the next IPO to the public. All the underwriter has to do is point to the previous IPO performance.

However, IPOs are not a license to print money. More skeptical IPO market observers point out that in many cases, IPO stands for "it's probably overpriced." That statement is even truer in years when the IPO market is not as hot as it was in 1999. Even in the hot 1999 IPO market, there were a number of IPOs that performed poorly on the first day of trading. For instance, MotherNature.com lost 21 percent in value after the first day of trading. Despite the substantial overall positive record of the 1999 IPO market, approximately 26 percent of 1999 IPOs fell below their offer prices by the end of the first trading day.

In the long run, the IPO picture is not very bright. Most companies turn out not to be the next Microsoft or Dell. As the IPO luster fades, the IPO stock prices return to Earth. A few scant years later, many IPOs are no longer listed because they were most likely bought out by a competitor or they were out of business. In fact, 17 percent of all 1998 and 1999 dot-com IPOs are now penny stocks that trade for $5 or less.

One academic study published in the *Journal of Finance* in 1991 by Jay Ritter revealed that the 3-year return on IPOs was approximately 34 percent, whereas a broad sample of companies in the same industry generated an approximate 62 percent return. This is not to say that IPOs are not a profitable long-term investment, because they are. Rather, equity investments in more mature or seasoned companies provide a higher rate of return with a lower risk.

However, as you will discover later in this chapter, the volatility of IPO stock performances can make them risky but rewarding stocks for swing traders. Before getting to that, however, we first need to discuss the process by which IPOs are disseminated to the public.

The Prospectus

All of the information about an IPO is disclosed in the prospectus, and subsequently it is a massive and difficult-to-read legal document. Indeed, the company lawyers go to great lengths to disclose all possible risks of the business in order to avoid lawsuits from disgruntled shareholders. If you do not want to read all seventy-plus prospectus pages, at least read the summary of the consolidated financial statements. The prospectus can be downloaded electronically from several Internet sites, such as Hoover's IPO Central site (www. IPOcentral.com), FreeEDGAR (www.freeEDGAR.com), or the SEC EDGAR database site (www.sec.gov). The other option is to call the lead underwriter or the issuer and request a copy of the preliminary prospectus.

Underwriters

A new issue is normally sold through a syndicate of investment bankers referred to as an underwriting syndicate. The issuer appoints a syndicate manager or a group of investment bankers as comanagers. The underwriters play by far the most important part in the IPO show. The IPO underwriter or the investment banker determines the price of the offering and helps in drafting the prospectus and other SEC filing documents. In addition to many federal laws, the underwriters must navigate through the myriad of state laws that regulate IPOs. These state laws are called blue-sky laws, because a judge in a nineteenth-century court case referred to an IPO sale as someone selling the blue sky. Finally, and most importantly, the underwriter must sell the new issue to the investment community. In other words, the lead underwriter has sole discretion regarding the pricing and timing of the new issue.

The importance of the underwriters cannot be overstated. Very often it is the underwriters themselves who can mean the difference between success and failure of the IPO. Therefore, IPO traders should make sure they know what banking firms are underwriting any IPO they are considering buying. There are approximately 410 listed investment banking firms in the United States today (see table 17.1). In my view, the investment bankers can be grouped into three general types of IPO underwriters:

1. Large global investment banks, which have a huge capital base, experienced investment bankers, and many thousands of brokers across the world. A short and incomplete list of the largest would include Goldman Sachs, Credit Suisse First Boston, Morgan Stanley Dean Witter, and Merrill Lynch. These four investment banks were the lead underwriters for 61 percent of all new issues in 1999. These banks underwrite the highest-quality IPOs that have the institutional support and perhaps the best chance of a positive long-term return on the investment.

2. Medium-size national investment banks, which have a smaller capital base and fewer brokers than the international investment banks and who are based mostly in the United States. A short and incomplete list would include Prudential Securities, Warburg Dillon Read, U.S. Bancorp Piper Jaffray, Dain Rauscher Wessels, and Thomas Weisel Partners.

Table 17.1 *Investment Banks and IPOs in 1999*

Lead Underwriter	Proceeds ($ million)	Market Share (%)	Number of Issues
Goldman Sachs & Co.	14,638	22.0	54
Morgan Stanley Dean Witter	13,967	21.0	49
Merrill Lynch & Co.	7,843	11.8	42
Credit Suisse First Boston	5,913	8.9	59
Donaldson, Lufkin & Jenrette	3,892	5.8	39
Lehman Brothers	2,905	4.3	32
J.P. Morgan & Co.	2,785	4.2	10
Fleet Boston Corp.	2,695	4.0	45
Salomon Smith Barney	2,587	3.9	23
Deutche Banc Alex Brown	2,087	3.1	27
Bear Sterns	2,086	3.1	26
Chase Manhattan Corp.	1,317	2.0	23
Warburg Dillon Read	1,249	1.9	7
Mediobanca	611	0.9	2
Banc of America Securities	518	0.8	8
Prudential Securities Inc.	356	0.5	9
CIBC World Markets	352	0.5	8
U.S. Bancorp Piper Jaffray	326	0.5	8
Thomas Weisel Partners	264	0.4	6
Dain Rauscher Corp.	244	0.4	4
TOTAL	66,635	100	546

3. Small regional boutique investment banks, which have a much smaller capital base and a few brokers, and which are based in a specific region in the United States. A sample list would include Blue Stone Capital, Capital West Securities, Chatfield Dean, Cleary Gull Reiland & McDevitt, and Dakin Securities.

From the investor's point of view, having a large global investment bank such as Morgan Stanley Dean Witter as the managing underwriter for an IPO is a step in the right direction. Analysts will most likely continue to monitor the stock in the secondary market, which indirectly promotes the stock in the long run and attracts attention from the broad investment community. Keep in mind that stock market analysts are employees of the same brokerage firm with the investment banking department. If the same brokerage firm had underwritten a deal, it is highly unlikely that analysts would issue "sell" or even "hold" recommendations for an IPO firm in the secondary market. As a rule of thumb, research opinions from the "not so independent" analysts will invariably come out positive following the public offering.

Let's suppose, for example, Morgan Stanley Dean Witter, as the lead underwriter, sells a large block of the new issues to institutional investors, which is always a good sign (large institutional ownership is an important predictor of the IPO's long-term success). With luck, Morgan Stanley Dean Witter's army of stockbrokers will then continue to recommend the stock to their clients in the secondary market and thus generate a built-in demand for the stock.

Venture Capitalists

Another important player in the IPO arena is the venture capitalist (VC). Before the owners of any private company can decide to go public, they must stay in business and grow for a few years in order to develop a track record. To get there, owners of promising small businesses often resort to asking venture capitalist firms to provide them with capital.

VCs are not benevolent organizations, and thus the "help" does not come cheap. Most likely, VCs end up controlling the business. Having the VC stamp of approval is important for the IPO, though, because it implies that professional management heads the company. Empirical evidence indicates that the IPO companies that have VC backing tend to outperform the IPOs that do not have such backing. In addition to supplying professional management, VCs provide personal contacts with the executives of large investment banks and institutional investment firms, whose support is crucial for any new issue.

Because the new IPO firms seldom have any strong earnings history, it is important to pay close attention to the firm's management. If the firm's management team is well experienced and respected in that particular industry, the institutional money will follow that IPO. The IPO prospectus provides sufficient biographical information on the IPO firm's management team. It would be favorable to see that the managers were also part of the management team from another successful publicly traded company in the same industry.

Financial Analysts and Auditors

In addition to the underwriter and the venture capitalist, another important player is the financial auditing firm, which assures that the firm's financial accountants are following the generally accepted accounting principles (GAAP). All IPOs are inherently risky, because the firms are new and without any historical stock price records. Fundamental analysis is the only form of stock evaluation at this point in time, and thus the accuracy of the firm's financial statements (i.e., the balance sheet and income statements) is crucial. Having a large and established national financial auditing firm as the independent financial auditor for the IPO firm is a clear advantage. It will alleviate any concerns that institutional investors or small investors might have about the integrity of the firm's financial statements.

In the current technology-driven stock market, it is extremely difficult to evaluate the IPO firm's financial statements. Most likely the corporate earnings are simply not there. In addition, most of the fundamental evaluation guidelines simply do not apply in the tech-driven stock market. Does this mean that fundamental analysis does not apply to IPOs? In my opinion, investors do not have any other options. They must use some form of analysis to ascertain the IPO's risk and reward. As there is no IPO historical stock price data, there is no technical analysis. If traders aren't using a fundamental-analysis tool, they are not using any form of analysis. Without the analysis, the IPO investment becomes a gamble.

Given limited corporate-earnings data, how would anyone know if this hot IPO would remain a hot company in the future? In such an event, one should look at the annual growth rate in gross revenues or sales, which should be an impressive number such as 40 percent or more. Compare the price of the IPO and the growth rate of the firm's revenues to the price and growth rate of competitors' revenues that are traded on the NASDAQ or NYSE. Read in the prospectus specifically how the firm's management will use the IPO proceeds.

Dot-Com IPOs

The 1999 IPOs introduced a new financial term into the investing public's lexicon—*concept stocks*. The so-called stocks, as exemplified by the Internet IPOs, defy any standard metrics of fundamental-analysis performance. Often there are no corporate earnings to be reviewed or even a product to be evaluated. Concepts stocks are based on speculation of emerging technological themes and trends that might drive future business opportunities. The new Internet themes are business-to-business (B2B) e-commerce, wireless Internet technology, broadband Internet, and DSL networks. The 1999 IPO market had a huge percentage of Internet IPOs. For instance, 197 (or 36 percent) of 1999 IPOs were Internet IPOs.

These dot-com companies were the best 1999 IPO performers. For instance, 57 percent of all 1999 IPOs and almost all of the Internet IPOs were founded less than five years ago. Moreover, 73 percent of 1999 IPOs had no earnings. The average IPO firm with no earnings generated $138 million in sales and had $24 million in net losses. Yet these companies had no problem raising money in 1999. What is astonishing is that these concept stock IPOs generated on average a 224 percent annual return in 1999.

On the other end of the 1999 IPO spectrum were the more conventional business enterprises that came from the more mundane industrial sectors. These 1999 IPO industrial firms represented banking and financial services, retail, leisure, specialty retail, drugs, consumer durables, utilities, transportation, real estate, manufacturing, and insurance. These "not-dot-com" firms had corporate assets, balance sheets, and—most importantly—a history of corporate earnings. Yet surprisingly, these 1999 IPOs with earnings generated only a 90 percent total annual return. This 90 percent is a high rate of return, but it compares poorly to the 224 percent annual returns from the 1999 IPOs that had little or no earnings.

Has the tech revolution in 1999 turned business valuations upside down? Does it mean that basic rules of stock analysis and valuations have changed just because information technology is changing the way we communicate, shop, and live? In my opinion, in the short run the answer is yes. In the long run, corporate earnings remain key to the creation of wealth in the stock market. All we have to do is take a closer look at the April 2000 stock market correction, which made major corrections to dot-com valuations.

The hot IPOs might be some of the very few high-tech firms that create a new technology that is appreciated by the stock market. When the dust settles a year or so later, IPO investors will discover whether they indeed invested their money wisely in one of those few promising technology companies. Until the dust settles, the IPO investors do not know whether they own diamond or zircon. Consequently, there is a great deal of speculation in the arena of IPO investments. And that fact alone makes these stocks potentially attractive to swing traders. But in the long run, the attributes of good business are still the same—corporate earnings. After all, that's how the stock market over the long run really keeps corporate score.

Selling IPOs

As a final step in the IPO process, the managing underwriter must organize a selling group to assist in the distribution or sale of the new issue. The selling group is comprised of broker-dealers who have no financial liability but earn part of the underwriting spread known as the selling concession. The selling group agreement outlines the amount of compensation to be earned.

The syndicate usually places an advertisement called a tombstone in a financial periodical announcing the sale of the new issue. The syndicate manager's name is at the top of the list of underwriters; other firms are listed alphabetically by the size of their participation

A hot issue is a new issue of stock that is in great demand. Because the hot issue is oversubscribed, it trades at an immediate premium in the market. Securities firms are restricted in the sale of hot issues to all broker/dealers' proprietary accounts and the accounts of officers, directors, partners, or employees of broker/dealers or their immediate family. Also, syndicate member firms may not withhold securities that are part of a new issue they are distributing if they have unfilled public orders. Withholding part of a hot issue for the member firm's own benefit is illegal and contrary to principles of equitable trading.

Some new issues, however, lack the investors' interest. To prevent an immediate drop in the price of the security during and after the distribution period, the SEC permits the managing underwriter to bid for the securities at or below the public offering price. This form of short-term price manipulation is called the price stabilization process. Most likely only the large underwriters have the financial resources and the will to support the declining IPO price at the public-offering price level. This is just another reason why the IPOs underwritten by firms such as Goldman Sachs, Credit Suisse First Boston, or Morgan Stanley Dean Witter are considered the safer IPOs.

Trading IPOs

When a hot IPO is released to the market, it is almost impossible for an outsider or a trader to purchase it at the inside price (i.e., the public offering price). That is simply a fact of the underwriting distribution process. Because the lead underwriter sets the initial IPO price and determines the timing of the IPO, the most likely net result is oversubscription. Thus, as the demand for the new issue exceeds the supply, it is almost impossible to acquire an IPO at the offering price.

The largest allotment of IPO shares goes immediately to the large institutional investors who are always the investment banks' most important clients. They are always first in line because their support is crucial for the success of this particular IPO as well as for the next round of IPOs. Then there is an allotment of 5 to 10 percent for the "friends and family" that goes literally to the issuer's pool of business friends and family members.

Then there is the practice of spinning. Spinning is the quid pro quo practice whereby the investment bank distributes shares of hot IPOs to its important clients (such as the venture capital firms' executives), in anticipation of receiving their underwriting business in the future. This practice is strongly discouraged by the SEC, and a few investment banks claim that they no longer do this.

Finally, the remaining shares are then divided among the underwriting syndicate members, who then individually distribute small IPO share allotments to their best brokers. However, only a few brokers have any clout with their employer (i.e., the syndicate member) when it comes to receiving an IPO allotment. At this time, the "lucky" few brokers can call their "best" retail clients and offer tiny portions of the IPO for sale.

For a retail client to be on that broker's call list, the client should have the following characteristics: a large and actively traded account worth millions of dollars with an established stockbroker who works for a brokerage firm that has a large and established investment banking practice.

In short, your best shot at getting the IPOs at the inside price is to be very wealthy and have an account with Morgan Stanley Dean Witter, Merrill Lynch, or Salomon Smith Barney. These large national brokerage firms accept individual accounts and also have active underwriting departments. Your second option is to have an individual account with regional underwriters, such as Raymond James or William Blair, although their underwriting volume is substantially smaller than that of the aforementioned. Still, you must satisfy the requirements of the first condition, which is always to be a wealthy investor. If you are not wealthy and do not have an account with any of these brokerage firms, you are at the bottom of the IPO food chain. It is not surprising that a great majority of investors in America do not receive IPOs at the public offering price.

I look at IPO distributions as a reward system. The retail client or the trader receives a few shares of an IPO as a reward for having a large account and doing a good business (i.e., generating a lot of commissions) with that brokerage house. The stockbroker receives an allotment because he or she is successful in generating a high volume of commission income for the brokerage house. The brokerage house receives the IPO allotment as a reward for having a successful investment banking department.

Some online brokers have tried to democratize the IPO distribution system by offering the IPO at the public offering price on a first-come, first-served basis. One online broker, the investment bank Donaldson, Lufkin & Jenrette, owns DLJ Direct, with whom a relatively small and actively traded account of $100,000 qualifies one for an IPO distribution. In addition, E-Schwab, E*Trade, and Fidelity have established a corresponding relationship with several underwriters. For instance, E*Trade has an alliance with Robertson Stephens and Goldman Sachs. Schwab has corresponding relationships with Credit Suisse First Boston,

J.P. Morgan, and Chase Manhattan Hambrecht & Quist. However, both Schwab and Fidelity require a $500,000 account balance in order for one to obtain IPOs.

Unfortunately, the IPO allotment given to online brokers has been extremely small, ranging from 10 to 1 percent. This is particularly true for the hot IPOs—online brokers often receive as little as 1 percent of the new issue. It appears that the online brokerage firms use and advertise this potential of purchasing the IPOs at the offering price as an enticement to open an account with their firm. The likelihood remains extremely small that the online investor would receive any shares of the hot IPO.

Digital IPOs

Another new twist in IPO distribution is the emergence of virtual IPOs, which were pioneered by Wit Capital (www.witcapital.com). Wit Capital was founded by a securities attorney, Andrew Klein, who in 1995 developed the prospectus and submitted it to the SEC and registered the blue-sky law filings for his microbrewery company, Spring Street Brewery. He then sold the new issues directly to investors over the Internet. In essence, he posted the prospectus online and collected $1.6 million from 3,500 investors for his microbrewery.

In 1997 Klein opened Wit Capital as the first online investment bank and established a corresponding relationship with other established investment bankers. Wit Capital offers online IPOs at the offering price on a first-come, first-served basis. There is no preferential treatment. Indeed, $1,000 can open an account with Wit Capital. All information, including the prospectus, is communicated electronically. In order to promote price stability and discourage the practice of flipping, Wit Capital requires that investors hold the IPO position for at least 60 days.

Flipping IPOs is a lucrative practice whereby investors immediately sell IPO shares after the start of trading in order to make a quick profit. The underwriters do not want to see anything in the aftermarket that exerts heavy selling pressure on the stock at the beginning of the IPO trading. Subsequently, all brokerage firms that offer IPO shares at the public offering price to their "elite" clients try to discourage the practice of flipping. The brokers condition a sale of an IPO to their clients with the requirement that prohibits sale of that IPO in the next 30 to 60 days. If the retail client sells the IPO within the 30-day frame, most likely that investor's name will be deleted from the broker's to-call list.

Spin-Offs

Spin-offs are a safer way to play the IPOs. A spin-off refers to a company that is selling a portion or all of a division to the public in the form of an IPO. There are a few compelling reasons for the parent company to spin-off a corporate division. The bottom line is that spin-offs tend to increase shareholder value. The following are a few reasons for a spin-off:

1. The parent company wants to raise capital because the company may be highly leveraged and wants to pay off some debt. In essence, the parent company is selling a corporate asset to the public to pay off debt.

2. The company might be restructuring its corporate operations by selling off a non-core business.

3. The parent company might be an old industrial corporation, while this particular corporate division might be a new-technology business. Many potential investors are not aware of this new-technology division as long as it is buried in the parent's corporate structure. AT&T and Lucent Technologies are a prime example of this. The stock of Lucent simply took off after the spin-off.

4. The parent company might elect to spin off a division to raise the stock price of the parent by selling a poorly performing corporate division. The parent might even transfer some of the corporate debt to the new spin-off company. In essence, the parent is unloading unproductive assets to the public at the high IPO-level price.

The spin-offs can have two distinct formats:

- *Traditional spin-offs, in which the parent company will end up owning 100 percent of the new company.* In essence, the parent company is dividing its corporate assets into two businesses, and the parent company's existing shareholders will own 100 percent of both companies.

- *Spin-offs with an 80-20 equity split cut up.* In other words, the parent company will retain 80 percent of the new company ownership, and 20 percent will be distributed to the public at the IPO offering price. The 80-20 equity split is standard because the 20 percent equity cut is a tax-free transaction. If the equity split is 75-25, then the transaction is a taxable event.

Spin-offs are attractive because the new company was in business as a separate corporate division for many years and has a performance history and most likely a track record of profitability, so the investors are buying a known factor. Experienced corporate management is already in place. Market share is already there, and thus spin-offs are considered to be less risky. Finally, the spin-offs can be a very large new issue.

IPO Trading Resources

Because the probability is great that the average swing trader will not get the IPO in the primary market at the inside price, the only alternative is to get the new issue in the secondary market. Swing and day traders armed with the latest IPO information, courtesy of the Internet, have made their presence felt in the 1999 IPO aftermarket trading. However, trading IPO stocks is a risky business, because some IPO stocks are thinly traded.

While the swing and day traders are moving quickly in and out of a particular IPO stock—almost all of them at the same time—the price volatility is substantial. If there is a massive panic selling, it would be difficult to get out of that stock at a reasonable price if there are only a few traders or investors on the other side of the market. In other words, if the stock is thinly traded, the price drop can be sharp and substantial. My recommendation is to trade IPO stocks in the secondary market only if there is a substantial trading volume, such as at least 500,000 shares traded daily.

The first day of trading of a new company's IPO is always tumultuous. The trader's first objective is to find out when the new issue will hit the market. There are a number of IPO Internet sites that provide a calendar of upcoming new issues. Some of the Internet sites are free, whereas other sites charge a monthly subscription fee.

The most popular free sites include Hoover's IPO Central (www.IPOcentral.com), Renaissance Capital (www.IPOhome.com), IPO.com (www.IPO.com), IPO Maven (www.IPOmaven.com), and Direct IPO (www.directIPO.com). Popular sites that charge a monthly subscription fee include Alert-IPO! (www.ostman.com/alert-ipo), IPO Monitor (www.IPOmonitor.com), IPO Spotlight (www.IPOspotlight.com), and IPO Data System (ww.ipodata.com). Most Internet financial directories, such as Yahoo! (www.Yahoo.com) and Silicon Investor (www.siliconinvestor.com), provide coverage on the domestic IPOs.

In addition, there are a few newsletters that charge subscription fees, such as the Thomson Financial Company's IPO Report (Tel: 212/765-5311). The IPO industry even has its own magazine that mainly covers the high-tech IPOs. This magazine is called, appropriately, the *Red Herring* (the name comes from the color of the initial or preliminary IPO prospectus that new companies distribute). *Red Herring* magazine also has its own online version (www.herring.com).

There are some sources of IPO information that nobody deserves or wants. First of all, stay away from the cold calls. Something must be wrong with the IPO if you receive a cold call from a broker offering you a "deal." You do not want that "deal." The brokers are going through a large phone list looking and dialing for your dollars. I must include here the old Wall Street adage that states that if you are a small investor and can buy the IPO at the public offering price, you do not want that issue.

Next, beware of rumors distributed through the Internet chat rooms. Do not buy any IPO in the aftermarket based on rumor alone. Some of the new issues are thinly traded and thus subject to stock manipulations. Do your own research before you buy any IPOs. Also, stay away from unsolicited mail advertisements and e-mail messages that promote particular IPOs. Those could be the so-called "pump and dump" offerings, which are handled through small fly-by-night investment banks. Most of these pump and dump stocks are purchased by brokers who first hype the stock (i.e., pump) and drive up the price. They then solicit retail customers through unsolicited mail pieces or cold calls. When the brokers sell their allotment (i.e., dump), the marketing stops, and demand for the stock simply disappears, and with that the stock value disappears.

IPO Alerts: First Day

It is difficult to generalize the first-day trading pattern for any IPO. I do not think that there is a typical chart pattern that can be applied to all IPOs. Usually, there is a pop-up at the beginning of the trading, because investors, who were unable to acquire shares at the offering price, jumped immediately into the aftermarket. Because there is huge imbalance at the beginning between the supply and the demand, the prices move up quickly. Also, there is a huge trading volume in the first 15 minutes of trading. If this is a hot IPO, prices will continue to go up after the initial pop-up. If this is a so-called broken IPO, prices will start to decline after the initial pop-up.

It is important to discuss the differences between the limit and market trade-order executions for the IPOs. (More information on the different types of trade order executions can be found in chapter 7.) If the trader submits a limit order during the first half-hour of trading, there is a distinct possibility that the order will not get filled. For instance, suppose that the price of the IPO is moving quickly, with small orders being filled in increments of 100 to 200 shares. This makes sense—the market makers can see that the prices are going up, so they are not willing to fill large orders. In order to display a continuous market and orderly price movement, the market makers are filling small orders and increasing the price rapidly by $1/_8$. If the trader submits a market order, he or she might end up buying at the top of the pop. If this is a hot IPO, then all is well, as most likely the stock price will continue to go up. However, if this is a broken IPO, then the trader is in trouble.

Hot IPO: First Day

Figure 17.1 depicts the first day of trading for one hot IPO that trades at a substantial premium on the offering price. Selectica Inc. is a San Jose, California, software company (www.selectica.com) with the ticker symbol SLTC. Selectica Inc. was founded in 1996 and at the time of its IPO had 269 employees who provided software for selling complex products on the Internet. The IPO's lead underwriter was CS First Boston, and the comanagers were Thomas Weisel and USB Piper Jaffray. The size of the IPO was 4 million shares and was offered on Thursday,

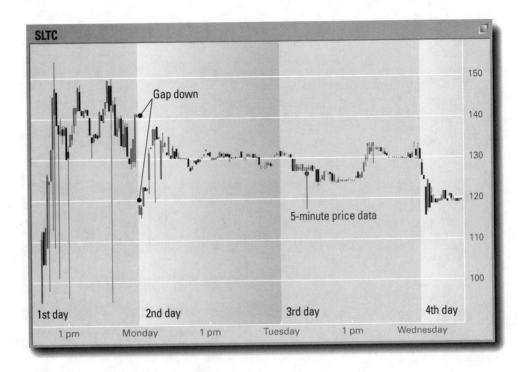

Figure 17.1 *Hot IPO: First Day of Trading for SLTC*

March 9, 2000, at the offer price of $30. In the aftermarket on Friday, the stock opened at approximately $90. It quickly popped up to almost $150 in one hour of trading. After the first day of trading, the stock closed at $141.

On Monday, the next day of trading, the stock opened at approximately $115, which was a huge down gap. If a trader purchased 1,000 shares of SLTC at the first-day closing price and carried the position over the weekend, he or she would begin the week with a $26,000 loss. Figure 17.1 is based on 5-minute candlestick data, so it is worth noting the length of the candlestick wicks, which demonstrates the huge price difference between the high and low prices during 5 minutes of trading and how these orders were filled.

Figure 17.2 depicts the first day of trading for one hot IPO that closed below the opening price. RADVision Inc. is an Israeli software company (www.radvision.com) with the ticker symbol RVSN. RADVision Inc. was

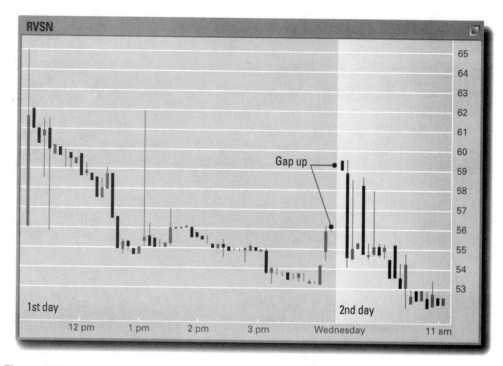

Figure 17.2   *Hot IPO: First Day of Trading for RVSN*

founded in 1992 and at the time of the IPO had 192 employees who provided software for enabling voice and data packets to move on the Internet. The IPO's lead underwriter was Lehman Brothers, and the comanagers were Salomon Smith Barney and USB Piper Jaffray. The size of the IPO was 3.8 million shares. RVSN was offered on Monday, March 13, 2000, at the offer price of $20. In the aftermarket on Monday, the stock opened at approximately $56. It quickly popped up to almost $65 in a few minutes of trading and then dropped dramatically in one hour of trading to approximately $55. At the end of the first day of trading, the stock closed at $55.

If you were one of the lucky few investors who bought the stock at the offering price of $20, then the IPO was hot. Most likely, you would have been one of the traders or investors who purchased this stock in the aftermarket. If that was the case, this IPO was not hot, at least for the first day of trading. The next day of trading, the stock opened with the large gap up of approximately $60. However, the stock prices immediately started to decline following the gap up. As you can see, the IPOs are very volatile.

Broken IPO: First Day

Figure 17.3 depicts the first day of trading for a broken IPO, which trades at a substantial discount on the offering price. Netpliance Inc. is an Austin, Texas, Internet company (www.netpliance.com) with the ticker symbol NPLI. Netpliance Inc. was founded in 1999 and at the time of the IPO had 156 employees who provided appliances and portals for the Internet. The IPO's lead underwriter was Donaldson Lufkin Jenrette, and the comanagers were Chase H&Q and Robertson Stephens. The size of the IPO was 8 million shares and was offered on Friday, March 16, 2000, at the offer price of $18. In the aftermarket on Friday, the stock opened at approximately $24. It quickly popped up to almost $26 in a few minutes of trading and then the stock price started to decline. After the first day of trading, the stock closed at $22. The next day of trading, on Monday, the stock opened at approximately the same closing price of $22. The stock then quickly dropped to $18, which

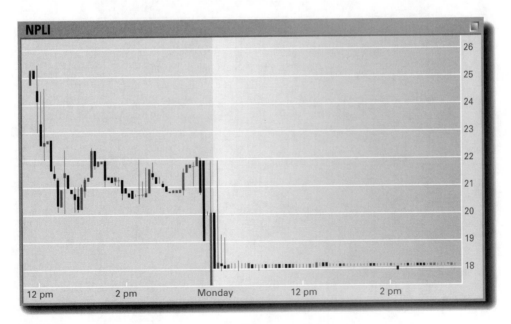

Figure 17.3 *Broken IPO: First Day of Trading for NPLI*

was the initial public offering price, and stayed in that price range for the rest of the day.

IPO Trading: First Months

A broader look at the first months of trading reveals that the hot IPOs tend to go up continuously, whereas the broken IPOs tend to decline continuously. Figure 17.4 depicts the Brocade Communications Systems IPO prices for the first six months, which by all accounts is considered a hot IPO. Brocade is a San Jose, California, computer network company (www.brocade.com) with the ticker symbol BRCD. Brocade provides fiber channel switches and software for storage area networks (SANs). The IPO's lead underwriter was Morgan Stanley Dean Witter. The size of the IPO was 3.25 million shares. BRCD was offered on Tuesday, May 25, 1999, at the offer price of $19.

In the aftermarket, the stock opened at $35. The stock closed at approximately $45 after the first day of trading. It reached its peak at

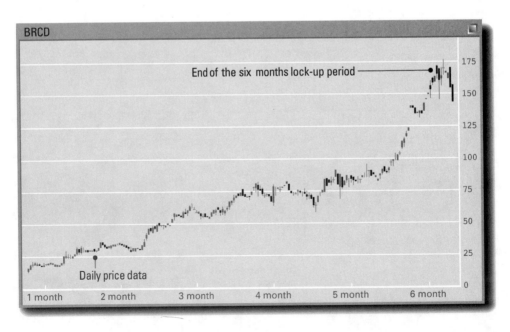

Figure 17.4 *Hot IPO: Six Months of Trading for BRCD (adjusted for 2-1 split)*

$352 and had already had a 2-1 split after only three months of trading. The average daily trading volume was 1.5 million shares, so the liquidity was good. After approximately six months of trading, the stock closed at $340, which was an approximate 970 percent increase from the first day's opening price.

Figure 17.5 depicts Value America Inc. IPO prices during the first six months, which clearly displays a broken IPO. Value America is a Charlottesville, Virginia, Internet company (www.valueamerica.com) with the ticker symbol VUSA. Value America was founded in 1996 and at the time of the IPO had 227 employees who provided e-commerce services on the Internet. The IPO's lead underwriter was Robertson Stephens, and the size of the IPO was 5.5 million shares. VUSA was offered on Friday, April 7, 1999, at the offer price of $23. In the aftermarket, the stock closed at $56 after the first day of trading. It reached $74 and then was in a steady decline after that point in time. After approximately six months of trading, the stock hit bottom at $3. The stock then inched up a little bit to about $6, which is an 89 percent decline from the peak price.

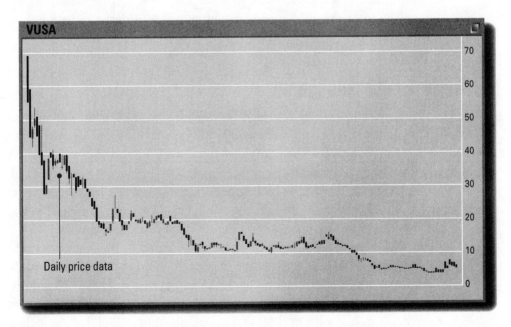

Figure 17.5   *Broken IPO: Six Months of Trading for VUSA*

IPO Alerts: The Quiet Period

After the IPO is priced, the issuer and the underwriters face further restrictions on issuing any research on the IPO. The SEC considers this to be the quiet period, which starts from the date of the IPO filing and lasts up to 25 days after the stock starts trading. The SEC wants to prevent any undue hype and thus only information from the prospectus can be disseminated to the general public. At the end of the quiet period, the underwriters (i.e., the brokerage firms) are free to issue their buy, hold, or sell recommendations. It is crucial for traders to know the Wall Street analysts' positions on the particular IPO at the end of the quiet period. The first recommendations will disclose if there is institutional support or backing for that particular stock.

In essence, first recommendations are the official Wall Street review for that stock. Traders can research the IPO calendars on any Internet IPO site and find a list of IPOs that are approaching the end of their quiet period. After the expiration of the quiet period, members of the selling syndicate and management of the new public company will most likely begin actively promoting or hyping the stock. Savvy swing traders anticipate a resurgence of public buying, and thus the expiration of the quiet period is commonly considered to be a bullish opportunity.

IPO Alerts: The Lockup Period

The lead underwriter restricts the company insiders from selling their shares for a period of time, usually 180 days. In other words, there is an agreement between the company doing an IPO and the underwriters that prohibits the company executives and large shareholders from selling the stock during the lockup period. However, the lead underwriter has the discretion of lifting the lockup period earlier. The objectives are to limit any selling pressures on the IPO and to stabilize prices.

Knowledgeable traders track the termination of the lockup periods, knowing that stocks may decline in price at about the 6-month mark. In other words, the termination of the lockup period is an alert to a short-selling opportunity. Most Internet IPO sites provide calendars where traders can find a list of IPOs that are approaching the end of the lockup period. One Internet site that tracks the IPO lockup expirations is the IPO Lockup.com (www.IPOlockup.com). Figure 17.4 illustrates this selling pressure and subsequent price decline for one hot IPO (BRCD) at about this point in time. As an additional example, table 17.2 depicts all IPO stocks with a lockup period that expired on the same day—January 25, 2000. In most cases, IPO stock prices declined after the expiration of the lockup period.

However, a word of caution is necessary here. The company executives—who are also large shareholders—have a vested interest in maintaining strong stock prices immediately after the expiration of the lockup period so that they can sell their shares into strong retail buying. Thus the company executives have a vested interest in timing any kind of favorable news that the company might have to coincide with the expiration of the lockup period. In other words, the company executives might announce at that point in time a stock split or a new promising business deal or a new product line.

Table 17.2 *IPO Lockup Expirations and Closing Prices (IPO Priced on July 29, 1999, and IPO Lockup Expiration on January 25, 2000)*

IPO Stock Symbol	Offering Price	Number of IPO Shares (million)	% of IPO Shares	% of Lockup Shares	Price 1 Day Before	Price Lockup Expires	Price 1 Day After
BPUR	$12	3.5	16%	76%	$47.00	$36.44	$33.38
CNSW	$8	2.5	28%	72%	$15.88	$16.69	$16.06
DIGX	$17	10.0	17%	83%	$90.88	$90.38	$90.06
NTWO	$13	5.0	24%	73%	$18.19	$18.19	$16.50
NTOP	$15	5.4	11%	89%	$48.88	$46.06	$44.19
NTIA	$22	5.5	21%	63%	$21.38	$20.50	$22.13
NTIQ	$13	3.0	19%	15%	$69.00	$68.81	$62.75

Short Selling and IPOs

The expiration of the lockup period corresponds with the large influx of IPO sellers and thus the short-selling opportunities appear. When the IPO price-ascending movement stops and the price reverts in value, there is a sudden influx of sellers who are trying to get out of the stock quickly. Sellers rush to close their long positions in order to minimize losses or to protect profits. There is little movement, however, on the demand side. Buyers are waiting for the bargain. They are waiting for the price to decline further in value before stepping in and buying the stock. Subsequently, the IPO price tends to drop quickly.

As a review, short selling basically means that the trader is selling a stock that he or she does not own. In essence, the seller is "short" and does not own the stock. The seller will borrow and deliver the "shorted" stock to the buyer at the settlement date, which is the standard T + 3 date (or trade plus three business days). Because the seller has sold a stock that he or she does not own, the brokerage firm must first lend him or her the stock. In other words, the stock must be on the brokerage firm's "short" list of shortable stocks.

Both the NASDAQ and the listed exchanges, such as the NYSE, have a short-sale rule that prohibits short selling on a downtick. This short-sale rule was developed to prevent speculative selling in NASDAQ or exchange-listed securities from accelerating a further decline in the price of that security. In essence, short selling can exert downward pressure on a stock's price and thus force the price to drop abruptly and significantly within a single trading day.

Listed exchanges such as the NYSE have a tick test, which states that the last reported sale price on the consolidated tape must be a plus tick. In essence, the SEC short-sale rule prohibits short sales of exchange-listed securities if the current price is below the previously reported last-sale price (i.e., a minus tick or zero-minus tick). In other words, the last sale must be a plus tick before the trader can execute the short sale. The rule is simple and enforceable because the trade reports in most exchange-listed securities occur on a single exchange floor by a single specialist, who ensures the sequential trade reporting.

The NASDAQ market is a different matter. The trade reporting in NASDAQ securities involves different market makers for the same stock, who are reporting trades from different locations to the NASD via computer interface. NASD requires that all trades must be reported within 90 seconds after execution. That means that two sequential trades might not be reported to the NASD at the same time and thus they do not appear on the NASDAQ tape in sequential order. Subsequently, the NASDAQ short-sale rule was designed as a BID test rather than the tick test.

The NASD short-sale rule prohibits the short sales if the new and current BID price is below the old BID price for a NASDAQ security. The trading software system automatically calculates if the current BID is an up BID or a down BID so that traders will have that information at their fingertips when attempting to execute the short sales. In essence, the trader would pay close attention to whether the current BID price tick arrow is up or down, or whether the current BID color is green or red. If the current BID color is green or the current BID tick arrow is up, then the short sale is legal. The trader can then short the stock.

The other short-selling requirement is that traders must open a type II account or a margin account. In essence, the margin account means that the purchase of a stock is partially financed, up to 50 percent, with borrowed money. The brokerage firm will issue a credit to the trader and charge interest so the trader can buy securities on credit and also borrow against the securities held in his or her account. The established margin account will be in the name of the trader and will carry his or her Social Security number as a tax-identification number (see chapter 8).

Assume that the stock market is facing a major correction and that most stocks, particularly the hot IPOs, are declining in value. The only way the trader can make money in the down market is to short sell. Because stock prices tend to fall at a faster pace than they tend to increase, traders can earn substantial sums of money in a short period of time by taking short-sell positions. This is even truer for the IPOs because they are even more volatile (or speculative) than the seasoned stocks. Keep in mind that NASD rules prohibit the short selling of IPOs within 30 days from the initial offering. Clearly, the expiration of the lockup period is one of the short-selling alerts, as illustrated in table 17.2. This is not surprising considering that a large percentage of IPO shares theoretically could be supplied in the market at that time.

It is important that traders are proficient and comfortable with the mechanics of short selling. (See chapter 7 to learn how to short sell a stock on an ECN without the required up-tick rule.) Short selling is clearly the other half of the stock-trading equation. Traders cannot expect to go long on every single trade. There will be days when the overall market is declining, and at that time the traders will need to go short. It is difficult to make money on long positions when the overall market values are descending.

Short selling is also potentially very lucrative. The short sellers can make a lot more money a lot more quickly than the traders or investors that utilize mostly long positions. Prices tend to decline much faster than they tend to appreciate in value. A brief look at any price chart will generally reveal a gradual price increase followed by a sharp decline. The quick drop in value can be attributed to panic selling. Fear of losing money is always a powerful motivator.

VI

Why the Trade Is or Is Not Working

"You've got to be careful if you don't know where you're going 'cause you might not get there."

—*Yogi Berra*

I ADMIT THAT FUNDAMENTAL STOCK ANALYSIS IS MUCH MORE RELEVANT TO THE stock investor than to the stock trader. Nevertheless, fundamental stock analysis provides traders with the foundation to understand and appreciate the broader relationship between the stock market and the business environment in general. In other words, traders that understand stock market fundamentals are able to answer many "why" questions. In the long run, the trader who understands why the stock is moving will master the field of trading. And the facts are the stock market fundamentals.

18

Fundamental Stock Analysis

"God does not play dice."

—*Albert Einstein*

Who cares about fundamental analysis? That's a good question. As a stock trader, you might ask, Why do I need to invest time and effort reading the company's financial statements? The fact is, not all traders consider fundamental analysis. But it may be important for longer-term traders such as swing traders and active investors. In this and subsequent chapters, a simple yet detailed methodology will emerge showing how swing traders can perform and profit from fundamental analysis.

But for now, here's the short answer to the question posed above. If you hold an overnight stock position, you have, in essence, become an investor, and thus you should care about the company's financial performance and its fundamentals. Because you are holding an open long (or short) position overnight, you do not have full control over the position during that time. So that there are no overnight surprises, it is in your best interest that the stock position is in a company that has sound business fundamentals.

In essence, stock fundamentals provide to traders the underlying reasons that explain why a particular price movement might (or might not) materialize in the next several days. Swing traders expect to observe a price movement in a specific direction of a magnitude of several points in one week, which is a substantial price change. There has to be a certain underlying fundamental reason for the stock's supply and demand schedules to dramatically shift in order for this large price movement to materialize. In other words, the fundamental stock analysis might explain why there is a sudden influx or exodus of stock buyers and sellers. At the very least, swing traders should be comfortable with fundamental stock analysis language and application.

Moreover, traders who have a good grasp of a company's fundamentals will be better prepared to react to news and other events that might impact that company's stock price. For example, if you know the depth of experience of a company's management team, you'll be able to quickly estimate the impact if the CEO suddenly announces he or she is quitting. Similarly, if you understand the company's debt structure, you'll be able to estimate what impact an interest-rate hike will have on the bottom line. And as a final example, if you know who a firm's clients are, you'll be able to gauge the effect of the loss or addition of a new client. Perhaps the market will overreact at first, affording you the opportunity to buy the stock on a dip and profit from the stock's quick recovery. Or, just as likely, the market may overestimate the effect of positive news and bid up the stock's price, giving savvy traders the opportunity to short the stock when it peaks.

For example, I read about a trader who explained that he recently purchased Advanced Micro Devices (AMD) shares because the company announced a new high-end chip that was superior to Intel's product. At the same time, the competitor Intel was experiencing supply problems (i.e., increased costs) and trading at the relatively high PE ratio (i.e., overpriced stock). This is all fundamental analysis. A trader took a position in AMD because the stock exhibited fundamental strengths at that point in time. Remember, as a trader you'll be pitting yourself against professionals who have access to detailed analysis of a company's fundamentals. To compete effectively, you should arm yourself with this knowledge as well.

Fundamental analysis is the practice of analyzing all economic and political factors that can influence a company's financial performance. Security analysts and traders attempt to forecast the company's future stock prices based on fundamental analysis. And their collective opinions greatly affect the prices. If the majority of investors and traders believe that the company's underlying fundamentals are strong, they will buy the stock and its price will increase. Conversely, if the majority of investors and traders believe that the company's underlying fundamentals are weak, they will sell their stock and its price will decline.

Top-Down Approach

At its core, fundamental analysis is a search for the intrinsic value of a company. That search is performed on two distinct levels:

1. The macroeconomic level, which starts with an analysis of the global or national economic environment and continues with an analysis of the company's industry or sector.

2. The microeconomic level, which is fundamental analysis of the particular firm's business performance. Financial analysts devote most of their time and effort to microlevel fundamental analysis.

If one is a long-term investor, then macroeconomic fundamental analysis is important. Firms do not exist in a vacuum. Understanding the underlying business environment will help investors to ascertain whether the company will continue earning profits in the future. In essence, the overall business success of the firm in the long run will be greatly impacted by the macroeconomic events that are completely outside the company's control. It is unreasonable to expect a bullish stock market (or rising stock prices) if the general economic output and the expected corporate earnings are declining.

Why would a short-term trader care about the anticipated Federal Reserve Board change in the monetary policy that will increase interest rates a month from now, when the trader plans to exit that particular short-term holding position long before higher interest rates trickle down to affect the company's earnings? The answer to that is, because rumors and consensus assumptions about interest-rate change affect stock prices immediately. And traders react strongly to the ways in which interest rates will affect a firm's future performance.

My favorite information source on the U.S. economy is the Dismal Scientist Internet site (www.dismalscientist.com). The site was so named because economics was labeled in the nineteenth century as the "dismal science." Another useful Internet source is the U.S. Commerce Department's Bureau of Economic Analysis site (www.bea.doc.gov), which provides national and international macroeconomic data. Both of these sites post macroeconomic data such as that which we are about to discuss.

Macroeconomic Analysis

Periods of economic expansion and contraction, of course, greatly affect stock prices, both in the short and long term. The most basic measure of the past national overall economic performance is the gross domestic product (GDP). GDP represents the total current market value of all goods and services produced by U.S. residents in one year. The key component of this definition is *current market value,* which means that all produced goods and services are expressed in the nominal or present price terms. For instance, the nominal GDP in the United States for 1999 was approximately $9,295 billion. If the U.S. inflation rate were substantial, the GDP value would increase simply because the overall price levels in the United States have increased. An increase in the nominal GDP would not necessarily coincide with any increase in economic output.

To alleviate this problem, the nominal GDP is converted into real GDP by dividing the nominal GDP value by a price deflator, such as the Consumer Price Index (CPI). The U.S. Department of Labor (Bureau of Labor Statistics) compiles this measure of the nation's inflation rate. The CPI represents the average change over time in the prices paid by urban consumers for a fixed-market basket of consumer goods and services. The CPI deflator provides a way for economists and financial analysts to compare what the market basket of goods and services costs this month with what the same market basket cost in baseline year of 1992, for instance. (The annual inflation rate between 1996 and 1999 was approximately 2 percent, which represents a historically low rate of inflation.) Therefore, dividing the nominal GDP by the CPI results in the real GDP, whereas the value of all goods and services produced is expressed in constant dollars (or 1992 prices).

The real GDP in 1999 was $8,897 billion. In other words, U.S. residents produced $8,897 billion worth of goods and services as expressed in 1992 prices. It's key to look at the growth rates in the real GDP. The Bureau of Economic Analysis releases the real GDP data a month after the end of the quarter. The growth in the real GDP indicates continuing economic expansion (and increased corporate earnings), whereas the declining real GDP indicates recession (or declining corporate earnings). A real GDP growth rate between 2 and 3 percent is considered normal. However, the real GDP growth rate between 1996 and 1999 was approximately 4 percent, which translated into fears that a booming economy would ultimately lead to a higher inflation rate.

The GDP is further segmented into four basic spending components:

1. Consumption (C), which represents consumer spending and which accounts for most of the economic output, with approximately 68 percent of the GDP.

2. Investment (I), which represents U.S. business expenditures for the equipment, machinery, and infrastructure that will enhance its future production. Investment spending accounts for about 17 percent of the GDP.

3. Government (G), which accounts for all federal, state, and local government expenditures on public goods and services, which account for approximately 18 percent of the GDP.

4. Net exports (X – M), which represent the international component of this dynamic and global U.S. economy. It is the annual U.S. exports (X) minus the U.S. imports (M). Historically speaking, the United States has always had a trade deficit and thus the net export figure is negative and accounts for approximately –3 percent of the GDP.

Thus the U.S. GDP can be expressed as:

$$GDP = C + I + G + (X - M)$$

The key is to monitor the four components of the GDP and see if there is a trend developing among the components. The largest component of the GDP is consumer spending (68 percent). If real GDP growth rates decline, then most likely consumer spending has already begun to decline as well. If consumer spending continues to decline, that would eventually mean lower corporate revenues and, as a result, lower corporate expected earnings. We know that the expected earnings are the most important factor in determining the stock's price in the long run.

Leading Economic Indicators

The big problem for traders is that GDP is a historical measure. GDP figures are published too late (one month after the end of the quarter) to provide any early warnings. By the time the real GDP statistic is published, the stock market has already reacted to the news. The truth is that the financial market reacts quickly and early because there are several leading economic indicators that provide early warning signs.

For instance, macroeconomists look at broad market stock prices, such as the S & P's 500 index, as one of the leading economic indicators that points where the GDP might be going. Again, the reason for this is rather simple: Investors evaluate securities based on expected corporate earnings. The expected earnings are a function of the future economic conditions and not a function of past or historical economic conditions. Figure 18.1 depicts a typical relationship between the stock prices (S & P's 500 index) and economic output (GDP). Subsequently, any perceived changes in expected corporate earnings will impact the short-term stock prices. And thus the stock market prices will turn before the GDP shows this change in direction.

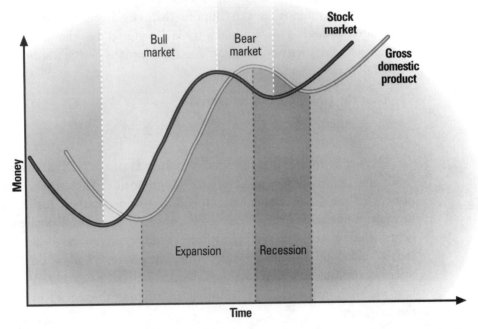

Figure 18.1 *Hypothetical Relationship Between Stock Prices and Economic Output*

The Conference Board, a nonprofit business-research organization with a membership composed of 2,800 large companies, releases the index of leading economic indicators on the first few business days of the month and two months after the reporting month. The financial impact of the index is rather small. Financial markets are not sensitive to this report because of the sizable reporting lag (two months). All of the indices and data components have previously been individually reported. In addition, the purpose of the index is to forecast the future economic output and not future stock prices. A rule of thumb is that three consecutive months of decline in the leading index is a sign that the economy will fall into recession. Indeed, the index of leading economic indicators has successfully predicted each of the eight U.S. recessions since 1950.

The composite index is constructed as a weighted average of ten key economic data series, which are designed to predict economic conditions in the near future. Each of the ten economic indicators impacts the GDP. The degree of relative importance is measured by the statistical measure of correlation "R square," which ranges from 0 to 1, with 1 being the measure of a perfect fit (or the highest correlation). Table 18.1 lists the economic indicators that comprise the index.

Table 18.1 *Leading Economic Indicators*

Economic Indicators	R Square
Spread between the 10-year Treasury and the federal funds rate, which represents the difference between the short- and long-term interest rates	0.46
M2, or broad definition of money supply	0.45
Building and housing permits	0.43
Stock prices of the S & P's 500 index	0.36
Index of consumer expectations	0.33
Average weekly initial unemployment claims	0.28
Vendor performance component of the NAPM index	0.25
Manufacturers' new orders for consumer goods	0.25
Manufacturers' new orders for nondefense capital goods	0.25
Average workweek in manufacturing	0.24

In addition to the leading indicator, the Conference Board also issues the coincident and lagging economic indicators. The coincident economic indicator consists of four series of economic data, such as non-farm employment, industrial production, manufacturing sales, and personal income, which all describe the current economic situation. The lagging economic indicators consist of several economic data series, such as changes in manufacturing labor costs, the level of inventories, the prime interest rate, and commercial and industrial loan volume. The purpose of the coincident and lagging economic indicators is to confirm any turning points in the leading economic indicator and to direct attention to structural imbalances that may be developing in the economy. In essence, the coincident and lagging indices provide a more complete picture of economic performance, rather than predicting slowdowns in the economy.

Fiscal Policy

Depending on your political views, it is either fortunate or unfortunate that the federal government has a limited ability to intervene and interfere with the market forces. Because the federal, state, and local governments account for only about 17 percent of the total economic activities, the government's ability to determine the level of the GDP is rather limited.

Nevertheless, the federal government does have the power to change the level of government spending and taxation; it is these changes in government spending and taxation that constitute its fiscal-policy instruments. Fiscal policy is designed to counterbalance cyclical macroeconomic events, such as an economic recession. The objective of fiscal policy is to intervene and favorably impact two GDP components: Consumption (C) and government spending (G). Ultimately, changes in fiscal policy impacts the GDP, which subsequently impacts corporate earnings and stock prices.

Monetary Policy

The federal government, through the actions of the Federal Reserve System, can impact the nation's credit supply and subsequently impact short-term interest rates and, consequently, the cost of capital. The financial market grinds out a wide array of interest rates, depending on the maturity of the loans, the relative loan risk, and the liquidity of the loan instruments. The most common short-term interest-rate benchmark is the prime rate, which is the rate charged by the commercial banks to their best customers.

The interplay between the demand for capital and supply of capital determines the interest rate. Consumers and businesses require borrowed funds in order to purchase goods and services on credit or to make investments. The money demand schedule is the standard negatively sloped demand line. At a high interest rate or high price of credit the public would demand less credit, whereas at the lower interest rate consumers and businesses would borrow more funds from the commercial banks. The federal government does not control that credit demand. However, the Federal Reserve System can control the supply of credit in this country.

The Federal Reserve System, or "the Fed," was established in 1913. Its primary function is to control the amount of bank reserves in the United States and thereby determine the amount of money or credit available. The supply of credit schedule is the standard positively sloped supply line. At a high interest rate or high price of credit the commercial banks would be willing to offer (or sell) more loans to public, whereas at a lower interest rate banks would offer less funds to the public. The Fed has only two options, which are illustrated in figure 18.2:

1. Increase the supply of money or shift the supply schedule to the right and thus reduce the short-term interest rate, which constitutes the expansionary monetary policy.

2. Reduce the supply of money or shift the supply schedule to the right and thus increase the short-term interest rate, which represents the restrictive monetary policy.

When the Fed, through its open market committee—which is the most common monetary tool—decides to sell Treasury bonds from its vast bond reserves, it is essentially giving the public pieces of paper and accepting money in return. The net result is that the commercial banks will end up with lower cash deposits in their banking system. In this way the sale of the bonds in the open market reduces the money supply and results in higher short-term interest rates.

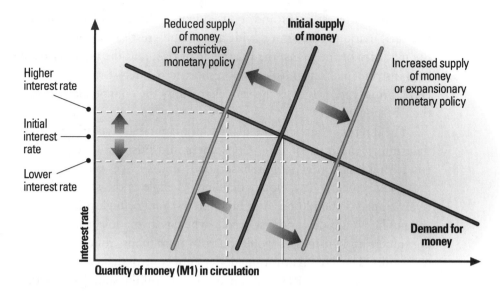

Figure 18.2 *Federal Reserve Bank's Monetary Policy*

Conversely, when the Fed's open market committee decides to buy Treasury bonds for its portfolio, it is essentially taking from the public pieces of paper and giving out money in return. The net result is that the commercial banks will end up with higher cash deposits in their banking system. In this way the purchase of the bonds in the open market increases the money supply and results in lower short-term interest rates.

Table 18.2 provides a summary of the fiscal and monetary policies and their relevance to the overall stock market signals. It is important to note that, in reality, all GDP components do not move in unison. It is common to see one or more of the aggregate demand components move in one direction, and the remaining components exhibit a different growth pattern. What is ultimately important is the overall movement in aggregate demand (i.e., expansion or reduction), which will ultimately determine the GDP.

Table 18.2 *Fiscal and Monetary Policies and Stock Market Signals*

	Bullish Stock Market Signals	Bearish Stock Market Signals
Aggregate Consumption	Increased aggregate consumer spending	Reduced aggregate consumer spending
Aggregate Investment	Increased aggregate investment	Reduced aggregate investment
Aggregate Government	Increased aggregate government spending	Reduced aggregate government spending
Exports and Imports	Trade surplus	Trade deficit
Aggregate Demand	Increased aggregate demand	Reduced aggregate demand
Fiscal-Policy Instruments	Increased government spending	Lower government spending
	Reduced taxes	Increased taxes
	Budget deficit	Budget surplus
Money Supply	Increased money supply	Reduced money supply
Monetary Policy Instruments	Fed buys Treasury bonds	Fed sells Treasury bonds
	Fed lowers discount rate	Fed increases discount rate
	Fed lowers reserve requirement	Fed increases reserve requirement

Macroeconomic Analysis and Individual Investors and Traders

Short-term traders should be aware of the changes in the economic environment because the stock market is an integral part of that environment. However, traders do not need to forecast or anticipate these macroeconomic changes. They need only to react quickly to the obvious changes in the broad economic atmosphere. For example, if the Federal Reserve Bank increases the discount rate, it is a clear signal that the Fed's policy is to reduce the nation's money supply and thus investors and traders can expect with a great deal of certainty that short-term interest rates will go up. If the trader owns bank stocks, which are clearly interest-rate sensitive, then this Fed announcement will have an immediate and adverse impact on that position. The only thing that the short-term investor or trader can do is to react quickly and close the position with hopefully a small loss.

It is impossible for traders to predict with any degree of accuracy and success the actions of the Federal Reserve Board. Investing time and effort to analyze the Fed's actions might not be a prudent use of the trader's limited time. For instance, the short-term investors and traders plan to take a long position in the bank stock. It is likely that the holding period for a long position is short enough so that the Fed will not change its monetary policy during this period.

The opposite is true for the long-term investor who has a long position in a bank stock that is interest-rate sensitive. Long-term investors have no choice but to pay close attention to the Fed's monetary policy because it will dramatically influence the bank's long-term stock price. Higher interest rates will simultaneously increase the cost of the loanable funds and lower the customers' demand for loans. The net outcome for the bank, of course, is lower corporate earnings.

Changes in short-term interest rates impact other capital-intensive businesses that customarily carry large debts. For example, the stock prices of utility companies are linked to changes in the interest rates. Utility companies borrow a great deal of money to build expensive power plants, and thus any change in the interest rate will impact their cost structure dramatically and thus their expected earnings.

In addition, home-building companies are extremely vulnerable to changes in interest rates. A higher mortgage interest rate will discourage many potential customers from making that financial commitment or qualifying for a mortgage loan. Automakers are also extremely sensitive to changes in the interest rates because those changes will directly influence the consumer interest rates for auto loans. Because most new car purchases are financed, high auto-loan rates tend to discourage auto sales. Subsequently, there is an inverse relationship between the interest rates and stock prices for the utility, auto, and home-building companies. In other words, swing traders should pay more attention to interest-sensitive stocks when the interest rates are changing.

That seems simple and direct, but consider the following: Interest-rate changes can impact the stock prices of companies whose core business is completely insensitive to fluctuations in interest rates. Why is it that the core business of these companies has only a remote link to interest rates and yet the stock prices of these companies are extremely sensitive to changes in the interest rate? These companies tend to pay large dividends, or in other words, the companies have relatively large-dividend yields. Income investors purchase these high-yield stocks specifically for the income. Consequently, a Treasury bond is considered a close investment substitute for high-dividend stocks. The interest-rate increase will result in the Treasury issuing a higher interest or yield for the Treasury securities. The higher yield would make the riskless Treasury bonds much more attractive. The shift in investor preferences toward the riskless high-yield Treasury bonds would result in lowered demand for stocks. Similarly, transportation companies are very sensitive to changes in oil prices because any change directly impacts their costs. And changes in exchange rates will dramatically impact the stock prices of those companies that have a large import-export business component.

Finally, some companies' earnings are very sensitive to the overall business cycle. These so-called cyclical stocks move with the general business cycle. Consumer demand for the companies' products tends to be very responsive to changes in overall consumer income. In other words, a company's products are highly "income-elastic." A small percentage decrease in consumer income due to a minor recession will decrease consumer demand dramatically, which would also result in the lowering of the product's price. The lower product price will translate into lower corporate earnings, and that will result in lower stock prices.

Some companies, however, seem to be insulated from general economic downturns. These stocks are commonly referred to as defensive stocks because the corporate earnings seldom fluctuate in response to the general business-cycle expansion or recession. The established pharmaceutical and food companies, for instance, tend to weather economic downturns better than other companies because their goods and services are consumer necessities. In other words, the demand for their products or services is "income-inelastic."

Industry Analysis

Industry analysis is the second step in the macroeconomic fundamental analysis. The focus of industry analysis is to ascertain if there are any predictable changes in demand for the company's product(s) or changes in the industry cost structure. Such developments will have a large impact on a company's future earnings.

Some financial analysts argue that analysis of one particular industry has less and less meaning because the large U.S. companies are well diversified across several industry lines, and most large companies have multiple product lines that transcend one narrow industry definition. However, smaller companies are most likely specialized and limited to one or a few product lines, and thus the industry study is important to ascertain the full degree of the investment risk.

Most analysts and investors prefer to start their fundamental analysis with the macroeconomic question, Which industry today will maximize my investment return tomorrow? Different industries perform very differently over the same period of time. The objective is to identify industries that have the potential to perform well in the present economic environment and whose component companies have the potential to perform better than the S & P's 500 index. The strategy here is quite simple—identify the industry in which there is a pent-up demand for its products or an industry that is experiencing a sharp revival.

Performance varies dramatically among different sectors. For instance, the S & P's 500 index increased in value 19.5 percent in 1999. Although this annual broad stock market performance is impressive by all historical accounts, it pales in comparison to the individual annual performance of several high-technology sectors. Investors' insatiable demand for the stocks of companies that are involved in any way in the business of the Internet generated the incredible increase in stock prices for such companies.

For instance, stock prices went up dramatically in 1999 for these sectors: the Internet (175%), electronics (112%), computer software (83%), computer hardware (75%), and telecommunications (72%). Conversely, several industry sectors had negative returns even in the strong bull market in 1999. The average stock prices dropped dramatically in 1999 for tobacco (53%), specialty retail (25%), utilities (19%), and aerospace and defense (14%). The underlying fundamental economic reasons for this precipitous decline are the threats of continuing class-action litigation (tobacco), competition from the Internet retail companies (specialty retail), utility-market deregulation (utilities), and the prospect of continued global peace (aerospace and defense).

After the economic sector is identified, the next step is to identify companies who are the leaders within that sector. That of course can be done using the tools of the microeconomic fundamental analysis. Within any industry, there is a substantial variance between individual companies' returns. Even if the particular industry is experiencing tremendous growth, there are always companies who are faltering. Some of the financial ratios are highly industry-specific, and thus it is important to compare the firm's financial ratios against the industry average.

Essentially, the industry analysis requires answering the following questions:

- What is the nature of the product or service?
- What is the market size of this industry?
- What are the competing or complementary industries?
- What is the industry growth rate?
- What stage is the product in the industry's life cycle (i.e., development, expansion, maturity, or decline)?
- What is the growth rate in demand for the industry product?
- What is the cost structure for the industry?
- Is the industry sensitive to changes in the interest rate or inflation?
- Which are the top firms in the industry?
- Is there foreign competition?

As you can imagine, it takes a great deal of time and effort to answer these questions. Subsequently, savvy swing traders tend to specialize in a few price-volatile industries, and thus they become experts on a few firms within these industries.

19

Analysis of Balance Sheet and Income Statement

"A nickel ain't worth a dime anymore."

—*Yogi Berra*

This chapter will explain how to interpret the financial information found in a company's balance sheet and income statement, what the application of related financial ratios is, and how swing traders can make use of this information. I plan to use Dell Computer Corporation as an example throughout this chapter. I need to state up front that I do not own any Dell stock, although I wish I did. Dell was the world's leading direct marketer of computer systems and one of the top computer vendors in the world. Indeed, Dell was the top stock of the 1990s. Dell stock had an average compound annual return of 97 percent during the bull-market decade of the 1990s. This is an astronomical return compared to the average 18 percent increase for all other S & P's 500 stocks traded on the major exchanges.

Dell stock appeals to swing traders because it has substantial long-term capital-appreciation potential, plenty of liquidity, and short-term volatility. I will first explain the components of Dell's consolidated statement. After we cover the basic terminology, we will look at the different fundamental-analysis indicators that are commonly used by traders. All of the fundamental stock market information for any publicly traded company is provided in the annual report, which has several standard components, including the two most important financial summaries—balance sheet and income statement.

The starting point of any fundamental analysis is the company's annual report. This formal report enumerates the company's business performance in the previous year. The report is a formal communication between the company's management team and the Wall Street community. It not only includes the company's annual financial statements, such as the balance sheet and income statement, but it also elaborates on the company's business mission and management philosophy. It is the easiest and best place to gather the stock's fundamental data.

Letter from the CEO

All annual reports will include a letter from the chief executive officer (CEO) to the shareholders. The letter provides a brief summary or review of the company's overall performance during the previous year. In addition, it will most likely outline the business plan for the upcoming year. The letter will try to put a positive spin on the business's overall performance and endorse the current management. Still, it is a starting point and does provide a quick overview of the company's overall business performance during the previous year.

In his letter to Dell's shareholders, CEO Michael Dell summarized the company's 1999 performance—everything went up. Dell has become the largest manufacturer and marketer of personal computers in the United States and second in the world. Other indicators of business performance also increased: net income (27%), earnings per share (28%), and return on invested capital (243%). Finally, Dell's stock price rose nearly 39 percent in 1999, and $100 invested in Dell at the June 1988 IPO price was worth more than $42,000 at the close of fiscal year 2000. In short, Dell Computer Corporation made a lot of people happy and rich and thus I speculate that Michael Dell had an easy task in writing this letter.

Annual reports will also name the entire management team, as well as the board of directors. Many investors pay close attention to changes in the management team, as well as to the representation of independent directors who are not part of the company's senior executive team.

Financial Statements

The financial statements and accompanying notes contained in the annual report illustrate the company's overall financial performance in the past year, as well as the historical trend. These financial statements will reveal the company's financial strengths and weaknesses, and thus ultimately pinpoint whether the company's stocks are a good investment. If the company is a large business enterprise, all financial statements will be consolidated so that they represent all components or divisions of the company. Usually at the end of the financial statement, the company will include related financial notes. The company's management team will attempt to explain in these notes, in much greater detail, any business event that impacted the provided financial statements. The related financial notes will often provide a clearer picture of any financial difficulties.

Balance Sheet

The first thing you should look at in an annual report is the balance sheet. Traders can use the information from the balance sheet to assess the company's financial liquidity (by comparing current assets to current liabilities) or to ascertain the company's leverage (by comparing debt to stockholders' equity). The following section will describe how swing traders can analyze this information to make better investments or trades.

Creating the company's balance sheet simply requires adding up all of the components: current assets, fixed assets, intangible assets, current liabilities, long-term liabilities, and stockholders' equity. One side of the balance sheet will combine all of the company assets—from the most liquid, such as cash, to the least liquid, such as equipment and buildings. The other side of the balance sheet will record all of the company's financial obligations or liabilities in order of immediacy. In other words, the most immediate financial obligations will constitute current liabilities, whereas the least immediate liability will represent the long-term debt. Finally, the aggregate company's assets must add up to total liabilities and stockholders' equity.

The balance sheet represents a snapshot of the company's financial position on a specific date, usually at the end of the calendar year (December 31). Dell elected to change its fiscal year from the 52-week period ending on the Sunday nearest January 31 to the Friday nearest January 31, which had no material effect on the company's consolidated financial statements. Table 19.1 depicts Dell's consolidated balance sheet over a period of three years.

The balance sheet has three major components: assets, liabilities, and stockholders' equity. The basic accounting equation is rather simple:

$$\text{Assets} - \text{Liabilities} = \text{Stockholders' equity}$$

The objective of any corporation's management team is to maximize assets and minimize liabilities in order to increase stockholders' equity (stockholders equity in this case is synonymous with the company's net worth). From our basic accounting equation, one can conclude the following:

$$\text{Assets} = \text{Liabilities} + \text{Stockholders' equity}$$

That is the reason that the balance sheet is so named—liabilities and stockholders' equity must always be equal or balanced to the assets. Assets represent all items owned by the corporation, which can be

Table 19.1 *Dell Computer Corporation Consolidated Balance Sheet—1998, 1999, 2000 (in $ millions)*

	Jan. 28, 2000	Jan. 29, 1999	Feb. 1, 1998
Total current assets	$7,681	$6,339	$3,912
Plus total fixed assets	765	523	342
Plus intangible assets	304	15	14
Plus long-term investments	2,721	0	0
Total assets	**$11,471**	**$6,877**	**$4,268**
Total current liabilities	$5,192	$3,695	$2,697
Total long-term liabilities	971	861	278
Total liabilities	**$6,163**	**$4,556**	**$2,975**
Total stockholders' equity (assets minus liabilities)	5,308	2,321	1,293
Total Liabilities and Stockholders' Equity	**$11,471**	**$6,877**	**$4,268**

grouped into three basic categories: current assets, fixed assets, and intangible assets.

Current Assets

Current assets are all assets that can be converted into cash within a short period of time, such as one year. The current assets are the following:

- Cash, such as currency, balance in checking account, and other bank deposits.
- Marketable securities that can be quickly converted to cash, such as stocks, corporate notes and bonds, and Treasury bills or bonds.
- Accounts receivable, which represents money owed to the company by the company's customers. The company expects to secure these funds within one year.
- Inventories, which translate into the value of finished products or work in progress. Accountants like to differentiate which accounting method was utilized in establishing the inventory value. If the "last in, first out" (or LIFO) method is used, then the cost of the last item produced is applied to the price received from the last sold item. If the "first in, first out" (or FIFO) method is used, then the cost of the first item produced is applied to the price received from the last sold item. If there is substantial price inflation in the economy, and if there is a substantial time lag between the first produced item and the last sold item, then FIFO will overstate the company's profits and maximize the company's tax liability. LIFO, however, tends to report lower profits and taxes.

Current assets are relatively easy to value, calculate, and liquidate. Dell inventories are stated on a FIFO basis. In Dell's example, the current assets for 1998, 1999, and 2000 are depicted in table 19.2.

Fixed Assets

Fixed assets, such as buildings, land, furniture, and equipment are used by the corporation in its daily business activities. Fixed assets are quite real, but they are difficult to value, calculate, and liquidate. All of Dell's

Table 19.2 *Dell Computer Corporation Current Assets—1998, 1999, 2000 (in $ millions)*

	Jan. 28, 2000	Jan. 29, 1999	Feb. 1, 1998
Cash	$3,809	$520	$320
Marketable securities	323	2,661	1,524
Accounts receivable	2,608	2,094	1,486
Inventories	391	273	233
Other	550	791	349
Total Current Assets	**$7,681**	**$6,339**	**$3,912**

property, plants, and equipment are carried at a depreciated cost. Depreciation is provided using the straight-line method over the estimated economic lives of the assets, which range from 10 to 30 years for buildings and 2 to 5 years for all other assets. Leasehold improvements are amortized over the shorter of either five years or the lease term. In Dell's example, the fixed assets for 1998, 1999, and 2000 are depicted in table 19.3.

Table 19.3 *Dell Computer Corporation Fixed Assets—1998, 1999, 2000 (in $ millions)*

	Jan. 28, 2000	Jan. 29, 1999	Feb. 1, 1998
Land and buildings	$229	$172	$137
Computer equipment	277	205	135
Machinery	383	252	171
Fixtures and furniture	251	146	66
Less depreciation	(375)	(252)	(167)
Total Fixed Assets	**$765**	**$523**	**$342**

Intangible Assets

Intangible assets are proprietary and nonphysical assets such as trademarks, patents, and copyrights. The value of intangible assets depends largely on the company's future potential earnings, which are derived from the company's reputation in the marketplace. Another component of intangible assets is goodwill. A company's goodwill asset is an intangible asset that adds value to the worth of the company and includes the reputation of its products, services, and staff. Table 19.4 depicts Dell's intangible assets over a period of three years. It seems to me that the tech companies preferred by swing traders must have a lot of goodwill on their books, as they're lacking in tangible assets.

Current Liabilities

On the other side of the balance sheet is the liability section, which chronicles the company's debts. If the debts must be repaid within a relatively short period of time, such as one year or less, then these liabilities are considered to be current liabilities. It is not difficult to identify current liabilities on a company's balance sheet—the word "payable" is attached. Current liabilities are the following:

- Accounts payable, which represents the amount that the company owes for materials and services purchased on credit, or rent owed to landlords

- Notes payable, which represents the payment amount that the company must pay banks and/or other creditors for short-term loans with an amortization schedule less than one year

- Dividends payable, which represents the cash payment to shareholders as declared by the board of directors

---

Table 19.4 *Dell Computer Corporation Intangible Assets—1998, 1999, 2000 (in $ millions)*

	Jan. 28, 2000	Jan. 29, 1999	Feb. 1, 1998
Intangible assets	$304	$15	$14

- Taxes payable, which represents the amount of tax owed to federal, state, or local governments

Table 19.5 depicts Dell's current liabilities over a period of three years.

Long-Term Liabilities

Long-term liabilities represent the debts that a company must pay after a year or more. The level of long-term debt will vary dramatically from one industry to another. For instance, capital-intensive industries, such as utility companies or real-estate companies, carry a substantial amount of long-term debt. However, the long-term debt was often needed to purchase or develop the long-term assets, such as the power plants or commercial real-estate properties. Table 19.6 represents Dell's long-term liabilities.

Stockholders' Equity

The components of stockholders' equity are the following:

- Common stock, which is listed on the company's balance sheet in excess of par value of the outstanding common-stock shares.

- Preferred stock, which is listed on the company's balance sheet in excess of par value of the outstanding preferred-stock shares. Preferred stock is a class of stock with a claim on the company's future earnings before any payments can be made on the common

Table 19.5 *Dell Computer Corporation Current Liabilities—1998, 1999, 2000 (in $ millions)*

	Jan. 28, 2000	Jan. 29, 1999	Feb. 1, 1998
Accounts payable	$3,538	$2,397	$1,643
Accrued notes, dividends, and taxes payable	1,654	1,298	1,054
Total Current Liabilities	**$5,192**	**$3,695**	**$2,697**

Table 19.6 *Dell Computer Corporation Long-Term Liabilities—1998, 1999, 2000 (in $ millions)*

	Jan. 28, 2000	Jan. 29, 1999	Feb. 1, 1998
Long-term debt	$508	$512	$17
Other long-term commitments	463	349	261
Total Long-Term Liabilities	**$971**	**$861**	**$278**

stock. Preferred-stock shareholders are entitled to a dividend at a specified rate when declared by the corporate board of directors. In addition, preferred-stock shareholders have priority over common-stock shareholders on the company's assets if the company liquidates.

■ Retained earnings, representing the net profits of a company, which have been retained by the company for future use, such as business expansion or company stock buybacks. Retained earnings do not necessarily mean that the company has that amount in cash; rather, it means that the company withheld such amount in profits from the dividend distribution for various business purposes. Profitable public companies that focus on growth tend to pay no or small dividends, and thus keep most of the profits in retained earnings. The management of such companies is basically telling its owners that the retained earnings will be a better investment for the shareholders because the money will be put back into the company to finance growth and the company stock will appreciate. Many investors, however, feel that distributed dividends would be a better individual choice for them because the management could simply waste that money.

■ Capital surplus (or paid-in capital), which represents the amount received from the sale of the company stock in excess of the stock's par value.

Table 19.7 depicts Dell's stockholders' equity over a period of three years.

Table 19.7   *Dell Computer Corporation Stockholders' Equity—1998, 1999, 2000 (in $ millions)*

	Jan. 28, 2000	Jan. 29, 1999	Feb. 1, 1998
Common stock	$3,583	$1,781	$747
Preferred stock	0	0	0
Retained earnings	1,260	606	607
Capital surplus	(465)	(66)	(61)
Total Stockholders' Equity	**$5,308**	**$2,321**	**$1,293**

Income Statement

The income statement examines the company's financial performance during a specified time period, which most commonly is one year or one quarter. The objective of the income statement is to document the company's net income or loss by subtracting all of the company's expenses from the revenues during this time period. Subsequently, the income statement is also called the profit and loss statement.

In essence, the income statement shows all of the revenues, expenses, depreciation, taxes, and any extraordinary revenue or expense amount. Analysis of the company's income statement will reveal its overall business performance. First, take a look at revenues or sales, which will state all of the operating revenues from the products and services sold. In essence, the company's financial accountants aggregate all of the money received from all of the company's revenue sources. At that time all of the business-revenue expenses or the costs of the goods sold are subtracted from the gross revenues. These are expenses directly related to producing goods or services. For instance, Dell must pay for the raw materials that make computers and cover wages to employees and the cost of overhead expenses. The difference between the company's total sales and its cost of sales is listed as the gross margin or gross profit.

In addition, the annual depreciation amount is subtracted to reflect depreciation of the company's fixed assets over the life of these assets. Depreciation is not an actual expense that the company must pay. It is an accounting charge or bookkeeping entry against the company earnings. In some cases the depreciation money is specifically earmarked for the fixed-assets replacement fund.

After all the operating and depreciation expenses from gross revenues have been subtracted, the result is the company's operating income for that year or quarter. At that time, "other income" is added to the calculated operating income. Other income reflects the company's investment income from the earned interest and dividends. When other income is added to operating income, the result is "earnings before interest and taxes." The company can use that amount to service the company's debt and to pay taxes. After the interest on corporate bonds is paid, the company will pay corporate taxes.

Finally, we come to net earnings or net income, which is literally the company's bottom line on the income statement. If the company's aggregate revenues were sufficient to pay for all of the operating expenses, depreciation, interest charges, and taxes, then the residual is positive, and the company would report a positive net income. In short, the company is profitable. Conversely, if the company's aggregate revenues were not sufficient to pay for all of the operating expenses, depreciation, interest charges, and taxes, then the residual is negative, and the company would report a net loss. At that time, the company would have to absorb the loss by borrowing funds or selling assets. Either way it is not a pretty picture. Table 19.8 depicts the income statement for Dell over a period of three years.

In addition to the company's balance sheet and income statement, the company's statement of cash flow is another important financial report. This report makes a positive adjustment to the net income or net earnings for the depreciation expenses, which are not actual physical expenses. All bookkeeping deductions, such as depreciation allowances and any extraordinary charges to reserve, are credited back or added to the net income. The cash flow statement is important because it registers how much cash is physically available to the company.

Other Financial Reports

The SEC requires all public companies to file several financial forms on a regular basis, which will provide additional financial information about the company. Form 10-K is submitted annually to the SEC and provides more detailed financial information than the company's annual report

Table 19.8 *Dell Computer Corporation Consolidated Income Statement—1998, 1999, 2000 (in $ millions)*

	Jan. 28, 2000	Jan. 29, 1999	Feb. 1, 1998
Revenue or sales	$25,265	$18,243	$12,327
Less cost of revenue	(20,047)	(14,137)	(9,605)
Equal gross margin or profit	$5,218	$4,106	$2,722
Less selling, general, and administrative costs	(2,387)	(1,788)	(1,202)
Less research, development, and engineering costs and depreciation	(568)	(272)	(204)
Equal operating income	$2,263	$2,046	$1,316
Less financing costs	(188)	(38)	(52)
Equal income before income taxes	$2,451	$2,084	$1,368
Less income taxes	(785)	(624)	(424)
Less extraordinary loss	(0)	(0)	(0)
Net income	$1,666	$1,460	$944

financial statements. Form 10-Q is a quarterly financial report submitted to the SEC. The 10-Q report is good in that it provides the most current financial data on the company. Unfortunately, the 10-Q report is not audited and tends to be less comprehensive than the 10-K report.

In addition to the 10-K and 10-Q reports, all public companies are required to immediately disclose all material events that might impact the company's future financial performance. This report is published in the SEC form 8-K. When the CEO decides to "retire" unexpectedly or "pursue other business opportunities," that information is disclosed in the 8-K report.

There is an easy and efficient way to retrieve all of this financial information. Anyone with Internet access can make use of the Electronic Data Gathering, Analysis & Retrieval system (EDGAR). EDGAR is an electronic database maintained by the SEC. Just go to the Internet site www.sec.gov and look for the EDGAR link.

In the end, financial accounting is not an exact science. Securities analysts might take the information from the financial notes and disagree with the company accountant's or auditor's conclusions. Securities analysts might then amend the company's income statement for their own analysis to reflect their—in all likelihood—more conservative approach. Subsequently, the figures presented by the company's accountants and auditors might be different from the financial indicators as developed and reported by different securities analysts.

20

Analysis of Earnings Ratios

"Lack of money is the root of all evil."

—*George Bernard Shaw*

Understanding the balance sheet and income statement is only the first half of fundamental analysis—developing and analyzing the financial ratios is the other half. As discussed in chapter 19, all financial analysts begin their fundamental stock analysis with the basic financial information that can be found in the company's balance sheet and income statement. These financial figures are then used in a larger context to develop several financial ratios, which are instrumental in identifying the company's strengths, weaknesses, and future trends. In essence, the practical nucleus of the fundamental analysis is embedded in the financial ratios.

Financial Ratios

A ratio is a measure of the relative size of two different numbers. These ratios are commonly expressed as a percentage or as a multiplier number. The objective of any financial ratio is twofold:

1. To provide a quick and concise method to compare different companies. In short, the first objective is to compare and contrast the

company's overall business performance relative to the established industry and the broad market benchmarks or standards.

2. To ascertain any trends by looking at a given company's financial ratios over time.

In my opinion, financial ratios can be grouped into three broad categories—earnings, liquidity, and assets-utilization ratios. First, let us cover the company's earnings ratios.

Earnings Ratios

Economists have long argued that there is a strong and positive correlation between a company's earnings and its stock price. In the short run, the company's stock prices are influenced by a myriad of different rational and often irrational factors, such as, for example, interest-rate changes, unfavorable news articles, profit taking, or stock selling by a large mutual fund. However, in the long run, the company's earnings will be the most important driving force behind its stock price.

Although the positive correlation between the company's market stock price and its earnings seems self-evident, measuring the relative value of the company's earnings is not an easy task. Financial analysts have therefore developed several ratios that are designed to ascertain whether the stock price is overvalued or undervalued relative to the value of the company's future earnings. If the long-term value-seeking investors perceive that the company's market price is undervalued relative to the company's earnings, then that would constitute a clear buy signal. Conversely, if the long-term investors who are seeking value perceive that the company's market price is overvalued relative to the company's earnings, then that would be a clear sell signal.

A negative earnings surprise can send a shock into the stock market and the stock could enter into a short-term price dive. An earnings surprise represents the difference between what financial analysts expected to see and what the company announced. It can be represented in absolute terms as cents per share or in relative terms as a percentage difference. Financial analysts devote a great deal of time to estimating a company's future earnings, such as the expected earning per share. Analysts then are able to develop a consensus of what that estimate should be.

If the company's announced earnings per share figures are dramatically different from an established consensus of analysts, then Wall Street will react (or often overreact), and thus there will be a short-term price correction. It is essential that traders be cognizant of the company's calendar so that they can anticipate and monitor the company's earnings announcement and the subsequent Wall Street reaction.

The most common earnings ratios are:

- Earnings per share (EPS)
- Diluted earnings per share
- Price earnings ratio (PE)
- Dividend payout ratio
- Current yield

Earnings Per Share and Diluted Earnings Per Share   Earnings per share (EPS) is defined as the following:

$$\text{Earnings Per Share} = \frac{\text{Net income} - \text{Preferred stock dividends}}{\text{Number of outstanding shares}}$$

The EPS formula incorporates only the company earnings that are available to common shareholders, and thus any preferred dividends are then subtracted from the net income. This generates the income that is available to the common shareholders, which is then divided by the number of the company's outstanding common shares. At that time we have the uniform standard of comparison: an earnings ratio that can be used as a measuring stick to compare earnings among different public companies at any point in time. The management can only impact the company's net income in order to influence its EPS. The number of the company's outstanding shares is already given and the preferred stock dividends are already declared. Obviously, the high net income figure translates automatically into a high EPS. Management then has an incentive to maximize the company's net income.

To further complicate our analysis, the companies will often issue convertible securities, such as convertible bonds, convertible preferred stock, warrants, or stock rights. Because these securities could be converted into common shares, the number of outstanding shares will increase. This will then result in a decrease in the EPS. Financial analysts will then calculate EPS on a fully diluted basis. The revised earnings per share is called diluted earnings per share, which assumes that all convertible securities have been converted into common stock.

Table 20.1 depicts Dell Computer Corporation's EPS and diluted EPS over a period of three years. The analyst would like to see a positive trend. Increasing EPS and diluted EPS over time will translate into a bullish sign, whereas decreasing EPS and diluted EPS would read as a bearish sign. Clearly Dell is doing well.

A pattern or a trend in the historical EPS is clearly significant. However, it is a common axiom in finance that past performance is not necessarily a guarantee of future performance. In my opinion, using only historical data to anticipate the future is like driving a car forward with only the benefit of a rearview mirror and without the benefit of looking ahead. Would it not be more productive to develop a forward or leading indicator?

EPS Estimate   Fortunately for us, there is such an indicator, called "EPS estimates." Most brokerage firms employ analysts who follow 15 to 20 stocks within a certain industry. Their job would be, for example, to track Dell Computer Corporation and its competitors in the PC industry to provide estimates and recommendations about Dell's future performance.

Table 20.1   *Dell Computer Corporation, Earnings per Share and Diluted Earnings per Share*

	Fiscal Year Ending			
	Jan. 28, 2000	Jan. 29, 1999	Feb. 1, 1998	Feb. 2, 1997
Earnings per share	$0.66	$0.58	$0.36	$0.18
Diluted earnings per share	$0.61	$0.53	$0.32	$0.17
Basic average shares outstanding	2,536	2,531	2,631	2,838
Diluted average shares outstanding	2,728	2,772	2,952	3,126

I want to differentiate here between the buy-side and sell-side financial analysts. A buy-side financial analyst is employed by a firm that invests or buys securities, such as a mutual fund, an insurance company, or a pension fund. A sell-side analyst, however, is employed by a NASD brokerage firm that is always promoting or selling securities. As you can imagine, the buy-side firms are distinctly different from the NASD broker/dealer firms that sell these securities. Buy-side analysts tend to be much more conservative, objective, and independent. Unfortunately, the ratings, estimates, and opinions of buy-side analysts are commonly not available outside their own firms.

Estimating future EPS for Dell is not an easy task. The analyst must forecast the gross revenues for the next four quarters as well as Dell's overall operating efficiency (i.e., its profit margin). To accomplish this task the analyst must have a complete understanding of the PC industry and Dell's products and its technology, as well as the overall economic conditions. In addition, the analyst must identify and measure Dell's cost centers and structure. Finally, to gain more insight about the company and its future, the analyst must invest a great deal of time into investigating the company's management and its business practices. As you can see, forecasting future earnings is an act of clairvoyance.

There are three possible sources of errors in forecasting the future company's earnings:

1. Errors from misjudging the overall future of the U.S. economy
2. Errors from misjudging the future of a particular industry
3. Errors from misjudging the future performance of a particular firm

Most analysts will agree that the most frequent errors in earnings estimates result from the last source—misjudging the future performance of a particular firm. It is not easy to secure detailed information about one company's future business performance. Financial analysts receive their information about the company's expected earnings directly from its management, and management usually has overly optimistic expectations about its future performance. In addition, financial analysts develop their own personal biases. They might simply like or prefer one computer firm in that industry, for example.

Ultimately, a brokerage-firm analyst will issue quarterly and annual EPS estimates for Dell. That information alone represents only the opinion of one analyst. Accuracy of the forecast will depend on the analyst's experience in that industry, skill, and training. Even the most experienced analyst can be wrong by a large margin. To mitigate this risk of having a wrong forecast, industry professionals pool together the EPS estimates from many analysts and develop a consensus or average EPS estimate. There are a few financial services companies, such as Zacks Investment Research (www.zacks.com), that compile and publish such consensus EPS estimates. Table 20.2 depicts an example of such diluted EPS estimates for Dell.

In this particular example, 33 securities brokers' analysts reported their EPS estimates for the next fiscal year, whereas only 28 analysts developed quarterly EPS estimates. A quick glance between Dell's previous year diluted EPS presented in table 20.1 ($0.53) and the consensus diluted EPS estimates for the upcoming fiscal year as presented in table

Table 20.2   *Dell Computer Corporation, EPS Estimates (2000)*

Sample of 33 Brokers	ANNUAL		QUARTERLY		In Five Years (%)
	In One Year	In Two Years	In Three Months	In Six Months	
Regional broker	$0.73	$1.03	$0.18	$0.21	41
Regional broker	$0.73	$1.05	$0.20	$0.20	37
Institutional broker	$0.73	$1.03	$0.18	$0.21	35
National broker	$0.73	$1.00	$0.18	$0.20	37.5
National broker	$0.73	$1.01	$0.18	$0.20	50
Regional broker	$0.75	$1.03	$0.18	$0.22	25
Institutional broker	$0.74	$1.02	$0.18	$0.21	32
Institutional broker	$0.73	$1.00	$0.18	$0.20	35
	Last 120 Days Consensus				
Total number of brokers	33	28	28	28	23
Low estimate	$0.70	$0.94	$0.17	$0.19	17
Mean estimate	$0.73	$1.02	$0.18	$0.21	33
High estimate	$0.78	$1.08	$0.21	$0.23	50

20.2 ($0.73) indicates a bullish sign. In addition, all analysts that follow Dell believed that the company would announce higher earnings this year.

The EPS estimates table is continuously being revised. As new information about the company and its business becomes available to the Wall Street community, the financial analysts will revise their estimates. The upgrades or downgrades in the EPS estimates become even more important than the initial EPS estimates. In essence, the changes in the EPS estimates become a leading indicator. Such announcements (or the anticipation of such announcements) are the kind of information that swing traders can trade on.

A change in the EPS estimates represents a change in the sentiment among the Wall Street professionals about the immediate future of the company. A downward revision in the EPS estimates will be conveyed quickly to professional fund managers who are buying or selling large blocks of shares. The fund managers are valuable institutional clients for any brokerage firm, and thus analysts will make sure that this information is quickly disseminated to them before it becomes public. Also, a change in the EPS estimates will be conveyed to the brokerage firm's sales force (i.e., the stockbrokers), who are providing daily buy-and-sell recommendations to thousands of their retail clients. The resulting large sell-off of that particular stock will quickly bring about a decline in price.

Conversely, an increase in EPS estimates will translate into higher expectations of the company's earnings by investors. Higher earnings could ultimately translate into higher dividends, which will make this stock more attractive to investors and Wall Street professionals. Higher demand for the stock, as more investors buy the stock, and reduced supply of the stock, as more investors refrain from selling the stock, will ultimately result in a higher price for the stock.

If the measures of the broad stock market (the S & P's 500 index) indicate the conditions of a bull market, then the stocks that have positive changes in the EPS estimates will tend to exhibit a higher increase than the broad market itself. If the changes in the EPS estimates were negative, then the stock would have a distinct probability of underperforming as compared to the S & P's 500 index performance. Conversely, if the S & P's 500 index indicates a condition of a bear stock market, then the stocks that have negative changes in the EPS estimates will tend to exhibit a greater price decrease than the broad market. If the changes in the EPS estimates were positive, then the stock would tend to perform better than the declining S & P's 500 index.

EPS Surprises Another variation on the EPS estimates is the EPS surprise. We have learned so far that 33 different regional, national, and institutional brokerage firms "follow" Dell business activities and issue estimates of its future EPS on a regular basis. Dell, like any other public company in the United States, will release to the public on a quarterly basis its actual quarterly earnings. The U.S. companies will publish their earnings reports just a few days or weeks after the end of the company's fiscal year, which most commonly will correspond with the end of March, June, September, or December. Several Internet-based information services companies, such as www.zacks.com and www.yahoo.com, will post the earnings announcement calendar for most U.S. public companies.

Most of the time the reported EPS is very close to the projected or estimated EPS, and thus there are no EPS surprises. However, every now and then there will be a substantial discrepancy between the reported EPS and the consensus EPS estimate. The EPS surprise can either be expressed as a percentage difference between the reported EPS and the consensus EPS estimate, or as an absolute-dollar difference between the two values. Once the positive or negative EPS surprises are announced to the public, they tend to have an immediate and dramatic impact on the stock prices.

EPS surprises may also have a dramatic impact on financial analysts. They are forced to go back to the drawing board to figure out why they had miscalculated. They will take a closer look at the next level of the company's EPS estimates so that they are not surprised again. The result of such a review will most likely be a universal adjustment to their estimates of the company's quarterly EPS. That again will have a secondary impact on the company's stock price.

If the EPS surprise was negative, rather large, and without any extraordinary justification, the financial analysts will then revise their estimates of the company's earnings downward. Some analysts will even downgrade their buy-and-sell recommendations, for instance, from buy to hold, or perhaps even to a sell recommendation. Reducing the company's future EPS estimates and downgrading its buy-and-sell recommendation will result in a flood of negative news about the company. Financial information services companies, such as CNBC or Bloomberg, will keep broadcasting to the general public that, one after another, brokerage firms are downgrading the company's financial status.

Price Earnings Ratio (PE)   One of the most important concepts in economics is the notion of value. Value is the relative worth of a commodity, product, or service. Value has two distinct components: benefit and price. It is easy for everyone to relate to the concept of benefit. The EPS is a clear benefit to shareholders. However, to reach the value of the benefit, one must incorporate the price that one must pay for such a benefit. To determine whether the reported benefit, such as the EPS, is overvalued or undervalued the financial analyst will incorporate the stock price into the measurement. That is accomplished by dividing the stock price by the benefit (EPS).

The price earnings ratio is calculated as follows:

$$\text{Price Earnings Ratio} = \frac{\text{Market price}}{\text{Earnings per share}}$$

The PE ratio, which is sometimes called the PE multiple or earnings multiple, is a broad benchmark used to compare the intrinsic value for any company. If the market price of the stock is $10 and the EPS is $1, then the PE ratio is 10. In other words, it takes $10 to buy a claim for $1 of the company's income. If the company distributed all of the earnings ($1) as dividends, then it would take 10 years to recover the initial $10 investment.

If, however, the market price of the stock is $100 and the EPS remains at $1, then the PE ratio becomes 100. It now takes a lot more money ($100) to buy a claim for the same $1 of the company's income. Again, if the company were to distribute all of the earnings ($1) as dividends, then it would take 100 years to recover the initial $100 investment. One can argue that a stock with such a high PE multiple, such as 100, is overvalued. In essence, the high PE multiple indicates that the public is paying a high market price for the company's present earnings. The stock with a lower PE ratio is clearly a better value.

The PE ratio is commonly computed by using the EPS calculations from the past 12 months. However, some financial analysts use the estimated or projected EPS in order to generate a "leading" PE ratio. The underlying rationale is that you are buying stock today and claiming future earnings potential, not past earnings. My preference is to keep the financial ratios as simple as possible, and thus the "trailing" or previous year EPS figure will suffice.

The PE ratio will change daily as the market price changes daily. If the EPS remains the same and the stock price goes up, then the PE ratio will go up as well. Conversely, if the stock price goes down and the EPS remains the same, then the PE ratio will go down as well. When comparing PE ratios of different companies, it is important to compare these ratios at the same time. The company with an increasing PE ratio will be viewed by financial analysts as becoming increasingly more speculative or overvalued.

Also, PE ratios vary dramatically from industry to industry. New companies in the dynamic growth industries, such as high-tech, will most likely show a high market price and a low EPS. Such companies tend to spend a disproportionate amount of the company's gross income on research and development or new marketing campaigns. Such companies tend to exhibit a lower net income and thus they report a lower EPS. In addition, investors and traders will bid up the price of high-tech stocks in anticipation of even greater future-earnings potential, which may or may not happen. Subsequently, the PE ratio for high-tech companies is high. For example, a recent average PE ratio for the PC industry was 49. In addition, many Internet companies have no earnings whatsoever to report (thus far only losses), and subsequently there is no PE ratio to be calculated. How can you divide a positive number (i.e., the market price) with zero or negative EPS (i.e., losses)?

Earnings Growth Rate   Is a stock with a high PE ratio automatically a bad investment? For instance, Dell Computer Corporation has a PE ratio of 70, whereas the average PE ratio for the S & P's 500 companies is about 31. Indeed, the average PE ratio for the S & P's 500 over the last decade is approximately 17. Does this mean that Dell stock is currently overvalued or a speculative investment? Moreover, does this mean that all stocks are currently overvalued or speculative investments?

The answer is maybe. In absolute terms, compared to other S & P's 500 stocks—and even the other high-tech stocks—Dell is clearly an expensive stock. Being expensive is not necessarily a bad attribute as long as the company has a track record of increased earnings. A conventional rule of thumb is that the company's PE multiple should be close to the company's earnings growth rate. The best measure of the earnings growth is to compare the growth rate in the company's EPS. EPS is the best measure of a company's earnings because it is based on the net earnings or net income figure, which takes into account both the changes in the company's revenues and its expenses. Comparing the PE multiple to the EPS growth rate is quite important for evaluating growth companies that pay little or no dividends.

Here's how this is done: To answer the question of whether Dell is overvalued, we need to compare the absolute number of the company's PE multiple (or PE ratio) against the absolute number of the company's growth rate in EPS. For instance, figure 20.1 showed that Dell's EPS in 1999 and 1998 were $0.58 and $0.36, which demonstrates a 61 percent increase in one year. Thus, Dell's trailing EPS for the last 12 months increased by 61 percent. The absolute number of the PE multiple of 70 is higher than the value of 61, and thus one can conclude that Dell is overvalued.

However, traders and short-term investors probably don't plan on keeping Dell in their portfolio for a long period of time. Their objective is to trade Dell stock and exploit its relative price volatility. If traders take a long position in Dell, most likely it is only for a few days or a few weeks. Instead of asking whether Dell is a good long-term buy investment, the traders and short-term investors would like to know if there is a strong probability that Dell will not decline in value. In this case, the PE multiple of 70 is relatively close to Dell's EPS growth rate of 61. Thus, based on this information alone, it's likely that traders won't foresee any dramatic drop in Dell's stock price. In essence, it is OK to keep Dell overnight because Dell has strong fundamentals.

Imagine if Dell did not have such strong earnings growth over time. Imagine that Dell's PE ratio is still 70 given the 1-year EPS performance, but that there is no growth in earnings or EPS over time. Suppose that the EPS growth rate from 1998 to 1999 is only 20 percent. The absolute number of the PE multiple of 70 is dramatically higher than the EPS growth rate of 20. There is a distinct possibility that many investors would consider Dell stock to be grossly overvalued, and thus they might sell Dell's long position to take any profits, or they might even short sell Dell stock. At this time, having a long position in Dell is risky because the market can react forcefully to any negative news on Dell with a large sell-off during after-hours trading. Dell stock might open for trading the next day with a large downward price gap.

Dividend Payout and Current Yield   Both dividend payout ratio and current yield measures attempt to depict how much of the company's earnings were distributed to shareholders. They are indicators of how much profit is returned to shareholders in the form of dividends. Comparing dividend payout and current yield is rather important for evaluating large "blue chip" companies that operate in a more stable, mature, or government-regulated business environment.

The dividend payout ratio measures the percentage of net income paid to common stockholders as cash dividends. It is calculated by dividing annual dividends by EPS.

$$\text{Dividend Payout} = \frac{\text{Annual dividend paid on common stock}}{\text{Earnings per share}}$$

A high dividend payout ratio would indicate that this is an income stock. Many utility companies that emphasize high and steady dividends have historically high dividend payout ratios of 60 to 80 percent. These companies are in mature, stable, or regulated industries and thus their future earnings potential is rather limited. If they cannot offer investors capital appreciation, then they must offer income or dividends. Traders and short-term investors often ignore income stocks because the stocks are not volatile. You have to have significant price volatility to make money as a trader or short-term investor.

However, an excessively high dividend payout ratio is not necessarily a good thing. Company management might wish to maintain a certain dividend level on a regular basis. However, if the EPS is declining, then the dividend payout ratio will increase. It is not that the company is declaring higher dividends, but rather that the company's earnings are declining. Imagine that the dividend payout ratio is approaching 90 percent. Sooner or later the company's management will have to cut back on the declared dividends (as the company cannot offer more than 100 percent), and this will send a clear message to Wall Street. Many income investors who purchased the stock based on expected high and steady dividends will sell the stock, and thus the stock price will decline in value. Such a situation would offer short-selling possibilities to traders.

Current Yield   The current yield or dividend yield for common stock depicts the rate of return that the dividend represents on the stock's current market price. It is calculated by dividing the annual dividend by the current market price:

$$\text{Current Yield} = \frac{\text{Annual dividend per common share}}{\text{Market price}}$$

The current yield values will oscillate daily with the fluctuations in the stock price. A current yield of 2 percent at the end of the trading day would basically mean that the investor would receive a 2 percent rate of return on declared dividends given the price of the stock at that time. Clearly a 2 percent yield is not a very attractive rate of return. However, dividends are only one source of investment income. Capital appreciation is by far a much more important source of income to investors. It contributes substantially more toward the total return on common stocks.

"Total return" is the sum of the stock's appreciation value at the time of sale and any paid dividends, divided by the stock's starting price. The calculated total return is the best way to compare a stock's overall performance because it takes into account both the distributed dividends and change in the stock market value. Many companies emphasize future growth and do not issue dividends. Subsequently, there are no current yield and dividend payout ratios to be calculated.

Traders will most likely seek stocks that emphasize growth over income. These companies offer no dividends or very small dividends even though the companies are profitable. The company executive management is basically stating to shareholders, "Trust us. The retained earnings will increase the company's equity and the company will obtain a high rate of return on that equity." Companies that emphasize growth over income are thus considered to be more speculative, and thus more price-volatile. Traders and short-term investors need to pay close attention to a company's future earnings announcement because the market can react dramatically to any earnings surprises.

21

Analysis of Liquidity and Assets Utilization Ratios

"A criminal is a person with predatory instincts who does not have sufficient capital to form a corporation."

—*Howard Scott*

After reading chapter 20, it is my hope that you are now convinced that financial ratios are instrumental in identifying a company's strengths, weaknesses, and future trends. I also discussed my preference for grouping financial ratios into three broad and general categories—earnings, liquidity, and assets utilization ratios. As we have already covered the earnings ratios, let us next cover a company's liquidity ratios.

Liquidity Ratios

Liquidity ratios are an important measure of a company's short-term stability because they measure a company's ability to convert its current assets into cash. In other words, liquidity ratios reveal how well the company can survive any short-term financial challenges.

The most common liquidity ratios are the following:

- Cash flow
- Net working capital

- Current ratio
- Quick asset ratio
- Cash asset ratio
- Debt coverage ratio
- Debt-to-equity ratio

Cash Flow

Cash flow value reflects all of the money generated by a company's operations. To calculate cash flow, annual depreciation expenses are added back into a company's net income (because depreciation is not an actual expense but only a bookkeeping entry). A positive cash flow value demonstrates that the company has sufficient income to pay all of its expenses and possibly declare dividend distributions. A negative cash flow value means that the company is losing money and may have trouble meeting its short-term obligations.

The company's income statement gives us the information required to calculate cash flow. Cash flow is calculated as follows:

Cash Flow = Net earnings (or loss) + Annual depreciation

Once again I will use Dell Computer Corporation as an example. Dell's income statement (table 19.8 in chapter 19) disclosed that the company had earned at the end of fiscal year 1999 (January 28, 2000) $1,666 million in net income and $375 million in depreciation expenses, and thus its cash flow is $2,041 million.

Net Working Capital

Any company must have working capital to finance its daily business operations. Think of working capital as the fuel that keeps the business running. Maintaining a prudent level of working capital at all times is important. Working capital is required in order for the company's existing financial obligations to be met and to expand its production if necessary. Net working capital is calculated as follows:

Net Working Capital = Current assets − Current liabilities

For Dell, at the end of 1999 the net working capital figure is extracted from the consolidated balance sheet information and is the substantial amount of $2,489 million. It seems that Dell is well poised to finance its immediate growth. Dell's net working capital figure is derived from table 19.1.

Net Working Capital ($2,489 million) =
Current assets ($7,681 million) – Current liabilities ($5,192 million)

Current Ratio

Net working capital basically provides us with an absolute-dollar figure. However, it doesn't answer such questions as whether it is an adequate amount and how it compares to the industry standards, which the current ratio does. The current ratio indicates whether or not the company has an adequate amount of working capital simply by comparing current assets to current liabilities. A high current ratio indicates sufficient net working capital, whereas a low current ratio indicates a working capital problem.

$$\text{Current Ratio} = \frac{\text{Current assets}}{\text{Current liabilities}}$$

For Dell Computer Corporation, the current ratio is 1.48 ($7,681 million in current assets divided by $5,192 million in current liabilities). The ratio of 1.48 basically means that there is $1.48 in current assets for each $1.00 in current liabilities. Is this current ratio of 1.48 adequate? Conservative investors look for companies that have a relatively high current ratio of 2 and greater. Does that mean that Dell Computer Corporation does not have sufficient working capital? A closer look at Dell's current assets schedule reveals that the largest components of Dell's current assets are the cash ($3,809 million) and marketable securities ($323 million). Other current assets are not quite as liquid, namely, inventories ($391 million) and accounts receivable ($2,608 million). Indeed, Dell is known in the computer industry for keeping only six days of supplies on hand in its inventory. The point here is that Dell, with a lot of cash and marketable securities on the one hand and small inventories and easily collectible accounts receivable on the other hand, is capable of operating with a current ratio of less than 2.

Quick Asset Ratio

The quick asset ratio is a more stringent or restrictive measure of liquidity than the current ratio because it doesn't take into account inventories that are not as liquid as cash, marketable securities, or accounts receivable. In essence, the quick asset ratio is the current assets reduced by inventories, then divided by current liabilities:

$$\text{Quick Asset Ratio} = \frac{\text{Current assets} - \text{Inventory}}{\text{Current liabilities}}$$

For Dell Computer Corporation, the quick asset ratio is 1.40. It is derived from $7,681 million in current assets reduced by $391 million in inventories, which is then divided by $5,192 in current liabilities. This means that there is $1.40 of quick assets available for every $1.00 of current liabilities, indicating that Dell is able to pay its bills for a short period of time without receiving any additional revenues. Again, a quick asset ratio of greater than 1 is considered to be a safe measure of liquidity.

Cash Asset Ratio

The cash asset ratio is the most restrictive test of a company's ability to meet its short-term debt. It takes into account only cash and marketable securities, and thus it represents the company's emergency cash-liquidity position. Cash asset ratio is calculated as follows:

$$\text{Cash Asset Ratio} = \frac{\text{Cash} + \text{Marketable securities}}{\text{Current liabilities}}$$

For Dell, the cash asset ratio is calculated as follows:

$$\frac{\text{Cash (\$3,809 million) + Marketable securities (\$323 million)}}{\text{Current liabilities (\$5,192 million)}} = 0.79$$

This basically means that Dell has 79 cents of cash and marketable securities available for every $1 of current liabilities. Obviously, the higher the cash asset ratio value, the stronger the company's liquidity position.

Debt Coverage Ratio

Debt coverage ratio is designed to measure the company's overall ability to meet debt payments (due to its bondholders) and dividend payments (due to preferred stockholders). Financial analysts often call this ratio the "bond interest coverage ratio." Failing to meet interest payments to bondholders would place a company in default on its debt, which could push the company into bankruptcy proceedings. A financial analyst can assess a bondholder's and an investor's degree of safety by comparing the money available for debt service to the amount of money required for the bond interest payments. The debt coverage ratio is found by dividing the company's operating income, which is the income before interest and tax payments, by the annual interest expense. The formula is as follows:

$$\text{Debt Coverage Ratio} = \frac{\text{Operating income}}{\text{Annual bond interest expense}}$$

Debt-to-Equity Ratio

The debt-to-equity ratio measures a company's financial leverage. Companies with a high percentage of outstanding debt compared with their respective equity positions are considered to be highly leveraged. In addition, stock prices of highly leveraged companies tend to be greatly impacted by any changes in interest rates.

The debt-to-equity ratio compares the company's securities that have fixed-interest charges, such as bonds and preferred stock, to those securities without fixed charges, such as common stock, for which dividends do not have to be declared. In essence, bond interest payments and preferred-stock dividends must be paid, whereas the common-stock dividends need not be declared or issued. Bankers use the debt-to-equity ratio to evaluate the credit strength of the corporation. Clearly, too much debt compared to equity is considered risky. The formula is as follows:

$$\text{Debt-to-Equity Ratio} = \frac{\text{Bonds} + \text{Preferred}}{\text{Common stock at par} + \text{Capital surplus} + \text{Retained earnings}}$$

Because Dell does not have any preferred stock outstanding, the debt-to-equity ratio would be found by dividing bonds by the value of the common stock, plus capital surplus, plus retained earnings.

Assets Utilization Ratios

Assets utilization calculations show the level of earnings that a company generates from each dollar of assets. Assets utilization ratios indicate a company's ability to utilize its current assets to generate income. The most common assets utilization ratios are as follows:

- Return on assets
- Operating profit margin
- Net profit margin
- Book value per common share

Return On Assets

Return on assets measures the company's overall effectiveness in utilizing the existing assets at hand to generate income. This measure of asset utilization is closely monitored for the asset-based industries, such as the banking industry. In addition, financial analysts will pay close attention to this financial indicator's trend for several years because it indicates whether the firm's relative efficiency is improving or declining. The formula for the return on assets is as follows:

$$\text{Return on Assets} = \frac{\text{Net income}}{\text{Total assets}}$$

For Dell Computer Corporation, the return on assets is calculated by dividing $1,666 million of net income by $11,471 million of total assets, which is approximately 14 percent. This financial indicator compares well against the PC-industry standard of 7 percent.

Operating Profit Margin

Financial analysts often examine operating profits and net profits to assess a company's overall profitability. To determine the operating profit margin, analysts divide the company's operating income by sales. For Dell, the operating profit margin is approximately 10 percent. Operating profit margin is calculated as follows:

$$\text{Operating Profit Margin} = \frac{\text{Operating income (\$2,263 million)}}{\text{Sales (\$25,265 million)}}$$

For Dell Computer Corporation, this means that 9 cents of gross profit is generated from each dollar of sales. The other way of expressing this ratio is to state that operating expenses account for 91 cents from each dollar of sales. In essence, Dell is spending 91 cents to produce one dollar of sales.

In addition, analysts commonly compare the operating profit margin figure with the industry standard to ascertain the company's relative efficiency. For instance, the operating profit margin industry standard for the PC industry is approximately 7. Analysts will then compare Dell's ratio over a few quarters to determine if the company's production efficiency is improving or declining.

Net Profit Margin

Net profit margin is a more meaningful indicator of asset utilization because the ratio takes into account debt service payments and taxes. To calculate the amount of net profit earned from each sales dollar, net income is divided by sales. For Dell Computer Corporation, the net profit margin is 6.5 percent. After taking into consideration interest expenses and taxes, Dell is earning a net profit of 6.5 cents for every dollar in sales.

$$\text{Net Profit Margin} = \frac{\text{Net income (\$1,666 million)}}{\text{Sales (\$25,265 million)}}$$

Book Value Per Common Share

Financial analysts will often try to link the price of securities that are issued by the company to the assets, which are backing these securities. This is often referred to as "book value." The company's book value, or its net tangible assets, are then divided by the number of outstanding common shares. The formula for the book value per common share is the following:

$$\text{Book Value Per Common Share} = \frac{\text{Net tangible assets}}{\text{Outstanding common shares}}$$

where

$$\text{Net Tangible Assets} =$$
$$\text{Total assets} - \text{Total liabilities} - \text{Intangible assets} - \text{Preferred stocks}$$

For Dell Computer Corporation, the book value per common share is $1.94:

$$\text{Book Value Per Common Share} = \frac{\$11,471 \text{ million} - \$6,163 \text{ million} - \$304 \text{ million} - 0}{2,575 \text{ million shares}}$$

Clearly, the company's book value has no relationship to the company's market value. Market value is determined by the market forces of supply and demand for the shares of that company. Most companies in the world are worth much more than their book value. For instance,

Dell Computer Corporation trades at a substantially higher price than the calculated $1.94 per share.

However, many companies in the world are asset-based companies—banks are an example—whereby accumulation of assets is the core of their business activities. The assets and liabilities of these companies are easily calculated and easy to interpret. Value investors look for such companies whose stock prices are so beaten by the stock market that the book value per share exceeds the stock price. In essence, the value investors are looking for a "turnaround situation."

Book value must not be confused with liquidation value or breakup value. The actual liquidation value of a company will depend on the amount a company receives for assets on the open market, which is dramatically different than the accounting values for such assets. Accounting procedures generally favor conservatism and thus the assets are calculated at their historical cost and depreciated over time. Subsequently, a fixed asset such as the company's office or factory building might have little value on the books when in fact they might be worth millions.

Interpreting Financial Analysis Ratios

Analyzing the company's financial statements and ratios is only a starting point. In order to obtain the full picture, one must invest time and effort to understanding the company's product, industry, and management philosophy. That information is always included in the narrative or nonfinancial section of the company's annual report.

It is important that traders develop a certain understanding of the company's business and its industry. This basic understanding will help traders sift through a myriad of news developments and determine quickly whether the news will have a large potential to impact the company's stock price. Understanding the company and its industry will help traders answer many "why" questions. The company's financial statements, such as the income statement and balance sheet, will reveal the current financial status of the company. The company's income statement and balance sheet will also paint a picture of the company's current financial health, but it will not explain "why" there are changes in that picture. For instance, does the company have a new product or service that explains the higher net income, or is that higher net income the result of cost-cutting measures?

The first step in conducting a financial analysis is to examine the changes in the financial ratios from year to year. That change, in both relative terms (ratios and percentages) and absolute terms (raw numbers), will indicate a trend. It is difficult to declare what constitutes a "good" rate of change, as this rate will vary from industry to industry and from year to year. Table 21.1 depicts the trend for Dell Computer Corporation over a 10-year time span.

The second step in performing a financial analysis is to compare and contrast the company's performance today across the industry and broad market standards. That comparison, in both relative terms (ratios and percentages) and absolute terms (raw numbers), will indicate a pattern. The comparison will answer any questions about whether the company is an industry leader or not. Table 21.2 depicts that comparison for Dell Computer Corporation for the previous year.

It is clear from the comparison of financial ratios that Dell is an industry leader. It is also clear from table 21.1 that Dell shows a consistent increase in sales, net income, and cash flow. In addition, Dell has a strong balance sheet with relatively little debt, although there is a large increase in debt for 1999. With the exception of that one year, Dell has a consistent record of profitability. All indicators of the company's financial well-being indicate that Dell is a profitable business.

Does this mean that Dell is a good investment opportunity? My personal answer is yes. To confirm my opinion, let us take a look at the buy-and-sell recommendations from the Wall Street brokerage firms. Zacks Investment Research of Chicago (www.zacks.com) compiles such recommendations from 230 brokerage firms, which collectively employ approximately 3,000 financial analysts. In addition to compiling brokerage firms' recommendations, Zacks also provides to investors and traders information on consensus analysts' opinions on future EPS estimates.

Table 21.3 depicts brokerage firms' recommendations for Dell Computer Corporation for the previous three months. The five possible recommendations have an assigned standardized ratings scale: strong buy (1 point), moderate buy (2 points), hold (3 points), moderate sell (4 points), and strong sell (5 points). For instance, the consensus or average recommendation among Wall Street analysts for the last three months for Dell Computer Corporation is 1.8, or moderate buy.

Table 21.1 *Dell Computer Corporation, 10-Year Summary of Selected Financial Indicators*

Financial Indicators	Jan. 2000	Jan. 1999	Jan. 1998	Jan. 1997	Jan. 1996	Jan. 1995	Jan. 1994	Jan. 1993	Jan. 1992	Jan. 1991
Current assets ($ million)	7,681	6,339	3,912	2,747	1,957	1,470	1,048	852	512	236
Current liabilities ($ million)	5,192	3,695	2,697	1,658	939	751	538	493	229	141
Depreciation ($ million)	375	252	167	47	38	33	30	19	13	9
Long-term debt ($ million)	508	512	17	18	113	113	100	48	41	4
Revenues ($ million)	25,265	18,243	12,327	7,759	5,296	3,475	2,873	2,013	889	546
Operating income ($ million)	2,263	2,066	1,353	714	377	249	−38	139	68	45
Net income ($ million)	1,666	1,460	944	531	272	149	−35	101	50	27
Earnings per share (EPS)	0.66	0.58	0.36	0.19	0.09	0.06	−0.02	0.05	0.03	0.02
Diluted earnings per share	0.61	0.53	0.32	0.18	0.09	0.05				
Price earnings ratio (PE) average in 1 year	70.8	59.2	26.1	14.9	12.0	10.5	NA	10.1	9.8	7.3
Dividend payout ratio	0	0	0	0	0	0	0	0	0	0

continues

Table 21.1 *Dell Computer Corporation, 10-Year Summary of Selected Financial Indicators (continued)*

Financial Indicators	Jan. 2000	Jan. 1999	Jan. 1998	Jan. 1997	Jan. 1996	Jan. 1995	Jan. 1994	Jan. 1993	Jan. 1992	Jan. 1991
Current yield	0	0	0	0	0	0	0	0	0	0
Debt coverage ratio	NA	NA	457	107	26.5	18.5	NA	NA	41.8	30
Debt-to-equity ratio	0.10	0.22	0.01	0.02	0.12	0.17	0.21	0.13	0.15	0.04
Return on assets	14.5	21.2	22.1	17.7	12.7	9.4	–3.1	11	9.1	10.3
Net profit margin	6.5	8.0	7.7	6.8	5.1	4.3	–1.2	5	5.7	5
Book value per common share	1.94	0.90	0.50	0.29	0.32	0.26	0.19	0.06	0.12	0.06

Computed ratios are based on the previous 12 months.

If you are a long-term investor, then Dell Computer Corporation stock is a good long-term investment opportunity. But you are not a long-term investor. You are reading this book because you are a short-term trader looking to make money trading stocks. Do you need to understand all of the presented financial analysis to conclude that Dell stock is a strong stock for the long run?

My personal opinion is yes, particularly if your stock trading style requires overnight long positions. If you have overnight long positions, regardless of the time length, you are an investor. As a short-term investor you should know how to use and understand the tools used by the professional investment community—fundamental analysis. More stock investing and trading knowledge is always better than less knowledge. More knowledgeable investors and traders perform better than less knowledgeable investors and traders. More knowledge is preferred to less!

Table 21.2 *Dell Computer Corporation, Summary Comparison of Selected Financial Indicators*

Financial Indicators	Dell (Jan. 2000)	PC Industry (Jan. 2000)	S & P's 500 (Jan. 2000)
Revenues growth rates (% change in 1 year)	31.5	10.9	22.1
Operating income growth rates (% change in 1 year)	21%	17.9%	21.6%
Earnings per share (EPS) growth rates	18.8%	15.8%	15%
Price earnings ratio (PE) average in 1 year	70.8	63	29.8
Current ratio	1.5	1.4	1.3
Quick asset ratio	1.3	1.1	0.9
Debt-to-equity ratio	0.1	0.04	1.1
Return on assets	15.3	6.8	3.0
Book value per common share	$1.94	$5.50	$10.56
Income per employee	$48,000	$26,000	$20,000
Revenues per employee	$740,000	$616,000	$277,000

Computed ratios are based on the previous 12 months.

Table 21.3 *Dell Computer Corporation, Buy, Hold, and Sell Brokerage Firm Recommendations*

Recommendation	Current	1 Month Ago	2 Months Ago	3 Months Ago
Strong buy	13 analysts	12 analysts	13 analysts	13 analysts
Moderate buy	12 analysts	13 analysts	12 analysts	12 analysts
Hold	8 analysts	9 analysts	7 analysts	7 analysts
Moderate sell	0	0	0	0
Strong sell	0	0	0	0
Average Recommendation	1.8 Moderate buy	1.8 Moderate buy	1.8 Moderate buy	1.8 Moderate buy

Recommendations are based on the previous 3 months from 33 analysts.

22

Summary of Swing Trading Recommendations

"The only source of knowledge is experience."

—*Albert Einstein*

Trading is not an exact science, and there is no "bulletproof" trading method or strategy that can sustain scientific scrutiny. The ten trading recommendations below are presented as a list, not necessarily in order of relative ranking. Readers might disagree with one or more suggestions, and that is OK, as every trader develops his or her own style.

I am not advocating that a novice trader incorporate all of the following recommendations immediately. Only experienced swing traders should utilize some of the recommendations, such as the recommendation to trade expensive and volatile NASDAQ stocks in increments of 1,000 or more shares. Chapter 9 on risk management elaborated further on how the novice swing trader should move along the ubiquitous learning curve. All of the following suggestions have been previously mentioned throughout the book; the list here serves as a summary of trading recommendations. Therefore, experienced swing traders should consider the following:

1. Consider trading volatile stocks. A stock's *relative price volatility* is measured by the *Beta coefficient*, which tells how much a stock moves in relation to the S & P's 500 index. A stock with a Beta

value of 1.5 or higher (i.e., a stock that is 50 percent on average more price-volatile than stocks on the S & P's 500 index) would be a good start. Technology stocks usually fit these criteria. Appendix 3 of this book lists the 100 NASDAQ and NYSE stocks with high price volatility and high daily trading liquidity. Many traders attempt to trade stocks that are not volatile. It is difficult to make money trading if the trading stocks are not moving, and there is no point in monitoring stocks if prices are historically stable.

2. Consider trading stocks that have high *absolute price volatility*, that is, stocks with a daily price range of at least 1 point and a weekly price range of at least 5 points. In other words, the difference between the intraweek high and low stock prices should be 5 points or higher. That is how swing traders make their money—exploiting the high weekly absolute price movement. It is possible to have high relative price volatility (high Beta) and low absolute volatility (low intraweek price range) if a stock is inexpensive. Again, technology stocks tend to be expensive and volatile; thus they have both high relative and absolute volatility.

3. Consider trading stocks that have high *absolute liquidity*. A stock's liquidity is measured by the average daily trading-volume statistics, which show how many shares are traded on average every day. The daily trading volume should be at least 500,000 shares. It is crucial that there are many buyers and sellers for a stock. If there is no liquidity (that is, if fewer than 500,000 shares are traded daily), traders could have a difficult time getting out of the trade at the desired price. For instance, the price could drop very quickly, and the trader might simply get stuck in a long and losing position.

4. Consider trading stocks in the right size. Swing traders should start trading with 200-share increments. But eventually they need to graduate to trading in increments of 1,000 or more shares. Ultimately, the objective of swing trading is to trade in increments of several thousand shares and to profit from the intraweek price movement. A small relative gain of 1 point or $1 per share would result in a large absolute profit of $1,000 if 1,000 shares were purchased in that single trade. If the trader were to purchase only 100 shares, the profit would be only $100.

5. Trade stocks that are expensive. Again, the objective of swing trading is to profit from relatively small intraweek price movements. For an expensive stock ($100 or more per share), a small relative change of 1 percent is 1 point, which would constitute a $1,000 potential profit if 1,000 shares were purchased. This is quite common and feasible. Stocks easily move up or down 1 percent during the trading day and as much as $10 to $20 in the course of five trading days. For an inexpensive stock ($10 per share), however, a 1-point price change would be a large relative change of 10 percent. If 1,000 shares were purchased, the stock price would need to move up or down 10 percent to earn a $1,000 potential profit. Although, there are a few low-priced stocks that often move 10 percent daily and have substantial daily trading volume—General Magic, Inc. (GMGC) is one stock that comes to mind.

6. Have a reason to trade that particular stock at that particular point in time. In other words, traders should observe trading signals to buy or sell a stock. A trading signal could be a combination of several technical-analysis indicator events occurring simultaneously. A trader should trade stocks that have a momentum or price trend at that point in time, and should not purchase or sell short a stock that is not moving at that time. Otherwise, the trader is just gambling by hoping for an appropriate outcome. By guessing, the trader would have only a 50 percent probability of making a winning trade if there is no observable price momentum or direction. Before the trader takes a long or short stock position, he or she needs to observe a series of upticks or downticks that would indicate or prove a price trend. Traders do not need to be proactive and anticipate the price movement; they need only be reactive and follow the observable price movement.

7. Take the stock position (long or short) that coincides with the broad market price movement. For example, you could follow the trend of the S & P's 500 index or the trend of a particular industry sector, such as the Semiconductor index if you are trading Intel (INTC) or Advanced Micro Devices (AMD). At the least, a trader should be cognizant of the S & P's 500 index or the NASDAQ 100 index price movement. It would be difficult to expect that one stock would appreciate in value if there were a broad stock market sell-off. The

probability of making a winning trade declines if the trader takes a position against the broad market.

8. Be cognizant of the stock's intraday and intraweek price support-and-resistance levels before entering the trade. The Bollinger bands indicator is an excellent and dynamic technical-analysis tool that shows real-time intraday and weekly price support-and-resistance levels. The problem is that traders often enter a long or short trading position too late. For example, if the price was already at the upper Bollinger band level (at the intraweek price resistance level), a trader should not purchase a stock at that point in time. This is the time to seek short-selling opportunities. Conversely, the trader should not sell short a stock if the stock is at the price-support level or at the lower Bollinger band at that time. Instead, the trader should look for buying opportunities.

9. Be cognizant of the stock's intraday and weekly price support-and-resistance levels when preparing to exit the trade. Some traders often wait too long to exit or close their long or short trading positions. For example, the price may have already peaked and started to decline when the trader decided to exit the long position. By then, it could be too late. It is always better and easier to sell at the price strength, when the price is still increasing or is stable and not declining. Traders should look to exit their short positions when the price is at the price-support level or the lower Bollinger band level. Conversely, traders should seek to close their long positions when the price is at the upper Bollinger band or at the price-resistance level.

10. Consider predominately using limit buy orders rather than market buy orders, so you are thus controlling the entry price. Limit orders will help traders who wish to buy at the BID price and sell at the ASK price. Consider using the ECNs when trading on the NASDAQ. That will help in buying the stock at the BID price and selling it at the ASK price.

I mentioned earlier that a trader must first observe a signal to buy or sell a stock before executing a trade. Too many times, traders enter a trade based on a gut feeling. A gut feeling is not good enough. As there is no such thing as a crystal ball to predict future outcomes, the next best device would be a technical analysis signal that indicates a potential for price movement. It is unrealistic to expect that all signals must occur simultaneously to generate a clear buy or sell signal. The trading universe does not have to be lined up perfectly for the trader to decide to buy or sell a security. However, the trader must be able to recognize and understand the correct signals in order to detect a trend.

In summary, stock trading has always been a risky business that does not have many "home runs." Success in this business does not come suddenly (or with any certainty). It takes many good as well as bad trades to become successful, and most new traders will never get there. Success appears only after many incremental profits from numerous trades.

Thus swing trading—or any other style of stock trading—is a business. Trading is not a hobby or a pastime, but is rather a profession that requires hard work, acquired knowledge, and discipline. As a final note, I present the same Latin quote I used to end my first book, *Electronic Day Trading Made Easy:* "Natura non facit saltum"—Nature does not make leaps. Any success in stock trading comes only in many small incremental steps.

APPENDIX

1

Electronic and Print
Trading Information

*"My sources are unreliable,
but their information is fascinating."*

—*Ashleigh Brilliant*

The Internet has transformed the way stock information is delivered. A few years ago, most stock market information was proprietary and costly. Investors and traders had to subscribe to and pay the financial information companies dearly for the expensive real-time quotes, news, and research. Even the delivery of that information was cumbersome and expensive. Investors and traders had to lease or purchase satellite dishes, computers, and software to process this continuous flow of data.

Today, all of the financial information companies have Internet sites, where they post the same quality of financial information free of charge. Although some sites charge a nominal monthly fee, investors and traders can still research a stock on demand at their convenience at any time of day—all at a fraction of what it would have cost fewer than five years ago.

Because the Internet phenomenon is truly an information revolution, these financial information sites are extremely dynamic. The content and format of these sites tend to change frequently, and new sites from new companies emerge continuously. Throughout this book, I mention relevant Internet resources. Nevertheless, I would like to offer here a brief list of my favorite sites, which provide useful and educational information in attractive and easy-to-use formats.

My favorite general financial directory and reference Internet sites are the Yahoo! Finance (www.finance.yahoo.com) and Microsoft Network MoneyCentral (www.moneycentral.MSN.com). These two sites deserve special mention because they are so complete, and they are absolutely free. At these sites, investors and traders can receive stock quotes, charts, company fundamentals, news, and discussion boards.

Other free general financial sites are Invest-O-Rama (www.investor ama.com), Online Investor Magazine (www.onlineinvestor.com), Thomson Financial Network (www.thomsoninvest.net), and INVEStools (www.investools.com). Among the sites that charge a nominal fee, but that provide great deal of value, is Wall Street City (www.WallStreet City.com).

In addition to these general stock market information sites, there are several rather specialized and focused Internet sites. For fundamental stock research, I suggest Zacks Investment Research (www.my. zacks.com), Multex Investor Network (www.multexinvestor.com), and BestCalls (www.BestCalls.com). Among the fundamental research sites that charge a nominal fee, I like Hoover's Online (www.Hoovers.com).

For technical stock analysis, I recommend BigCharts (www.Big Charts.com), BigEasy (www.BigEasyInvestor.com), FreeRealTime (www. FreeRealTime.com), and ClearStation (www.ClearStation.com). For stock market news analysis, I like CBS MarketWatch (www.CBSMarket Watch.com), CNN Finance Network (www.CNNfn.com), CNBC (www. CNBC.com) and Reuters MoneyNet (www.moneynet.com). Among the news sites that charge a nominal fee, but that provide great deal of value, are The Wall Street Journal (www.wsj.com), The Street (www.The Street.com), and Briefing.com (www.Briefing.com).

For an education in general stock investing and trading, I suggest the Internet sites from the American Association of Individual Investors (www.AAII.com), The Investment FAQ (www.invest-faq.com), and Armchair Millionaire (www.armchairmillionaire.com). For anyone interested in chat rooms for investors and traders, Silicon Investor (www.siliconinvestor.com) and Raging Bull (www.RagingBull.com) have some good resources. Also, the Web site for the Federal government's Securities and Exchange Commission (www.sec.gov), as well as those for the NYSE (www.NYSE.com) and NASDAQ (www.NASDAQ.com)

stock exchanges, provides useful information. FreeEDGAR (www.free EDGAR.com) is another useful Internet site that compiles and provides a ton of free fundamental stock research data from the SEC EDGAR database.

In addition, electronic stock traders and investors have the opportunity to eavesdrop electronically on conference calls between corporate management and Wall Street analysts. There are several Internet sites that specialize in broadcasting corporate earnings conference calls: Best Calls (www.BestCalls.com), Street Events (www.StreetEvents.com), Street Fusion (www.StreetFusion.com), and VCall (www.Vcall.com). Keep in mind that it is very difficult to sort through the wealth of information transmitted during the long conference calls and to pick up on the fine points. In addition, several Web sites, such as Earnings Whispers (www.earningswhispers.com), Whisper Numbers (www.whispernumbers.com), and Street IQ (www.streetiq.com), were created to provide the so-called "whisper earnings" figures. These Internet sites collect earnings estimates from numerous Internet message boards, as well as poll their site users.

It is important to expand on where investors and traders can find stock market data on the Internet. There are several Internet-based data feed providers that provide delayed and real-time stock quotes and news for a fee or sometimes free of charge: Standard & Poor's ComStock (www.spcomstock.com), PCQuote (www.pcquote.com), Quote (www.quote.com), Bloomberg (www.bloomberg.com), eSignal (www.esignal.com), and Data Broadcasting Corporation (www.DBC.com).

Print Media

I believe strongly that reading books on stock investing and trading, such as this book and many other similar titles, is the most cost-effective way to acquire the required knowledge of the stock market. Investors and traders can pick up a great deal of concise information in a single book.

In addition to books, there is a new kid on the block: *Active Trader* ($4.95 per issue), a monthly magazine (www.ActiveTraderMag.com) designed specifically for swing and day traders. Also, the Online Investor (www.OnlineInvestor.com) is a monthly magazine ($24.95 for annual subscription) that provides timely and quality electronic trading information.

There are also several time-tested sources of printed stock market information. Standard & Poor's *Corporation Records* is the major reference for the historical corporate financial information. Moody's Investor Services prints similar annual information in its various manuals. Value Line also has corporate financial information in its "Value Line Investment Survey." *The Wall Street Journal* and *Investors Business Daily* are standard daily reading fare for most professional investors and traders. Finally, many daily newspapers in America provide summaries of financial data in their finance sections. *The New York Times* has, by far, the best financial section among the daily newspapers in America.

Another form of print media includes market newsletters, which contain buy or sell stock recommendations. A typical newsletter contains a brief analysis of a particular stock, along with the recommendation. Potential subscribers should ascertain whether the newsletter is appropriate in terms of the following:

- Does the newsletter cover the appropriate financial product?
- Does the newsletter cover the appropriate trading or investment strategy?
- Does the newsletter cover the appropriate time holding strategy?
- Is the delivery mechanism appropriate in terms of time (e-mail, fax, or mail)?
- What is the newsletter writer's reputation or track record, if there is any?
- Do you agree with the newsletter writer's reasoning and logic?

There are several Internet sites devoted exclusively to market newsletters. These sites provide quick comparisons among several newsletter categories, such as product, strategy, rates, and frequency of publication, as well as links to the Internet sites. The sites are INVEStools (www.investools.com), Newsletter Network (www.margin.com), and the Hulbert Financial Digest (www.hulbertdigest.com). My personal feeling about the overall value of newsletters is one of healthy skepticism. If there is a Holy Grail to stock trading and investing, and in my opinion there is no such thing, why would anyone disclose it for a minor subscription fee? If you are thinking of subscribing to a market newsletter, my recommendation is to ask for a free examination copy or a free trial subscription.

Finally, consider attending a stock trading conference, such as the Online Trading Expo (www.OnlineTradingExpo.com), which are organized throughout the year in major metropolitan U.S. cities. You might also consider enrolling in a trading seminar, such as the Online Trading Academy (visit www.OnlineTradingAcademy.com for more information). The price range for the seminars varies from a few hundred to a few thousand dollars. Just as you would when purchasing any product or service for the first time, do the research and check the offering company's references and credentials—before you sign up for the seminars.

2

Traders and Taxes

"The trick is to stop thinking of it as 'your' money."

—*IRS auditor*

It is axiomatic that death and taxes are unavoidable. This book would be incomplete without the topic of trader's tax issues. Here I attempt to cover this complex issue briefly. This appendix is not designed to be an authoritative source on traders' tax issues, especially because I am not a tax attorney or tax accountant. There are only a few books that deal specifically with the tax issues that face stock investors and traders. I strongly encourage you to do your own research on this topic. One good reference is Ted Tesser's *The Trader's Tax Survival Guide*.

Tax Rates

Because this is not a tax book, it covers only the basic tax concepts. I would like to reiterate that "cash basis accounting"—a method of reporting income when it is received and expenses when they are incurred—is the foundation of the trader's tax return. All income is subject to progressive or graduated federal tax. In other words, as the individual income increases, the average and marginal tax rates increase as well. There are five marginal tax rates, or tax brackets, in the United States; they vary from 15 to 39.6 percent. Table A2.1 shows the 1999

Table A2.1 *1999 Tax Rate Schedule*

| Single Filing Status | | | Married Filing Jointly Status | |
Taxable Income Over	Taxable Income Under	Marginal Tax Rate	Taxable Income Over	Taxable Income Under
$0	$25,750	15%	$0	$43,050
$25,750	$62,450	28%	$43,050	$104,050
$62,450	$130,250	31%	$104,050	$158,550
$130,250	$283,150	36%	$158,550	$283,150
$283,150	—	39.6%	$283,150	—

tax rate schedule for taxpayers who are filing returns as single or married and filing jointly.

According to table A2.1, if your filing status is single, you pay a 15 percent tax rate on the first $25,750 and a 28 percent tax rate on income higher than $25,750 and lower than $62,450.

In addition to paying taxes to the federal government, individuals also pay income taxes to the state in which they live. However, there are a few states, such as Florida or Nevada, that do not have a state income tax.

Income

The next step is to define income. The federal tax law defines income as any acquisition of wealth that excludes gifts and inheritances. In other words, income may be defined as any gain derived from capital and labor. In fact, the Internal Revenue Service (IRS) defines the following fourteen specific categories of income:

1. Compensation for services
2. Income from business
3. Gains from dealings in property
4. Interest
5. Rents
6. Royalties

7. Dividends

8. Annuities

9. Income from life insurance policies

10. Pensions

11. Partnership income

12. Income from ownership interest in an estate or trust

13. Income from discharge of debt

14. Alimony payments

Traders and stock investors need to know what is specifically excluded from the definition of income:

1. The return of capital or return of an original investment, such as the cost of stocks

2. Unrealized stock gain or appreciation, meaning that the investor is not liable for stock appreciation until the stock is sold

The U.S. Tax Reform Act of 1986 also differentiates between three different types of income:

1. Earned income

2. Investment income

3. Passive income

The different types of income are taxed at the same rate as regular income, with the exception of long-term capital gains. This income differentiation becomes important when determining which losses can be deducted on tax returns. The IRS tax code has always had earned income and investment income categories. But, in 1986, the U.S. Congress created for the first time a new type of income—passive income. Passive income comes from passive activities. A passive activity is one in which the taxpayer is not directly and materially involved. This definition covers all rental income and the income from limited partnerships in which limited partners do not participate in management decisions.

Earned income is compensation received for providing goods or services. Investment income is portfolio income that includes interest, dividends, royalties, annuities, as well as gains or losses from the disposition of an investment. Earned and investment incomes are considered ordinary incomes and are thus taxed at the individual tax rate.

Capital Gains and Losses

The other important tax issue is the concept of capital gains and losses. Capital gain (or loss) is defined as a gain (or loss) that comes from the sale of capital assets. The IRS defines a capital asset to be any business or nonbusiness property. The exceptions are inventories, accounts receivable, and properties that are held for sale in the normal course of trading. Securities are considered to be capital assets. If a capital asset, such as stock, is sold for less than its cost, the IRS considers this to be a capital loss. If the capital asset is sold for more than its cost, the IRS considers this to be a capital gain.

Capital losses may be used to offset capital gains. Furthermore, within certain IRS limits, capital losses may be used to offset ordinary income. The IRS also differentiates whether capital gains are short term or long term. The holding period starts on the day the buy order was executed, or the trade date. Conversely, the holding period ends on the day the sell order was executed. All capital gains or losses are considered short term if the holding period is less than one year and long term if the holding period is more than one year.

Another tax concept is the issue of the stock cost basis. The cost basis of a security is the total price paid for the stock, including the commission cost. The cost basis will be adjusted periodically for any stock dividends or stock splits. A stock split occurs when a company decides to divide its shares in two, three, four, or more. In the event of a 2:1 stock split, the stockholders would get twice as many shares, but each share will be worth half as much. Since nothing else about the company has changed, shareholders aren't better or worse off. All capital gains or losses are realized or recognized in the tax year of the trade date on which the security has been sold.

The final step is to determine the net impact of the capital gains and losses. Given the stock cost basis, the holding period, and the final stock-selling price (including the cost of the commission, which would be deducted from the proceeds), the trader or investor can determine the level of short-term and long-term capital gains and losses. The trader would net the short-term losses against the short-term gains, and the long-term losses against the long-term gains.

If the trader or investor has a poor year and the net result is both short-term and long-term losses, the net short-term and long-term losses are combined and deducted from ordinary income, up to a $3,000 maximum. If the net losses exceed $3,000, the unused portion can be carried forward and used to offset ordinary income for the next tax year. The losses can be carried forward indefinitely. This is an apparent double standard. There is no limit on capital gain that is subject to federal taxation. If you made money, the federal government wants a percentage cut of that entire gain.

If a trader or investor has a mixed performance and the net result is a short-term gain and long-term loss, the long-term loss can be used to offset the short-term gain. If the net is positive, the net gain is added to the ordinary income and taxed at the ordinary tax rate based on the progressive tax schedule.

If the trader or investor has an overall positive performance and the net result is both short-term and long-term gains, the positive short-term net gain is added to ordinary income and is taxed at the ordinary tax rate. The positive long-term net gain is taxed at the ordinary tax rate, up to a maximum of 28 percent, even if the taxpayer's other ordinary income is taxed at the higher rate.

Expenses

The first half of the tax equation is income; the second half is expense. The IRS looks keenly at what expenses can be deducted from income. The IRS test on whether expenses are allowed has four questions:

1. Is the expense necessary to produce that income?
2. Is the expense ordinary and common in conducting that type of business activity?
3. Is the expense reasonable with regard to the level of the generated income?
4. Is the expense allowed or legal under the existing federal tax code?

Whether expenses incurred in trading are necessary, ordinary, and reasonable is clearly subjective. Because each tax return is unique, the answers to these questions will vary from one trader to another. This variety means that traders have the ability or potential to interpret what constitutes necessary, ordinary, and reasonable expenses. A word of caution—there are many self-employed individuals who are clashing with the IRS over business expenses that they think are necessary, ordinary, and reasonable.

The best tax preparation strategy is to be prepared to document and explain to the IRS why certain trading expenses are claimed to be necessary, ordinary, and reasonable. The trader who might someday be audited must be prepared to back up (with supporting documents) and substantiate his or her trading expense claims.

Ted Tesser's tax book for traders lists several trading expenses that are commonly accepted by the IRS, including the following:

- Computer and software expenses, if trading from the home
- Real-time data feed costs
- Brokerage fees
- Margin interest expenses
- Cost of books, seminars, and other educational tools on trading
- Subscriptions to professional magazines, papers, and publications
- Tax advice
- Trading advice
- Legal fees
- Accounting fees
- Safe deposit box fees for the storage of trading documents
- Portion of home expenses that qualify as home office deductions, if trading from the home

The IRS code also differentiates among three classes of investors: market maker, investor, and trader.

Market Maker

The definition of market maker, for tax purposes, is clear. The market maker is the NASD broker or dealer who is a merchant of securities. The NASD broker/dealer might be an individual, a partnership, or a corporation. The market maker has an established place of business and regularly buys and sells securities in the ordinary course of business. Securities are the market maker's inventory; they are not capital assets.

All of the income made by the market maker is automatically considered to be ordinary income. There are no short-term capital gains or losses. The market maker can claim an unlimited amount of losses. Because the market maker is a business, a self-employment tax must be paid. All expenses, such as interest charges, are treated as business-related expenses.

Investor

The IRS defines an investor as an individual who buys and sells securities for his or her own account. All expenses incurred in investment activities are considered to be investment expenses, and not business expenses. Therefore these expenses are deducted as miscellaneous itemized deductions on Schedule A of the investor's tax return. Investment expenses are subject to a 2 percent limitation. All income is treated as an investment income, not ordinary income. Finally, the maximum net loss that can be used to offset ordinary income is $3,000.

Trader

For the IRS, the trader is clearly a hybrid between the investor and the market maker. The U.S. courts have always recognized this tax classification, although the tax forms do not specifically list this category. In addition, in 1997, Congress recognized that "traders are taxpayers who are in the business of actively buying, selling, or exchanging securities or commodities in the market." Congress also stated that market makers are the securities dealers who deal directly with the customers. In other words, traders are actively involved in the exchange of securities on the market, rather than in the exchange of securities directly to the customer—a fine distinction that has significant tax implications.

And what separates the traders from investors? The IRS does not have a hard number or a specific test that will differentiate investors from traders. To consider a taxpayer as a trader rather than an investor, the IRS looks at the following:

- Regular, continuous, and frequent trading
- Substantial number of trades
- Short-term trading style
- Small, if any, income derived from dividends
- Expenses declared on Schedule C

Traders buy and sell securities for their own accounts, just as investors do. Unlike the investor, however, the trader's level of trading activity is dramatically higher. Subsequently, the IRS looks at the frequency of the trades, the length of the holding period, and the source of profit. A typical day trader makes several dozen trades every day, while holding the stock for only a few minutes or a few hours. He or she profits from the daily short-term price fluctuations. On the other hand, the investor holds the securities for a longer period of time (sometimes more than one year), performs fewer securities transactions, and earns profit from dividends as well as from capital appreciation.

Tax Treatment

One of the main points of this book is that trading is a business. The trader must treat this business seriously if he or she has any hope of being successful. It is a business that requires individual time commitment, dedication, and hard work. Thus it is not surprising that the IRS treats equities trading as a business as well.

A **swing** trader makes several trades every week while holding the stock for a few days and profits from the short-term price fluctuations. Therefore, it is my opinion that swing trading is trading and not investing.

All trading expenses are considered to be business-related expenses and are 100 percent deductible on Schedule C of the individual's tax return. However, trading income is considered to be short-term capital gains and thus must be reported on Schedule D. Recall that there is a $3,000 limit on the amount of short-term losses that can be applied on Schedule D to offset ordinary income for that year.

However, this $3,000 limit can be avoided if the trader elects to mark-to-market his or her position under IRS section 475. According to mark-to-market accounting rules, traders can put all of their trading income and losses on Schedule C and thus not carry anything into the next year. In essence, Congress allows traders to use section 475 to show all income or expenses on schedule C and yet not be subject to self-employment tax. There is no self-employment tax because the trader's income is considered to be a short-term capital gain and not ordinary income. There is no box on the tax form to select section 475; it must be noted on Schedule C. (My advice is to hire a tax accountant to prepare the trader's tax return properly.)

Traders must use two forms to report income and expenses from trading activities. They report the trading income as investment income (short-term capital gains) on Schedule D, and trading expenses as ordinary business expenses on Schedule C. In terms of tax liability, one can argue that traders are better off than market makers. Both market makers and traders can claim trading expenses. However, market makers are subject to self-employment tax, whereas traders are not—one of the few times that market makers do not have an advantage over traders.

Because the IRS treats traders as a hybrid between investors and market makers, there are certain tax advantages available to traders that are not available to investors. For example, for traders:

- Itemized deductions are not necessary to claim and deduct trading expenses. Traders can take the standard deduction and still take additional expense deductions on Schedule C.

- All trading educational seminars are tax deductible business expenses.

- All investment interest expense (i.e., the margin interest expense) is considered trading expense and is allowed as a normal business expense.

- The home office expense is routinely allowed as a business expense, if the trader trades from home.

- All trading business expenses are not subject to any floor or minimum value, such as the 2 percent to 3 percent floor on Schedule A that investors must pay.

Table A2.2 summarizes the IRS tax treatment for the three classifications.

IRS Tax Audits

It is always a good practice to expect the best and be prepared for the worst. There is always a possibility that the IRS will audit a trader. This section covers that worst case scenario—the IRS tax audit.

First of all, to be classified as a trader, it is not necessary to create a separate legal entity. An individual is entitled to achieve the trader status simply by being a trader. However, many tax accountants, including Ted Tesser, argue that Limited Liability Partnership, Limited Liability Company, or Corporations Subchapter C or S entity forms are preferred

Table A2.2 *IRS Tax Classification Summary*

Tax Issue	Market Makers	Traders	Investors
Profits treated as	Earned income	Short-term capital gains or losses within investment income and reported on Schedule D (with 475 exception, gains, and losses reported on Schedule C)	Short-term capital gains or losses within investment income and reported on Schedule D
Loss limits applied against earned income	No limits	$3,000 limit per year with carry forward to next year (with 475 exception)	$3,000 limit per year with carry forward to next year
Subject to self-employment tax	Yes	No, even if trading is your only source of income	No
Expenses treated as	Business expenses	Business related expenses with 100% deductible and reported on Schedule C	Investment related expenses itemized and reported on Schedule A

legal vehicles for stock trading. In general, these forms can offer more tax, retirement, and estate planning options to traders than the individual entity structure can.

In his book, Ted Tesser argued that there is no such thing as a one-size-fits-all entity structure that is the most preferred. In some cases, multiple ownership structures might be created to maximize benefits. Tax attorneys and accountants call this tax planning, and, as with anything else, tax planning can be as complicated or as simple as you wish it to be.

We all have an interest in minimizing our tax liabilities. None of us wants to pay more to the government than is necessary. In fact, most Americans believe, rationally or irrationally, that we already pay too much in taxes. However, minimizing taxes does not mean cheating on your tax returns. That is clearly illegal. It also does not mean finding tax loopholes in the IRS code and exploiting them. Minimizing taxes legally means obtaining knowledge of the IRS code (as applied to your individual tax circumstances) and using current allowable deductions and exemptions to the fullest advantage.

Investors and traders often push the envelope of IRS code interpretation on their tax returns. Consequently, their returns are selected for IRS audits. It is always important to keep good records of your trading transactions and expenses. In the event that the IRS audits your return, these records can substantiate your deductions and expense claims.

It is also preferred that these records be in an electronic format. Because traders may conduct thousands of trades in a single year (for swing traders, this number is lower), it can be difficult to provide a quick summary of all trades. Trading software often has the capability to export, or copy, the daily trade activity records onto a disk. This copy can then be imported at a later date into any spreadsheet program.

The Probability of Being Audited

The good news is that the odds are in your favor that you will not get audited. The IRS simply has a colossal task. Every year the IRS collects more than $1.5 trillion to fund the U.S. government. It processes more than 200 million tax returns from more than 110 million U.S. taxpayers. It issues over 80 million refunds and distributes over 1 billion forms and publications. In addition, the IRS must enforce the tax laws of this country and ensure that the taxpaying public pays the proper amount of tax. As you can see, the IRS is overwhelmed. Consequently, only a small portion of the 110 million taxpayers will ever be subject to an IRS audit. The IRS audits approximately only 3 million tax returns annually.

The news is even better. The first target of the IRS audit is the known criminal. (Let us hope that this does not apply to you.) The next targets are certain highly paid professionals. The IRS customarily targets doctors, dentists, lawyers, and CPAs because of their relative high-income levels and their propensity for practicing creative accounting. The next groups of targeted individuals are salespeople, airline pilots, flight attendants, and business executives, because they tend to have unusually high expense deductions relative to their income. Often these expenses are poorly documented. If you are not in any of these listed professions, then your chances of being audited are often fewer than 1 percent.

The process of selecting individual tax returns for an audit is highly computerized. The IRS computer program selects tax returns that do not comply with the IRS code or that have certain discrepancies between the reported incomes as being reported by the taxpayer and other businesses that issue the W-2 or 1099 forms. Therefore, you must make sure that all income is reported.

It is also important that tax returns are clean and fully completed. All questions must be answered completely. Avoid including large sums of money under the "miscellaneous income" or "miscellaneous expenses" sections. It is always better to be specific. Avoid making sloppy or careless mathematical mistakes. There are several computerized tax preparation software packages on the market that will ensure that your completed tax return is clean, complete, and mathematically correct.

Avoid using certain deductions that customarily trigger the IRS audits. The home office deduction is one item that commonly raises IRS scrutiny. But if you are an Internet trader, this home expense is legal and allowed. Avoid using rounded-off expense deductions, as they indicate guessing. It is always a good idea to work with a professional and capable tax accountant. If the IRS suspects that a tax accountant is too aggressive or unscrupulous, it can trigger IRS audits for the accountant's entire client base. The IRS will notice if an individual reports millions of dollars of gross sales from trades. However, the same trading activity will not raise any IRS flags if the legal entity doing the trading is a corporation or limited partnership. The IRS is very accustomed to seeing large dollar figures on corporate or limited liability partnership returns.

Unfortunately, a small number of IRS audits are randomly selected. The IRS uses this type of random selection to ascertain the overall taxpayers' compliance with the tax laws. In addition, each IRS district office has a different percentage of returns audited. Some districts are more aggressive (or efficient) and, therefore, perform substantially more audits, while some districts are more relaxed. The bottom line here is that the probability is great that you will not be audited.

3

Good Trading Stocks for 2000

Large Relative Volatility and Trading Volume

Symbol	Company Name	Industry Name	Avg. Daily Vol. Last Year	Beta	52-Week High	52-Week Low	Exchange
SGNT	Sagent Technology, Inc.	Application Software	691,400	6.82	45.38	6.28	NASDAQ
WEBT	WebTrends Corp.	Internet Software & Services	561,100	5.98	86.63	11.94	NASDAQ
AIPN	American International Petroleum Corp.	Oil & Gas Drilling & Exploration	1,679,000	5.32	2.06	0.38	NASDAQ
NITE	Knight/ Trimark Group, Inc.	Investment Brokerage, Regional	4,974,900	4.9	81.63	21.69	NASDAQ
TFSM	24/7 Media, Inc.	Internet Software & Services	641,600	4.58	65.25	15	NASDAQ
DRIV	Digital River, Inc.	Business Software & Services	552,200	4.36	43.63	10	NASDAQ

continues

379

Large Relative Volatility and Trading Volume (continued)

Symbol	Company Name	Industry Name	Avg. Daily Vol. Last Year	Beta	52-Week High	52-Week Low	Exchange
IDCC	InterDigital Communications Corp.	Wireless Communications	958,400	4.1	82	4	NASDAQ
DCLK	Double Click Inc.	Internet Software & Services	5,065,500	3.92	135.25	30.25	NASDAQ
BAMM	Books-A-Million, Inc.	Specialty Retail, Other	572,600	3.92	16.63	4	NASDAQ
CPTH	Critical Path, Inc.	Business Services	788,800	3.71	119.5	28.06	NASDAQ
VERT	Vertical Net, Inc.	Internet Information Providers	2,770,600	3.6	148.38	13.56	NASDAQ
ANCR	Ancor Communications, Inc.	Communication Equipment	1,234,600	3.48	94.13	6.5	NASDAQ
ALLR	Allaire Corp.	Internet Software & Services	589,000	3.42	94.13	19.94	NASDAQ
YHOO	Yahoo! Inc.	Internet Information Providers	15,847,300	3.4	250.06	55	NASDAQ
EGRP	E*TRADE Group, Inc.	Internet Software & Services	7,412,300	3.35	60.44	16.06	NASDAQ
EBAY	eBay Inc.	Internet Software & Services	4,239,200	3.33	255	70.28	NASDAQ
LWIN	Leap Wireless International, Inc.	Telecom Services, Domestic	518,400	3.25	110.5	14.56	NASDAQ

Large Relative Volatility and Trading Volume (continued)

Symbol	Company Name	Industry Name	Avg. Daily Vol. Last Year	Beta	52-Week High	52-Week Low	Exchange
NSOL	Network Solutions, Inc.	Internet Software & Services	2,070,300	3.21	255.63	24.5	NASDAQ
USIX	USinternet-working, Inc.	Internet Software & Services	1,161,300	3.18	71.7	6.37	NASDAQ
NTBK	Net.B@nk, Inc.	Savings & Loans	1,101,900	3.16	64.89	8.56	NASDAQ
BVEW	BindView Development Corp.	Application Software	677,900	3.16	45.75	7.5	NASDAQ
LCOS	Lycos, Inc.	Internet Information Providers	3,223,800	3.12	93.63	28.56	NASDAQ
CMGI	CMGI, Inc.	Internet Software & Services	10,320,900	3.11	163.5	33.13	NASDAQ
EXDS	Exodus Communi-cations, Inc.	Internet Software & Services	6,988,400	3.11	179.63	16.5	NASDAQ
BYND	Beyond.com Corp.	Internet Software & Services	1,288,700	3.01	33.5	1.59	NASDAQ
ENTU	Entrust Technolo-gies Inc.	Security Software & Services	1,049,500	2.98	150	16.88	NASDAQ
GNET	Go2Net, Inc.	Internet Information Providers	917,900	2.93	111.75	44.06	NASDAQ
PCLN	Priceline.com Inc.	Internet Software & Services	3,054,600	2.86	145.75	45.5	NASDAQ
AMES	Ames Department Stores, Inc.	Discount, Variety Stores	612,500	2.81	48.88	10.5	NASDAQ

continues

Large Relative Volatility and Trading Volume (continued)

Symbol	Company Name	Industry Name	Avg. Daily Vol. Last Year	Beta	52-Week High	52-Week Low	Exchange
COOL	Cyberian Outpost, Inc.	Internet Software & Services	634,400	2.77	15.94	3.63	NASDAQ
PXCM	Proxicom, Inc.	Business Software & Services	575,800	2.75	67.5	9.03	NASDAQ
ITWO	i2 Technologies, Inc.	Application Software	2,761,400	2.69	223.5	13.06	NASDAQ
INSP	InfoSpace.com, Inc.	Internet Information Providers	4,542,500	2.67	138.5	8.81	NASDAQ
BRCM	Broadcom Corp.	Semiconductor, Integrated Circuits	4,243,200	2.67	253	40.75	NASDAQ
TRAC	Track Data Corp.	Information & Delivery Services	1,209,700	2.66	12.25	1.59	NASDAQ
CLS	Celestica Inc.	Computer Peripherals	684,000	2.66	62.25	19.09	NYSE
KMAG	Komag, Inc.	Data Storage Devices	594,900	2.66	5.31	1.56	NASDAQ
GTS	Global TeleSystems Group, Inc.	Telecom Services, Domestic	2,648,400	2.63	45.84	11.75	NYSE
ASYT	Asyst Technologies, Inc.	Semiconductor Equipment & Materials	620,600	2.62	67	8.56	NASDAQ
AMZN	Amazon.com, Inc.	Internet Software & Services	13,074,900	2.61	113	40.81	NASDAQ
LRCX	Lam Research Corporation	Semiconductor Equipment & Materials	3,838,100	2.59	56.81	8.68	NASDAQ

Large Relative Volatility and Trading Volume (continued)

Symbol	Company Name	Industry Name	Avg. Daily Vol. Last Year	Beta	52-Week High	52-Week Low	Exchange
ISSX	ISS Group, Inc.	Internet Software & Services	706,100	2.59	141	20	NASDAQ
SCI	SCI Systems, Inc.	Diversified Electronics	1,084,000	2.58	58.38	18.59	NYSE
FLEX	Flextronics International Ltd.	Printed Circuit Boards	2,024,800	2.53	79.75	21.25	NASDAQ
OMKT	Open Market, Inc.	Internet Software & Services	1,410,100	2.52	66	7.88	NASDAQ
ATHM	Excite@ Home	Internet Information Providers	7,824,200	2.51	80.69	15.88	NASDAQ
CNCX	Concentric Network Corp.	Internet Service Providers	1,075,200	2.49	61.88	16.69	NASDAQ
MFNX	Metromedia Fiber Network, Inc.	Diversified Communication Services	4,884,200	2.48	51.88	10.56	NASDAQ
RNWK	Real Networks, Inc.	Internet Software & Services	3,824,200	2.45	96	25.5	NASDAQ
GSTRF	Globalstar Telecommunications Ltd.	Telecom Services, Foreign	2,711,500	2.44	53.75	7.88	NASDAQ
LEH	Lehman Brothers Holdings Inc.	Investment Brokerage, National	1,003,300	2.44	107.5	47.56	NYSE
AOL	America Online, Inc.	Internet Information Providers	32,565,200	2.42	95.81	38.47	NYSE

continues

Large Relative Volatility and Trading Volume (continued)

Symbol	Company Name	Industry Name	Avg. Daily Vol. Last Year	Beta	52-Week High	52-Week Low	Exchange
GBLX	Global Crossing Ltd.	Telecom Services, Foreign	9,347,900	2.39	64.25	20.25	NASDAQ
WCII	WinStar Communications, Inc.	Telecom Services, Domestic	1,792,900	2.39	66.5	24.01	NASDAQ
INKT	Inktomi Corp.	Internet Software & Services	3,675,800	2.36	241.5	42	NASDAQ
TWRS	Crown Castle International Corp.	Diversified Communication Services	983,800	2.36	44.75	14.69	NASDAQ
GWRX	Geoworks Corp.	Application Software	922,100	2.33	54.88	1.94	NASDAQ
CKFR	CheckFree Holdings Corp.	Internet Software & Services	1,287,000	2.31	125.63	23.13	NASDAQ
VISX	VISX, Inc.	Medical Appliances & Equipment	2,417,700	2.24	103.88	14	NASDAQ
ATML	Atmel Corp.	Semiconductor, Memory Chips	5,322,900	2.23	61.38	8.72	NASDAQ
SCH	Charles Schwab Corp.	Investment Brokerage, National	4,645,900	2.23	67.13	26.94	NYSE
IFMX	Informix Corp.	Application Software	4,302,300	2.21	21.25	6.38	NASDAQ
PCS	Sprint PCS Group	Wireless Communications	3,811,400	2.19	66.94	20.75	NYSE

Large Relative Volatility and Trading Volume (continued)

Symbol	Company Name	Industry Name	Avg. Daily Vol. Last Year	Beta	52-Week High	52-Week Low	Exchange
AFCI	Advanced Fibre Communications, Inc.	Communication Equipment	2,155,500	2.19	89.38	8	NASDAQ
VIGN	Vignette Corp.	Internet Software & Services	4,313,800	2.16	100.57	6.99	NASDAQ
PVN	Providian Financial Corp.	Credit Services	1,326,200	2.13	130.88	58.13	NYSE
KLAC	KLA-Tencor Corp.	Semiconductor Equipment & Materials	4,179,800	2.12	98.5	21.19	NASDAQ
PRGN	Peregrine Systems, Inc.	Application Software	1,866,900	2.12	80.63	9.13	NASDAQ
TLAB	Tellabs, Inc.	Communication Equipment	5,170,400	2.11	77.25	41.81	NASDAQ
QCOM	QUAL-COMM Inc.	Communication Equipment	19,970,000	2.09	200	21.52	NASDAQ
MWD	Morgan Stanley Dean Witter & Co.	Credit Services	4,129,300	2.09	97.38	40.5	NYSE
AMTD	Ameritrade Holding Corp.	Investment Brokerage, National	4,518,600	2.08	43.5	12.31	NASDAQ
AMAT	Applied Materials, Inc.	Semiconductor Equipment & Materials	14,648,400	2.05	115.13	26.38	NASDAQ

continues

Large Relative Volatility and Trading Volume (continued)

Symbol	Company Name	Industry Name	Avg. Daily Vol. Last Year	Beta	52-Week High	52-Week Low	Exchange
ASML	ASM Lithography Holding N.V.	Industrial Electrical Equipment	1,995,700	2.05	50.2	12.82	NASDAQ
KRB	MBNA Corp.	Credit Services	2,000,200	2.03	33.25	19.5	NYSE
NVLS	Novellus Systems, Inc.	Semiconductor Equipment & Materials	4,863,300	1.98	70.25	15.28	NASDAQ
VRSN	VeriSign, Inc.	Internet Software & Services	3,073,700	1.95	258.5	24	NASDAQ
TER	Teradyne, Inc.	Semiconductor Equipment & Materials	2,027,800	1.94	115.44	23.25	NYSE
CD	Cendant Corp.	Business Services	4,345,200	1.93	26.94	13.63	NYSE
DISH	EchoStar Communications Corp.	Electronic Equipment	3,894,600	1.92	81.25	11.88	NASDAQ
ADI	Analog Devices, Inc.	Semiconductor, Broad Line	2,815,800	1.89	94.69	17.63	NYSE
DELL	Dell Computer Corp.	Personal Computers	28,433,000	1.87	59.69	31.38	NASDAQ
NOVL	Novell, Inc.	Application Software	6,055,800	1.86	44.56	9.75	NASDAQ
NOK	Nokia Corp.	Wireless Communications	12,572,800	1.85	60	16.92	NYSE

Large Relative Volatility and Trading Volume (continued)

Symbol	Company Name	Industry Name	Avg. Daily Vol. Last Year	Beta	52-Week High	52-Week Low	Exchange
ADCT	ADC Telecommunications, Inc.	Communication Equipment	3,965,900	1.84	64.5	17.19	NASDAQ
ONE	Bank One Corp.	Money Center Banks	4,877,600	1.77	63.56	23.19	NYSE
INTU	Intuit Inc.	Application Software	3,098,700	1.77	90	22.48	NASDAQ
NXTL	Nextel Communications, Inc.	Wireless Communications	4,575,700	1.73	165.88	34	NASDAQ
C	Citigroup Inc.	Money Center Banks	10,575,900	1.66	65.44	40.13	NYSE
PSIX	PSINet Inc.	Internet Service Providers	3,653,000	1.65	60.94	15.53	NASDAQ
MSFT	Microsoft Corp.	Application Software	30,279,800	1.62	119.94	65.13	NASDAQ
LU	Lucent Technologies Inc.	Processing Systems & Products	14,208,800	1.6	84.19	49.81	NYSE
BVSN	BroadVision, Inc.	Internet Software & Services	8,089,700	1.59	93.2	4.48	NASDAQ
LSI	LSI Logic Corp.	Semiconductor, Specialized	4,330,000	1.59	90.38	16.75	NYSE
JDSU	JDS Uniphase Corp.	Diversified Electronics	13,586,400	1.58	153.42	15.2	NASDAQ
MU	Micron Technology, Inc.	Semiconductor, Memory Chips	11,410,200	1.55	72.56	17.13	NYSE

continues

Large Relative Volatility and Trading Volume (continued)

Symbol	Company Name	Industry Name	Avg. Daily Vol. Last Year	Beta	52-Week High	52-Week Low	Exchange
SLR	Solectron Corp.	Printed Circuit Boards	3,785,100	1.54	49.5	24.59	NYSE
PMTC	Parametric Technology Corp.	Technical & System Software	4,860,700	1.52	35.94	7.38	NASDAQ
IMNX	Immunex Corp.	Biotech-nology	5,757,300	1.51	83.92	13.76	NASDAQ
CPWR	Compu-ware Corp.	Application Software	6,043,300	1.5	40	10.44	NASDAQ

Note: The table is organized by Beta coefficient, from high to low.

4

Key NASDAQ Market Makers

Symbol	Market Maker Name
ABSA	Alex Brown & Sons, Inc.
AGIS	Aegis Capital Corp.
BEST	Bear Stearns & Co., Inc.
BTSC	BT Securities
CANT	Cantor Fitzgerald & Co., Inc.
CHGO	Chicago Corp.
CJDB	CJ Lawrence Deutsche Bank
COST	Coastal Securities
COWN	Cowen & Co.
DAIN	Dain Bosworth, Inc.
DEAN	Dean Witter
DLJP	Donaldson Lufkin & Jenrette
DOMS	Domestic Securities
EXPO	Exponential Capital Markets
FACT	First Albany Corp.
FAHN	Fahnestock & Co.
FBCO	First Boston Corp.
FPKI	Fox-Pitt, Kelton, Inc.
GRUN	Gruntal & Co., Inc.

continues

Symbol	Market Maker Name
GSCO	Goldman Sach & Co.
GVRC	Gvr Co.
HMQT	Hambrecht & Quist, Inc.
HRZG	Herzog, Heine, Geduld, Inc.
JEFF	Jefferies Co., Inc.
JPMS	J.P. Morgan
KEMP	Kemper Securities, Inc.
LEHM	Lehman Brothers
MADF	Bernard Madoff
MASH	Mayer & Schweitzer, Inc. (Charles Schwab)
MHMY	M .H. Meyerson & Co., Inc.
MLCO	Merrill Lynch
MONT	Montgomery Securities
MSCO	Morgan Stanley & Co., Inc.
MSWE	Midwest Stock Exchange
NAWE	Nash Weiss & Co.
NEED	Neddham & Co.
NMRA	Nomura Securities Intl. Inc.
OLDE	Olde Discount Corp.
OPCO	Oppenheimer & Co.
PERT	Pershing Trading Co.
PIPR	Piper Jaffray
PRUS	Prudential Securities Inc.
PUNK	Punk Siegel & Knoell, Inc.
PWJC	Paine Webber, Inc.
RAGN	Ragen McKenzie, Inc.
RBSF	Robertson Stephens & Co., Lp
RPSC	Rauscher Pierce Refsnes, Inc.
SALB	Salomon Brothers
SBNY	Sands Brothers & Co., Ltd
SBSH	Smith Barney Shearson, Inc.

SELZ	Furman Selz, Inc.
SHWD	Sherwood Securities Corp.
SNDV	Soundview Financial Group, Inc.
SWST	Southwest Securities, Inc.
TSCO	Troster Singer Corp. (Spear Leads)
TUCK	Tucker Anthony, Inc.
TVAN	Teevan & Co., Inc.
UBSS	UBS Securities
VOLP	Volpe Weity & Co.
WARB	S. G. Warburg & Co., Inc.
WBLR	William Blair & Co.
WEAT	Wheat First Securities, Inc.
WEDB	Wedbrush morgan Securities
WEED	Weeden & Co., LP
WERT	Wertheim Schroder & Co., Inc.
WSEI	Wall Street Equities, Inc.
WSLS	Wessels, Arnold & Henderson

Glossary

absolute liquidity   Total shares being traded on an exchange in a day.

absolute price volatility   Total dollar change in the price of the stock.

accounts payable   Amounts companies owe suppliers for goods and services. Listed under current liabilities on statement of financial position. See also *current liabilities, debt, income taxes.*

accounts receivable   Amounts customers owe a company from sales of goods or services that the company expects to collect within one year. Listed under current assets on statement of financial position. See also *assets, current assets, fixed assets, goodwill.*

accumulation   Addition to trader's original market position; first of three distinct phases in a major trend in which investors are buying. Compare with *distribution.*

advance-decline   Each day's number of declining issues is subtracted from the number of advancing issues. The net difference is added to a running sum if the difference is positive, or subtracted if the difference is negative.

aftermarket IPO performance   Describes how the stock of a newly public company has performed, with the offering price as the typical benchmark.

all or none IPO   Offering that can be canceled by the lead underwriter if it is not completely subscribed. Most best-effort deals are all or none.

annual report   Stockholders' report from a company, published at the end of each fiscal year. Includes such required elements as auditor's report and company's statements of earnings, financial position, and cash flows. Also includes letters and articles by company executives, information on financial condition, and significant events.

arbitrage   Simultaneous purchase and sale of two different and closely related securities to take advantage of a disparity in their prices.

ASK   Price at which a holder of a security is willing to sell. Asked price is the price paid when a security is bought. It is usually lower than the bid. In over-the-counter trading, securities dealers or market makers profit from the spread between BID and ASK so much that they are often willing to pay discount brokers for order flow. Compare *BID.*

ASK size   Number of shares associated with current ASK price or number of shares the seller(s) is (are) offering for sale at the ask price.

assets   Anything companies own—physical assets (e.g., buildings, trucks, inventories of products, equipment, cash) and intangible assets (e.g., goodwill, trademarks, patents). Listed as a category on the statement of financial position. See also *accounts receivable, current assets, fixed assets.*

auditor   Firm of certified public accountants that a company hires as an independent third party to review financial information. Main purpose is to make sure statements of earnings, financial position, and cash flows fairly present the company's financial condition.

average daily volume   Number of shares traded in a given number of days, divided by that number of days. Useful for judging how liquid a stock is and whether any one day's volume marks a sharp departure from the norm. The latter usually indicates some news or change of circumstances that could be relevant to shareholders.

balance sheet   See *statement of financial position.*

bar chart   Displays a security's open, high, low, and close prices using one vertical line for each time period, whether for a day, week, month, etc. Most popular type of security chart. On the left side of the bar is a tick that indicates the opening price. The tick on the right side of the bar is the closing price. The vertical length of the bar shows the price range.

basket trades   Large transactions made up of a number of different stocks.

bear or bearish market   When stocks trend downward for a long period of time, it's a "bear" market. The term comes from the fact that when bears attack, they strike downward with their paws.

best effort IPO   Deal in which underwriters only agree to do their best to sell shares to the public, as opposed to much more common bought, or firm commitment, deals.

beta   Regression of the estimated coefficient that belongs to a particular variable.

beta (coefficient)   Measure of the market/nondiversifiable risk associated with any given security in the market. A ratio of an individual's stock historical returns to the historical returns of the stock market. If a stock increased in value by 12% while the market increased by 10%, the stock's beta would be 1.2.

BID   Price at which a market maker is willing to buy a security from an investor. The BID price is the price received when an investor sells a security.

bidding   Act of buying securities at the posted BID price.

BID size   Number of shares associated with the current BID price or the number of shares the buyer(s) is (are) offering to buy at the posted BID price.

Bollinger bands   John Bollinger created trading bands (upper and lower boundary lines) plotted at standard deviation levels above and below a moving average. Because standard deviation measures volatility, the bands widen during volatile markets and contract during calmer periods.

bond   Form of debt security issues by a government or corporation. Promises payment of original investment plus interest on specified future dates.

book value   Value of asset, liability, or stockholders' equity account. For a fixed asset, it is typically the cost of the asset less accumulated depreciation. As companies continue to use fixed assets to generate revenue, the book values lessen and sometimes ultimately reach zero. See also *depreciation.*

breakout   If a stock has traded in a narrow range for some time (built a base) and then advances above the resistance level, this is an upside breakout. Breakouts are suspect if they do not occur on high volume (compared with average daily volume). Some traders use a buy stop, which calls for purchase when a stock rises above a certain price.

bull, or bullish, market When stock prices have risen steadily over several months, experts call it a bull market. The term comes from the way the animal attacks. When a bull rushes forward, it holds its head low and then gores upward with its horns.

bull/bear ratio Market-sentiment indicator based on a weekly poll of investment advisors as to whether they are bullish, bearish, or neutral on the stock market. Published by Investor's Intelligence of New Rochelle, New York. Historically, readings above 60% have indicated extreme optimism on the part of the public and even professionals (bearish for the market). Readings below 40% have indicated extreme pessimism (bullish for the markets).

buy on margin Practice of buying stock with money borrowed from a broker. The loan is collateralized by the security purchased, which is held in a margin account. The broker charges interest, but the rate is usually attractive compared with other forms of debt, as it is secured by an easily marketable stock.

call option Contract that gives the buyer of the option the right, but not the obligation, to take delivery of the underlying security at a specific price within a certain time.

candlestick chart Chart that displays open, high, low, and close prices of a security for each time period and that illustrates the relationship among these prices. Chart elements look like candlesticks with wicks at both ends. The actual candle portion is called the real body and is determined by the day's open and close prices. The wicks, called shadows, show the price range for the day. When the close is higher than the open, the body is green (if color is available).

cash Currency and checks on hand and deposits in banks. Listed in the current assets section on the statement of financial position. Also called *cash equivalents*.

cash equivalents See *cash*.

change Dollar difference between the preceding day's closing price and the most recent price. (Prices are delayed by at least twenty minutes.)

close Final trading price for a security at the end of the most recent trading day.

closed trades Positions that have been liquidated.

commission Fee that brokers charge for executing a transaction. Amount is usually based on number of shares or the total dollar amount of the trade.

common stock Ownership stake in a company. Holders of common stock shares are last in line in terms of claim to dividends and assets.

confirmation Indication that at least two indices—in the case of Dow theory, the industrials and the transportation—corroborate a market trend or turning point.

correction Sharp, short drop in stock prices, after which the market resumes an upward climb. Of course, when the correction is happening, it's hard to distinguish it from the beginnings of a bear market. Any price reaction within the market leading to an adjustment by as much as one-third to two-thirds of the previous gain.

current assets Assets a company can convert to cash within one year. For example, accounts receivable and inventories of products to sell. Listed in the assets category on the statement of financial position. See also *accounts receivable, assets, fixed assets.*

current liabilities   Obligations a company has to others, such as creditors, suppliers, and tax authorities, payable within one year. Listed in the liabilities category on the statement of financial position. See also *accounts payable, debt, income taxes.*

current offer   Price at which the owner of a security offers to sell it at the posted ASK price.

daily range   Intraday price volatility, or the difference between the high and low price during one trading day.

daily volume (13-week average)   Average number of shares of a company's stock traded daily over the previous 13-week period. Daily volume is one indicator of how liquid a security is. A low daily volume could imply low interest in a stock, a limited float (number of shares outstanding), and/or a highly volatile share price, since even relatively small trades will have an exaggerated effect. Low-volume stocks, also known as thinly traded, are usually seen as riskier than more heavily traded shares.

day order   Trade order to buy or sell a security during the market hours in a trading day.

day's high   Highest price of the security during the current day's trading. By comparing with day's low, traders can get an idea of how much the stock is fluctuating.

day's low   Lowest price of the security during the current day's trading. By comparing with the day's high, traders can get an idea of how much the stock is fluctuating.

day trader   Person who buys and sells stocks rapidly during the day to exploit the stocks' intraday price volatility.

debt   Money a company has borrowed and must repay, frequently with interest. Listed in the liabilities category on the statement of financial position. See also *accounts payable, current liabilities, income taxes.*

depreciation   Allowance for wear or age made to the value of a fixed asset, allocating its cost over its estimated useful life. Listed in the assets category on the statement of financial position. See also *book value.*

derivatives   Financial contracts the value of which depends on the value of the underlying instrument commodity, bond, equity, currency, or a combination.

distribution   Any set of related values described by an average (mean), which identifies its midpoint, a measure of spread (standard distribution), and a measure of its shape (skew or kurtosis). Also, the act of selling stocks, or when the traders or investors use the current rally to liquidate old positions in the face of good news. Compare with *accumulation.*

divergence   Two or more averages or indices that fail to show confirming trends.

diversification   Investing strategy that seeks to minimize risk by diversifying among many types of investments. Diversification and risk are directly related. The more diversified a portfolio, the less risk there is.

dividends Cash or stock payments from a company's profits distributed to stockholders, an equal amount for each share of stock owned. Listed as dividends on the statement of stockholders' equity.

Dow Jones Industrial Average Probably the most widely watched indicator of American stock market movements. More than 100 years old, it is well known. By including only thirty stocks, it is manageable. These stocks tend to be those of the largest, most established firms and represent a range of industries. Unfortunately, there are only thirty of them, and they are not always an ideal proxy for the thousands of stocks that make up the market as a whole. Broader indices such as the Standard & Poor's 500 (for large companies), the Russell 2000 (for smaller companies), and the Wilshire 5000 (for an especially broad measure) have gained popularity.

downtick Indicates that the current BID price is lower than the previous BID.

drawdown Reduction in account equity as a result of a bad trade or series of bad trades.

dynamic data updates Ability to update an application automatically from within another application.

earnings Profit, or net income; in this case the sum of the trailing four quarters' net income from continuing operations and discontinued operations.

earnings per share (EPS) Net income divided by common shares outstanding. A company that earns $1 million for the year and has a million shares outstanding has an EPS of $1. This EPS figure, which represents how much of earnings each share is entitled to, is important as the basis for various calculations an investor might make in assessing a stock's price.

earnings report See *statement of earnings.*

earnings surprise Difference between what analysts expected a company to earn and what was actually earned. Earnings estimates have gained importance in recent years, and companies that don't measure up often find their shares hammered. (The difference can also be expressed as a percentage.)

earn the spread Act of buying a stock at the BID price and selling a stock at the ASK price, thus earning the difference between the BID and ASK prices.

Electronic Communication Networks (ECNs) Allow market makers and any traders to post and display BID and ASK prices on a national system, so that others can fill these orders. Most often the ECN buy or sell orders would become the best buy and sell prices for the security. All ECNs are proprietary systems. To participate in the marketplace, they must be registered with the NASDAQ and NASD. To date, there were eight ECNs on the NASDAQ system: Instinet Corporation (INCA), Island ECN (ISLD), Archipelago (ARCA), Bloomberg Tradebook (BTRD), Spear Leeds & Kellogg (REDI), Attain (ATTN), BRASS Utility (BRUT), and Strike Technologies (STRK).

equilibrium market Price region that represents a balance between demand and supply.

equity The part of a company's assets that belongs to the stockholders. In other words, the amount that would remain if a company sold all of its assets and paid off all of its liabilities. Listed as stockholders' equity on the statement of financial position and on the statement of stockholders' equity.

exchange Organization that provides for the trading of a listed security. The biggest, most established companies usually trade on the New York Stock Exchange (NYSE), but many giants in technology and other newer companies trade on NASDAQ.

expenses Costs such as salaries, rent, office supplies, advertising, and taxes. Listed in the operating expenses category on the statement of earnings.

exponential moving average (EMA) Mathematical-statistical method of forecasting that assumes future price action is a weighted average of past periods. Mathematics series in which greater weight is given to more recent price action.

extreme Highest or lowest price during any time period; a price extreme.

fade Act of selling a stock at rising price or buying a stock at falling price.

fast market Declaration that market conditions in the trading pit are so temporarily disorderly with prices moving rapidly that floor brokers are not held responsible for the execution of orders.

52-week high Highest price for a security or fund during the past 52 weeks, or one year.

52-week low Lowest price for a security or fund during the past 52 weeks, or one year.

fill Executed order; sometimes refers to the price at which an order is executed.

fill order Trade order that must be filled immediately on the floor or immediately canceled.

filter Device or program that separates data, signal, or information in accordance with specified criteria. Moving average line is considered to be a filter.

Financial Accounting Standards Board (FASB) Association of accounting professionals that decides, maintains, and communicates generally accepted accounting principles (GAAP).

first trade price See *opening price for IPO*.

fixed assets Anything companies use for more than one year to manufacture, display, store, and transport products. Often called property, plant, and equipment because that's what fixed assets usually are. Listed after current assets in the assets category on the statement of financial position. See also *accounts receivable, assets, current assets*.

flipping IPO Buying an IPO at the offering price and then selling the stock soon after it starts trading on the open market. Greatly discouraged by underwriters, especially if done by individual investors.

floor brokers Employees of brokerage firms working on exchange trading floors.

footnotes Annual report section that provides information essential to understanding the financial statements fully. Explain the financial statement's numbers and any significant events affecting them. Also provide additional detail and provide supplementary financial information. Also called *notes*.

Form 10-K See *SEC Form 10-K*.

Form 10-Q See *SEC Form 10-Q*.

fundamental analysis Analytical method by which only the sales, earnings, and value of a given tradable's assets may be considered. The analysis holds that stock market activity may be predicted by looking at the relative company performance data, as well as at the management of the company in question.

futures Contracts to make or accept delivery of a given commodity on a given date at a prearranged price. Traded on all sorts of things, including corn, pork bellies, S & P's 500 index, and Treasury securities. However, hardly anyone actually delivers (or accepts) all the bacon implied by a futures contract on pork bellies. Investors simply settle up with money. Futures (in the case of S & P's 500 index futures) are a legal way to bet on the direction of a broad stock market, or (in the case of Treasury securities) on the direction of interest rates.

gap Day in which the daily range is completely above or below the previous day's daily range.

goodwill Intangible asset that adds value to the worth of a company; for example, the reputation of its products, services, or personnel. Listed in the assets category (sometimes as Investments and sundry assets) on the statement of financial position. See also *assets, intangible assets*.

gross income Difference between a company's total sales and its cost of sales. Listed as a category on the statement of earnings. Also called *gross profit*.

gross profit See *gross income*.

gross spread for IPO Difference between an IPO's offering price and the price the members of the syndicate pay for the shares. Usually represents a discount of 7% to 8%, about half of which goes to the broker who sells the shares. Also called the *underwriting discount*.

head and shoulders For technicians or chartist, a chart pattern indicating a peak, a decline, a second even higher peak, a decline, a rebound to the level of the first peak, and yet another decline. A head and shoulders pattern is supposed to be bad news, indicating the stock is headed downward.

historical data Series of past daily, weekly, or monthly market prices (open, high, low, close, and volume).

income statement See *statement of earnings*.

income taxes Fees placed by federal, state, local, and foreign governments on a company's earnings. Listed on the statement of earnings. See also *accounts payable, current liabilities, debt*.

index Composite of securities that serves as a barometer for the overall market or some segment of it. The best known of these are the Dow Jones Industrial Average and the Standard & Poor's 500, both of which reflect the performance of large American companies. Other indices include the Russell 2000, which is an index of smaller stocks. Many indices are much more specific.

initial public offering (IPO) First stock sold by a company when going public. A feature of runaway bull markets, as there is proven demand for stock and it makes sense to sell shares when they are likely to bring the highest prices. The hottest IPOs can make their purchasers a quick profit by soaring soon after trading begins.

in play Stock that is the focus of a public bidding contest, as in a takeover.

insider trading Buying and selling by a company's own officers and directors for their personal accounts. When investors buy or sell based on material nonpublic information, they are engaged in illegal insider trading.

Instinet   Established in 1969 to serve large institutional investors. Offers to participating institutions the ability to trade NASDAQ and NYSE stocks among themselves 24 hours a day. A private market with often better prices.

institutional ownership   Percentage of a company's shares owned by banks, mutual funds, pension funds, insurance companies, and other institutions, all of them characterized by a propensity to buy and sell in bulk. Big institutional trades are having an increasing impact on the securities markets, as the institutional share of savings increases.

intangible assets   Anything nonphysical, such as goodwill, trademarks, and patents, that has value for a company. Listed in the assets category (sometimes as Investments and sundry assets) on the statement of financial position. See also *assets, fixed assets, goodwill.*

interest-sensitive stock   Stock whose price is very much affected by rising or falling interest rates. Auto makers, homebuilders, mortgage lenders, financial institutions, and others find that when rates soar, their business dries up. But some stocks can show rate sensitivity because these are stocks that pay hefty dividends. When rates fall, this dividend looks even better. But when rates rise, this dividend is less appealing compared to Treasury securities and other riskless investments.

inventories   All goods and materials available for sale (in the case of wholesalers, retailers, and distributors) or raw materials and supplies, works in process, and finished goods (in the case of manufacturers). Listed in the current assets section on the statement of financial position.

investments   Company's equity ownership in unconsolidated subsidiaries and affiliates. Listed in the category of assets on the statement of financial position.

IPO premium   Difference between the offering price and opening price. Also called an *IPO's pop.*

IPO's pop   See *IPO premium.*

Island   Established in 1996. The fastest growing ECN. Increasingly more popular trading platform among day traders because it is fast, reliable, and relatively inexpensive.

lag   Number of data points that a filter, such as a moving average, follows or trails the input price data.

last price   Current trading price of one unit of a particular security.

last trade size   Most recent number of shares traded of the security.

lead IPO underwriter   Investment bank in charge of setting the offering price of an IPO and allocating shares to other members of the syndicate. Also called *lead manager.*

lead manager   See *lead IPO underwriter.*

leverage   Use of debt to increase returns. Investors also use leverage when buying stocks on margin. Associated with risk: An investor who buys stock on margin may run into trouble if the stock falls, leaving the loan insufficiently collateralized.

liabilities   Company's debts to a lender, a supplier of goods and services, a tax authority, a landlord, and others. Listed on the statement of financial position.

limit order   Order to buy or sell when a price is fixed. When traders or investors instruct a broker to buy shares at or below a certain price, or sell shares at or above a certain price, they've entered a limit order. These reduce the risk that an order will be filled at a price the traders or investors don't like. The down side is that by waiting for that particular stock price, the stock you want may get away from you, or the stock you want to unload just keeps falling in price.

line chart   Displays only the closing price for a security for each time period. A line connects closing values from each period. Often used for plotting mutual funds, which typically only have a daily close value. Over time, these points present a telling performance history for the security.

liquid asset   Asset that can be quickly converted into cash; for example, cash and marketable securities.

liquidity   Ability to quickly convert or sell an asset, such as a stock, into cash.

lockup period for IPO   Time period after an IPO when insiders at the newly public company are restricted by the lead underwriter from selling their shares. Usually lasts 180 days.

long   Establishing ownership of the responsibilities of a buyer of a tradable; holding securities in anticipation of a price increase in that security.

long-term debt   Debt a company will repay after one year. Listed in the liabilities category on the statement of financial position.

margin account   In stock trading, an account in which purchase of stock may be financed with borrowed money. This amount varies daily and is settled in cash. In essence, a brokerage account that lets an investor or trader buy securities on credit or borrow against securities held in the account. Interest is charged on such borrowing, but usually at attractive rates compared with other forms of debt. Trading on margin can enhance investment returns considerably, but like all leveraged activities, can also backfire. The federal government limits the extent to which margin can be used in equities trading.

margin call   Request for additional capital to bolster the equity in an investor's or trader's margin account. If the trader or investor cannot provide additional cash or securities, the broker will sell the shares.

marketable securities   Financial assets, such as stocks and bonds, that companies can convert to cash. Listed as assets on the statement of financial position.

market on close   Order specification that requires the broker to get the best price available on the close of trading, usually during the last five minutes of trading.

market maker   Broker or bank continually prepared to make a two-way price to purchase or sell for a security or currency.

market order   Instructions to the broker to immediately sell to the best available bid or to buy from the best available offer.

market risk   Uncertainty of returns attributable to fluctuation of the entire market.

market sentiment   Crowd psychology; typically a measurement of bullish or bearish attitudes among investors and traders.

market timing   Using analytical tools to devise entry and exit methods. Technique used by traders or investors who believe they can predict when the market will change course. If the traders or investors can time the market correctly, then they can make huge profits.

market value Company value determined by investors, obtained by multiplying the current price of company stock by the common shares outstanding.

mean Result of dividing the sum of the values by the number of observations.

momentum Time series that represents change of today's price from some fixed number of days back in history.

momentum indicator (MOM) Market indicator that uses price and volume statistics for predicting the strength or weakness of a current market and any overbought or oversold conditions, and to note turning points within the market.

money flow Technical indicator that keeps a running total of the money flowing into and out of a security. Money flow is calculated daily by multiplying the number of shares traded by the change in closing price. If prices close higher, the money flow is a positive number. If prices close lower, the money flow is a negative number. A running total is kept by adding or subtracting the current result from the previous total.

most-active list Stocks with the highest trading volume on a given day.

moving average Mathematical procedure to smooth or eliminate the fluctuations in data and to assist in determining when to buy and sell. Moving averages emphasize the direction of a trend, confirm trend reversals, and smooth out price and volume fluctuations, or "noise," that can confuse interpretation of the market. The sum of a value plus a selected number of previous values divided by the total values.

moving average convergence/divergence (MACD) Crossing of two exponentially smoothed moving averages that are plotted above and below a zero line. The crossover, movement through the zero line, and divergences generate buy and sell signals.

moving average crossover Point at which the various moving average lines intersect each other or the price line on a moving average price bar chart. Technicians use crossovers to signal price-based buy and sell opportunities.

moving window Snapshot of a portion of a time series at an instant in time. The window is moved along the time series at a constant rate. For instance, a three-minute moving average line takes into account continuously the observation of the last three minutes.

narrow range day Trading day with a smaller price range relative to the previous day's price range. In other words, the stock prices were stable during that day.

National Association of Securities Dealers (NASD) Industry organization that regulates the behavior of member securities dealers. Owns and operates NASDAQ, the automated quotation system for over-the-counter trading. Derives its authority from the federal government. Every securities dealer in the country is required by law to be a member.

National Association of Securities Dealers Automated Quotation system (NASDAQ) Electronic stock exchange run by the NASD for over-the-counter trading. Established in 1971, it is America's fastest growing stock market and is a leader in trading technology shares. Has more listed companies than the New York Stock Exchange, and handles more than half the stock trading that occurs in the United States.

negative divergence Two or more averages, indices, or indicators that fail to show confirming trends.

net earnings Company's total revenue less total expenses, showing what a company earned (or if lost, called net loss) for a set period, usually one year. Listed often literally as the bottom line on the statement of earnings. Also called *net income, net profit.*

net income See *net earnings.*

net profit See *net earnings.*

net sales Company's total sales less returned merchandise and discounts. Listed on the statement of earnings.

net worth Amount of a company's stockholders' equity. Listed as total stockholders' equity on the statement of financial position.

New York Stock Exchange (NYSE) America's biggest and oldest securities exchange. Has the most stringent requirements for being listed. Where most of the nation's largest and best-established companies are listed. Although computers are used, the NYSE remains old-fashioned in that buyers and sellers (representing investors all over the globe) shout orders at one another face to face. In fact, the NYSE's auction system, in which buyers and sellers meet in the open market, usually produces fair market pricing. To maintain an orderly market, specialists on the trading floor manage buying and selling of assigned stocks and have the responsibility of buying when no one else will.

noise Price and volume fluctuations that can confuse interpretation of market direction.

nontrend day Narrow range day lacking any discernible movement in either direction.

normal distribution For the purposes of statistical testing, simulated net returns are assumed to be drawn from a particular distribution. If net returns are drawn from a normal distribution, low and high returns are equally likely, and the most likely net return in a quarter is the average net return.

notes See *footnotes.*

odd lot Order to buy or sell fewer than 100 shares of stock.

offering Act of trying to sell a stock at the posted ASK price.

offering price for IPO Price that investors must pay for allocated shares in an IPO. Not the same as the opening price, which is the first trade price of a new stock.

on-balance volume (OBV) Plotted as a line representing the cumulative total of volume. Volume from a day's trading with a higher close compared with the previous day is assigned a positive value, whereas volume on a lower close from the previous day is assigned a negative value. Traders look for a confirmation of a trend in OBV with the market or a divergence between the two as an indication of a potential reversal.

open Price paid in a security's first transaction of the current trading day.

opening price for IPO Price at which a new stock starts trading. Also called *first trade price.*

opening range Range of prices that occur during the first thirty seconds to five minutes of trading, depending on the preference of the individual analyst.

open trades Current trades that are still held active in the customer's account.

operating expenses   Costs related to a company's operations; for example salaries, advertising, sales commissions, travel, and entertainment. Listed on the statement of earnings.

operating income (or loss)   Result of deducting the cost of all sales and operating expenses from a company's net sales. Listed on the statement of earnings.

opportunity cost   Income foregone by the commitment of resources to another use.

oscillator   Technical indicator used to identify overbought and oversold price regions; an indicator that trends data, such as price.

overbought market   Market prices that have risen too steeply and too quickly.

overbought or oversold indicator   Attempts to define when prices have moved too far and too fast in either direction and thus are vulnerable to a reaction.

oversold market   Market prices that have declined too steeply and too quickly.

oversubscribed IPO   Deal in which investors apply for more shares than are available. Usually a sign that an IPO is a hot deal and will open at a substantial premium.

preferred stock   Stock that acts much like a bond but that confers an ownership stake in the company. Preferred shares typically pay a fixed dividend and give their holder a claim to earnings and assets prior to that bestowed by common stock. In general, the higher the preferred yield, the greater the risk. Preferred stock often comes with a conversion clause permitting it to be traded in for common shares.

previous close   Price of the security at the end of the previous day's trading session.

price   Current market price of a security or the amount paid to buy one unit of a security.

price/earnings (P/E) ratio   Stock price divided by annual earnings per share. Also known as the P/E multiple. P/E is the single most widely used factor in assessing whether a stock is pricey or cheap. In general, fast-growing technology companies have high P/Es, because the stock price is taking account of anticipated growth as well as current earnings.

program trading   Trades based on signals from computer programs, usually entered directly from the trader's computer into the market's computer system.

prospectus   Document, included in a company's S-1 registration statement, that explains all aspects of a company's business, including financial results, growth strategy, and risk factors. The preliminary prospectus is also called a red herring because of the red ink used on the front page, which indicates that some information, such as the price and share amounts, is subject to change.

proxy   Written authorization from a shareholder for another person to represent him or her at a shareholders' meeting and to exercise voting rights.

put/call ratio   Volume of put options divided by the volume in call options. A high ratio (put volume much higher than call volume) is considered by technical analysts to be a sign of bearish sentiment, indicating the market is headed south.

put option   Contract to sell a specified amount of a stock or commodity at an agreed time at the stated exercise price.

pyramid   To increase holdings by using the most buying power available in a margin account with paper and real profits.

quiet period for IPO Time in which companies in registration are forbidden by the Securities and Exchange Commission to say anything not included in their prospectus, which could be interpreted as hyping an offering. Starts the day a company files an S-1 registration statement and lasts until 25 days after a stock starts trading. The intent and effect of the quiet period have been hotly debated.

range Difference between the high and low price during a given period, such as one day.

ratio Relation that one quantity bears to another of the same kind, with respect to magnitude or numerical value.

reaction Short-term decline in price.

registration statement See *S-1*.

relative strength Comparison of the price performance of a stock to a market index, such as Standard & Poor's 500 stock index.

resistance Price level at which rising prices have stopped rising and have either moved sideways or reversed direction; usually seen as a price chart pattern.

retained earnings Total of a company's net earnings since its inception, minus any payments made to stockholders. Retained earnings is actually part of stockholders' equity and represents the portion of a company's assets that are financed from profitable operations rather than from selling stock to investors or borrowing from external sources. Listed on the statement of financial position.

retracement Price movement in the opposite direction of the previous trend.

revenue Total flow of funds into a company, mostly for sales of its goods or services. Listed as the first category on the statement of earnings.

risk Chance that something bad (a loss) will happen. Risk in the context of trading and investing simply refers to the variability of returns.

risk tolerance Amount of psychological pain the trader or investor is willing to suffer from the investments.

road show for IPO Tour taken by a company preparing for an IPO in order to attract interest in the deal. Attended by institutional investors, analysts, and money managers by invitation only. Members of the media are forbidden.

round trip Buying and selling the same stock or opening and closing the trade position, especially in a relatively brief period.

running market Market wherein prices are changing rapidly in one direction with very few or no price changes in the opposite direction.

S-1 Document filed with SEC announcing a company's intent to go public. Includes the prospectus. Also called *registration statement*.

screening stocks Practice, abetted by computers, whereby investors or traders search for all stocks meeting a given set of criterion. For instance, traders can screen for all NASDAQ companies with market capitalization above $500 million, daily trading volume 500,000 shares, and Beta value greater than 1.5.

SEC Form 10-K Financial report that the SEC requires companies to submit yearly. This audited form contains more detailed information than the financial statements in the annual report.

SEC Form 10-Q   Financial report that the SEC requires companies to submit quarterly. This unaudited form includes briefer, less detailed financial statements than those in the annual report.

securities   Investments, including stocks and bonds. Listed as assets on the statement of financial position.

Securities and Exchange Commission (SEC)   Federal agency charged with regulating the securities markets.

SelectNet   Introduced in 1990 and designed so that market makers could communicate and execute trades electronically among themselves. Orders are broadcast to NASDAQ market makers only. Provides day traders with a tool to electronically submit orders directly to the market makers at a better price than the posted best BID and ASK prices. Not a mandatory system for market makers. Market makers have the option to accept or to ignore that offer; a SelectNet order is filled only if the market maker chooses to execute that order.

selling short   Selling a security and then borrowing the security for delivery with the intent of replacing the security at a lower price.

selling stockholders for IPO   Investors in a company who sell part or all of their stake as part of that company's IPO. Usually considered a bad sign if a large portion of shares offered in an IPO comes from selling stockholders.

settlement   Price at which all outstanding positions in a stock or commodity are marked to market; typically, the closing price.

share   Certificate of ownership in a company. Also called *stock*.

shareholder   Owner of part of a company. Also called *stockholder*.

short covering   Process of buying back stock that has already been sold short.

short interest   Shares that have been sold short but not yet repurchased; shares sold short divided by average daily volume.

short interest ratio   Indicates the number of trading days required to repurchase all of the shares that have been sold short. A short interest ratio of 2.50 indicates that, based on the current volume of trading, it will take two and a half days' volume to cover all shorts.

signal   In the context of stock or commodity time series historical data, usually daily or weekly prices.

signal line   In moving average jargon, the first moving average, such as the fast moving average line of three-minute data, is smoothed by a second moving average, such as the slow moving average line of nine-minute data. The second moving average is the signal line.

simple moving average   Arithmetic mean, or average, of a series of prices over a period of time. The longer the period of time studied (that is, the larger the denominator of the average), the less impact an individual data point has on the average.

slippage   Difference between estimated transaction costs and actual transaction costs.

smoothing   Mathematical technique that removes excess data variability while maintaining a correct appraisal of the underlying trend.

specialist Trader on the market floor assigned to fill bids or orders in a specific stock out of his or her own account, when the order has no competing bid or order, to ensure a fair and orderly market.

spike Sharp rise in price in a single day or two; may be as great as 15% to 30%, indicating the time for an immediate sale.

spinning IPO Practice by investment banks of distributing IPO shares to certain clients, such as venture capitalists and executives, in hopes of getting their business in the future. Outlawed at many banks.

split Occurs when a company decides to divide its shares into two, three, four, or more. Thus a stock worth $100 might be the subject of a 2 for 1 split, resulting in a share price of $50. Holders in this case get twice as many shares, but each is worth half as much as before, and since nothing else about the company has changed, shareholders aren't better or worse off. Traditionally seen as a good sign; companies split their shares when the price of each share is considered high enough to discourage ownership.

spread Trade in which two related contracts/stocks/bonds/options are traded to exploit the relative differences in price change between the two.

Standard & Poor's 500 Widely followed benchmark of stock market performance. Includes 400 industrial firms, 40 financial stocks, 40 utilities, and 20 transportation stocks. All the firms are large. Also the basis of a large amount of index investing. Inclusion in the index usually causes a stock to rise.

standard deviation Positive square root of the expected value of the square of the difference between a random variable and its mean; a measure of the fluctuation in a stock's monthly return over the preceding year.

statement of cash flows Financial statement that reports the flow of cash in and out of a company for a set period, usually one year. It reports the operating activities, investing activities, and financing activities of the company.

statement of earnings Financial statement that reports the results of a company's business operations (revenue and expenses) for a set period, usually one year. Also called *earnings report, income statement, statement of operations*, and *statement of profit and loss*.

statement of financial position Financial statement that reports a company's assets and the claims against them (liabilities and stockholders' equity) at a set date noted on the statement. Also called *balance sheet*.

statement of operations See *statement of earnings.*

statement of owners' equity See *statement of stockholders' equity.*

statement of profit and loss See *statement of earnings.*

statement of stockholders' equity Financial statement that reports the changes in the owner's interests (equity); for example, by detailing changes in net earnings or dividends paid to stockholders. Usually separate, although a company may prepare a statement of retained earnings instead. Also called *statement of owners' equity.*

stochastic Literally means "random."

stochastics oscillator Overbought/oversold indicator that compares today's price with a preset window of high and low prices. These data are transformed into a range between zero and 100 and then smoothed.

stock Certificate of ownership in a company. Also called *share.*

stockbroker Individual registered with the National Association of Securities Dealers (NASD) who is authorized to buy and sell securities for his or her customers.

stockholder Owner of part of a company. Also called *shareholder.*

stock index futures Futures contract traded that uses a market index, such as the S & P's 500 index, as the underlying instrument. The delivery mechanism is usually cash settlement.

stock symbol Unique, market-approved code that identifies a particular security on an exchange. Generally reflects the name of the security. Also called *ticker symbol.*

stop loss Risk management technique in which the trade is liquidated to halt any further decline in value.

stops Buy stops are orders placed at a predetermined price over the current price of the market. They become "Buy at the market" orders if the market is at or above the price of the stop order. Sell stops are orders placed with a predetermined price below the current price. They become "Sell at the market" orders if the market trades at or below the price of the stop order.

street name Name under which a brokerage firm holds the securities of its customers. Most brokerage companies hold their customers' securities in the firm's street name rather than in the name of each customer. By using its street name rather than an individual's name, the brokerage firm can process trades faster.

support Historical price level at which falling prices have stopped falling and either moved sideways or reversed direction; usually seen as a price-chart pattern.

syndicate Group of investment banks that buy shares in an IPO to sell to the public. Headed by the lead manager and disbanded as soon as the IPO is completed.

target price Price that investors or traders hope a given security will reach within a certain period of time.

technical analysis Form of market analysis that studies supply and demand for securities and commodities based on trading volume and price studies. Using charts and modeling techniques, technicians attempt to identify price trends in a market.

technology sector Category that includes computer hardware, software, electronics, electrical equipment, and wireless communications companies.

tick Last reported stock transaction. Is reported in increments of $\frac{1}{8}$, $\frac{1}{16}$, or $\frac{1}{32}$.

ticker tape or screen Real-time report that states the last price and the unique, market-approved code that identifies a particular security on an exchange.

ticker symbol See *stock symbol.*

tick indicator Number of stocks whose last trade was an uptick or a downtick.

time series Collection of observations made sequentially in time and indexed by time. All stock price data is the time series data.

trading bands Lines plotted in and around the price structure to form an envelope or a band, answering whether prices are high or low on a relative basis and forewarning whether to buy or sell by using indicators to confirm price action. Bollinger bands are an example of trading bands.

trading range   Difference between the high and low prices traded during a period of time.

trailing stop   Stop-loss order that follows the prevailing price trend.

trend   General drift, tendency, or bent of a set of statistical data as related to time.

trend following   Moving in the direction of the prevailing price movement.

trending market   Price moves in a single direction.

trendless   Price movement that vacillates to the degree that a clear trend cannot be identified.

trendline   Line drawn that connects either a series of highs or lows in a trend. Can represent either support, as in an uptrend line, or resistance, as in a downtrend line. Consolidations are marked by horizontal trendlines.

triple witching hour   Last hour of trading on the third Friday of March, June, September, and December, when investors rush to unwind their positions in index options and futures, all of which are expiring on the same day. Triple witching hour has produced some major price swings as investors buy and sell both the derivatives and the underlying securities.

turning point   Approximate time at which there is a change in trend.

underwriting account   See *gross spread for IPO.*

uptick   Indicates that the current BID price is higher than the previous BID.

value stock   Stock that is undervalued by the current stock market. Can be identified on the most basic level simply by examining the key ratios.

venture capital   Funding acquired during the pre-IPO process of raising money for companies. Done only by accredited investors.

volatility   Measure of a stock's tendency to move up and down in price, based on its daily price history over the latest twelve months.

volume   Total units of a security traded on the most recent trading day. An unusually high volume means that important news has just come out, or will come out soon. Rising volume coupled with a rising share price is considered a bullish indicator for a stock, while the opposite is considered a bearish indicator. Technical analysts also track a volume price trend to relate volume and price. Technical analysts believe that the biggest price gains are associated with the heaviest volume trading.

whiplash or whipsaw   Alternating buy and sell signals that result in losses; an investment or trade where the price goes in the opposite direction from that which was anticipated right after the transaction is made. A trade is made based on a buy signal generated by a technical indicator. Then, shortly thereafter, the price moves in the opposite direction giving a sell signal. Results frequently in a trading loss. Can also substantially increase the trading commission cost.

Index

A

Achelis, Steven, 162
Advance decline, 229, 231; value, 224
Alerts. *See* Trading alerts
America First Trader, 68
American Express, 63, 66
Ameritrade, 62, 66, 68
AMEX, 52, 57; centralized specialist system, 52; members, 52; NASDAQ acquisition of, 52
Analysis, fundamental. *See* Fundamental analysis
Analysis ratios, 34
Appel, Gerald, 202
Archipelago (ARCA), 53, 54, 58, 72, 125; extended trading hours, 58; order-execution system, 58
Arms, Richard, 232
Assets utilization ratios, 328, 341, 346–349; book value per common share, 348–349; net profit margin, 347–348; operating profit margin, 347; return on assets, 346–347
Attain (ATTN), 53
Ax analyst, 19
Axes, 48, 114. *See also specific firms*

B

Back testing, 40–41; accuracy of, 40
Balance sheet, 315–321; assets, 316–317; current assets, 317, 318; current liabilities, 319–320; fixed assets, 317–318; intangible assets, 319; liabilities, 316; long-term liabilities, 320; stockholders' equity, 316, 320–321, 322
Banc of America Securities, IPO underwriter, 275
Basket trade, 18
Batten, William, 45
Bear/bearish market: charting, 174–175, 179; signals, 307
Bear Sterns & Co., IPO underwriter, 273
Berber, Philip, 67
Bidding, 106, 108
Bloomberg, 71, 258, 334
Bloomberg Tradebook (BTRD), 72
Blue chip companies, 50, 258, 338
Blue-sky laws, 272, 280
Blue Stone Capital, IPO underwriter, 273
Bollinger, John, 211
Bollinger bands, 17, 18, 23, 149, 211–214, 235, 261, 358
Brass Utility (BRUT), 53
Broad market measures, 223; market breadth indicators, 229–232; market indices, 224–229
Brokerage firms, full-service retail, 48, 49
Bull/bullish market: charting, 173–174, 178; signals, 307
Buying, 106, 107, 108
Buy orders, 358

C

Candlestick charting, 17, 18; Japanese origins, 169. *See also* Candlestick charts; Candlestick patterns

Candlestick charts, 170; price information displayed, 170; wicks, 170. *See also* Candlestick charting; Candlestick patterns

Candlestick patterns, 171–179; bearish, 174–175; bearish engulfing lines, 175, 179; bullish, 173–174; bullish engulfing lines, 173–174, 178; buy signal, 177, 178; dark cloud, 174; doji, 173, 176, 178, 179; double doji, 176; evening star, 175; hammer, 173, 174; hanging man, 174; harami, 176; harami cross, 176; morning star, 174; neutral, 175–176; neutral market, 172–173; piercing line, 173, 174; price downtrend, 172, 178; price uptrend, 171–172, 179; sell signal, 177–178; short-sell signal, 179; spinning tops, 175, 176, 178, 179

Capital, minimum required, 127

Capitalization levels, 129

Capital West Securities, IPO underwriter, 273

Cash dividends, 251–253. *See also* Settlement dates

Charting, 51; vs. mathematical technical analysis, 160–161; as subjective art, 161, 182

Charting patterns, 161, 194; ascending triangles, 191, 193; breakout gaps, 187; breakouts, 183; common gaps, 186; descending triangles, 191, 192; double bottoms, 161; double tops, 161; downside flags, 193, 195; flags, 193–195; gap down, 185, 186; gaps, 185–187; gap up, 185, 186; head and shoulders, 187–189; horizontal lines, 182–185; inverse head and shoulders pattern, 188, 189; multiple bottoms, 189–190; multiple tops, 189, 190; saucers, 161; symmetrical triangles, 191–192, 194; trend lines, 183–185; triangles, 190–192; upside flags, 193–194. *See also* Price resistance; Price support

Charting software packages, 170

Chartists, 160; objective, 183

Chase Manhattan, IPO underwriter, 273

Chase Manhattan Hambrecht & Quist, 64; IPO underwriter, 280, 287

Chatfield Dean, IPO underwriter, 273

Chicago Board Options Exchange (CBOE), 228

Chicago Mercantile Exchange, 228

CIBC World Markets, IPO underwriter, 273

Clearing firms, 76; securities, 76

Clearing trades, 76

Cleary Gull Reiland & McDevitt, IPO underwriter, 273

CNBC, 20, 33, 71, 289, 334–335

CompuTEL Securities, 64

Concept stocks, 276. *See also* Internet stocks

Conference Board, 303, 304; index of coincident economic indicators, 304; index of lagging economic indicators, 304. *See also* Index of leading economic indicators

Consumer Price Index (CPI), 300

Control stocks, 268

Credit Suisse First Boston, 64; IPO underwriter, 273, 278, 279, 284

Current market value, 300

Cutting the spread, 105

CyBerCorp, 21, 67, 69, 74, 76, 240

CyberTrader, 18, 56, 72, 74, 105, 116, 118, 125, 243

Cyclical stocks, 309

D

Daily high and low alert, 247–248, 258–259

Dain Rauscher Wessels: IPO underwriter, 272, 273

Dakin Securities, IPO underwriter, 273

Datek, 62, 63, 66, 68

Day traders, 14–15, 46, 64, 81, 87, 177; goal, 6; IPO information and, 282; losing money, 71–72; number of trades, 6, 15; stock-holding period, 14; stop-loss limit, 9; stress, 9; vs. swing traders, 3, 5, 8, 9–10, 14; technical analysis tools, 163, 165; trading increments, 6, 18; vs. value/growth investors, 5, 14; work, 9. *See also* Day trading

Day trading, 6–7, 10, 13, 147; analysis tools, 17, 197–198; holding period, 17, 86; number of trades, 17; objective, 14–15, 162; risks, 140; stop loss per trade, 17; strategies, 112, 119–120; vs. swing trading, 6, 10, 17; swing trading similarities, 13–14; target gain per trade, 17; total commission cost, 17; trading objective, 17; trading size, 17; vs. value/growth investing, 6, 10. *See also* Day traders; Precision trading

Day trading firms, 55, 56, 57, 72–73, 74, 151; branch offices, 73; electronic, 155; minimum capital required, 127; scalper swing traders in, 22; as SOES order-entry firm, 115; trading with, 70–74

Dean Witter Reynolds (DEAN), 48, 61

Designated Order Turnaround (DOT), 49–51, 102

Deutsche Banc Alex Brown, IPO underwriter, 273

Discover Brokerage, 62, 63

"Dismal science," 299

Dismal Scientist Internet site, 299

DLJ Direct, 61–62, 63, 66, 68; IPOs and, 279

Dogs of the Dow, 34, 37

Donaldson, Lufkin & Jenrette (DWP), 61, 63; IPO underwriter, 273, 279, 287

Dow, Charles, 159, 229

Dow Jones: Composite index (COMP), 229; Industrial Average (INDU), 34, 224, 225, 229; as lagging indicator, 229; Transportation index (TRAN), 229; Utilities index (UTIL), 229

E

Earnings per share (EPS), 29, 329–330, 335–336, 337, 338; estimate, 330–334; growth rate, 29, 39, 336–337; historical trend, 330; surprises, 334–335

Earnings ratios, 328–339, 341; current yield, 338–339; diluted earnings per share, 329–330; dividend payout ratio, 338; price earnings ratio (PE), 335–336. See also Earnings per share; Value

Earnings reports, 248–251; price reaction and, 250

Earn the spread, 47

Earthman, Bobby, 67

Elder, Alexander, 182

Electronic Communication Networks (ECNs), 43, 45, 46, 52–55, 59, 69, 72, 74, 105, 106, 107, 111, 116–117, 119, 144, 243, 244, 294, 358; advantages, 53–54; cost effectiveness, 53; disadvantages, 55; future of, 59; online brokers and, 52–53; outside market prices, 143; preferred order-execution vehicle, 125; SEC definition, 52

Electronic Data Gathering, Analysis & Retrieval system (EDGAR), 272, 324

Electronic stock trading, risk, 139

Electronic Traders Association (ETA), 71–72, 140

Empire, 66, 68

E-Schwab, IPOs and, 279–280

E*Trade, 49, 62, 63–64, 66, 68; IPOs and, 279–280; Power E*Trade, 75

Exponential moving averages (EMA), 198–199; fast, 17, 18, 199, 200, 201, 202, 203, 204; slow, 17, 18, 200, 201–203, 204, 214

F

Fading the breakout, 183

Fading the gaps, 187

Fama, Fisher, Jensen, Roll study, 252, 254

Fast trading, 154; trading increments, 154

Federal Reserve Bank: discount rate, 308; monetary policy, 304–307

Federal Reserve Board, 127, 130, 304; monetary policy, 260. See also Regulation T, SEC Act of 1934

Federal Reserve System, 305

Fidelity Investments, 61, 62, 63–64, 66, 68; IPOs and, 280

Fiedler, Edgar, 43

Field name, 37

52-week alert, 247–248

Fill or kill orders, 124–125

Financial analysis ratios, interpreting, 349–353

Financial analysts/auditors, IPOs and, 275

Financial Network, 61

Financial ratios, 327–328; categories, 328; objective, 327. See also Assets-utilization ratios; Earnings ratios; Liquidity ratios

Financial software, trading instruments in, 72

Financial statements, 315

First in, first out (FIFO), 124, 317

FirstTrade, 63, 64, 68

Fleet Boston, IPO underwriter, 273

Freeman Welwood, 64, 66

FreeTrade.com, 63

Full-time trading, vs. part-time trading, 10–11

Fundamental analysis, 14, 16, 297–298, 313–314; balance sheet, 315–321; cash flow statement, 323; CEO letter, 314; financial statements, 315; fiscal policy, 304; income statement, 322–323; leading economic indicators, 302–304; macroeconomic analysis, 299–300, 301; microeconomic analysis, 299–300; monetary policy, 304–306; SEC Form 8-K, 324; SEC Form 10-K, 323–324; SEC Form 10-Q, 324; top-down analysis, 399–300. See also Financial ratios; Gross domestic policy; Macroeconomic analysis, individual investors/traders

G

Generally accepted accounting principles (GAAP), 275

Goldman Sachs & Co. (GSCO), 48, 64; IPO underwriter, 272, 273, 278, 279

Gomez Advisors Inc., 65; customer profiles, 67; scoring methodology, 66

Graham, Benjamin, 159

Granville, Joseph, 233

Gross domestic product (GDP), 300–301, 302, 303; components, 304, 306; consumption, 301, 304; government, 301, 304; as historical measure, 302; investment, 301; net exports, 301

Growth companies, 31; mature/established, 31

Growth investing, 26, 29–32, 35; difficulty of, 31–32; vs. value investing, 29. See also Growth investors

Growth investors, 27, 32, 35, 38–39. See also Growth investing

H

Haugen and Lakonishok study, 264–265

Hertzog Hein & Geduld (HRZG), 48

High current yield, 33–34. See also Dogs of the Dow

High-tech stocks, 19, 30–31, 154, 260

Howell, Jim, 67

Hypothecation process, 130

I

Income-elastic products, 309

Income statement, 322–323

Initial public offerings (IPOs), 269–270; aftermarket trading, 282; alerts, 290–291; broken, 284, 287–288, 289; distributions as reward system, 280; dot-com, 276–277; first months, 288–289; first trading day, 282, 284–288; flipping, 280–281; hot, 284–287, 288, 293; insiders and, 267–268; Internet brokers and, 63–64; Internet sites, 283; limit vs. market trade-order executions, 284; lockup, 290–291; magazines, 283; newsletters, 283; 1999, 270–271; price volatility, 282; prospectus, 271; risky information sources, 283; rumors concerning, 283; selling concession, 277; spinning, 278; spin-offs, 281–282; three-year return, 271; tombstone advertisement, 277; trading, 278–280, 282–283, 284–289; trading resources, 282–283; virtual, 280. See also

Financial analysts/auditors; IPO underwriters; Venture capitalists

Index of leading economic indicators, 303

Insiders, 266–268

Insider trading, 255, 266–268; material insider information, 268; tracking, 268

Instinet (INCA), 15, 54, 57–58, 63, 72, 74, 86

Interest rates: automakers and, 308; changing, 309; home-building companies and, 308; prime rate, 305; utility companies and, 308

Internet brokers, 48, 56, 72, 74–76; after-hours trading, 63; capital required, 127; commission-free trades, 63; ECN access, 65; IPO allotment, 280; IPO distribution and, 279; IPOs and, 63–64; issues related to, 65–67; Level II quote screen, 64; technical support, 65; top ten volume market share, 62; top twenty, 66; top twenty most active traders, 68; trading with, 61–64; trading with direct-access, 67–69

Internet index (INX), 228

Internet Investing, 65

Internet service providers (ISPs), 67; broadband service, 59

Internet stock chat rooms, 21

Internet stocks, 18–19, 152, 154; broadband Internet, 276; business-to-business (B2B), 276; as concept stocks, 276; DSL networks, 276; IPOs, 276; wireless Internet technology, 276

Internet trading, criticism, 129–130

Investing, value/growth, 10. See also Investors, value/growth

Investing strategies, 25, 26. See also Growth investing; Value investing

Investment banks, IPO underwriters, 273. See also specific investment banks

Investors, value/growth: vs. day traders, 5, 8, 14; objective, 8; stock-holding period, 8; vs. swing traders, 3, 5, 8, 14

IPOs. See Initial public offerings (IPOs)

IPO underwriters, 272–274, 275, 278; large global investment banks, 272; medium-sized national investment banks, 272; 1999, 273; small regional boutique investment banks, 273. See also specific investment banks

Island (ISLD), 53–57, 58, 63, 72, 74, 107, 111, 125, 144; extended trading hours, 59; Level II screen display, 55, 56; order fills, 56; trade-order execution system, 56. See also Island trade orders

Island trade orders, 122–125; Island book, 122–124; Island fills, 124–125; Island order mechanics, 125; placing, 125

J

J.P. Morgan (JPMS), 64; IPO underwriter, 273, 280

K

KeyTrade Online, 68
Klein, Andrew, 280
Knight-Trimark (NITE), 49

L

Lane, George, 215
Large cap stocks, 35
Last in, first out (LIFO), 317
Lee, James, 140
Lehman Brothers (LEHM), 48, 63; IPO underwriter, 273
Level I information screen, 69, 70, 72, 75, 82–87, 88, 245; BID and ASK, 82–83; BID-to-ASK ratio, 84; change, 87; close and open, 86–87; high and low, 85–86; spread, 83–84; volume, 84–85
Level II information screen, 23, 48, 50, 51, 69, 70, 72, 75, 81–82, 87–99, 102, 111, 115, 118, 120, 121, 122, 124, 144, 240, 241, 245, 248, 261; BID and ASK, 88–93, 113; dynamics, 93–99; market depth, 101; price decrease, 97–99; price increase, 95–99; real-time, 258; share size, 113; supply-and-demand forces, 93–99
Leverage, 145; size, trading styles comparison, 10
Limit orders, 105, 108–109, 112, 150, 358; on NYSE, 111–112; vs. market orders, 110–111. *See also* Orders, type of
Liquidation value, 349
Liquidity, 84. *See also* Liquidity ratios
Liquidity ratios, 328, 341–346; cash asset ratio, 344–345; cash flow, 342; current ratio, 343–344; debt coverage ratio, 345; debt-to-equity ratio, 345–346; net working capital, 342–343; quick asset ratio, 344
Liquid stocks, 210
Losing money, 145, 151, 155
Losing streak, 146–147

M

Macroeconomic analysis, 299–301; individual investors/traders, 309–311; industry analysis, 312–313. *See also* Gross domestic product
Malkiel, Burton, 160
Margin, trading on: dangers, 6–7. *See also* Margin accounts; Margin calls
Margin accounts, 6, 127–129, 145, 293; credit balance, 134; long, 131–134, 136; restricted, 133; restrictions on purchasing power, 128; short account, 134–136. *See also* Hypothecation process; Intraday margin calls; Margin agreement; Margin maintenance requirement; Regulation T, SEC Act of 1934; Special memorandum account
Margin activity statements, reading/interpreting, 135–136
Margin agreement, 130
Margin calls, intraday, 136–137
Margin maintenance requirement, 134
Market breadth indicators, 229–232; TRIN, 229, 231–232. *See also* Advance decline
Market capitalization, 35; stock categories, 35
Market indices, 224–229; construction, 225–227; correlation among, 224; divergence between, 224–225; market-capitalization weighted, 225–226; price-weighted, 225, 226. *See also* Dow Jones Industrial Average; NASDAQ Composite index; NASDAQ 100; NYSE Composite; Russell 2,000; S & P's 500; Wilshire Small Cap
Market makers, 23–24, 46, 51, 53, 69, 70, 83, 99, 114–116, 144, 147, 185, 244; accessing through SelectNet, 118–120; basic trading strategy, 24; collective earnings, 47; identification codes, 48; making money, 47–48; movement, 261; role, 46–47. *See also* *specific market makers*; Axes; Level I information screen; Level II information screen
Market making business, 47
Market making firms, number of, 48
Market orders, 108, 112–113, 150. *See also* Orders, types of
Market ticker, 243–245, 258; ticker reports, 244
Market value, 348
Market variables: current price, 162; last closing price, 162
Mathematical technical analysis, 161–162; charting vs., 160–161

Mayer and Schweitzer (MASH), 49

Mediobanca, IPO underwriter, 273

Merrill Lynch & Co. (MLCO), 48, 64; buying IPO stock through, 279; IPO underwriter, 272, 273

Micro cap stocks, 35

Mid cap stocks, 35

Momentum indicator (MOM), 214–215, 235; plotted as histogram, 214

Momentum traders, 27, 38

Momentum trading, 26–28, 35; opportunities, 51

Morgan Stanley Dean Witter (MSCO), 48, 63, 64; buying IPO stock through, 280; IPO underwriter, 272, 274, 275, 278, 288; online, 66

Moving average, 17, 197, 198. *See also* Moving average indicator

Moving average convergence/divergence (MACD), 202–205; histogram, 204–205; as oscillator tool, 202; signal lines, 204, 205

Moving average (MA) indicator, 197–198, 205; drawback, 198; simple (SMA), 198; uses, 197; weighted (WMA), 198. *See also* Exponential moving average

Murphy, John, 161

My Discount Broker, 66, 68

N

NASDAQ Composite index (COMPX), 30, 224, 225, 262

NASDAQ market makers. *See* Market makers

NASDAQ National Market System (NNMS), 113, 114, 116

NASDAQ 100 (IQX), 224, 228

NASDAQ securities market, 147

NASDAQ SelectNet system. *See* SelectNet

NASDAQ stocks, 19, 47, 50, 51, 52, 58, 86, 111, 144, 148, 150, 243, 244, 245, 246, 247, 355; expensive, 356; high-tech, 151; minimum maintenance requirement, 133–134, 135; volatile, 355

National Association of Securities Dealers Automated Quotation system (NASDAQ), 22, 46–47, 56, 108, 113, 114, 116, 130, 148, 149, 276, 292–293, 358; brokers, 46; computer system, 70; dealers, 46; vs. ECNs, 45; going global, 59; initiating trading transaction, 46; Level I stock quotes, 82; market-order execution system, 22; number of stocks, 35, 48; vs. NYSE, 45; Osaka Stock Exchange and, 59; trading information, 81; volatility, 51. *See also* NASDAQ Composite index; NASDAQ National Market System; NASDAQ 100; NASDAQ securities market; NASDAQ stocks

National Association of Securities Dealers (NASD), 46, 115, 116, 133; broker/dealer, 65, 69, 76, 115, 130, 131; rules, 293. *See also* SOES; SOES orders

National Discount Brokers (NDB), 62, 66, 68

News, 256–261; about mergers and acquisitions, 256–257; direct company, 260; macroeconomic, 259; as recent business events, 256–257; time factor, 260. *See also* Noise, market

New York Stock Exchange (NYSE), 22, 45, 49–51, 57, 108, 129, 130, 148, 149, 231, 276, 292; ease of trading, 50; vs. ECNs, 45; Level I stock quotes, 82; limit orders on, 111–112; market-order execution system, 22; vs. NASDAQ, 45, 49; number of stocks, 35; safety in trading, 50; stock prices, 50; tick test, 292; trading information, 81; trading volume, 262. *See also* Designated Order Turnaround; NYSE Composite; NYSE securities market; NYSE stocks; NYSE trading information screen; Specialists

NexTrade (NTRD), 54

Nison, Steve, 171

Noise, market, 200; investment, 258

North American Securities Administrators Association (NASAA), 71–72

NYSE Composite (NYA.X), 224

NYSE securities market, knowledge of, 147

NYSE stocks, 19, 47, 49, 51, 58, 86, 148, 230, 240, 243, 244, 245, 247, 356; minimum maintenance requirement, 133–134, 135

NYSE trading information screen, 99–103; buy and sell orders filled, 101–102; help for swing traders, 103; inside market size, 101; poor trading stock, 102–103; ratio field, 100

O

Offering, 106–107

On-balance volume (OBV) indicator, 233–235

Opportunists, traders as, 13

Options trading, 51

Order qualifiers, 109–110; all or none, 110; at the close, 110; at the opening, 110; day order,

109; fill or kill, 110; good 'til canceled order, 110; immediate or cancel, 110; not held, 110; open order, 110

Orders, priority of, 112

Orders, types of, 108; buy limit, 107–109; buy stop, 108, 109; buy stop-limit, 108; market makers/specialist buying, 107, 108; market makers/specialist selling, 107, 108; sell limit, 107–108; sell stop, 108; sell stop-limit, 108; stop-limit order, 109; stop order, 109; trader's aggressive buying, 107; trader's aggressive selling, 107; trader's buy market, 108, 110; trader's passive buying, 107; trader's passive selling, 107; trader's sell market, 108. *See also* Limit orders; Market orders

Oscillator indicators, 207, 211, 221. *See also* Bollinger bands; Momentum indicator (MOM); Price volatility; Relative strength index (RSI); Stochastic oscillator

P

Pacific Stock Exchange (PCX), 58

Paine Webber, Inc. (PAIN), 49, 64

Paper trading, 149–151

Part-time trading, 10–11

PEG ratio, 29

Philadelphia Exchange, 228

Position trading. *See* Swing trading

Precision trading, 9

Price congestion, 182, 183, 192

Price-momentum shift, 240

Price-momentum trading strategy, 13–14, 28

Price resistance, 182, 184–185, 191, 211

Price reversal, waiting for, 9

Price stabilization process, 278

Price support, 182, 184–185, 191, 211

Price-to-book ratio, low, 33

Price trend, 261

Price volatility, 221; absolute, 208–209; in industries, 311; relative, 207, 209–211. *See also* Volatility

Prudential (PRUD), 49; IPO underwriter, 272, 273

Pump and dump stock schemes, 21, 283

Purchasing power, 128; calculating, 132

Q

Quick & Reilly, 66

R

Raymond James, IPO underwriter, 279

Redibook (REDI), 54, 63

Regulation T, SEC Act of 1934, 127, 130; current margin requirement, 130, 131–137

Relative strength index (RSI), 218–221; reading, 221

Rendleman, Jones, Latane study, 248

Risk: day trading, 140; electronic stock trading, 139; market, 140; monitoring, 221; reward and, 139; trading execution, 140. *See also* Losing money; Losing streak; Risk-management tools

Risk-management tools, 141–145; pyramiding stock position, 144–145; setting loss limits, 142–143; using market orders, 143–144

Ritter, Jay, 271

Robertson Stephens & Co. (RBSF), 63; IPO underwriter, 279

Russell 2,000 (IUX), 224

S

Salomon Brothers (SALB), 48

Salomon Smith Barney, 64; IPO underwriter, 273

S & P's 500 (INX), 34, 40, 85, 226, 228–229, 253, 262, 265, 302, 310, 333, 356, 357; as lagging indicator, 229; prices, 209; return, 254

S & P's 500 futures, 228; as leading indicator, 229

SAPI slugs strategy, 34

Scalper swing traders, 20–22; number of trades, 22; percentage of winning trades, 22; as risk takers, 22; screening stock data, 20–21; stock holding period, 21–22; using Internet chat rooms, 21. *See also* Scalping; Stock screening tools

Scalping: as day trading style, 20; as swing trading style, 20

Schwab, Charles, 48, 61, 62–64, 66, 75

ScotTrade, 68

Scottsdale Securities, 64

Search engines: financial, 209; stock, 265

Seasonal events, 261–265; day-of-the-week effect, 264; January effect, 262–263; month-end effect, 263–264; pre-holiday effect, 263; presidential-election effect, 264–265; summer doldrums effect, 262; weekend effect, 264

Sector indices, 227

Securities and Exchange Commission (SEC), 113, 266–267, 278, 280, 290; Form 8-K, 324; Form 10-K, 323–324; Form 10-Q, 324; rule No. 144, 268; rules, 266–267; short-selling rule, 292
Securities discount retailers, 49
Securities Investor Protection Corporation (SIPC), 65
Securities market, two-tiered, 53
SelectNet, 56, 57, 58, 72, 107, 111, 113, 116–117, 122, 125, 144, 243. See also SelectNet orders
SelectNet orders, 116–122; broadcast orders, 117; order-execution mechanics, 118–119; preference buy-order trading strategy, 119–121; preference orders, 117–118; preference sell-order trading strategy, 121–122
Selling, 107–108
Semiconductor index, 228
Settlement dates, 251–252
Sherwood Securities Corp. (SHWD), 49
Short selling, 292; IPOs, 292–294
Short-term trading. See Day trading; Swing trading
Siebert, 66
Slow trading, 151–154; minimizing cost of mistakes, 152; minimizing mistakes, 152; selecting "slow stocks," 152; 200-share increments, 153–154
Small cap stocks, 35
Smith Barney Shearson, Inc. (SBSH), 49
SOES, 106, 107, 113; rules, 113, 116. See also NASDAQ National Market System (NNMS); SOES mechanics; SOES orders
SOES mechanics, 114–116
SOES orders, 55, 56, 113–116, 143–144; execution priority, 113; execution speed, 114; mandatory, 113, 116; placing, 115; trading execution school, 113
Software index (CWX), 228
Specialists, 46, 69, 70, 74, 83, 102, 107, 109, 147, 186; basic trading strategy, 24; collective earnings, 47; making money, 47–48; role, 46–47, 49; vs. market makers, 49
Specialist swing traders, 19–20; advantages, 20; profit potential, 20; as risk takers, 19–20
Specialist swing trading, 22. See also Specialist swing traders
Special memorandum account (SMA), 132

Squawk boxes, 71
Stochastic oscillator, 215–220; fast, 216–217; slow, 216–217
Stock diversification, 25
Stock dividends, 257
Stock exchange, 45
Stock market signals: bearish, 307; bullish, 307; fiscal policies 307; monetary policies, 307
Stock prices: decline in, 310–311, rise in, 310
Stocks, good-trading for year 2000, 379–388
Stock screening, 20, 25, 35–40, 265. See also Stock screening tools
Stock screening tools, 20, 36–40
Stock splits, 253–256; reverse, 255–256; stock price reaction to, 255
Stock trading, vs. investing, 25
Stock trading styles, 4–5, 10. See also Day traders; Day trading; Investing, value/growth; Investors, value/growth; Swing traders; Swing trading
Stop price, 109
Strike (STRK), 54
SuperSOES. See NASDAQ National Market System (NNMS)
SureTrade, 62, 63, 66, 68
Swing traders, 15–19, 45, 46, 65, 81, 85–86, 105, 177, 187, 210, 214, 239, 245, 247, 256, 259, 260, 265, 297–298; account capital, 18; annual return, 9; competing with day traders, 4; competing with long-term investors, 4; vs. day traders, 3, 5, 8, 9, 15; goal, 7; IPO information and, 282; multiple stock positions, 18; objective, 7, 15, 28, 162; prevalence, 4; recommendations, 355–358; stock-holding period, 3, 7, 9, 15; stop-loss limit, 9; technical analysis tools, 163, 165; vs. value/growth investors, 3, 5, 8, 9, 14. See also Scalper swing traders; Specialist swing traders; Swing trading
Swing trading, 13, 139; alternate names, 3; analysis tools, 17, 199; vs. day trading, 10, 17; as day trading/investing hybrid, 10, 16; day trading similarities, 13–14; holding period, 17, 86–87; number of trades, 17; recommendations, 355–358; stop loss per trade, 17; target gain per trade, 17; total commission cost, 17; trading objective, 17; trading size, 17; vs. value/growth investing, 10. See also Swing traders

T

Taxes, traders and, 367–398; auditing probability, 377–378; capital gains and losses, 370–371; expenses, 371–374; income, 368–369; investor expenses, 373; IRS tax audits, 375–378; market maker expenses, 372–373; tax rates, 367–368; tax treatment, 374–375; trader expenses, 373–374

Tax planning, 267–268

TD Waterhouse, 66, 68

Technical analysis, 14, 28, 159; computerized, 197; criticism, 160; indicators, 16. *See also* Charting; Mathematical technical analysis

Technical analysis charts: constructing, 162–163; interpreting, 163; real-time, 23; with combined indicators, 235. *See also* Technical analysis formats

Technical analysis formats, 162–163; bar charts, 166–168, 170; line charts, 168; tick-by-tick price, 165–166; time frame, 163–165. *See also* Candlestick charting; Candlestick charts

Technical analysis software programs, 161, 162–163

Technical analysis tools. *See* Momentum indicator; Moving average convergence/divergence; Moving average indicator; Oscillator indicators

Technology index (TXX), 228

Terranova (TNTO), 72

The Financial Cafe, 63

Thomas Weisel Partners: IPO underwriter, 272, 273

Thomson Financial, 266

Time and sales window, 240–243, 258; purchasing trades, 241; selling trades, 242

Top advances and decline report, 245–247

T+3 settlement cycle, 59, 251

Trade, starting to, 151–152

Tradebook (BTRD), 54

TradeCast, 18, 21, 56, 67, 67, 72, 74, 76, 116, 118, 125, 240, 243

TraderBot, 36

TradeScape, 68, 76

TradeStation, 36, 40

Trading account, 129–130

Trading account requirement, trading styles comparison, 10

Trading activity, trading styles comparison, 10

Trading alerts, 241–242; IPO, 284, 290–291; longer-term, 240; shorter-term, 240. *See also* Cash dividends; Daily high and low alert; Earnings reports; 52-week alert; Insider trading; Level II information screen; Market ticker; News; Seasonal events; Stock screening; Stock dividends; Stock splits; Time and sales window; Top advances and decline report

Trading commission cost, trading styles comparison, 10

Trading Direct, 63, 68

Trading information sources, 361–365; conferences, 364–365; Internet sites, 362–363; print media, 363–365

Trading map, 147

Trading oversight, trading styles comparison, 10

Trading paralysis, 235

Trading plan, 147; questions to address, 148–149

Trading principles, general, 22–24

Trading recommendations, 355–358; buy right increments, 356; consider absolute price volatility stocks, 356; consider expensive stocks, 357; consider high absolute liquidity stocks, 356; consider limit vs. buy orders, 358; consider volatile stocks, 355–356; observe trading signals, 357; take broad market price movement stock position, 357–358; watch stock's price support-and-resistance levels before buying, 358; watch stock's price support-and-resistance levels before selling, 358

Trading risk: high, 14; trading styles comparison, 10

Trading signals: clear, 24; exit, 149; observing, 357. *See also* Stock market signals

Trading software, 18, 21, 22, 72, 74–75, 116, 118, 125, 149, 151, 162, 215, 227, 240, 243, 245, 247. *See also* CyberTrader; TradeCast

Trading strategies, 25, 26. *See also* Investing strategies; Momentum trading

Trading success: factors, 23; increasing probability of, 23–24

Trading suitability, 77; financial competence, 77; technical competence, 77

Trading terminology, 106–108. *See also specific trading terms*

Trading volume, 232–235. *See also* On-balance volume (OBV) indicator

U

U.S. Department of Commerce Bureau of
Economic Analysis, 299, 300
U.S. Department of Labor Bureau of Labor
Statistics, 300
U.S. economy, information sources on, 299
U.S. Bancorp Piper Jaffray, IPO underwriter, 272,
273, 284

V

Value, 38, 335; benefit component, 334; price
component, 335
Value investing, 26, 32–34, 35; tactic, 33–34. *See
also* Value investors
Value investors, 27, 32, 39; as market
contrarians, 33. *See also* Value investing
Value Line Inc., 266
Velocity, 74
Venture capitalists, IPOs and, 274, 275, 278
Vickers Stock Research Corporation, 266
Volatile stocks, 211, 356
Volatility, relative price: Beta coefficient
measurement, 355–356

W

WallStreet Electronica, 66, 68
Wall Street Online, 65
Wang Investments, 63, 64, 68
Warburg Dillon Read, IPO underwriter,
272, 273
Watch lists, 21
Waterhouse Securities, 62
Watley, A. B., 63, 64, 66, 68
Web Street Securities, 64, 66, 68
Weisel, Thomas, 284
Wholesalers, 48
Wilder, J. Welles, 218
William Blair & Co. (WBLR), IPO underwriter,
279
Wilshire Small Cap, 224
WingspanBank.com, 66
Wireless trading, 69–70

Z

Zacks Investment Research, 39, 332,
350

About the Author

Misha T. Sarkovich, Ph.D., once the managing partner for a day-trading firm, is the author of the bestselling day-trading book *Electronic Day Trading Made Easy* (Prima Publishing, 1999). He received his Ph.D. degree in economics from Florida State University in 1985, and has taught undergraduate and graduate courses in Economics and Finance at several universities in the United States and Australia. He holds an NASD series 7 general securities license. In addition, Dr. Sarkovich has conducted many stock-trading seminars and appeared on CNBC and CNNfn. He lives and trades from his home in Fair Oaks, California.